Languedoc
Roussillon

Languedoc-Roussillon made to measure

Languedoc-Roussillon à la carte

FOOD AND DRINK – LOCAL SPECIALITIES 18

RESTAURANTS 30

WINES AND VINEYARDS 42

HOME FURNISHINGS 50

CASTLES, CITADELS AND MANSIONS 62

HISTORY AND HERITAGE 68

EXCURSIONS – GENTLE AND ENERGETIC 80

BEACHES, WATER PARKS AND SPAS 96

SPORTS 102

FESTIVALS AND TRADITIONS 110

ARTS AND CULTURAL EVENTS 118

Languedoc-Roussillon in detail

Languedoc-Roussillon made to measure

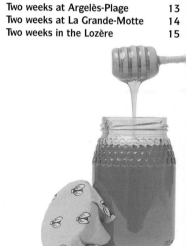

A weekend
in and around
Montpellier

The historic centre of the town (called l'Écusson – the shield) is a pedestrian precinct and you need to leave your car in one of the numerous underground car parks. Try and arrive on a Friday evening and have a drink at one of the numerous outdoor cafés (which stay open until 1am!) in the Place de la Comédie (the true town centre) where coloured easy chairs and canopies stretched over the tables give a festive air to the noble architecture. Other good places are Place de la Loge, Place du Marché-aux-Fleurs, Place Saint-Ravy, Saint-Côme or Saint-Roch. On Saturday, wander through the old town, the area bounded by the grands boulevards. Note the façades of the old mansions in the Rue de l'Ancien-Courrier, Rue de l'Argenterie and the Rue de l'Aiguillerie. There is a lively market in the Place Jean-Jaurès. After lunch, take a long walk on the Promenade

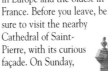

du Peyrou. Admire the view over the town and its surroundings right up to the Cévennes, then visit the Jardin des Plantes (botanical gardens, p. 225), one of the loveliest in Europe and the oldest in France. Before you leave, be sure to visit the nearby Cathedral of Saint-Pierre, with its curious façade. On Sunday,

start your walk in the Place de la Comédie and go up the Esplanade Charles-de-Gaulle, which is lined with vegetation. Stop to visit the Musée Fabre (p. 227) then carry on to the Corum. Return via the Jardin du Champ-de-Mars and wander through the Polygone shopping centre to get to the new district of Antigone, designed by Ricardo Bofill (see p. 226). Take the children on the little train that runs through the town centre to visit the Lunaret zoological park (p. 227). You could also take a bus from the bus station and have lunch at Palavas-les-Flots (p. 232), see the sea and the lagoons, or carry on to La Grande-Motte (p. 230) to enjoy its huge beach.

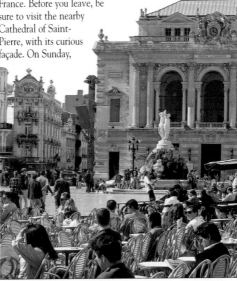

A weekend
in Carcassonne and Narbonne

The round trip will take you back to Carcassonne. Special events: there is a Medieval Festival every August in Carcassonne with jousting tournaments, *son et lumière* performances and concerts. On the next day, visit Narbonne (p. 180), the ancient capital of southern Gaul. The magnificent Cathedral of Saint-Just, started in 1272, the courtyards of the adjoining bishop's palace and the picturesque streets around the Canal de la Robine are of particular interest. The 710-ft (214-m) high Massif de la Clape (p. 185), which separates Narbonne from the sea, dominates the plain, the *garrigues* (scrubland) and vineyards. Lunch on seafood at Gruissan (p. 186), a fishing village built on a circular plan which is now also a modern seaside resort. An alternative would be to tour Narbonne and then visit Fontfroide Abbey (p. 177), the magnificent 12th-C. Cistercian abbey at Gruissan instead. You could then eat either at Gruissan or in Narbonne. The afternoon could be spent at the Sigean African Reserve (p. 189) where antelopes, monkeys and flamingoes roam over an area of more than 247 acres (100 ha) beside the lagoons of Bages and Sigean.

Begin the weekend in the medieval city of Carcassonne (p. 166) and by the Canal du Midi (p. 200). In the morning, walk around the ramparts, of which Viollet-le-Duc said: 'I do not know if such a complete and formidable set of defensive works exists anywhere else in Europe.' The city, its château and ramparts have been occupied in turn by the Gauls, Romans, Visigoths, Saracens, counts of Trencavel and many kings of France. Below the ramparts lies the grid-patterned lower town which also has many treasures including the Pont-Vieux, the Gothic Cathedral of Saint-Michel and several mansions. This is one of the most spectacular historic sites in France. Break for lunch in the Place Marcou in the old part of town. In the afternoon, take a boat trip on a barge on the Canal du Midi, which is lined with plane trees and winds through the vineyards of the Minervois.

A weekend
in and around
Nîmes

If you are lucky enough to be in Nîmes over Whitsun (Pentecost) weekend, you will have to book accommodation well in advance because the Féria will be at its height and more than a million visitors flock to the arenas. This festival offers five days of unforgettable celebrations. In Nîmes, as in Montpellier, the ancient town centre has been pedestrianised. First visit the Roman arena (p. 254) of this ancient city, then wander the narrow lanes behind the Place du Marché, the Rue Fresque, Rue de l'Aspic, Rue de la Madeleine and the Rue des Marchands. In the Place aux Herbes, admire the fine cathedral façade and visit the Musée du Vieux-Nîmes (p. 254). Have lunch at one of the outdoor cafés in the little squares, which also contain tempting shops and boutiques. The Maison Carrée and its contemporary counterpart the Carré d'Art (p. 252-253) are on the agenda for the afternoon, which you could complete, if you like antiquities, with a tour of the archaeological museum. The next day take a stroll through the gardens of La Fontaine to the Magne tower. Or you could take a trip to Uzès, 16 miles (25 km) away, whose medieval and Renaissance town centre has been so well restored. Have lunch in one of the numerous little squares or have a drink at the magnificent Duché (p. 272). You can also go and see the extraordinary Pont du Gard (p. 268), an incredible feat of Roman engineering stretching over the river Gardon, which stands in a lovely verdant landscape that has been particularly well preserved.

A weekend
in Collioure
and Roussillon

Start your weekend with a stroll through this delightful fishing port (p. 148) whose vibrant colours were immortalised by the artists Braque and Matisse. The little tour called *Chemin du fauvisme* (the Fauvist painters' route) (p. 148) is very pleasant and will take you right around the port. You can also visit the anchovy salting works, the local speciality. Then it is time for lunch in Collioure. In the afternoon, drive down the road beside La Côte Vermeille (p. 144), where there will be plenty of views over the promontories and beaches of the Catalan coast.

Stop to taste the dessert wine at Banyuls (p. 147), a seaside resort and yacht harbour overlooked by terraced vineyards. From Banyuls, you can either follows the tracks of the smugglers and customs officers of old or go for a swim off Cap Béar (p. 146). Alternatively you

could visit the aquarium of the Arago Laboratory. Return via Port-Vendres (p. 146), the old port of Venus, which is still a busy fishing port and whose main square contains a pink marble obelisk erected to the memory of Louis XVI. Don't miss the fish auction which takes place from 4pm. On the second day, drive along the corniche of the rocky coast to the old village of Argelès-sur-Mer (p. 144), where they hold lively markets; there is also an evocative regional folklore museum called the Casa des Albères (p. 145). Argelès-Plage (p. 145) is a long strip of sand which is ideal for either bathing or a family picnic. Free-flying eagles at the Château de Valmy (p. 145), at the foot of the Albères, are a fabulous sight. In the afternoon, drive through the orchards and vineyards of the Plain of Roussillon. Return to Collioure, where you could take a little trip out to sea or sample some of the regional wines at the Maison de la Vigne. If you intend to take one of these short breaks, it is a good idea to contact Sud Résa Vacances who specialise in these types of holidays and will help you choose the one that suits you best (Information, ☎ 04 67 92 78 08).

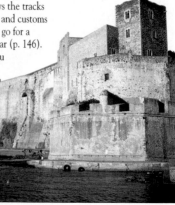

A week
in Font-Romeu

Font-Romeu is a mountain resort situated 6,000 ft (1,800 m) above sea level on the sunny slope on which the French national football team trained for its victory in the final of the 1998 World Cup. It has wonderful views, protected from the wind by thick forests of fir trees (p. 162). It is both a winter and summer resort. In summer you can go mountain and cross-country skiing, or swim and there is also an equestrian centre, an archery centre, a nine-hole golf course, a health farm, tennis and squash courts, a rock-climbing wall and a sauna. There are many hiking trails, as well as canoeing and kayaking, paragliding and mountain-biking. For weekly accommodation rental, contact the Tourist Office (p. 169). Font-Romeu is an ideal base for a tour of the Cerdagne (p. 162-3). The surrounding plateau is a sunny haven of greenery. You can also visit the Roman baths at Dorres, the largest solar-powered kiln in the world at Odeillo (p. 162-3), the lake of Lanoux, the panoramic view from the Pic du Canigou, the Musée de la Cerdagne at Sainte-Léocadie (p. 163), the abbeys of Saint-Michel-de-Cuxa (p. 159) and Saint-Martin-du-Canigou (p. 161), and take a wonderful trip in the little yellow train from Villefranche-de-Conflent (p. 156).

If you are looking for sun all year round, clean air and spectacular views, the mountains of Languedoc-Roussillon are ideal, whatever the season, for winter sports and summer holidays in magnificent settings.

A week
at Canet-Plage

Yachtsmen, sports enthusiasts and ordinary holiday-makers will love this part of the coast which is busy all year round (p. 140). Canet-Plage is the favourite resort of the residents of Perpignan, with a huge beach, aquarium, unusual museums and yacht harbour. The Place de la Méditerranée, in the centre of the resort, is symbolically, and fittingly, adorned with a monumental nude entitled *La Fille de la mer* (*Daughter of the sea*). A few miles away,

and easy to reach on foot, the old village of Canet-en-Roussillon, where a tradition of vines and market gardens (p. 140) lives on. The château and ice-well are of particular interest. If you are staying at the resort you can take several excursions, for instance from Canet to Saint-Cyprien (p. 142) by bicycle along the beach. Or you could hike or ride on horseback around the lagoon, spend a day sea-fishing or take a sea trip along the coast. The bird-watching path around the Étang de Canet and Saint-Nazaire is another possibility. Visits can also be made to Perpignan (p. 132), ancient capital of the kingdom of Majorca, the Byrrh cellars at Thuir (p. 154) and the medieval village of Castelnou (p. 155).
Tourist Office:
☎ 04 68 73 61 00 (Place de la Méditerranée).

A week at
Cap-d'Agde

Why do as many as a quarter of the tourists to the Languedoc-Roussillon region decide to stay at Cap-d'Agde (p. 214)? Of course, it's a great place to meet people of the opposite sex, but more especially it is because of all that the seaside here has to offer. There are 8¾ miles (14 km) of fine sandy beaches which are barred to traffic, which means that they can be explored on foot or by bicycle. The Richelieu beach has ⅝ mile (1 km) of sand, starting from the Île des Loisirs. Further to the west, at Rochelongue, there is a smaller beach, La Plagette, below the cliffs. La Conque is a beach of black, volcanic sand. The Plage du Môle is 2,000 ft (600 m) long and

is the busiest beach of them all. La Roquille is covered with large shells. Almost everywhere you go you can rent a sunshade, deck chair or steamer, and a lilo or a pedalo. There are holiday activity clubs for children, volley-ball courts, ice-cream parlours, snackbars, bars and fast-food outlets of all kinds. Anyone aged over seven can learn to sail and canoe, and there is also miniature golf and football. You can take to

the sea in a sailing-dinghy, a motor-boat or on a sailboard (p. 215). Why not get up early (or don't bother to go to bed at all) to go on a sea-fishing trip; day or night, you are sure to have a good catch. Take a break from sunbathing to visit the Musée Éphèbe. Take a trip to Agde (p. 212) where the lava-built houses cluster around the Cathedral of Saint-Étienne, and wander through the old Quartier de La Glacière (icehouse district). Continue on to Pézenas (p. 208), Molière's home town, where there are sign-posted walks indicating the most interesting 17th- and 18th-C. mansions.

WATER, WATER EVERYWHERE!
Whether you are seriously into surfing, fancy a quick dip in the sea to cool down, or want to test the curative powers of the spas and thermal baths, there are enough aquatic activities in Languedoc for everyone. Fancy trying a new sport? Check out the addresses on pages 104–107; where you will find lots to keep you and the children occupied. If you are stressed out, and want to treat your body like a temple, turn to p. 100 and prepare for a rejuvenating experience...

Two weeks in
Port-Leucate

This is a coastline of contrasts – of rocky outcrops and lagoons, and vineyards stretching far out to the horizon. Port-Leucate was a resort created in the 1960s, and is now entirely devoted to water-sports, mainly yachting and windsurfing. When you have seen all the resort has to offer, go and watch the funboarders on the lagoon, or visit the picturesque village and the ruins of the château. And you will still have plenty left to do. You can explore the Leucate cliff (p. 190) on foot, by bike or by mountain-bike, visit the oyster-farm and shrimp-farm, the flume at the aquatic park, and take a short trip on a pleasure boat. Then take time to learn about the history of the region by visiting Salses-le-Château (p. 137), then Tautavel (p. 138), to see the Musée de la Préhistoire. In summer, the prehistoric festivals even feature buffalo and kid on the menu! Stop at Rivesaltes for an apéritif of Muscat wine. Another interesting side-trip is to the Corbières region (p. 176), the frontier between France and Spain, which is still heavily fortified with citadels on rocky peaks, and where you can see the Cathar châteaux (p. 178). The surrounding countryside consists of *garrigues* and bare rock and is crisscrossed with numerous little roads which often run beside deep gorges. The châteaux of Quéribus and Peyrepertuse are enhanced by their magnificent countryside setting. After all this activity, take lunch in the village of Cucugnan (p. 178), one-time favourite haunt of Alphonse Daudet, and sample a glass of the Blanquette de Limoux, a local sparkling white wine, which will help you recover your strength after hiking over the area's stony paths.
Leucate Tourist Office:
☎ 04 68 40 91 31.

Two weeks at
Argelès-Plage

A rgelès-Plage, at the foot of the Pyrenees, is superb for diving. It is set in La Côte Vermeille (p. 144) which inspired the Fauvist and Cubist painters. You have a choice: you can either explore these lovely surroundings, or simply choose to laze around on the beach, depending on your mood. Behind their tourist façade, the little Catalan ports have retained their fishing traditions intact. Fishing for sea lampreys and the fish auction are two examples.

You can use Argelès as a base for exploring the region. The resort has much to offer, including the Mas Larrieu nature reserve, hiking trails on the Albères (p. 147), the easy Sentiers d'Émilie footpaths and a walk to the Massane Tower. The Cathedral of Elne (p. 143) on the plain of Roussillon has a magnificent Romanesque cloister with stonework friezes depicting flowers and stylised animals. Why not visit Céret (p. 152) on Saturday, market day, to see, sample and buy local produce. The museum of modern art is full of Cubist paintings, and works by Picasso, Braque and Chagall, all in a typically Catalan village which has retained its authenticity. Sit on a café terrace in the shade of the plane trees and watch the scenes Picasso observed with his keen eye. At the end of the day, at sunset, the port of Collioure (p. 148), another favourite of the Impressionist painters, is a wonderful place for a stroll.

AUX
TOREADORS
DU
MONDE

Two weeks at
La Grande-Motte

cypresses amid a landscape of lagoons, marshes and salt marshes. It has a huge beach, part of which is reserved for naturists. Take a side-trip to Frontignan, famous for its Muscat wine (p. 49). After tasting it, make your way to Sète (p. 218), a fishing village where you should sample the *bourride*, the local fish soup. Then visit the Musée Georges Brassens and the cemetery.

You may feel like doing nothing more than staying glued to the beach for the whole of your stay, of course, but La Grande-Motte offers much more than sunbathing (p. 230). Set in an expanse of greenery, the seaside resort of La Grande-Motte, with its famous pyramid-shaped seafront buildings, offers everything in the way of seaside fun – well-cared for beaches, fishing, scuba-diving, a marina and a huge aquarium containing a shark tank. If the pleasures of the above don't appeal, there is an excellent 18-hole golf course. Carnon-Plage is another resort to the south. Its Bridge of Lamentations crosses the channel that runs through it. Palavas-les-Flots is a 19th-C. seaside resort (p. 232). The cathedral stands in a grove of pines, nettle-trees and

Two weeks in
the Lozère

If you prefer the countryside to the sea and have decided to explore inland, the Lozère will not disappoint you. You can use Mende (p. 306) or Florac as a base and explore the limestone plateaux of the Causse de Sauveterre and the Causse Méjean (p. 298) as well as the gorges of the Tarn and the Jonte (p. 300) which can attain depths of up to 2,000 ft (600 m)! The Corniche offers magnificent views and passes through delightful villages with narrow lanes, terraces and vaulted passageways, such as Sainte-Énimie, Saint-Chély-du-Tarn, Le Rozier and Meyrueis. From La Malène, rent a flat-bottomed boat, with a boatman, and float down to the Cirque des Baumes. If you prefer something more active, rent a canoe or kayak from the many water-sports centres. Or explore the Margeride (p. 306), a district of moorland, broom and forests, as well as that of the Beast of Gévaudan, the 200-year-old legend which continues to intrigue and enrich local folklore. The Aubrac (p. 304) remains one of the least populated regions of France, and is most famous for its fine landscape of vast meadows, lakes and magnificent forest. You will travel through it from Marvejols, once a busy weaving centre and now a pleasant and popular inland holiday resort.

Languedoc-Roussillon à la carte

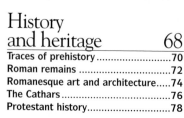

Food and drink – local specialities

With its wonderful seafood, regional delicacies and traditional cooking, Languedoc-Roussillon has something to tempt every palate.

Chocolate and sweet delights

1. Perpignan:
   Chocolaterie Cantalou,
   Biscuiterie-Confiserie Lor.
   p. 134.
2. Tautavel: Écomusée de
   l'Abeille et du Miel.
   p. 139.
3. Limoux: nougat.
   pp. 40 and 175.
4. Fontfroide: honey from
   Clauses Montseret.
   p. 177.
5. Narbonne: *Galets de la
   Clape* (chocolate almonds).
   pp. 183-184.
6. Bédarieux:
   beehives and honey.
   pp. 204-205.
7. Paulhan:
   Rouquette honey.
   p. 211.
8. Pomérols: Guy Bouzigues'
   chocolates.
   p. 216.
9. Lodève: the *lodévois*,
   (walnut tart).
   p. 249.
10. Uzès: Mas de Tessan bee-
    hives; Haribo sweet factory.
    pp. 274 and 275.
11. Florac: sugar and
    chestnuts.
    p. 292.
12. Mende:
    Maison Gribet,
    jams.
    p. 307.

Local specialities

13. Amélie-les-Bains:
    Antoine Alaminos,
    Catalan specialities.
    p. 150.
14. Boule-d'Amont:
    Relais de Serrabone,
    local cuisine.
    p. 155.
15. Bize-Minervois:
    L'Oulibo (olive oil).
    p. 199.
16. Clermont-l'Hérault:
    olive oil cooperative.
    p. 206.
17. Lodève:
    Pélardon (cheese).
    p. 250.
18. Uzès: truffle market,
    garlic fair, La Caracole
    (snails).
    pp. 273-275.
19. Alès: Maison Lagarde,
    wild mushrooms.
    p. 281.
20. Meyrueis:
    Jontanels farms.
    pp. 294 and 295.
21. Hures-la-Parade:
    Hyelzas, an old-fashioned
    farm.
    p. 299.

Montagne Noire

Béziers

29 N113 Canal du Midi 15

Carcassonne A61 5 **Narbor**

Limoux 3 4 2 23

Aude Corbières

2

Perpignan 1 N9

Têt

Tunnel de Puymorens •Prades 14 A9

ANDORRA N20 N116 Tech **Collioure**

Pic du Canigou 13 •Céret Col du Perthus

9,132 ft (2,784 m)

SPAIN

A75

A75

Orb

N112

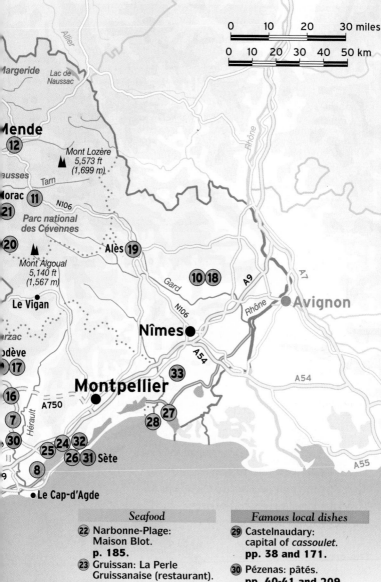

Seafood

22 **Narbonne-Plage: Maison Blot.** p. 185.

23 **Gruissan: La Perle Gruissanaise (restaurant).** p. 187.

24 **Bouzigues: The oyster route** p. 217.

25 **Balaruc: tour of the oyster-beds.** p. 216.

26 **Sète: La Marine.** p. 218.

27 **Aigues-Mortes: Salt-pans of the Mediterranean.** pp. 26 and 265.

28 **Port-Camargue: Poissons d'Argent, fish-farm.** p. 267.

Famous local dishes

29 **Castelnaudary: capital of *cassoulet*.** pp. 38 and 171.

30 **Pézenas: pâtés.** pp. 40-41 and 209.

31 **Sète: *tielle* (squid pie).** p. 219.

Drinks

32 **Bessan: Ricard factory.** p. 213

33 **Vergèze: Perrier spring.** p. 258.

From the olive tree to olive oil

O live trees were brought to the Languedoc 2,500 years ago by the Greeks. These trees produce small, dry black olives or large, juicy green olives. Olives and olive oil can be bought everywhere and appear at almost every meal (50,000 tonnes are consumed each year!): green, black, peppery or thyme-flavoured olives, *tapenade* (olive paste) or olive oil sprinkled over tomatoes – always healthy and tasty.

The olive
The olive is an oval fruit, which is fairly fleshy. The stone may be small, large, pointed or rounded and the skin changes from pale green to black as it ripens. It matures between July and late September and is harvested until February (for the late oil-producing

The tree
Olea europea, the cultivated tree, belongs to the Oleaceae family (like the ash and the lilac) and is an evergreen so it does not shed its leaves. The leaves are bright green on top, silvery-green under-neath. The trees grow to about 10–13 ft (3–4 m) in height and flourish on poor, arid soil and the Mediter-ranean climate, with its (mild winters, warm, dry summers, wet autumns or springs) and brilliant light.

varieties). A cultivated olive tree produces an average of 33–66 lb (15–30 kg) of olives annually.

Harvesting

Olives have been harvested for centuries by beating the trees lightly with a stick to bring down the fruit without undue harm. They are also picked by hand: the picker wears thick gloves and scrapes the fruit off the twigs with a little plastic rake. A good picker will average 130 lb (60 kg) a day. Machines to shake, vibrate or even vacuum the trees (black olives only) are sometimes used, but these machines are not suitable for all types of tree or olive grove.

Traditional oil-pressing

The olives are weighed and brought to the press where they remain for anything from a few hours to and two or three days to get warm so that the yield is greater. They are then washed and crushed (without being stoned) to release their oil. This operation transforms them into a smooth paste, without any lumps of flesh, which is then kneaded. The pressing operation then allows the oil to be extracted and separated from the water (see inset).

Picholine

Picholine is the main French type of green olive, rustic and tough, and very suitable for pickling. It can be kept in brine for a very long time without losing its green colour. The Picholine is oval in shape, elongated, with a smooth, bright green skin and firm flesh. It is harvested in October and November.

Lucques

The Lucques is an olive that grows nowhere else in the world but the *départments* of Aude and Hérault. It is tasty and full of flavour and is recognisable by its crescent shape. It is harvested in September and

VIRGIN OLIVE OIL

Extra-virgin and virgin olive oil is produced from fruits which are only cold-pressed once. When the paste is heated and pressed a second time, an inferior quality is obtained. The separation of oil and water was performed for many years in large tanks. Since oil is lighter than water, it floated to the surface. Nowadays, centrifugation, a mechanical process, makes it possible to perform the separation instantly and much more thoroughly. Approximately 11 lb (5 kg) of olives are needed to obtain about 1¾ pints (1 litre) of oil.

then soaked in brine. It can thus be preserved naturally at room temperature until April or May when it is placed in a cold room. This technique helps it retain its bright colour and original texture.

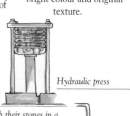

Hydraulic press

T he olives are crushed with their stones in a mill or press into cakes of pulp. These are then crushed in a hydraulic press. The oil and water extracted are then taken to a centrifuge which separates the two elements. The oil is then stored in vats before being bottled.

Oysters from the Languedoc

The Bassin de Thau, full of flocks of pink flamingoes and seagulls, lies on the rugged coastline of Languedoc, open to the sea. This is where Bouzigues oysters are cultivated (p. 217). The bay lies just south of Montpellier, on a coast where the locals have been farming this little sea creature for more than a hundred years. Flat or convex, large or small, eaten alone or with other shellfish, Languedoc oysters should be accompanied by a chilled white wine, preferably Picpoul-de-Pinet.

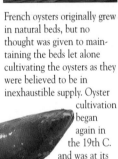

The oyster over the centuries

The oyster has long been a staple of peoples living near the coast and is exceptionally nutritious though low in calories. The Greeks ate oysters baked or boiled in honey and flavoured with parsley and mint. The Romans accorded the oyster a place of honour at their banquets. Increasing demand for the oyster led to a search for a way of cultivating them, which the Romans suceeded in doing, fattening them up in special ponds. However, the oyster fell from favour in the Middle Ages but was again accorded a place of honour under Louis XIV. At the time, there were about 2,000 shellfish merchants in Paris.

French oysters originally grew in natural beds, but no thought was given to maintaining the beds let alone cultivating the oysters as they were believed to be in inexhaustible supply. Oyster cultivation began again in the 19th C. and was at its height in 1850, but the flat oyster, the only one cultivated at the time, was subject to disease and the oyster-beds set up by Napoleon III were decimated.

'Our land is the sea'

The Bassin de Thau covers 18,525 acres (7,500 ha), and is cut off from the open sea by a sea-wall ⅝ mile (1 km) long, in which there are three sluice-gates enabling clean water to flow in and out. The basin has all the advantages of a lagoon in its shallowness, salinity,

temperature and nutritional elements, which provide a suitable environment for shellfish cultivation, in which the oyster can fatten and improve its flavour to the best advantage. More than 10,000 to 15,000 tonnes of oysters are produced by 800 farms. This represents 10% of national production and places oyster-farming as the second-largest industry in the Hérault after viticulture.

An original breeding technique

A highly original technique has been devised for breeding oysters in this part of the world. They are grown attached to ropes suspended from tables in the water. Up to 1,000 ropes can be suspended from each table. The spats, or baby oysters collected in the wild, are attached to the ropes and left to grow. After 12 to 18 months, they are removed and the largest are sold, while the smaller ones are individually returned to the ropes and left in the water for another year. Bouzigues oysters are of two kinds: flat and convex. The convex oysters, lined with mother-of-pearl, represent 80% of consumption.

A distinction is also made between the *détroquée* oyster which has been fattened for 15 to 18 months and the *spéciale*, which has been left for an additional 12 months to fatten. The *spéciale* is of a better quality and the shell is sharp-edged. The dark flat oyster, with its robust flavour, is also very popular.

Male or female?

The oyster is a mollusc with a complex internal organisation. The creature is completely contained within the shell. It has a mantle which contains the sensory organs enabling it to breathe and feed. It also has a digestive system consisting of a mouth and a round stomach with a heart, veins and arteries in which its colourless blood circulates. The reproductive organs of the oyster are extremely unusual, in that an oyster can be alternatively male or female. This hermaphroditism operates slightly differently, depending on whether the oyster is flat or convex. In the flat oyster, the change of sex

occurs after every discharge of semen and eggs, but in the convex oyster it only occurs once a season. The egg-laying season takes place three times a year. 500,000 to 1,500,000 ovules are produced in the flat oyster, whereas the convex oyster has between 20 and 100 million eggs. Of all of these, only 10 eggs (or spats),

whether from the flat or convex oysters, will ever reach complete maturity.

Spats, or baby oysters, are grown on collectors in the form of roof tiles, and removed either by machine or by hand.

The truffle
in pursuit of the black diamond

Around 50 tonnes of truffles are gathered in France each year – in the Dordogne and in the Lot, as well as in the *départements* of Gard, Drôme, Vaucluse, Bouches-du-Rhône, Hérault and Alpes-de-Haute-Provence. The Gard, though not part of the Périgord, is one of the main truffle-producing *départements*, supplying 15% of the national production of *Tuber melanosporum*. This underground fungus or mushroom is better known by the name of 'black truffle' or 'Périgord truffle'.

Where do truffles come from?

In order to develop and bear fruit, the truffle needs to grow in association with a tree, usually an oak, hazel or linden tree. Such a tree is known as a truffle-bearing tree (*arbre truffier*). The truffle becomes connected with a root via the little root-like filaments known as *mycorrhiza*, which enable the plants to exchange nutritive elements that benefit both fungus and tree. The black truffle grows in permeable limestone soil, where the summers are hot and stormy and winters are mild. However, it is still hard to cultivate truffles as not all factors required to promote its growth are known, hence its high price. Shrewd, trained observers can detect the existence of a truffle by studying the ground. To detect a truffle, look for a bare area around the tree trunk called the *brûlé* (burned patch).

Harvesting

The black truffle can only be harvested and sold fresh between November and 20 March. To find truffles in the ground, the hunter usually makes use of an animal with a good sense of smell, such as a pig or a dog (the latter must be specially trained, because it is not particularly fond of truffles, unlike the pig). Some experts can also detect truffles by watching for the truffle-fly, a little brown fly which lays its eggs in an over-ripe truffle. If you try and gather truffles by simply turning over the soil with a hoe, you will destroy the truffle-ground for many years to come. Truffle-hunting at night is strictly forbidden.

AN APHRODISIAC

This expensive delicacy is alleged to act as an aphrodisiac for women! Early pagan worshippers dedicated the truffle to the goddess Aphrodite and Mme de Pompadour and Madame du Barry, high priestesses of love in the 18th century, prepared many dishes based on truffles. Napoleon is alleged to have made use of its properties in order to conceive his son and heir. The famous gourmet, Brillat-Savarin, claimed that 'on certain occasions, it can make women more tender and men more lovable'. You will just have to try it out for yourself...

Keeping a truffle

Fresh truffles can be kept for a week or so in a refrigerator, unbrushed and unwashed, in an airtight jar with some kitchen towel. After having brushed them under cold water and dried them carefully, they must be sterilised or frozen. They must then be prepared before they are defrosted by cutting into slices or grating.

Eating a truffle?

Whether raw or cooked, all you need are a few grams to give the preparation an

inimitable flavour. For a *brouillade*, eggs in their shell and truffles are placed in a hermetically sealed container 24 hours in advance so that the flavours and scents of the truffles can be diffused (you

will need ½–¾ oz (15–20 g) of grated truffle per person which is sprinkled over a runny omelette). The strong fragrance of the truffle also goes wonderfully well with meat and pâtés. It can also be thinly sliced and eaten on buttered bread (use slightly salted butter) or in a green salad sprinkled with olive oil in which a few slices of truffle have been marinated for 4 or 5 hours.

Buying a truffle

A truffle market is held at Uzès every Saturday between November and March. Most of the truffles are sold to agents but in the Place aux Herbes, anyone can buy them from the growers (in January 1997, they cost almost 2,000 F for $2^{1}/_{4}$ lb (1 kg)!). For more information, contact the Syndicat des Producteurs de Truffes du Gard, at Uzès (24, Av. de la Gare, ☎ 04 66 22 58 36. Open from 8am-noon). On the third

Sunday of January, you can also buy seedlings that have been infected with truffle *mycorrhiza*. There are guided tours of the truffle grounds, tastings and sales at the Truffières du Soleil, Mas du Moulin de la Flesque, Uzès, ☎ 04 66 22 08 41 (p. 273).

Reading matter

Truffles, the Black Diamond and Other Kinds, preface by Peter Mayle and written by Jean-Marie Rocchia, past president of the National Association of Trufflegrowers. There are very few books exclusively about truffles in English, but any good book about mushrooms will include a section on truffles.

Salt and salt marshes

When you leave Aigues-Mortes and head towards the sea and Grau-du-Roi, the landscape is flat and marshy, dotted with ponds and lagoons. Your eyes are drawn to the white hills which rise up out of the surrounding vineyards. These are mounds of salt, belonging to the Compagnie des Salins du Midi and are waiting to be packaged before they reach your table.

Ancient history

Salt production in the region was begun by the Roman engineer Peccius, who lived around the beginning of the Christian era. By the late 17th C., 17 little salt marshes, under various ownerships, were being operated in the area. Serious flooding in 1842 led these small owners to work with a merchant in Montpellier and in 1856, the Compagnie des Salins du Midi was formed. Since then it has undergone several

changes. It is now a multi-national, belonging to the American group Morton, the world's biggest salt producer.

What is a salt marsh?

A salt marsh is a flat, slightly depressed area in the ground, rendered as watertight as possible, in which sea-water can circulate naturally or is pumped in and covers the whole surface in a shallow layer. At Aigues-Mortes, the salt marshes are fed from a

pumping station with a capacity of 33 cu. ft (10 m³) per second. The annual volume of water pumped from the sea is in the order of 150 million cu. ft (45 million m³).

The Aigues-Mortes salt marsh

The salt marshes cover an area of 26,650 acres (10,800 ha), which straddles the *départements* of Gard and the Bouches-du-Rhône. The perimeter is 11¼ miles (18 km) north to south and 8¾ miles (14 km) east to west, which is larger than the city of Paris! Of this, 212 miles (340 km) consist of roads and

paths crisscrossing the land in every direction. Guided tours are arranged to visit the area (see p. 265).

How does it work?

Once the water has been pumped in, nine-tenths of it must evaporate in order for the salt to be deposited. For this purpose, the water is circulated through 86 basins, a total evaporation surface of 1,235 acres (500 ha). Most of these pans are former ponds, ringed by more than 280 miles (450 km) of dykes. Thanks to the combined effect of sun and wind, evaporation is so effective that the salt content of the water increases from ½ oz to 4½ oz per 1¾ pints (29 to 260 g/l).

What happens then?

After covering 44 miles (70 km) by gravitation or pumping, the brine (water with a strong concentration of salt) thus obtained is introduced into 50 basins measuring between 12–24 acres (5–10 ha) and about 6–8 in (15–20 cm) deep. The brine now becomes pinkish in colour, thanks to the presence of a micro-organism called *Dunaliella salina*. At this stage, any further evaporation will cause the salt to crystallise and deposit itself in the basin or salt marsh.

Salt collection

An average of 3½ in (9 cm) of sodium chloride crystals are deposited annually from April to September. Before the autumn rains, the 'salt cake' is collected. This operation lasts for 30 days and requires a great deal of manpower and equipment. The salt is cleaned, any impurities being removed by washing in sterile brine. It is then stored in piles 73 ft (22 m) high called *camelles*.

More statistics

In the space of this one month of the year, about 15,000 tonnes of salt are collected and stored daily. This represents 450,000 tonnes of marketable salt, the result of a whole year's work. Salt is then gradually removed from the stockpile to be packed and delivered to various customers. The salt produced at Aigues-Mortes is for human consumption.

Mineral waters
straight from the source

There are approximately 1,200 mineral water springs in France. It is the French organisation, the Académie de Médecine which decides on whether they have any therapeutic use for French consumers and, of course, mineral water is marketed as being very good for you and having great health-giving properties. The marketing of mineral water has been a great success and now the spring waters of Languedoc-Roussillon are familiar sights on tables all over the world.

Mineral water treatment?

The French are major consumers of bottled water, drinking 190 pints (110 l) per person per year, although only a few decades ago they drank twice as much. Do mineral

waters really have the benefits ascribed to them? Do they aid slimming, improve digestion and reduce stress? The Académie de Médecine is not too specific, merely ascribing to them properties that are 'favourable to health'.

Table water, spring water or mineral water?

Table water is water from rivers or the water table that is made drinkable by chemical processing and then bottled. Spring water is naturally drinkable. Its mineral concentration may vary and it is bottled without being processed. Mineral water is recognised by the Académie de Médecine and the French Ministry of Health and must indicate the mineral content on the label of the bottle.

Which mineral water to drink?

Not all the 1,200 springs in France have therapeutic properties. If the mineral content of water is low – less than 0.005 oz/1¼ pints (500 mg/l) – the water suits everyone, especially the very young. If it is rich in mineral salts – more than 0.05 oz/ 1¼ pints (1,500 mg/l) – it is useful in combatting kidney stones, gout and dropsy but is not drinkable as a table water.

The Gothic bridge at Quézac has spanned the Tarn since the 14th C

Vernière

This natural mineral water from Lamalou-les-Bains has its iron content removed and is recarbonised with its own gas. Vernière is good for the digestion due to its bicarbonates, for the bones due

to its calcium, and for the metabolism, thanks to its magnesium and potassium. It is low in sodium (0.154 g/l) and can be drunk by anyone.

Salvetat

Salvetat is a spa resort and the source of the Rieumajou spring. This naturally sparkling water is produced by one of the branches of the Évian group.

Quézac

Quézac is in the Gorges du Tarn, about half a mile (1 km) from Ispagnac. The little village of Quézac is notable for its magnificent stone bridge across the river Tarn. This source of sparkling mineral water has been known since the 19th C. but was not bottled until 1995. It is now sold in supermarkets.

Perrier

The famous bubbles (more than 50 million per 1¾ pt/1 l) are the result of volcanic

activity in the region. The spring, which is called Bouillens, was discovered in 1891 by a Dr Perrier. In 1903, the newspaper proprietor Lord Harmsworth bought the Société des Eaux Minérales, Boissons et Produits Hygiéniques de Vergèze from Louis Perrier, retaining the name and logo which have remained unchanged since the reign of Napoleon III.

Lord Harmsworth invented the shape of the bottle, which is based on an Indian club. The bottling plant that conquered America can be visited

and there are tastings (p. 258).

Four bottles that are a healthy complement to any meal

Restaurants

A selection of restaurants at which you can sample Catalan cuisine, the riches of the sea, *cassoulet* or *foie gras*. Addresses and comments are on pages 32 to 35.

Pyrénées-Orientales

1. Banyuls-sur-Mer: La Littorine.
2. Castelnou: L'Hostal.
3. Céret: Les Feuillants.
4. Collioure: Le Tapas Café.
5. Perpignan: La Passerelle, La Casa Sansa.
6. Villefranche-de-Conflent: Auberge Saint-Paul.

Aude

7. Carcassonne: Château Saint-Martin Trencavel, Auberge de Dame Carcass.
8. Castelnaudary: Restaurant du Centre et de Lauragais.
9. Narbonne: Aux Trois Caves.
10. Villepinte: Aux Deux Acacias.

Lozère

11. Mende: La Safranière.
12. Meyrueis: Ferme-Auberge chez Rémi Baret.

Gard

20 Alès (Seynes): La Farigoulette.
21 Nîmes: Le Magister.
22 Port-Camargue: Le Spinaker.
23 Uzès: La Jasse.

Hérault

13 Béziers:
L'Ambassade,
Le Jardin.
14 Bouzigues:
Les Jardins de la Mer.
15 Clermont-l'Hérault:
Ferme-Auberge du Mas de Font-Chaude.
16 Ganges (Saint-Martial):
La Terrasse.
17 Montpellier:
Isadora,
La Maison de la Lozère.
18 Pézenas:
La Pomme d'Amour.
19 Sète: La Palangrotte.

Local restaurants

The following are some recommended restaurants, on a *département* by *département* basis. Their local cuisine which will enable you to discover the delicious food that Languedoc-Roussillon has to offer.

La gardiane de taureau, *a dish made with ox-cheek or stewing steak*

Pyrénées-Orientales
La Littorine
**Hôtel Les Elmes,
Plage des Elmes,
66650 Banyuls-
sur-Mer,
☎ 04 68 88 03 12.
Open daily.**
From 100 F to 300 F.

The chef worked in Portugal for a while hence the Portuguese influence in the very individual cuisine. Fish and shellfish are the main attraction, but the desserts and wines are also delicious. This is one of the best restaurants in Roussillon.

L'Hostal
**13, Carrer de na
Pastora,
66300 Castelnou,
☎ 04 68 53 45 42.
Closed Mon. and Wed.
evening except in
summer, and Jan.-Feb.**
From 95 F to 230 F.
A generous Roussillon table. It specialises in grilling over vine twigs, but it is also one of the last restaurants to serve *cargolade* (snails) (p. 36).

Les Feuillants
**1, Bd Lafayette,
66400 Céret,
☎ 04 68 87 37 88.
Closed Sun. evening and
Mon. except in July–Aug.**
From 250 F to 500 F.
Elegant and unusual cooking which is largely dependent on the riches of Catalonia for its raw ingredients. The surroundings are imposing and the wine list remarkable. For gastronomes on a budget, the Brasserie des Feuillants, on the opposite side of the courtyard, also offers excellent and more homely Catalan cooking at reasonable prices (menu at 130 F).

The three main ingredients for aligot (recipe p. 37)

Making aligot

anchovies, sardines, squid (*calamari*) and snails. An excellent choice.

Auberge Saint-Paul

7, Pl. de l'Église,
66500 Villefranche-
de-Conflent,
☎ 04 68 96 30 95.
Closed Mon. from Easter to Oct.; Tues. from Oct. to Easter.
From 130 F to 400 F.
Surprising combinations of top-quality ingredients are guaranteed to set the mouth watering. There is an excellent and extensive wine list. One of the best places to eat in the *département*.

Auberge de Dame Carcass

3, Pl. du Château,
11000 Carcassonne,
☎ 04 68 71 23 23.
Closed Mon. and Tues. lunchtime off-peak.
From 95 F to 250 F.
There is dining on three floors of this country inn. The recipes include food grilled over an open wood fire and there are excellent regional wines. A very good place to know in the old town, which is otherwise full of tourist traps.

Le Tapas Café

Av. de la République,
66190 Collioure,
☎ 04 68 98 30 32.
Closed Sun. evening.
From 80 F to 150 F.
The clue is in the name of course, you can make your own choice of *tapas* from the many dishes which are mouthwateringly displayed in the shop window. Don't forget to accompany your meal with a Collioure wine.

La Passerelle

1, Cours Palmarole,
66000 Perpignan,
☎ 04 68 51 30 65.
Closed Sun. and Mon. lunchtime.
From 100 F to 180 F.
A fish and seafood restaurant of incredible freshness. The cooking is aromatic and there are also some original Catalan dishes.

La Casa Sansa

2, Rue Fabrique-
d'en-Nadal,
66000 Perpignan,
☎ 04 68 34 21 84.
Closed Sun.
From 100 F to 350 F.
The decor is mixed but the atmosphere is convivial. The food is typically Catalan. The main ingredients are

Crème catalane, *a creamy custard under a caramelised crust*

Aude

Château Saint-Martin Trencavel

Hameau de Montredon,
11090 Carcassonne,
☎ 04 68 71 09 53.
Closed Wed. *From 165 F to 300 F.*
A magnificent setting for cuisine in the grand style. The wine list is a marvel and the service impeccable. The perfect place for a special occasion.

The petit violet Roussillon artichoke

Restaurant du Centre et de Lauragais

31, Cours de la République,
11400 Castelnaudary,
☎ 04 68 23 25 95.
Open daily.
From 90 F to 120 F.
Excellent regional cooking in elegant surroundings. Dishes include *foie gras* and *cassoulet*.

Aux Trois Caves

4, Rue Benjamin-Crémieux,
11100 Narbonne,
☎ 04 68 65 28 60.
Open daily.
From 100 F to 230 F.
The restaurant is situated inside old Roman cellars. The cuisine is of the very best. Dishes include *cassoulet*, snails and scampi and the menu is extensive.

Aux Deux Acacias
RN 113 (7 miles
(11 km) from
Castelnaudary on the
Rte de Carcassonne),
11150 Villepinte,
☎ 14 68 94 24 67.
Open daily.
From 70 F to 165 F.
This restaurant serves one
of the best *cassoulets* in the
region, in a warm and friendly
atmosphere.

Hérault

L'Ambassade
22, Bd de Verdun,
34500 Béziers,
☎ 04 67 76 06 24.
Closed Sun. and Mon.
evening.
From 115 F to 220 F.
The decor is slightly shabby
but the food is surprisingly
good and certainly something
to write home about. The
menu varies depending on
what is fresh and in season,
but the dishes are always
first-class.

Le Jardin
Av. Jean-Moulin,
34500 Béziers,
☎ 04 67 36 41 31.
Closed Sun., first week of
Jan., Feb. school holidays
and first fortnight of July.
Fresh ingredients which vary
depending on market avail-
ability and the season, so the
menu is always a delightful
surprise. There is a good wine
list and the wines are of
excellent quality.

Les Jardins de la Mer
Av. Louis-Tudesq,
34140 Bouzigues,
☎ 04 67 78 33 23.
Open daily except in Jan.
From 95 F to 135 F.
The name means 'gardens of
the sea' so seafood, and particularly shellfish, is the main
attraction. The recipes are
delicious and are typical of
this town famous throughout
France for its oysters.

Ferme-Auberge du Mas de Font-Chaude
Rte du Lac, Les Bories,
34800 Clermont-
L'Hérault,
☎ 04 67 96 19 77.
Open from 15 March to
15 Nov.
From 90 F to 150 F.
Excellent local cuisine served
outdoors under the trellis in
summer. Unforgettable
pastries and ice cream.

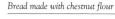

Bread made with chestnut flour

Isadora
6, Rue du Petit-Scel,
34000 Montpellier,
☎ 04 67 66 25 23.
Closed Sat. lunchtime
and Sun.
From 80 F to 150 F.
The restaurant is situated in a
13th-C. vaulted room and
specialises in seafood.

La Maison de la Lozère
27, Rue de l'Aiguillerie,
34000 Montpellier,
☎ 04 67 66 36 10.
Closed Sun. and Mon.
lunchtime; Aug.
From 125 F to 200 F.
As the name implies, the
produce of Lozère is the
house speciality, including
charcuterie from the mountains, *aligot* and local cheese.
There is also a shop attached
so you can buy local delicacies to take home.

La Pomme d'Amour
2 bis, Rue Alber-Paul-
Allies, 34120 Pézenas,
☎ 04 67 98 08 40.
Closed Mon. evening and
Tues., except in season.
From 80 F to 120 F.

*Tellines, tiny cockles from the
Camargues, eaten with an apéritif*

The art of using baby squid, known in French as supions

Simple local food and generous servings in the heart of the old town.

La Palangrotte
Quai de la Marine, 34200 Sète,
☎ 04 67 74 80 35.
Closed Sun. evening and Mon.except July–Aug., and Nov.–Jan.
From 120 F to 300 F.
This restaurant is a local institution. *Eausel*, a fish dish typical of Sète, is always on the menu and is delicious. There are other original, fine seafood dishes.

Gard

La Farigoulette
30580 Seynes, 12 miles (20 km) from Alès,
☎ 04 66 83 70 56.
Closed Sun.
From 70 F to 160 F.
An atmospheric country inn which serves fine local charcuterie and preserved (*confit*) goose and duck made by the owner and his family.

La Terrasse
30440 Saint-Martial, 9 miles (15 km) from Ganges,
☎ 04 67 81 33 77.
De 85 F à 180 F.
A mountainside inn serving food which does honour to the local dishes. Interesting specialities.

Le Magister
5, Rue Nationale, 30000 Nîmes,
☎ 04 66 76 11 00.
Closed Sat. lunchtime and Sun. evening.
From 150 F to 270 F.
An elegant atmosphere and enchanting menu. This is a truly gourmet restaurant. The chef trained and worked at the best establishments in France (Ritz, Tour d'Argent).

Le Spinaker
Pointe du Môle, 30240 Port-Camargue.
Closed Sun. evening and Mon. off peak, Nov.–Apr.
From 130 F to 395 F.
Seafood of the sun, as befits the location. The chef combines the flavours of the sea and the land, with great success.

La Jasse
Arpaillargues, 30700 Uzès,
☎ 04 66 03 10 92.
Open daily.
From 65 F to 120 F.
Delicious cooking with a local flavour. Tripe is one of the many specialities.

Lozère

La Safranière
Chabrits, 48000 Mende,
☎ 04 66 49 31 54.
Closed Sun. evening, Mon., and March.
From 95 F to 230 F.
Haute cuisine, concentrating on herbs and spices.

Ferme-Auberge chez Rémi Baret
Les Hérans, 48150 Meyrueis,
☎ 04 66 45 64 42.
1 April–30 Sept. Closed Sat. and Tue. evenings. Reservations a few days in advance.
From 60 F to 130 F.
Freshness and naturalness are the watchwords at this excellent restaurant which serves food typical of the Causse district, hence its popularity.

Cargolade, an Occitan snail dish

Local cuisine

The cuisine of Languedoc-Roussillon has something in common with that of Provence, in that it uses lots of garlic, olive oil and herbs and is accompanied by the local wines. However, there are some special local dishes such as snails with knuckle of ham or *aligot*. The main ingredient varies, depending on whether you are by the sea or in the mountains. At the seaside, there are plenty of shellfish and fish. Here are some of the outstanding dishes.

From mutton to fish

Sheep live and graze on the *Causses*, the limestone table-lands and are an important food. Leg of lamb and lamb cutlets are grilled over vine trimmings, and a few pinches of thyme from the *garrigue* are thrown over them at the last minute. Sausages and hams, smoked or unsmoked, are enjoyed in the Cerdagne and are used in Castelnaudary for *cassoulet*. By the sea, fish soups such as the *bourride* of Sète, *bouillinade*, mussels and oysters are the main dishes. Not many cheeses are made here except a sheep's cheese from the Causses. There are lots of local sweets and desserts (see p. 40).

The *escargot* divine

In Lozère, the fat snails that live on the vine are called *cagaroulettes*. They are first made to fast for two weeks on a bed of thyme and bayleaf, then cooked for one hour in a

court-bouillon with bacon, bayleaf, fennel and an onion pierced with cloves. The sauce consists of chopped bacon with fried onions, pounded anchovies, sausage meat and herbs. The snails are left to simmer in a pot so that they become impregnated with the flavours of the sauce. If cooked *à la sommiéroise*, they are flavoured with walnuts, rosemary and mint; *à la nîmoise*, with anchovies; *à la*

lodévoise, with wild thyme and chervil with Swiss chard; *en aillade*, with garlic and walnuts crushed with potatoes. A *bouillabaisse de cagarots* is a snail stew with the white parts of leeks and puréed tomatoes. Snails can also be cooked in lard, with chopped bacon, ham or pig's liver. In the Albères or on the Canigou, the snail dish is called *cargolada*. Snails are braised over vine trimmings, removed from their shells and coated with aïoli (garlic sauce). At Saint-Guilhem-le-Désert, on Holy Thursday, it is said that the pilgrims on their way to St. James of

Compostela paraded in procession in the light of tiny oil lamps made from snail shells.

The recipe for *aligot*

This is a speciality from Lozère. You first mash about 1 lb (600 g) of boiled potatoes. In a casserole rubbed with garlic, melt 5 oz (150 g) of butter and 4 fl oz (150 g) of crème fraîche over high heat. Add 14 oz (400 g) fresh thinly sliced tomme or Cantal cheese. Keep stirring the mixture with a wooden spoon, always in the same direction. Gradually beat in the mashed potatoes and continue to stir. When the thick paste no longer sticks to the sides of the pan, the *aligot* is ready.

Collioure anchovies

Anchovies are fished in September and October, at night, from boats lit with bright lights. They are salted as soon as they are unloaded. A few days later, they are gutted and their heads are cut off, they are then arranged in a ring in vats in alternate layers of salt and fish. They are

marinated like this for three months, in their own brine. They are then packed in olive oil or salt, in tins or jars (for the better quality), and marketed. Anchovies are a speciality of Collioure, which still uses the traditional method. Several small companies still make a living from this trade. These anchovies and their by-products such as *anchoïade* (creamed anchovies) and olives stuffed with anchovies are a frequent feature of Catalan food.

La bourride de lotte

Monkfish soup (*bourride de lotte*) is a speciality of Sète. Take a piece of monkfish large enough for four people. Cut it in slices. Place the slices in a pot with a chopped onion, thyme, bayleaf and fennel and moisten with seawater (or

salted water). Simmer for 10 minutes or so. In the meantime, make an *aïoli* by blending together 6 crushed cloves of garlic, 2 egg yolks and 2 ladlefuls of olive oil. Pour it slowly into the pot with the fish, stirring constantly until the mixture thickens slightly. Place a slice of freshly toasted bread rubbed with garlic in each serving bowl and pour the monkfish soup over the bread.

Cassoulet
filling and nourishing

K nown and loved in Castelnaudary since the 15th C., the authentic recipe for *cassoulet* was given to Catherine de Medici by an old woman in 1579, since the queen was seeking a remedy for the sterility of her daughter, Queen Margaret, wife of the king of Navarre, the future Henri IV. Despite everything, no child was born... perhaps the queen did not follow the recipe to the letter? Who knows? In any event, *cassoulet* continues to be lovingly prepared today, at Castelnaudary where it originated, but also throughout the Carcassonne district and even elsewhere in the Pyrenees. This is what it is and how to make it.

The origin of *cassoulet*
The dish takes its name from the vessel in which it is cooked, a clay pot from Issel, 5 miles (8 km) from Castelnaudary. The word in Occitan for small pot is *casso*, hence the diminuitive *cassolet* or *cassoulet* (the 't' is pronounced). A small casserole for great traditions.

Basic principles
There is no *cassoulet* without beans. Languedoc varieties of white haricot beans are called *monges* or *mongettes*, but the preferred dried white bean is the *lingot*, ideally from Lavelanet or Pamiers. The meat always consists of *confit* of goose, fresh pork hock, partridge, pork rinds and fresh local pork sausages. All should be from the Castelnaudary region, of course. Never use so-called Strasbourg sausages or lamb. Other essential ingredients are garlic and pork belly. If you are not in Castelnaudary you will not be able to use the local water, which is supposed to produce perfectly

cooked beans, or the gorse twigs from the Montague Noire to feed the fire.

Which wine?
For some people the richness of *cassoulet* can only be completely matched by a Grand

Fitou. Others prefer to temper the abundance with the flowery and wild fragrances of a Corbières from Lagrasse. Still others consider that the velvety 'preserved' flavours suit a Minervois des Terrasses. In any event, all are agreed that the wine should be red.

The recipe

In an *oulo*, an earthenware pot, cover the beans with cold water then blanch them for 5 minutes in boiling water. Discard this water and cover them again with warm water. Add the chopped pork rinds, diced salt pork and a dab of lard. Season with salt and simmer for 2 hours in a low oven. The beans should be firm but well cooked. Heat the *confit* of goose in a large frying pan so that the fat runs out, then brown all the meat. Arrange a layer of beans with their cooking water in a wide-mouthed casserole then add some meat and then another layer of beans. Fry the sausage in a pan and insert it into the last layer of beans. Sprinkle the contents of the casserole with the rest of the cooking liquid from the sausage and sprinkle generously with pepper.

Cooking

Bake the stew until a brown crust forms on the surface. Push the crust under, then continue cooking until another crust forms, and push this under. You should do this several times.

Do not allow the contents of the pot to dry out. Water can be added, but don't drown the *cassoulet*. It should be baked for 3 to 4 hours. The moral of the story is that you have to get up very early in the morning to enjoy your *cassoulet* in the evening!

SCANDAL IN CASTELNAUDARY

Cassoulet used to be made with broad beans before the American white bean invaded Europe (towards the end of the 16th C.). It has only been known by this French name since 1897. The French adopted many words from the languages of the French provinces, including Occitan. In Occitan, a stew of Occitan broad beans called *petit moine* (little monk) was also given the name of the pot in which it was cooked, but real *cassoulet* only comes from Castelnaudary!

La Belle Chaurienne
Cassoulet
au Canard
Conserverie du Languedoc
Castelnaudary
420 g

Sweets and candies
from nougat to honey

The best-known regional confections are the Galettes de Pont-Aven, Calissons d'Aix and Dragées de Verdun. In Languedoc-Roussillon, there is a passion for mouthwatering sweets – the locals have a sweet tooth. Before going to Perpignan, Limoux or Montpellier, don't forget to note the addresses of some of the best confectioners.

Nougat from Limoux

Using the white honey of the Aude and combining it with almonds from Roussillon, the Maison Labadie (p. 175) has been making its own nougat in copper cauldrons since 1895 and still packs it by hand! A variation is nougat made with almonds and pistachio nuts from neighbouring Bor.

The *croquants villarets* of Nîmes

These are little dry almond rusks. Their inimitable flavour comes from the evergreen oak twigs which Villaret, the *pâtissier* in the Rue de la Madeleine, Nîmes, first used to cook them in c.1775. Apparently he would often give out *croquants villarets* to customers in place of change. They are very popular in Nîmes.

The *grisettes* of Montpellier

Thanks to an farmer who is also a bee-keeper, these sweets, which have been a speciality of Montpellier since the Middle Ages, are now available once again. Pilgrims on their way to the Shrine of St. James of Compostella thronged the streets in their dark clothing which was grey with dust, hence the name *grisette*. Grisettes are balls of liquorice, honey and aniseed flavouring. They are only made by Breguiboul and

can be bought at Godiva, but only in Montpellier (p. 229)!

Tourron and *Rousquille* of Catalonia

These are two typically Catalan sweets. The first is a type of nougat containing almonds, pine nuts and hazelnuts. The second is an iced sponge ring. Here are two good places to buy them: Les Confiseries du Tech, Av. Saint-Gauderique, 66300 Casbestany, ☎ 04 68 50 69 63; Lor (established in 1848), 85, Rue Pascal-Marie-Agasse, 66011 Perpignan, ☎ 04 68 85 65 05.

The *Berlingot* of Pézenas

This speciality from Pézenas is not a humbug like the usual *berlingot* but consists of candy-striped sticks in various flavours (aniseed, mint, coffee, lemon, etc.) which were introduced to the city by an African peddlar. They have been known since the 17th or 18th C. and can be found throughout the town. M. Boudet makes them by hand (visit by appointment, ☎ 04 67 90 76 05).

The *petits pâtés* of Pézenas

Lord Robert Clive (1725–1774), the famous Clive of India, stayed in Pézenas in the

winter of 1768 for his health. These small topedo-shaped pies with golden crusts containing sweetened meat were first made by his Indian cook. Today they are eaten as an appetiser. The recipe is imitated in Béziers and Bordeaux, but never equalled.

The *biterrois* of Béziers

You will find these delicious cakes made with ground almonds and grapes soaked in

Muscat brandy in all *patisseries* in Béziers. Every *patissier* makes his own. The *bitterois* is a cake that travels well, and

can be kept for three weeks. It should be eaten with the local San-Andiu wine.

Beaucaire bread

Every baker in this town will give you his own recipe for *pain de Beaucaire*, which was once round but is nowadays made with a cut down the centre. Another delicacy is *patissoun*, or Easter pâté, a

little sweetmeat of crystallised fruit, similar to Arab cakes. It is only sold in the spring.

Honey

In the Languedoc-Roussillon region honey is collected from bees carrying thyme, rosemary, heather, sweet chestnut and acacia pollen. Bee-keepers even move their hives so that the bees are as close as possible to the best nectar from wild or cultivated flowers. Of the many places to buy honey, the best are Rouquette, 9 *bis*, Route de Saint-Martin, 34230 Paulhan, ☎ 04 67 25 04 40 (by appointment).
Near Narbonne, visit the Miellerie des Clauses Montseret (p. 177).

Other sweetmeats

When visiting the region, you will also have the delight of discovering Narbonne honey croquettes, crystallised fruit in Carcassonne, *coupetade* (toasted almonds, apricots and raisins in a sweet paste), *amélou* (ground almond and grated lemon peel cake) in Florac, orange-flower *navettes* in Sète and *titan*, a soft, delicious chocolate made in Béziers, as well as a host of other sweet-tasting goodies.

MEL I MATO AND CREMA CREMADA

Here are two Catalan specialities to prepare at home. The first one, which is very easy to make, consists of serving a smooth curd cheese coated with honey and sprinkled with nibbed almonds in a pretty ramekin (if possible made at a local pottery).
The second one is a delicious *crème caramel* delicately flavoured with aniseed, lemon or cinnamon, with a burned caramel topping.

Wines and vineyards

Languedoc-Roussillon, from the Camargue to the Spanish border, is the largest wine-making region of France. Make sure you taste a few wines during your holiday. Look for signs saying 'Dégustation'.

> *Wines and vineyards of the Aude*
>
> *Wines and vineyards of the Hérault*
>
> *Wines and vineyards of the Gard*
>
> *Wines and vineyards of the eastern Pyrenees and Rousillon*

Béziers
Cataroise de Béziers.
p. 197.
Minervois vineyards.
p. 198.

Portel-des-Corbières
Terra Vinea –
the Rocbère cellars.
pp. 176-177.

Lézignan-Corbières
Corbières vineyard.
p. 176.

Limoux
Aimery Sieur d'Arques
cooperative.
p. 175.

Tautavel
The wine-makers of
Tautavel.
p. 139.

Thuir
Byrrh cellars.
p. 154.

Banyuls-sur-Mer
Cave Coopérative l'Étoile.
p. 147.

A75

Lot

A75

Orb

N112

Montagne Noire

Minervois

Béziers

Canal du Midi

N113

A61

Carcassonne

● **Narbonne**

Limoux ●

Aude

Corbières

Perpignan

Têt

N116

N9

Tech A9

Collioure ●

SPAIN

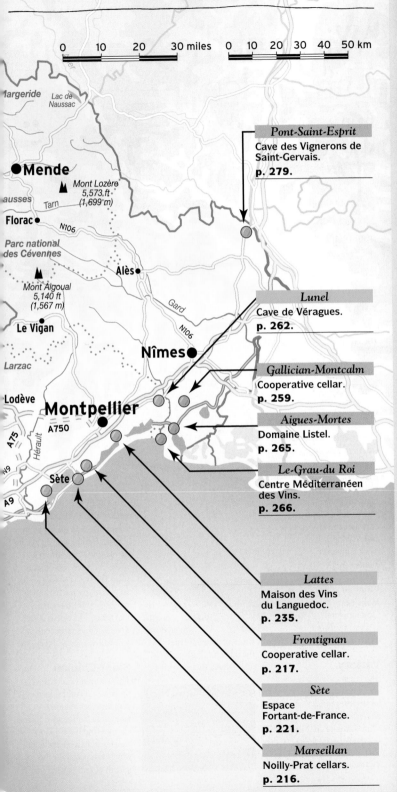

0   10   20   30 miles   0   10   20   30   40   50 km

Margeride   Lac de Naussac

●Mende

▲ Mont Lozère
5,573 ft
(1,699 m)

Florac●   Tarn   N106

Parc national
des Cévennes

Alès●

Mont Aigoual
5,140 ft
(1,567 m)

Le Vigan

Larzac

Lodève

Montpellier   A750

A75   Hérault

N9   Sète

A9

Nîmes●

Gard

N106

Pont-Saint-Esprit
Cave des Vignerons de
Saint-Gervais.
p. 279.

Lunel
Cave de Véragues.
p. 262.

Gallician-Montcalm
Cooperative cellar.
p. 259.

Aigues-Mortes
Domaine Listel.
p. 265.

Le-Grau-du Roi
Centre Méditerranéen
des Vins.
p. 266.

Lattes
Maison des Vins
du Languedoc.
p. 235.

Frontignan
Cooperative cellar.
p. 217.

Sète
Espace
Fortant-de-France.
p. 221.

Marseillan
Noilly-Prat cellars.
p. 216.

Wines of the Languedoc

fruity, robust and velvety

The *appellation* covers 120,000 acres (50,000 ha) of vines on the slopes and *garrigues* (scrubland) of Languedoc, from Narbonne to Nîmes, a total of 156 communes, of which five are in Aude, 14 in Gard, and the rest in Hérault. Annual production is 69,300 gallons (315,000 hectolitres) of red wine and rosé and 145,500 gallons (32,000 hectolitres) of white wine. The wines were praised by Cicero and Pliny the Younger, and received an Appellation d'Origine Contrôlée in 1985.

Finding your bearings

There are three main vineyards: Saint-Chinian, Faugères (north of Béziers), Clairette-du-Languedoc (north of Pézenas), and twelve others: Pic Saint-Loup, in the north; Montpeyroux, Cabrières, Pinet, Saint-Saturnin, in the central region; Saint-Georges-d'Orques and la Méjanelle around Montpellier; Saint-Christol, Saint-Drézéry, Vérargues in the east; Quatourze and la Clape in the far west.

possible to produce wines of different types, and the differences are carefully maintained, though with a constant eye to quality. The *garrigue* (scrub) contributes its aromas of thyme and rosemary, of broom and of rockrose. The red is perfect for an everyday wine but should not be kept for more than four years. The rosé is better than its Provençale equivalent which is more expensive.

Variety

The red grape varieties used are Carignan, Grenache, Mourvèdre, Syrah, Cabernet-Sauvignon and Merlot. The white varieties are Picpoul, Bourboulenc, Clairette, Chardonnay and Sauvignon. The diversity of soils makes it

Saint-Chinian

This vineyard was created by St. Benoît d'Aniane who planted vines around his monastery. Surrounded by the Carroux and the Espinouse, it benefits from a microclimate which also promotes the growth of mimosa and orange

trees. These are robust reds and rosés, produced at Ussignan, Cazedarnes, Creissan, Pierrerue, Quarante, Roquebrun, Saint-Chinian and Vieussan.

Faugères

Faugères is grown at an altitude of 500–1,000 ft (150–300 m) on a shale soil which imbues the Faugères with flavour. The vines are grown south of Bédarieux on steep terraces at Autignac, Cabrerolles, Caussiniojouls, Faugères, Fos, Laurens and Roquessels.

La Clape

The red, stony clay soil yields 132,000 gallons (6,000 hectolitres) a year. The white Blanc de blancs is the most typical, plus there is Malvoisie (Malmsey, which according to the Greeks, gave wisdom to those who drank it) and Bourboulenc; the red wines are spiced with the scents of the *garrigue*, and the Rosé de Saignée (from the ripest grapes) has salmon-pink highlights and an aroma of berries.

Clairette-du-Languedoc

This vintage was well known in Gallo-Roman times, taking its name from the vine stock itself. It is made at Adissan,

Le Bosc, Cabrières, Paulhan, Péret. The wine may be dry or mellow and is drinkable whether young or old.

ROUSSILLON WINE

In the past Roussillon wines have had a poor reputation but this is gradually fading. The reds have a nice bouquet (and can be kept for about 8 years), the white wines are flowery and the rosés pleasant (can be kept for 1–2 years). They are made at Bélesta, Cazes Frères, Château de Jau, Domaines Jammes, Sarda-Malet, Taichac and Terrassous.

Quatourze

The dry climate at the gates of Narbonne, near the Étang de Bages, is ideal for Mourvèdre. Nice rosés and powerful reds are produced here, not forgetting the white wines.

Chapel near Usclas-du-Bosc (Hérault), in the vineyard of Clairette-du-Languedoc

Cabrières

These shale soils benefit from a lot of sun and produce 1,500 gallons (7,000 hectolitres) a year. There is a Clairette and rosés with a good reputation, including the Estabel, as well as velvety reds that go well with the local game.

Picpoul-de-pinet

This vineyard overlooks the Étang de Thau and produces 7,300 gallons (33,000 hectolitres). The Picardin, a dry fortified wine dates from the Middle Ages and was much appreciated by the Dutch. Only white wines have the A.O.C. label. They are fruity, with a hint of aniseed, and can be served with shellfish and fish.

Montpeyroux

The vineyard extends along the edge of the the Causse du Larzac, at the foot of the Baudile peak. In the 14th C., the bishops of Montpellier had their summer residence here when the vineyard was already producing famous crimson wines, with the aroma of ripe fruit and the *garrigue*.

Saint-Saturnin

This rich vineyard is situated in the foothills of the Larzac, in a warm climate sheltered from the winds. Taste these supple, fruity 'night wines'

and the robust reds which smell of the *garrigue*, stewed fruit and spices.

Saint-Georges-d'Orques

From 1730, the consuls of the town stamped their barrels with a device representing a knight fighting a dragon. In 1804, Thomas Jefferson recommended reducing the import duty on these wines to combat alcoholism (due to addiction to spirits). The vineyard produces 4,500 gallons (20,000 hectolitres) of red wines and rosés annually.

Saint-Christol and Saint-Drézéry

The pebble terraces of Saint-Christol, exposed to sea breezes, produces 2,600 gallons (12,000 hectolitres) of generous reds, with a hint of spice. Saint-Drézéry, 9 miles (15 km) east of Montpellier, is a vineyard on a gentle slope producing 1,000 gallons (4,500 hectolitres) a year.

La Méjanelle

The pebbly soil at the gates of Montpellier makes this vineyard, which is affected by its closeness to the sea, exceptional. It produces heavy, concentrated wines, with a mixed bouquet of spices and ripe fruit.

Vérargues

In the east of the Hérault, you will find fruity, mellow red wines which Jean-Jacques

Rousseau praised to d'Alembert. This vineyard has been producing 'coffee wines' for a long time. The annual yield is 4,000 gallons (18,000 hectolitres).

Pic Saint-Loup

If you don't have a head for heights and are neither a hunter nor a rambler, you will still find grapes on the lower slopes. The Pic Saint-Loup is 18¼ miles (30 km) long, 9 miles (15 km) wide and its favourable soil produces 10,300 gallons (47,000 hectolitres) annually, including a very good Gravettes.

Conditions for having an A.O.C.

Conditions for an A.O.C. are a basic yield of 11 gallons (50 hectolitres) per 2½ acres (1 ha), 11° minimum proof and a density of 4,000 plants per 2½ acres (1 ha). The main varieties are Carignan, Cinsault,

Mourvèdre and Syrah; additional varieties are Counoise Noir, Grenache Rosé, Terret Noir and

Picpoul Noir. Most wines produced under the Coteaux-du-Languedoc Appellation are required to be blended.

Where to buy

Direct sales to individuals, which wine makers prefer, account for 30% of annual production. However, if you live in the United States, the United Kingdom, Germany, Switzerland or Belgium, you can also find them at home because commercial buyers come from all over the world. Keep your eyes peeled in the supermarkets and remember the names. Only costing around 12 to 14 F a bottle in France however, they'll be much better value than if bought back at home.

AOC, VDQS?
HISTORY OF THE INITIALS

AOC: Appellation d'Origine Contrôlée. This means that the origin and name of the wines is supervised by the INAO (Institut National des Appellations d'Origine) of which there are 400 for wines alone. Grape varieties, cultivation methods, yields, percentage of alcohol and vinification methods are laid down by law. VDQS: Vin Délimité de Qualité Supérieure. These wines are subject to the same supervision as those of the AOC, but since the yield is permitted to be greater, the overall quality is generally not as high.

A few vintage years

1988: Exceptional. Thanks to a warm, sunny summer the grapes matured well and were very concentrated. The wines are heavy and balanced with complex aromas. One of the best years for wines with keeping quality.

1989: Another great year. Lots of rain in the spring, high temperatures in August, producing concentrated rich wines, with a lot of ripe tannins. Powerful wines for keeping.

1990: A fine year, although with a little too much rain in the spring which encouraged fungal pests. But the Syrahs gave excellent results.

1991: early.

1992: rich wines of a very similar quality to the fine wines produced in 1988.

Muscat and sweet wine

From Montpellier to Perpignan, five vineyards draw their strength from the burning sun and are happy with just a few drops of rain a year. They produce a sweet wine, which may be as much as 16° proof with 4.5 oz (130 g) of sugar per 1¾ pt (1 l). These naturally sweet wines and other muscats are a beautiful golden colour, and are extremely powerful, so should be consumed in moderation.

Identity card

The appellation Vin Doux Naturel (VDN) is reserved for wines from only four grape varieties – Muscat, Grenache, Maccabeo and Malvoisie – produced in Languedoc-Roussillon and a few other *départements* in the Midi. They are made from ripe grapes in which pure grape spirit has been added to them during fermentation. For such a wine to be labelled *rancio*, a VDN must age in vats exposed to the sun in summer and be kept warm in winter for at least two years.

Natural sweet wine or muscat ?

Of the 12 appellations for natural sweet wines, only six are muscats. These are Rivesaltes, Frontignan, Saint-Jean-de-Minervois, Mireval, de Lunel and Beaumes-de-Venise (in Vaucluse). The other VDNs are Banyuls, Banyuls Grand Cru, Maury, Rivesaltes, Rasteau and Grand-Roussillon.

Rivesaltes

This wine, from a muscat grape originally from Alexandria and from other small muscat grapes, and has been produced since the 13th C., making it one of the oldest sweet wines of Europe. Its brick-red colour takes on fawn highlights after long maturing, promising sweet, fruity flavours. It is drunk young as a dessert wine.

Lunel

Lunel is made from small muscat grapes in the sandstone slopes of Lunel, Vérargues and Saturargues. The vineyard covers 642 acres (260 ha) producing 219,290

a sweet, dark red wine which can be kept for 40 years. It has great finesse and subtle aromas. For information about buying and sampling it, see p. 147.

Maury

On the hills north of Agly, 98,6850 gallons (45,000 hl) of this elegant, powerful wine is produced from Grenache Noir grapes. It is the colour of pomegranates when young, later turning mahogany. The bouquet is reminiscent of cocoa. For information, see p. 139.

(10,000 hl annually). The muscat has a fruity flavour but does not have the reputation it deserves. It is mainly drunk as an apéritif or with dessert.

Frontignan

This is another wine produced from a single variety of small, white muscat grapes. It is golden, fruity and with an aftertaste of honey. In the 17th C. it was said to 'surpass any other type of wine in its generosity'. Frontignan production is a real industry, with 430 vineyard owners and 1,778 acres (720 ha),

producing 43,860 gallons (20,000 hl) per year (2 million bottles), all from one cooperative cellar. (see p. 217).

Mireval

The vineyard covers the south side of the Gardiole range between Sète and Montpellier. Planted from a small muscat variety, it produces a sweet, natural, smooth, light and fruity wine.

Banyuls

This wine is a favourite of the Côte Vermeille, and is planted on narrow terraces. The vineyard produces

Saint-Jean-de-Minervois

This is the only Minervois muscat (p. 198), and is the jewel of the appellation, produced from a vineyard planted at an altitude of 667 ft (200 m) (which is why it is harvested three weeks later than the other muscats).

WHAT GOES WELL WITH MUSCAT?

Some people drink it as an apéritif or with *foie gras*. Its exotic flavours of pineapple, lychee and mango marry well with a sorbet or apricot, lemon or plum tart or even a *crème brûlée*. These sweet wines also go well with blue cheese (Roquefort or Stilton) and goat's cheeses (with raisin bread). An opened bottle will keep well for about ten days.

Home furnishings

From the finest silk to Catalan fabrics, pottery and glass, you will find that the region has a lot to offer.

① Perpignan

Maison Quinta:
Les Toiles du soleil,
Catalan weavings.
p. 135.

② Perpignan

Centre d'Artisanat d'Art.
pp. 134-135.

③ Sorède

Les Micocouliers:
whip factory.
pp. 145-146.

④ Arles-sur-Tech

Catalan woven fabrics.
p. 151.

⑤ Saint-Laurent-de-Cerdans

Catalan woven fabrics:
Les Toiles du Soleil,
Musée de l'Espadrille.
pp. 150-151.

⑥ Céret

Mértiers d'Art Saint-Roch: regional arts and crafts centre.
pp. 152-153.

⑦ Castelnaudary

Poterie du Castel.
p. 171.

⑧ Lamalou-les-Bains

Hérépian:
bell foundry.
p. 205.

⑨ Villeneuvette

Woollen
cloth mill.
p. 207.

⑩ Pézenas

Pottery.
p. 210.

⑪ Couloubrines

Glassworks.
p. 57.

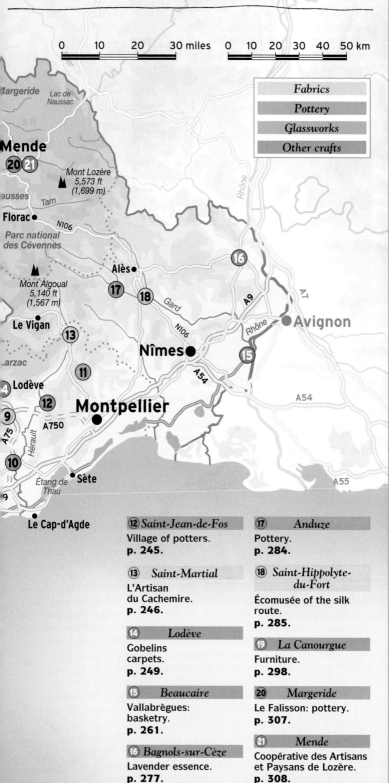

0   10   20   30 miles   0   10   20   30   40   50 km

| Fabrics |
| Pottery |
| Glassworks |
| Other crafts |

Margeride   Lac de
             Naussac

Mende
20 **21**
                  Mont Lozère
                  5,573 ft
ausses   (1,699 m)
           Tarn

Florac ●
                  N106
Parc national
des Cévennes

Mont Aigoual
5,140 ft   Alès ●
(1,567 m)   **17** **18**   Gard
                                              A9   A7
Le Vigan ●
          13   N106   Rhône   ● **Avignon**
arzac
                          Nîmes ●
Lodève   **11**   **15**
4
9   **12**   **Montpellier**   A54
           A750   A54
10
          Hérault   A55
          Étang de   ● **Sète**
          Thau

● **Le Cap-d'Agde**

⑫ Saint-Jean-de-Fos
Village of potters.
p. 245.

⑬ Saint-Martial
L'Artisan
du Cachemire.
p. 246.

⑭ Lodève
Gobelins
carpets.
p. 249.

⑮ Beaucaire
Vallabrègues:
basketry.
p. 261.

⑯ Bagnols-sur-Cèze
Lavender essence.
p. 277.

⑰ Anduze
Pottery.
p. 284.

**⑱ Saint-Hippolyte-
du-Fort**
Écomusée of the silk
route.
p. 285.

⑲ La Canourgue
Furniture.
p. 298.

⑳ Margeride
Le Falisson: pottery.
p. 307.

㉑ Mende
Coopérative des Artisans
et Paysans de Lozère.
p. 308.

The silk industry

Silkworm farming was invented in China and reached its zenith in 18th-C. France, then declined at the beginning of the 20th C. The rich fabrics with which kings and courtesans clothed themselves were produced at the workshops of Saint-Hippolyte-du-Fort (p. 285) or Saint-Jean-du-Gard (p. 292). There is still an active craft industry which perpetuates the tradition in the heart of the Cévennes.

The silk-puller

In Cévennes, the earliest evidence of silk manufacture dates from 1296, where there is evidence that a 'silk-puller' was working in Anduze. In the 14th C., silk weavers became rich and their families powerful. In the 16th C., the advent of Protestantism coincided with the favour in which farmers and botanists found themselves. Olivier de Serres, counsellor to King Henri IV, encouraged him to develop the silk industry. Later, after the Wars of Religion, Colbert (1619–1683), minister to Louis XIV, continued the work of his predecessors, helped by Basville, superintendant of the region.

Undivided attention

From seed to cocoon, every stage needs to be monitored, the temperature controlled, the silkworm 'nest' cleaned and the silk worms fed.

The seeds are the eggs laid by the female Bombyx moth immediately after mating. The incubation period lasts for 15 days. Women would put the seeds into little bags which they slipped down their cleavage or under their petticoats, but in the 19th C., incubators were introduced, and then later collective incubation chambers (one per valley).

The giant appetite of the silkworm

The silkworm larva emerges after a fortnight as a tiny, hairy black caterpillar and requires constant care. Silkworms must be fed huge amounts of leaves. As much as 2,867 lb (1,300 kg) of mulberry leaves are required for 1.16 oz (33 g) of seeds! In one month, after four moults, the silkworm's weight increases 10,000 fold!

Traditional de-cocooning equipment

Silence for the spinners!

After the last moult the worm stops eating and looks for a support. Large branches of white heather are arranged in arcs on the screen of the nest-box. The worm climbs up and starts secreting a continuous

silken thread from its mouth. The thread measures 2,330–5,000 ft (700–1,500 m) long. It spins its cocoons uninterruptedly for three days and must not be disturbed or disrupted. Even a thunderstorm could prove disastrous. The last stage consists of

removing the heather and sorting the thousands of golden or white cocoons. This is the de-cocooning stage. Some cocoons are retained for reproduction, the rest are smothered to prevent the moth emerging from the cocoon and tearing it.

'The golden tree'

In 1709, there was a terrible frost which decimated the sweet chestnut and olive trees, and the farmers replanted the forests with mulberry trees. Silk mills multiplied. From 1752 onwards, the land of silk was defined as extending from Vigan to Privas via Alais, whose silk fair on 24 August became the most important in the kingdom. The silken thread was sold to merchants and was then

THE SILK ROADS

Interested in silk? Try this tour which covers Gard, Hérault and Lozère and offers the visitor a new insight into the places affected by the history of silk. Mulberry trees, silk-worm farms, spinning mills (milling consists of twisting together the threads from several cocoons in order to form a silk thread), museums and crafts-manship are all be covered. Contact: Association pour le Développement de la Sériciculture, Pl. du 8-Mai, 30170 Saint-Hippolyte-du-Fort (p. 285), ☎ 04 66 77 66 47, fax: 04 66 85 44 71.

milled at Uzès or Nîmes. In the Cévennes, silk manufacturing was confined to stockings, which do not require milling. Stockings from the Cévennes were worn on aristocratic calves in all the courts of Europe.

The golden age of silk

After the Revolution, the market declined, but the Restoration in 1820 relaunched production and there was another 30 years of prosperity. The introduction of steam marked the transition from craftsmanship to industry. At its zenith, around 1855, silk production was suddenly ruined by a terrible epidemic. Pasteur contained the disease in 1865, but the opening of the Suez Canal made it much easier to import oriental silks and French silk could not compete. The *coup de grâce* came in the 20th C., with the invention of artificial fibres, and the farms shut in 1965.

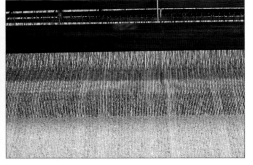

Fabrics
woollen cloth and hand-woven fabrics

Languedoc-Roussillon has always been a cloth-weaving region, quite apart from its silk. Fabrics range from woollens to the famous denim for jeans. Some industries have disappeared, but others are perpetuating the tradition. At any rate, we're not yet ready to clothe ourselves entirely in paper or plastic!

Cloth from Villeneuvette...

There was a famous woollen mill near Clermont-l'Hérault from the 17th C. It produced fine, light woollen cloth known as *londrin* (from the word 'London') dyed in bright colours and exported to the Levant and other countries in the Mediterranean. After the Revolution, it specialised in cloth for the army and mainly fulfilled government contracts. It was one of the last woollen mills in Languedoc to close, but it did so in 1954.

...from Lodève...

The clothing industry had its heyday here in the 18C. In 1730, Lodève had the monopoly for supplying the Royal army and in the year 1747 it produced more than 20,000 items. Wars kept the mill in production until 1860 when its privilege ceased and

this marked the start of its decline. In 1960, the last mill closed its doors, making 400 workers redundant.

...and from the Montagne Noire

There were 240 looms operating in the villages of the region (such as Montolieu and Cuxac-Cabardès) in the early 18th C. At the Royal

FROM NÎMES OR FROM GENOA?

In San Francisco in 1850, an Austrian tailor, Levi Strauss, had the idea of making hard-wearing trousers for miners from cloth made in Nîmes (de Nîmes), a very tough type of serge which came from the Italian port of Genoa (in San Francisco, it was pronounced 'Djinn') normally used as sailcloth. From the workplace to fashion, via leisure, denim jeans have progressively become an essential item in every wardrobe.

As for the colour scheme, these are a hymn of praise to the south, whether they are the 'blood and gold' combination in homage to spices or inspired by the deep blue of the Mediterranean.

Factories and museums

The production centre for Catalan fabrics is Vallespir. At Saint-Laurent-de-Cerdans, Les Toiles du Soleil (p. 150) has been carrying on the tradition since 1860 and has used old documents to either reproduce old designs or adapt them for modern tastes.

The Musée de l'Espadrille (p. 150) retraces the history of this cloth shoe which has become a summer classic and explains how it is made. In Arles-sur-Tech (p. 151), Les Tissages Catalans is a new enterprise that has opened up in the premises of a former weaving mill. It is both a museum displaying old dying workshops and weaving shops retracing the history of the Catalan weaving mills, as well as a workshop where table linen is still produced for sale commercially.

Manufacturers cloth was woven for export to Smyrna, Constantinople, Cairo and Aleppo. Unfortunately, from the late 18th C., competition from the British caused a slowing down and finally the demise of this regional activity.

a taste for geometric motifs and patterns as well as weaving in relief. The patterns that most typically appear on this closely woven, coarse fabric include stripes, which were used for deck-chairs and table linen as well as for the famous espadrilles.

Catalan weaving

Catalan hand-loom weaving is centuries old but was really only developed in the late 19th C. No one knows who the first weaver was nor when he lived. It is quite likely that some of the influences came from Catalonia's centuries of conquests and war, which left

Glass and glass-making

Between the Middle Ages and the Revolution, the gentlemen glass-makers of Languedoc worked on the Hortus *causse*, 19 miles (30 km) from the Mediterranean, Montpellier and Nîmes. They made bottles, flasks and flagons for the apothecaries and wine-makers of the region. A signposted route enables you to visit the various manufacturers. Take the D 107 to Claret, Ferrières-les-Verreries, Lauret, Sauteyrargues, Valflaunes and Vacquières.

Origins

The tradition of the master glass-makers of Languedoc is not fully understood, but it is clear that the Hortus *causse* is particularly well-suited to glass-making. Its forests of evergreen and deciduous oaks supply the wood needed for the furnaces

which heat the sand and iron in the production of molten glass. The glass-makers sold their products in the markets of Ganges, Sommières and Montpellier. It may well be due to them that Languedoc wine could be exported and became so popular.

Who were the glass-makers?

In the 15th C. glass-making was an industry governed by a strict code. The impoverished nobility were allowed to make glass with consent of the King. In 1455, the Sommières charter stipulated that only the descendants of these gentlemen glass-makers, who owned their own glassworks, were entitled to pursue this occupation. The privilege was thus hereditary and the secrets and skills were passed down from generation to generation.

Decline and revival

The Revolution abolished such privileges which damaged the trade. With the Industrial Revolution coal came into use. It was less expensive than the charcoal used hitherto and made it possible to reach the ideal

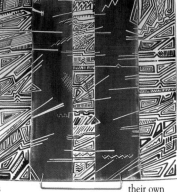

The glass-maker's tools

Tongs for pulling the glass

Rod for collecting, blowing and turning the glass

Wooden mallets for roughly shaping the glass

Scissors for cutting the glass from the rod

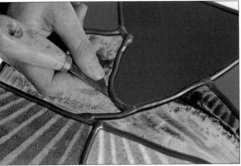

temperature for melting glass much faster. This industrialisation accelerated the decline of the industry as a craft. Since 1989, a few enthusiasts have revived the tradition which has led to the foundation of the glassworks at Couloubrines and at Ferrières-les-Verreries.

Couloubrines
☎ 04 67 59 06 39.
Open: Jul.–Aug, 4-7pm;
Sun. and bank holidays 2-5pm.
Closed 1 Oct.–15 May.
This is an open-air glassworks, so avoid going on a rainy day. It claims to reproduce the old atmosphere of the glassworks of the Renaissance. An oven has even been reconstructed based on ancient techniques.

Art glassworks at Claret
Open daily, Jul.–Aug. 10am-7pm; Jun. and Sept. except Wed. 10am-noon and 2-6pm.
Closed 1 Jan.–15 Feb.
Research establishments, training schools and exhibition premises have joined forces to raise the standard of contemporary glass-making techniques. Eric Lindgren,

a glass-blower from the Swedish school of Orrefors, ☎ 04 67 59 08 60, and a stained glass artist, Béatrice Jaillet ☎ 04 67 59 07 48, are resident workers here.

On the route
Campagne is the gateway to the glass-making road and was once a stop on the route to St. James of Compostella. Saint Martin also

stopped here and allegedly cured the population of the 'white evil'. There are no more iron mines at Gallargues, but if you make the effort to climb the Pene you will have a magnificent view to the sea. Garrigues and Sauteyrargues, are delightful villages with a lovely Romanesque church. Vacquières with the famous Cammaous bridge is followed by Valfalaunes below the Pic Saint-Loup and cliff of the Hortus.

The future
A third workshop is free at the time of writing and is used for temporary exhibitions. An artist working in an activity complementary to glass-blowing and stained glass would be very welcome. Steve Linn, a sculptor in glass, has been working at Claret recently, but more craftsmen are needed.

The Anduze vase

T he clay soil of Languedoc-Roussillon lends itself well to the creation of pottery and earthenware, a tradition that dates back thousands of years. Anduze (p. 284) has been renowned for its pottery since the 5th C. According to legend, a potter from this town visited the fair at Beaucaire and noticed an Italianate vase in the Medici style. It had an elegant shape and was decorated with flowers and fruit. He was inspired by it to create what became the Anduze vase, in which Florentine exuberance is tempered with the austerity of the Cévennes.

a dynasty of potters who made crockery, jugs, green-oil jars, casseroles and basins for the local silk-spinning industry. It was not until the 18th C. that

Why Anduze ?

The red clay needed for making this type of pottery is found here at Anduze. A little further away, in the Hérault, the thick Ganges clay supplies the slip, a clay coating with which the vase is covered before firing. A mineral extract from Durfort was used for the glaze. When enriched with copper oxide it produces green glaze; when manganese oxide is added, the result is a rich chestnut brown glaze.

What the vase looks like

It is a short, circular vase with a thick lip, decorated on the sides with various traditional designs which are typical of the region. The size of the vase varies enormously from 2.5–40 in (6.5cm– 1 m). The colours are marbled in a mixture of honey yellow, olive green and chestnut brown glazes.

Who makes them?

The oldest known vase dates from 1782, and was made by Gautier,

the signatures of the oldest families appeared on the famous Anduze vases.

cracks – the potter's nightmare. Finally, it is ready for glazing and firing.

Rediscovered craftsmanship

The pottery was made in the traditional way until the first quarter of the 20th C. The advent of new materials for pottery caused many of the factories to disappear. Today, the old techniques are still used with the introduction of some new ones (in the colouring, for instance, blues, cerise and white enamel are making an appearance).

How they are made

The clay is dried, crushed and milled. Water is then pumped through it for 10 days. The paste thus obtained is then put into a ball-clay machine and aged for at least a month. The vase is pre-shaped in a calibrator (the potter's wheel is no longer used because of the heavy work involved; you need more than 220 lb (100 kg) of clay for a 3.4 ft (1 m) high vase). It is made in two parts, the foot and the body.

The decoration

When it has hardened (after a week in a plaster mould), the decorations are applied, as is the foot, and the vase is dried again. Then it is covered in white slip to enable the glaze to fix properly. The vase must dry before firing, or it could develop

Anduze... and the others

Anduze is a well-known name, but there are many other places in Languedoc-Roussillon where contemporary artist-potters are at work (see map pp. 50-51), especially in Saint-Jean-de-Fos (p. 245), where the potteries developed mainly in the 17th and 18th C., and at Saint-Quentin-la-Poterie (p. 274), the capital of earthenware and terracotta in the *département* of Gard.

Reed cutting
an ancient tradition

In Provençal, the word for a reed is *sagno*. Between Vauvert and Saint-Gilles, the little D 779 side-road which runs beside the lagoons of Charnier and Grey in the Petite Camargue (p. 258) offer an insight

into an occupation stretching back aeons – that of the reed-cutter, or *sagneur* as they are known locally. These *sagneurs* have abandoned tractors in favour of flat-bottomed boats which take them down the channels into the labyrinthine marshes.

A closed shop

Only the inhabitants of Vauvert and Gallician have the right to harvest reeds over the 4,448 acres (1,800 ha) of the communally owned marshes. There were about 120 reed-cutters in the 1960s, who always cut them by hand. Today, they number fewer than twenty, though their ranks are swelled by a few casual workers during the harvest season. This secret

environment is silent but for the sound of water-fowl, coypu (which have replaced beavers) and frogs. The reed-cutters know the area like the backs of their hands.

Portrait of a reed-cutter

The reed-cutters work in water up to their knees. They wear rubber waders and the only tools they use are a long-handled sickle called a *sagnadou* and a sharpening-stone. They tie the cut reeds into bundles 24 in (60 cm) in circumference. Back on dry land, the bundles will be combed, sorted and bound with wire. They fill their boats with the bundles and when it is full, the *sagneur* tranports them to a larger boat called *la bête* ('the beast'). A good cutter can make as many as 100 bundles per day.

Harvesting time

The reed-cutting season lasts from November to March, although in the old days cutting was done in the summer. Reeds are cut when their leaves have fallen and before the regrowth. The reed bunches are lined up along the edges of the roads awaiting shipment to the United Kingdom, the Netherlands, Brittany, Paris or Normandy as well as to a few local workshops which process them.

Uses of reeds

Reed has exceptional properties. It is tough, waterproof and non-rotting, an excellent heat and sound insulator and light and flexible (it bends but does not break, as the saying goes). It can be converted into cellulose, woven cloches, forage and cladding. It is used to make mats for household purposes or the woven braids used by horticulturalists in cold climates to protect tender plants. The main use of reed is, of course, as thatch. A roof covered with reed thatching from the Camargue is said to have a lifespan of up to 30 years.

In the Camargue

The stone huts, sheepfolds and farmhouses (*mas*) of the Camargue are no longer built of traditional materials. But for those that remain, where the thatched roof needs repairing or replacing, the thatcher gets to work. He nails battens to the rafters and places the bales of thatch on them. The rows overlap from the bottom, over two-thirds of the surface. In the last row, the bales are arranged the other way round so that that the roof-ridge is even under its cement coping.

A mechanised future

In privately-owned marshes, machines for harvesting, beating and baling the reeds have replaced manpower. These machines range from a heavy harvester which damages the marsh by crushing and compacting it, to a machine that rolls – or rather hovers – over the water thanks to its low pressure pneumatic tyres. The most sophisticated machinery can harvest up to 2,000 bundles a day. Machines are popular with birds, who like to eat the insects left by the machines in their wake.

A skill that should not be lost

The traditional reed-cutter not only harvests reeds but he is also vital for the survival of the ponds and lagoons in the Petite Camargue. Since the Rhône has now been harnessed and no longer floods the marshes naturally, the reed-cutters play the role of regulators. By cutting their reeds beneath the water, they renew the ecological balance of this environment. If the marsh were to disappear, so would the unique flora and many nesting and migrating birds.

Castles, citadels and mansions

From the Cathar citadels perched on limestone peaks to the 18th C. mansions surrounded by luxurious gardens, the array of architectural styles is quite stunning. Take the time to explore.

Castles and châteaux

1 Perpignan: the 14th C. Castillet-Casa Pairal. **p. 133.**

2 Salses-le-Château: 15th-16th C. fortress. **p. 137.**

3 Tautavel: 13th C. feudal castle. **p. 138.**

4 Canet-en-Rousillon: 11th-14th C. viscount's castle. **p. 140.**

5 Formiguères: 9th C. château des rois de Majorque. **p. 165.**

6 Carcassonne: 12th C. château Comtal. **p. 169.**

7 Béziers: 19th C. château de Belle-Île. **p. 197.**

8 Pézenas: 17th C. château de Lézignan-la-Cèbe. **p. 211.**

9 Montpellier:18th C. Montpelliérain châteaux. **pp. 236-239.**

10 Prades-le-Lez: 18th C. domaine de Restinclières. **p. 240.**

11 Sommières: 11th C. fortified castle, 11th-16th C. château de Villevieille. **pp. 242 and 243.**

12 Beaucaire: 11th C. château Royal. **p. 260.**

13 Alès: 19th C. château du Colombier, 12th-16th C. château de Portes. 17th C. château de Rousson, **pp. 280 and 282.**

14 Florac: 17th C. château. **p. 292.**

15 Saint-Chély-du-Tarn: 15th C. château de la Caze. **p. 302.**

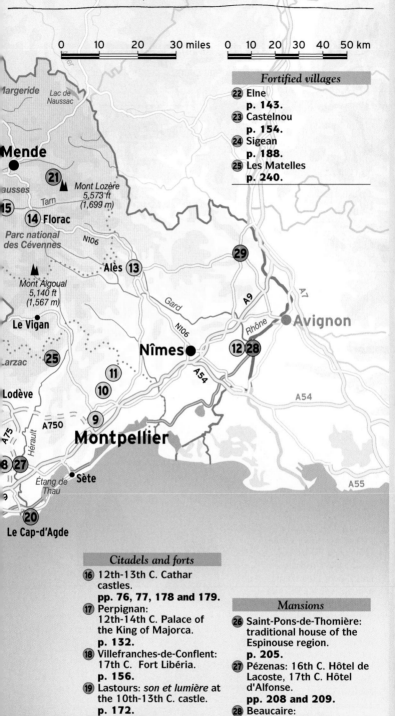

0 10 20 30 miles **0 10 20 30 40 50 km**

Fortified villages

22 Elne
p. 143.
23 Castelnou
p. 154.
24 Sigean
p. 188.
25 Les Matelles
p. 240.

Margeride Lac de Naussac

Mende

21 Mont Lozère
5,573 ft
(1,699 m)

ausses Tarn

15

14 Florac

Parc national des Cévennes N106

Mont Aigoual
5,140 ft
(1,567 m)

Le Vigan

Alès 13

Gard

A9

N106 Rhône **Avignon**

Nîmes 12 28

A54

arzac 25

Lodève

11
10

A54 A55

9

A750

Montpellier

A75 Hérault

8 27 Sète

Étang de Thau

20

Le Cap-d'Agde

Citadels and forts

16 12th-13th C. Cathar castles.
pp. 76, 77, 178 and 179.
17 Perpignan:
12th-14th C. Palace of the King of Majorca.
p. 132.
18 Villefranches-de-Conflent:
17th C. Fort Libéria.
p. 156.
19 Lastours: *son et lumière* at the 10th-13th C. castle.
p. 172.
20 Cap-d'Agde:
Brescou fort.
p. 214.
21 Mont Lozère: 10th C.
Citadelle de La Garde-Guérin.
p. 297.

Mansions

26 Saint-Pons-de-Thomière:
traditional house of the Espinouse region.
p. 205.
27 Pézenas: 16th C. Hôtel de Lacoste, 17th C. Hôtel d'Alfonse.
pp. 208 and 209.
28 Beaucaire:
17th C. town hall.
p. 260.
29 Bagnols-sur-Cèze:
17th-18th C. private mansions.
p. 276.

Citadels forts and follies

From the fortresses of the Cathar country, perched on the rocky spurs of the Corbières (p. 178), to the 18th-C. follies of the Montpellier district (p. 236), the great houses of Languedoc-Roussillon are a permanent reminder of this region's turbulent history. They are proof of how this frontier territory was coveted and became an

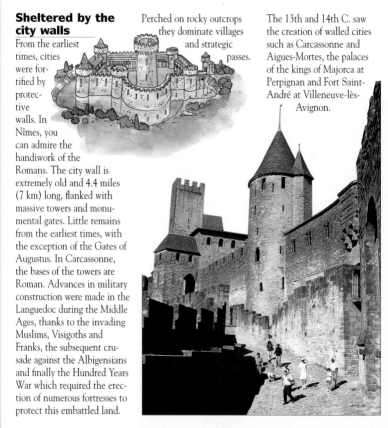

Fortification in the style built by Vauban

almost permanent battleground. Once peace was finally established, the follies of Montpellier were built, evidence of the elegant lifestyle of the Age of Enlightenment.

Sheltered by the city walls

From the earliest times, cities were fortified by protective walls. In Nîmes, you can admire the handiwork of the Romans. The city wall is extremely old and 4.4 miles (7 km) long, flanked with massive towers and monumental gates. Little remains from the earliest times, with the exception of the Gates of Augustus. In Carcassonne, the bases of the towers are Roman. Advances in military construction were made in the Languedoc during the Middle Ages, thanks to the invading Muslims, Visigoths and Franks, the subsequent crusade against the Albigensians and finally the Hundred Years War which required the erection of numerous fortresses to protect this embattled land.

Perched on rocky outcrops they dominate villages and strategic passes.

The 13th and 14th C. saw the creation of walled cities such as Carcassonne and Aigues-Mortes, the palaces of the kings of Majorca at Perpignan and Fort Saint-André at Villeneuve-lès-Avignon.

SIGNALLING TOWERS: EARLY COMMUNICATION

Roman texts report the existence of watchtowers on the hilltops which produced smoke signals during the day and bonfire signals at night. Warnings were thus given to the people – as on the arrival of the Carthaginian fleet, anchored in the bay of Tarragona in Spain as well as the movements of Roman ships. The system was improved in the face of constant danger from the Muslims and the number of tall buildings in the region increased. Later, the lords of Anduze created a new system of signalling towers in the Cévennes, thus controlling the means of communication and reinforcing their power. The same system of beacons was used during the Hundred Years War. It is amazing to realise that the Tour de Sauve could therefore communicate with the Tour de la Canourgue, nearly 50 miles (80 km) away as the crow flies.

Vauban in Roussillon

It is thanks to Louis XIV that the military engineer Vauban (1633–1707) visited Roussillon several times to see how it could be protected. The Treaty of the Pyrenees, signed in 1659, meant that Roussillon was the frontier of France and hence required protection. Vauban made a detailed on-site study of the places requiring fortification, sometimes electing to build an entire fortification, as at Amélie, Perthus and

Mont-Louis and sometimes reinforcing an existing structure, as at Perpignan, Collioure and Villefranche-de-Conflent. The buildings have made Roussillon into a living record of Vauban's work for the Sun King (Louis XIV).

Follies in the Age of Enlightenment

When peace was finally established, civilian architecture gave the old town centres the look that we are familiar with today. In the 18th C., a time of wealth and prosperity for Montpellier, the nobility and the wealthy built mansions in the centre of town, and on the outskirts they built *les folies* or follies (from the Latin *folium*, meaning a 'leaf'): little châteaux in flower gardens, which vied with each other for refinement and architectural superiority. These opulent settings were used for receptions, masked balls, spectacles and soirées. The follies include Flaugergues, La Mogère, and the châteaux of O, Bonnier, Assas and Alco. If you would like to step back in time, they are open to the public.

Rural architecture
from shepherds' huts to farmhouses

Each part of France has its own distinctive style of country buildings. In the Cévennes and in Aubrac cowherd's huts or *burons* are common, whereas in Lower Languedoc it is the *chai* or wine-cellar which you will often see. Local materials such as stone tiles and shale were used for the construction.

Houses in the Causses

These solid buildings have additional stonework at the edges as protection against the cold and are several storeys high with thick stone walls. Sheep were given shelter on the ground floor in a space that protected the lambs from cold winters and hot summers. There is an outside staircase to the upper floors of the building, at the top of which there is a *pailher*, or hay-loft. The rooms are thus insulated by the warmth of the sheepfold below and the straw and hay in the loft above.

Cowherd's hut (buron) in the Aubrac

They consist of a kitchen, living room, bedrooms and a scullery. The houses are usually clustered into hamlets which are situated beside rivers or near farmland. A water-butt stands close to the kitchen to collect rainwater.

Burons

These are typical cowherds' huts in Aubrac, built in the meadows; some are still in use.

They are built of basalt and granite with a single opening, and are a temporary shelter for a cowherd when the cows are at their summer grazing, between May and October. The single room under the stone roof is used as a living room and dairy.

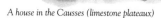

A house in the Causses (limestone plateaux)

Houses in the Cévennes

These are designed to resist the harsh climate and are generally built of shale (including the tiling of the main room) and chestnut (for the flooring). Sometimes the small window openings are edged with sandstone or limestone blocks. The ground floor is the cowshed and barn. The living quarters are on the first floor, the top floor is reserved for breeding silkworms. There may be a chestnut-drying hut, known as a *clède*, as an outbuilding. The floor is covered with wooden slats on which the chestnuts are strewn. A fire beneath them dries and preserves them.

The *pailher* in the Espinouse

The Espinouse is a mountain range which extends from La Salvetat-sur-Agout to Lamalou-les-Bains (p. 204). It is covered in forests of beech, oak and chestnut, pastures and moorland. The walls are built of granite and gneiss and thatched with broom. Where the walls are exposed to wind and rain, they are tiled with hard-wearing slates.

Capitelles and *mazets*

Capitelles are drystone huts used by shepherds in the meadow or for storing tools. The circular wall is made of blocks of shale and limestone, with a hole left for the entrance. The roof consists of stone tiles arranged inside in a fish-scale pattern. The roof-ridge consists of a large stone slab. A *mazet* is a little

House in the Cévennes

square shelter with a sloping roof, which stands among the vineyards.

Wine-growers' houses

In Lower Languedoc, these houses have small doors and windows (to keep the inside cool). The walls are painted ochre or pink and there are two doors at the front, one large and semi-circular leading to the cellar or *chai* and a smaller one leading to the staircase, which then leads to the living quarters on the first floor.

Farms of the Upper Languedoc

These are long, low houses. The living quarters and barns for storing grain and farm machinery are all under the same roof. They often have a stone or half-timbered pigeon-loft which was a privilege (*droit de seigneurs* meant only the lords had the right to breed pigeons). The pigeon lofts are square and and are crowned by a lantern with pigeon holes to enable the birds to fly out.

History and heritage

From prehistoric times to the 19th C., Languedoc-Roussillon boasts many interesting historical sites.

Cities and towns of historic interest

1 Perpignan: Saint-Jean quarter.
p. 133.
2 Carcassonne
pp. 166 and 169.
3 Castelnaudary
pp. 170 and 171.
4 Narbonne
pp. 180-185.
5 Béziers
pp. 192 and 197.
6 Clermont-L'Hérault
pp. 206 and 207.
7 Pèzenas
pp. 208 and 211.
8 Agde
pp. 212 and 213.
9 Montpellier
pp. 222-229.

10 Nîmes
pp. 252-257.
11 Beaucaire
pp. 260 and 261.
12 Aigues-Mortes
pp. 264 and 265.
13 Villeneuve-lès-Avignon
pp. 270 and 271.
14 Uzès
pp. 272 and 275.
15 Pont-Saint-Esprit
pp. 278 and 279.
16 Alès
pp. 280-283.
17 Anduze
pp. 284-285.
18 Gorges of the Tarn and the Jonte
pp. 300-303.
19 Marvejols
pp. 304-305.
20 Margeride
pp. 306-307.

Prehistoric sites

21 Tautavel:
Musée de la Préhistoire.
p. 138.

22 Viols-en-Laval:
prehistoric village.
p. 241.

History-based performances

28 Lastours: *son et lumière* at
the 10th-13th C. castles.
p. 172.

29 Limoux: Catharama.
p. 175.

30 Ouveillan: Cistercian barn
at Fontcalvy.
p. 185.

Roman remains

23 The Domitian Way
p. 73.

24 Narbonne:
Archaeological museum.
p. 181.

25 Nîmes: Maison Carrée,
Musée Archéologique,
Les Arènes.
pp. 252-255.

26 Pont du Gard:
Roman aqueduct.
p. 268.

27 Laudun: Caesar's camp.
p. 277.

Religious buildings

31 Serrabone:
Serrabone Priory.
p. 154.

32 Prades: Abbey of Saint-
Michel-de-Cuxa.
p. 159.

33 Casteil: Abbey of Saint-
Martin-du-Canigou.
p. 161.

34 Formiguères:
tour of the Capcir
churches.
p. 165.

35 Fontfroide (old town):
Fontfroide Abbey.
p. 177.

36 Ouveillan: Cistercian barn
at Fontcalvy.
p. 185.

37 Saint-Papoul:
Benedictine Abbey.
p. 173.

38 Sète: The Deaconate
Church of Saint-Louis.
pp. 220-221.

39 Palavas-les-Flots:
Maguelone Cathedral.
p. 232.

40 Saint-Guilhem-le-Désert:
Abbey of Saint-Guilhem.
p. 245.

41 Saint-Gilles: Abbey.
p. 259.

Traces of prehistory

As you cross the limestone plateaux of the windswept Grands Causses, the *garrigues* vibrating to the buzz of the crickets and cicadas or the rushing waters of the river Roussillon, you may see ancient standing stones, evidence of a prehistoric past lost in the mists of time. This region was one of the earliest to be inhabited by humans and, located between the Atlantic Ocean and the Mediterranean, was an extremely important trade route and passage.

À la carte menu, home delivery

The earliest humans found the right conditions for settling in the Languedoc-Roussillon region. There was abundant game and the soil was stony so providing perfect material for Stone-Age tools. In the Palaeolithic period, *homo erectus* lived in harmony with nature; hunting and gathering were sufficient to meet his needs for food.

From 400,000 BC, when man discovered how to make fire, living conditions became a little more comfortable. In the Aldène cave in the Hérault, for example, the ground has been covered with limestone tiles and pebbles; the first easy-clean floor was born!

Neanderthal and beyond

During the Ice Age, cold and warm periods alternated for tens of thousands of years. During one of the cold spells, the reindeer arrived and were hunted as a favourite game animal. Caves came to be used as dwellings and in many of them traces of a spiritual life were found.

A dolmen

From 80,000 BC, Neanderthal man seems to have been preoccupied with the afterlife, treating the dead with respect and clearly believing in the existance of another world. The hunter-gatherer civilisation attained its zenith. As the climate warmed up, in 10,000 BC, the nomadic people started to settle in one place.

A revolution in action

The Neolithic revolution began in the Near East with the birth of agriculture, animal husbandry and the making of pottery. In c. 5500 BC, the first Neolithic civilisation reached the Mediterranean. A wave of megalithic building swept over the area from the Atlantic coast towards the Mediterranean and scores of menhirs and dolmens were erected. At Cambous (p. 241), you can see one of the earliest villages of houses with drystone walls.

A menhir

In c. 2,000 BC, bronze was discovered – an alloy made of copper and tin. This made it possible to develop lethal weapons and warfare broke out all over Europe and the old Neolithic society crumbled.

Prehistoric terms

Megalith: from the Greek words *mega* (big) and *lithos* (stone). In Languedoc, these are usually of limestone, but its poor resistance means that it cannot be cut into the huge slabs encountered in Roussillon, which are cut from shale and granite.

Menhir: from the Breton words *men* (stone) and *hir* (long). What purpose the menhir, a monolithic standing stone, served is still unknown today. Was it planted by the giant Gargantua, the fairies or the legendary Roland? This is what popular legend claims but the experts believe they may have had something to do with a fertility rite due to the phallic look of the standing stones. Others believe they were connected with sun worship or astronomy and still others believe they were simply milestones.

Tumulus: (from the Latin) a pile of stones or earth in an oval, round or rectangular shape, covering a burial-place. Some tumuli are simply piles of stone, covering one or more corpses.

Cromlech: from the Breton words *crom* (round) and *lech* (standing stone). A megalithic monument formed from menhirs arranged in a circle. Why were they arranged in a circle? The purpose of the stone circle or henge is still being discussed by archaeologists today.

Dolmen: from the Breton words *dol* (table) and *men* (stone). A communal grave, built of megaliths and covered with a stone slab resting on pillars and with a slab at one side. The whole was covered by a tumulus. Some of these rooms could contain several hundred bodies.

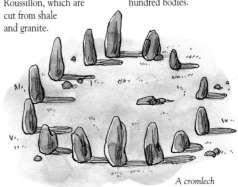

A cromlech

Roman remains
Caesar's legacy

The Roman history of Languedoc-Roussillon is long and has left some spectacular traces. These include the Ephebus at Agde, the Pont du Gard and the Maison Carrée at Nîmes… The names of many towns in the Languedoc, as well as christian names such as Auguste (Augustus) and Pauline have obvious links with Roman times. The recent restoration of the Antigone district in Montpellier by Ricardo Bofill is evidence of modern architects' continuing fascination with antiquity. As for the region's heady *vins de pays* and the custom of cooking with olive oil, these might never have existed had the Romans not passed this way.

Three thousand years of history

The seafaring peoples of the Mediterranean began to land on these shores from the 6th C. BC. They introduced grape and olive cultivation and soon began trading with the local population inland. Collioure and Agde were founded by the Phoenicians and the Greeks of Phocea in Asia Minor founded Massilia (Marseille). Trade increased rapidly and caused the port to expand. The people of Massilia gained control of Agde. A cooperative relationship developed with Arles, and the Rhône corridor became a highway for trade between northern Europe and the Mediterranean.

Benefits of the *pax romana*

The region was conquered by the Romans in 123 BC, and this marked a turning-point. The Romans founded the first colony outside Italy at Narbonne in 118 BC, and went on to found Nîmes. Roman colonisation was slow at first but speeded up during the reign of Julius Caesar, who founded Béziers, and was even more rapid under Augustus and his successors, with the foundation of

the colonies of Pézenas and Lodève. In 27 BC, the province of Narbonnensis was founded, covering about the same area as today's Languedoc. For several centuries, the region prospered under the *pax romana* (Roman rule). The vineyards, mining and pottery were the foundation of busy trading and monumental architecture flourished in the cities. Although the Maison Carrée and the arenas at Nîmes still survive as evidence, many other monuments, for example all the buildings of Roman Narbonne, have totally disappeared. However, traces of Roman colonisation can still be seen in the foundation of most of the towns of Languedoc (Carcassonne,

Castelnaudary, Beaucaire, Uzès and Sommières, among others). Roman influence also extended to the hinterland, which was less colonised but not abandoned, thanks to the excellent network of roads that the Romans created, linking it to the Domitian Way.

An impressive road system

For eight centuries, after the construction of the Appian Way in 312 BC, which linked Rome to Naples, the Romans created a huge road system consisting of more than 62,500 miles (100,000 km) of highways. These roads, which were built either by consuls or governors, under the watchful eye of the emperor, bore the name of the builder or that of the important towns they served. Thus, the Domitian Way was laid in 118 BC by Domitius Ahenobarbus, proconsul of the Province of Narbonnaise.

The Domitian Way

The Via Domitia (Domitian Way) runs from Beaucaire on the river Rhône to Le Perthuis in the Pyrenees and started out as a military road leading to Spain. It later became a major highway for communication and trading.

The construction was a massive project which involved clearing the terrain, building a causeway on firm foundations, covering it with ballast of earth and gravel, held in place by vertical slabs, then draining the whole construction by means of ditches along the sides. The project was comparable to the motorway building programme of modern times. Apart from the trade between Rome and its colonies, a busy life developed along the road, at every crossroad and between neighbouring villages and posthouses, which activated the local economy. While visiting the region, you will find that some sections of the Domitian Way have been preserved and enhanced. They remain a formidable monument that left an indelible mark on the life and landscape of the whole of the Midi and Languedoc in particular.

Romanesque art and architecture

The Cathedral of Maguelone

Romanesque art first emerged in Languedoc-Roussillon in the early 11th C. and affected many buildings, ranging from little churches to large, important Cistercian abbeys.

Around the year AD 1000, the monk Raoul Glaber wrote of 'a white robe of churches' covering France. From the Pyrenees to the Causses, there are many such buildings of great beauty and craftsmanship hidden away in the depths of the countryside, which are well worth seeking out.

A period of magnificence

Between the 11th and 13th C., Languedoc was part of the rise of the West. Trade with the Orient was developing, people were on the move. New towns sprang up to rival the old Roman cities; for example Montpellier emerged in the 11th C. Towns began to claim autonomy and ran themselves with a committee, led by a *consuls*, like the cities of Italy. Intellectual life flourished. Troubadours sang in the main streets known as the Cours d'Amour in Narbonne and in Béziers. Montpellier became a seat of learning as early as the 12th C., setting up schools of law and medicine.

The province had a strong Roman heritage (see p. 72) which it never entirely abandoned, so there was a certain continuity between Romanesque art and the art of antiquity. The style was so popular here that it continued well beyond the period allotted to it in other parts of Europe.

Influences of the Languedoc School

This architectural style, which took a long time to take root, proved to be very well adapted to local tastes and requirements,

The Abbey of Saint-Michel-de-Cuxa

especially in the simplicity of its shapes. The earliest Romanesque art in the area came from Lombardy. The outline is austere but there are many sculptures and decorative bands and friezes, as well as arcades and crenelations, rather like the teeth of a gear-wheel. The Abbey of Gellone (1040), in Saint-Guilhem-le-Désert (p. 244), which was built to accommodate the pilgrims who came to venerate a piece of the Holy Cross, is one of the first examples. The link with antiquity can be seen in Saint-Gilles (p. 259), close to the border with Provence, whose façade imitates a triumphal arch, such as the one at Orange. In the Lot and Allier valleys, the predominant influence is that of the Auvergne and the Velay. The Pyrenees are a background for incomparable hilltop abbeys perched like eagle's nests such as that of Saint-Michel-de-Cuxa or

Romanesque bridge near Lagrasse

Saint-Martin-du-Canigou (p. 161). Along the coast, large fortified churches such as Maguelone were built to resist Saracen attacks.

The Abbey of Saint-Martin-du-Canigou on an outcrop in the Pyrenees

TO THE SHRINE OF ST. JAMES OF COMPOSTELLA

Most devout pilgrims around the year 1000 aimed to visit the shrine of St. James of Compostella in Spain. A devout pilgrim believed it his duty to visit either this shrine, or Rome, or Jerusalem, choosing a route which would take him to as many other shrines as possible on the way. There are four roads in France that lead to the shrine of St. James. One of them, the Route du Puy, runs through the Haut Gévaudan, in Lozère, of which the section between Le Puy and Conques traverses the Margeride and the Aubrac and has a Romanesque church roughly every 15½ miles (25 km). These churches not only dispensed the sacrament to pilgrims, but also housed them in their priories, fed them and generally ministered to their needs. Even if you are not a pilgrim, take a backpack and try walking this famous route.

The Cathars

maison du Sire de Trencavel

Nowadays, many impressive fortresses perched on dizzying heights and the ancient villages still bear witness to a lost religion. The inhabitants of the Corbières often talk about the Cathars. They say that their love of independence, their defiance of the government and their will to live their own way is because they still feel themselves to be 'Cathars'. In reality, there were fewer Cathars than is generally believed but their epic history has left its mark here.

Heretics

The Cathars were also known as the Albigensians because their revolt began near Albi. They called themselves the 'pure' or 'perfect' (from the Greek *katharos*). They were dualists who saw the visible world as the work of the devil and believed in another incorruptible and eternal world, created by God. They denied the existence of hell and believed in the transmigration of souls, condemning sacraments and the ecclesiastical hierarchy. To attain perfection, they had to renounce marriage and purify themselves through the *consolamentum*, the only person capable of interrupting the cycle of reincarnation. The Cathars advocated a return to the primitive church, the Christianity of the apostles in the face of the laxity of the Catholic church of the time. Their intransigence was quite against the spirit of the time and their independence threatened the emerging centralism.

Cathar country

Albigensianism spread like wildfire through southwestern France, around Toulouse and Albi, but also affected the western part of Languedoc-Roussillon (Aude and the western Hérault). Béziers

The Cathedral of Béziers only partially withstood the sacking of the town by the Crusaders (1209)

and Carcassonne were Cathar strongholds and in the early 13th C. they found refuge from their persecutors in châteaux owned by knights, such as Quéribus, Peyrepertuse and Lastours. They were gradually pushed back to the wild Corbières but resisted to the end. The countryside matched their predicament – arid, difficult and lonely. You can drive through the countryside, but it is only on foot that you will really be able to negotiate the paths that will lead you to

The Château de Quéribus

DO THE CATHARS LIVE ON?

'They have only seven centuries of history, they still live on. I still hear the clash of arms and often see the flames that lick the walls and the giant charnel-houses... The Cathar knights weep quietly...'
Francis Cabrel
(*Chandelle*).

Representation de ceux qui Sont Condannees au feu par la Inquisition

The execution of the last Cathars, as it was depicted in the 17th C

A monument to the memory of the 144 Cathars in front of the Church of Minerve, who preferred to burn themselves to death when the town surrendered in 1210

The Château de Peyrepertuse standing guard over the valley

some of the most spectacular remains. Many châteaux and towns in the area were touched by this sad episode of history.

The crusade against the Albigensians

The danger for the church was that the Cathars, with their heretical doctrine, recruited their members from among the rich merchant class and middle-classes of the towns, as well as among the noblemen. This élite, which represented about 10% of the population, would be able to influence the rest to adopt Catharism. In 1209, Pope Innocent III launched a merciless repression, a crusade against the heretics. The knights of the Île-de-France and northern France, attracted by the wealth of Languedoc, gathered in Lyon under the leadership of Simon de Montfort. They rode south and invaded the region, acting with the greatest brutality. The siege of Béziers was the most dreadful episode. Of its inhabitants – Catholics, Cathars and Jews – 20,000 were massacred indiscriminately. The papal legate told the invaders: 'Kill them all, God will recognise his own.' Most of the victims were burned to death. The movement continued in secret for many decades and it took more than a century to exterminate the Cathars. The Inquisition took it upon itself to deal the Cathars the death blow.

Protestant history
and religion

Protestantism and the armed uprising of the Camisards have created a true cultural identity that has left its traces on the countryside and to which the whole of the Cévennes still refers three centuries later. Jean-Noël Pelen claims 'the whole of the geographical horizon is peopled with memories of the Camisards, in the form of bridges, caves, ravines or ruined farmhouses, as well as place names'. Here is a brief outline of the story of this legendary revolt.

The Reformation

Protestantism emanated from Geneva in 1532, spreading along the Rhône valley, with the roving of merchants and peddlars, touching Nîmes and Montpellier, but establishing itself solidly in the Cévennes. The unusual feature of the Protestantism of Languedoc is that it established itself in the peasant class in a country which had been so heavily colonised by the Romans. The Cévennes was known for its coarse woollen cloth called *cadis* and it was through trade in this cloth with Languedoc, Nîmes and Beaucaire that the ideas of the Reformation arrived. As the peasant interacted with the travelling craftsman and merchant in these towns he began to hear about and finally adopt this new doctrine. 'Wool exudes heresy' wrote André Chamson.

The Wars of Religion

The two bloodiest episodes of the 16th C. are the massacre of the Catholics in

'The mountains of the Cévennes to which the fanatics of Languedoc retreated'. An 18th-C. engraving.

Nîmes in 1567 (*la Michelade*) and the massacre of the Protestants at Marvejols in 1586 by the Duc de Joyeuse. The Edict of Nantes, in 1598, merely restored peace on a temporary basis, the Protestants revolting again in 1621 under the Duc de Rohan. The Peace of Alès, in 1629, restored calm but the Protestants were forced to destroy their places of safety. Louis XIV revoked the Edict of Nantes in 1685 and sent missionaries and dragoons, who were billetted on the

'Heresy unmasked by truth'. An 18th-C. engraving.

Camisards Bridge at Mialet

local inhabitants. This caused many to recant and revert to Catholicism, but the Cévennes continued to resist. Protestants held 'assemblies in the Wilderness', at which laymen replaced the exiled pastors and at which 'prophets' announced the re-establishment of the 'true religion'.

Modern guerrilla warfare

These prophets, fed on the Old Testaments, were convinced that they were led by God and preached fervently as the repression grew worse. The War of the Camisards broke out in July 1702, which astonished the whole of Europe. How could weavers, pig-farmers and goatherds hold their own against the army of the most powerful sovereign on earth at the time? This was the first guerrilla war of modern times.

The War of the Camisards became a

legendary tale of a popular uprising. After defeat and repression, the famous Maréchal de Villars sued for peace in 1704, but the revolt persisted until 1713.

Maréchal de Villars

Protestant man

In the 16th C. the Protestant understood and spoke French as the Reformation required that Latin be abandoned and the vernacular adopted and defined as the language of the state.

Occitan was spoken in the provinces. As Protestantism spread, a new kind of French regionalism against the influence of Rome began to appear. In the 19th C., the Protestant community acquired social standing and became the most educated so that the valleys of the Cévennes supplied generations of primary school teachers for the whole of Languedoc.

Protestantism gave the people of the Cévennes a taste for individual thought and liberty, opposing all religious, moral and political power. They have retained their tradition of helping refugees and the oppressed throughout the years and during World War II, Spanish Republicans, Communists, anti-Fascists and Jews all benefited from their assistance. The Protestant regions were the areas of the *maquis*, the Resistance. Thus Daniel, Élie or Noémie (Old Testament names that are typical of the region), descendants of the Camisards, became *maquisards* (Resistance fighters). For more information, contact or visit the Musée du Désert (Mas Soubeyran, Mialet, ☎ 04 66 85 02 72), a museum dedicated to the Protestant tradition.

Protestant prayers in the Cévennes wilderness. An 18th-C. engraving.

Excursions – gentle and energetic

Energetic hikes or family walks, lasting for a few hours to several days, the possibilities are as numerous as they are varied.

Hiking, climbing and riding

1. **Pic du Canigou:** climbing.
p. 160.
2. **Pic Carlit:** high-altitude tour.
p. 164.
3. **Pic de Nore:** climbing or horse-riding.
p. 173.
4. **Lamalou-les-Bains:** Pic du Tantajo.
p. 205.
5. **Pic Saint-Loup:** climbing, Ravin des Arcs: rambling.
p. 241.
6. **Mont Aigoual:** Col de la Sereyréde, path of the 4,000 steps.
p. 295.
7. **Mont Lozère**
p. 297.

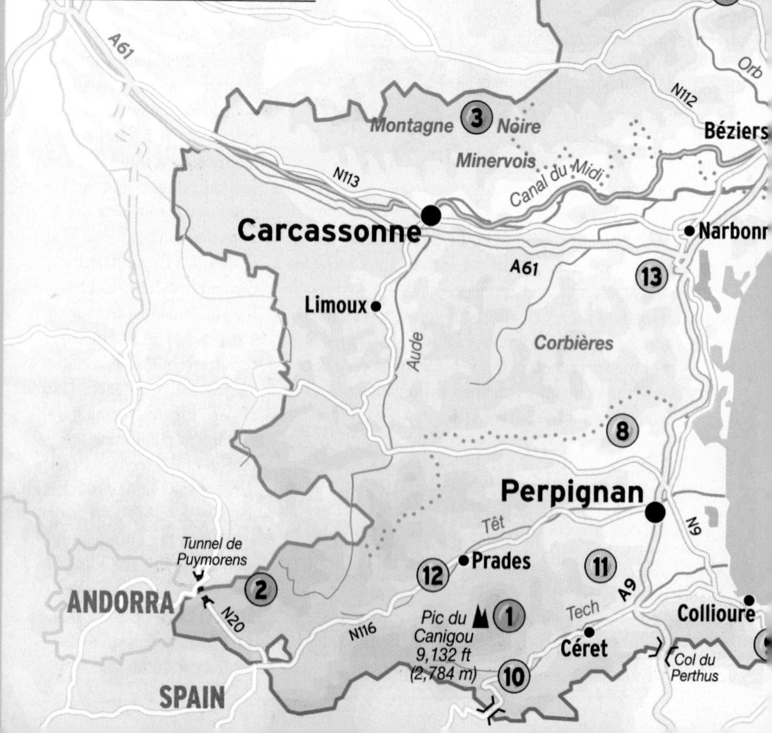

A75
4
A61
Orb
N112
Montagne 3 Noire
Béziers
Minervois
Canal du Midi
N113
Carcassonne
Narbonne
A61
13
Limoux
Aude
Corbières
8
Perpignan
Têt
N9
Tunnel de Puymorens
Prades
12
11
2
ANDORRA
N20
A9
N116
Pic du Canigou 9,132 ft (2,784 m)
1
Tech
Collioure
Céret
Col du Perthus
10
SPAIN

Walking, hiking & canoeing

⑧ **Tautavel: the Fenouillèdes.**
p. 139.

⑨ **Banyuls-sur-Mer:**
sanctuary and aquarium
of the Arago laboratory,
taking the tax collector's
path.
pp. 146 and 147.

⑩ **Prats-de-Mollo:**
Costabone, botanical
path and Gorges de
la Fou.
p. 151.

⑪ **Castelnou:**
Serrabone Priory.
pp. 154-155.

⑫ **Villefranche-de-Conflent:**
nature reserve.
p. 157.

⑬ **Portel-des-Corbières:**
Terra Vinea – the
Rocbère caves.
p. 176.

⑭ **Clermont-l'Hérault: Cirque**
de Mourèze, around the
Salagou.
p. 207.

⑮ **Agde: Mont Saint-Loup.**
p. 213.

⑯ **Saint-Guilhem-le-Désert:**
Vallée du Bout-du-Monde,
the Verdus.
pp. 244 and 245.

⑰ **Ganges: Gorges of the**
Vis, Cirque de Navacelles.
p. 247.

⑱ **Uzès: Gorges of the Gardon.**
p. 275.

⑲ **Pont-Saint-Esprit:**
Valbonne forest.
p. 279.

⑳ **Florac: Vallée Borgne.**
pp. 290 and 291.

㉑ **Le Rozier: Corniches**
of the Causse Méjean.
p. 299.

㉒ **Gorges of the Tarn**
and the Jonte.
pp. 300-303.

㉓ **Bagnols-les Bains:**
healthy walks.
p. 309.

The garrigue
sundrenched landscape

The word *garrigue* sounds right only when it is pronounced with an authentic Mediterranean accent. The origin of the word is *garric*, the Occitan name of the kermes oak (*Quercus coccifera*), the small evergreen oak which grows in this landscape of bright sunshine and eternal summer, of stony paths and aromatic plants whose subtle fragrances are carried on the wind.

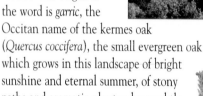

The hand of man

If there is a *garrigue*, it is because the forest, of mainly ever-green oaks and Aleppo pines, has disappeared at the hand of man, who has deforested, cultivated, turned into pasture and even set fire to these lands. But when nature is banished it returns... if not swiftly, at least by degrees, so much of the abandoned scrubland is now covered in vegetation and is returning once more to its original state.

Hardy bushes

The scrub generally reaches between 3½ and 24 ft (1 and 3 m) in height and is full of hardy plants thick with thorns. It consists of fragrant lentisk terebinth, rock-rose,

gorse, buckthorn, thorny juniper and kermes oak whose leaves are very thorny. These dominate the pale grey grass called the branched brachypod which grows where nothing else can withstand the scorching sun.

Bouquet garni

The ingredients for a bouquet garni are all to be found in the *garrigue* – a cook's delight. They include rosemary whose leaves are long and narrow, wild thyme, true lavender and Montpellier aphyllanth. If you feel like

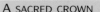

adding a little flavour of the *garrigue* to your cooking whilst on holiday, you can cut some, however, be careful of those vicious thorns.

Loved by all

The persecuted Protestants gathered there to hold services in secret. Textile workers set up their *capitelles*, drystone huts used for family outings; the perfumery and

dyeing industries have plundered it for raw materials. Many have made use of the *garrigue*.

Highs and lows...

Caves and canyons, moraine, cliffs and ravines punctuate the wide limestone plateaux. These include the Ravine des Arcs near Montpellier (cut by the river Lamalou), the peak of Saint-Loup, the Sauve sea of rocks, the Cirque de Mourèze in the Liausson mountain, the Orb gorges and the Montagnettes (little mountains) of Cathar country.

The wildlife

Many animals have adapted to the arid conditions, including locusts and grasshoppers, reptiles such as green or spotted lizards and grass snakes, butterflies (the Machaon and the Apollo) and many species

A SACRED CROWN

One of the shrubs that grows in the *garrigue* grows up to 13½ ft (4 m) high and bears the name of Christ's Thorn. In summer, its branches carry strange fruit enclosed within a yellow membrane. The branches are covered in large thorns and the flowers look like tiny red drops of blood. It is alleged to be the plant used to make Christ's crown of thorns.

of snail, which hibernate in summer and are only active during the rainy season. There are also the noisy cicada, the red partridge, and foxes, badgers and squirrels.

Eagles' wings

The Bonelli eagle haunts the lowland *garrigues*. It is a bird of prey which mainly hunts wild rabbit and red partridge. It is 27.5 in (70 cm) tall, with a wingspan of 5–6 ft (1.5–1.8 m) and is found in the eastern Corbières. The body is white or cream and the back dark brown. The wings are straight and dark. It is a protected species.

The Petite Camargue
dunes and marshes

The Petite Camargue, in Languedoc, is the part that lies west of the Petit Rhône river. It is quite a different world from the rest of Languedoc. Like the Camargue, in Provence, it has 280 days of wind and 20 inches (50 cm) of rain a year and 60 inches (150 cm) of water evaporate annually. As you enter the Petite Camargue, take in its wild beauty with your eyes and ears. Banish any idea of white horses galloping through the water – this is a cliché invented to attract tourists.

A short geography course

The Petite Camargue covers 155 sq. miles (400 km²) of lowland and lagoons. It extends through eight communes, including Saint-Gilles, Aigues-Mortes and Le Grau-du-Roi. The lagoons of Scamandre and Charnier in the north are surrounded by the largest reed-bed in France. The purple heron arrives in spring from Africa to nest in the reeds. The plain of the Vistre and the Vidourle is almost entirely farmland, except near Cailar where the lush grass is grazed by herds of bulls in summer.

The marshes

These form a belt around the lagoons and extend as far as the Canal du Bourgidou. They absorb rainwater, so their water is sweet or only slightly salted. This is where the phragmite reed grows, cut by the reed-cutters (see p. 60), as does the rush used by basket-makers. As far as the Petit Rhône, the marshes have been turned into rice paddy-fields with their characteristic chequerboard pattern.

The Sansouire

This is a salty plain of clay soil which cracks deeply when dry. It is covered in saladelle, a plant sacred to cowherds, and samphire, which crackles when crushed underfoot and is edible and sometimes pickled in vinegar. Many invertebrates live in the putrid mud, including slugs, worms and

snails which make a delicious meal for the flamingoes and other waders.

The dunes

The dunes are mounds of sand which separate the freshwater marshes from the salt marshes (like the plain of Montcalm which cuts through the marshes between Sylvéréal and Aigues-Mortes). Asparagus and vines (*vin de sable*) are grown on the dunes. There are just a few small dwellings in the flat landscape, which is dotted all

pastures of the Petite Camargue are inadequate to feed the 2,000 or so head of cattle which are there and so some herds have been moved to the *garrigues*.

Cowboys of the Camargue

The cowboys or herdsmen of the Camargue have a special saddle which helps them to

over with tamarisks, olive trees, parasol pines and juniper trees.

Domain of the birds

The lagoons are populated by many water-fowl, most of them migratory. There are ducks, herons (grey heron, oxpecker and egret), long-legged plovers, curlews, sandpipers, terns, sea-swallows, which fly as gracefully as swallows, seagulls and black-headed gulls. And of course, the pink flamingoes.

The Camargue bull

This bull has a narrow forehead and long, dark-grey horns which are blackish at the tip and curve in the shape of a lyre. The large eyes are alert, the neck and shoulders are extended and narrow and the haunches are long. The Petite Camargue bull is about 4 ft (1.30 m) high and only weighs 882 lb (400 kg). It likes to stay with the herd which clusters around the bogs, even in winter. Frightened of humans,

the poor creatures are also used for bull-running. Unfortunately, the remaining

sit in the saddle for many hours at a time. It has a padded *trusquin* (backrest) and a high pommel on the front to grip onto instead of the reins. The Pujols, in Nîmes, are specialist manufacturers of the Camargue saddle. They jealously guard its secret – the framework of curved metal elements and the type of leather used. It takes 80 working hours to complete one saddle, which costs more than 15,000 F (including the complete harness).

The Causes
stark beauty and absolute tranquillity

These wide limestone plateaux lie south of the Massif Central. Some are wooded, others are dry and exposed with strange rock formations. The plateaux, called *causses*, are among the most unique regions of France. They are bounded by the Cévennes, the Lot valley, the plains of the Hérault and lower Languedoc. More and more ramblers are attracted by the wild countryside and the stretches of water are popular with windsurfers.

Landscapes

The dry plains are 3,333 ft (1,000 m) above sea level interspersed with deep canyons and natural cave or *avens* (p. 90). It is a stony, lonely landscape, dotted with villages whose houses are built of drystone. Vegetation is sparse, thorny, burned by the sun in summer and frozen in the snow in winter. Only herds of sheep can graze there. Millions of years ago, the sea covered almost the whole area. When it retreated, it left deposits and sediments, limestone and fossils. The surface limestone, eroded by wind, rain and frost, has become striped, ragged and pierced over the years creating this stark, harsh landscape.

A subterranean world...

Limestone readily absorbs water, and is easily eroded. In this area, water circulating in underground rivers has carved out subterranean caves as vast as cathedrals. The action of the water slowly dissolves the limestone, forming grottoes and stalagmites and stalactites. It takes a whole century to create ½ in (1 cm) of limestone deposit. Vegetation finds a foothold in cracks in the stone. There are tufts of lavender, yellow star sedum, purple scabious and prickly thistles with blue flowers. There are plantations of black pine beside the Cévennes corniche (p. 290), and plateaux covered with beech, Austrian oak, fir trees and a few junipers, with their thorny leaves, which are resistant to extremes of temperature.

... and the sheep

The *Cause* has traditionally been sheep-grazing country, and this has done much to destroy the forest. Sheep eat leaves and young shoots in the pastures and on the peaks. Thanks to their wool, however, a textile industry developed, though the lure

A lavogne

of town life has caused its decline. Today flocks are kept for the ewes' milk which is mainly made into cheese, of which the famous Roquefort cheese is a prime example. The famous blue cheese called *Bleu des Causses* is made from cow's milk, however, and comes from the Millau region, which lies beyond the borders of Languedoc.

The canyons

These are deep, narrow valleys cut into the limestone. The best examples in France are the gorges of the Tarn and the Dourbie. Some canyons are as much as 1,670 ft (500 m) deep, with steep sides, ledges, cornices and caves that are called *baumes*, from the Provençal word *baoumo*, meaning a cave or grotto. The winding rivers continue to flow right at the bottom, fed by the resurgence of underground waterways. There are few plants that can live on the damp rocks, with the exception of the butterwort, a plant with a glistening appearance which is actually carnivorous and traps insects on its sticky leaves.

A LITTLE *CAUSSES* VOCABULARY ...

Lavognes: small pools used for watering the flocks, as long as the sun has not dried them out.
Cloups: little depressions made by rainwater, which has dissolved the carbonate of lime in the limestone.
Sotchs: larger depressions in which the dissolved limestone contains traces of salt or gypsum, imparting a reddish colour to the arable soil.
Avens: potholes, whose openings are often surrounded by brush. The best known are the Aven Armand and the Grotte de Dargilan.
Rochers ruiniformes: erosion has added to the work of the underground waters to sculpt stones in the shape of monuments or ruined villages.

... AND THE CANYONS.

Planiols: still, limpid waters.
Ratchs or rajols: white-water rapids.
Détroits or étroits: (straits) narrow passages in which the river flows between two steep walls.

Marmites de géants: (lit: giant's cooking-pots) circular caves dug into limestone walls beside the river. The fast-flowing water, carrying pebbles and gravel downstream with it, erodes the softer rocks that it passes, forming caves.

Cévennes National Park

The park lies at an altitude of 1,333 to 5,666 ft (400 to 1,700 m) and straddles the region of the Grands Causses (Causse Méjean), the Margeride (Mont Lozère) and the valleys of the Cévennes (Mont Aigoual). The terrain varies greatly, depending on the underlying rocks (shale, granite or limestone) and the climate (Mediterranean, Atlantic or mountain). The variety of habitats including forests, moorland, grassy slopes and rocks, results in there being 1,656 varieties of plant that grow in the park. It is a veritable paradise for all true nature lovers!

The park with a thousand faces

(Details p. 288)
The park has been classified as a National Biosphere Reserve and is one of the regions that has been most bio-logically enriched in Europe. Beginning in the early 1980s, many animals were re-introduced and certain habitats colonised by some species are now protected. The Cévennes has changed a

great deal since Robert Louis Stevenson wrote *Travels with a Donkey* in 1879. If he were to pass this way again, he would find many that had died out by the time he arrived have since been restored.

Mont Lozère

(Details p. 296)
The upland woods, moors and grasslands are varied environments that are rich in wildlife. The bogs (wetlands) are home to particularly interesting flora and fauna, whilst there are many wild boar, deer and chamois in the forests. The north face of Bougès was chosen for the re-introduction of the large grouse. Many birds of prey can be see in the open moorland.

Valleys of the Cévennes

The uneven terrain is covered with scrub and oak and chestnut plantations. Wild boar, the game that is most frequently hunted in the park, are prolific. Strangely, hunting is permitted in this national park as a way of culling certain animals. The Montpellier grass snake is also found here and the European beaver is quite common in

the Gardons, lakes which contain fish found only in the Mediterranean.

The *Causse*
(Details p. 300)
The limestone plateaux of the *Causse* are home to numerous species. The Causse Méjean, resembles steppe and this open countryside is one of the park's main attractions. Moufflons roam the cliffs overlooking the gorges and beavers colonise the river banks. Brown vultures hover over the Jonte gorges, where a colony of 200 birds lives. Monk vultures and other types of vulture, joined them recently.

Mont Aigoual
(Details p. 294)
The steep south face of the Aigoual is a favourite haunt of the moufflon. Local birds include the screech-owl and the black woodpecker, the largest woodpecker in Europe. These birds spontaneously recolonised this essentially forest environment. Migrating predators, such as the harrier eagle and the honey-buzzard, prefer to hunt in open ground. The red deer, fallow deer, chamois and wild boar are the most common mammals.

ORCHIDS AND BROWN VULTURES

The flora and fauna of the park are as varied as the environment. About 1,656 flowering plants have been recorded, one third of all French flora. Certain plants are considered to be rare, and the orchids are strictly protected. As for the fauna, the moors and woods are inhabited by fallow deer, red deer, beavers, grouse, peregrine falcons, eagle-owls and brown vultures. There is a brown vulture's eyrie at Truel in the Jonte gorges. In spring, you can see the migration of birds, in summer the blooming of the meadow cranesbill, in autumn the rutting of the deer and the moufflons. Here nature flourishes quite undisturbed.

The village of Merlet

Caves and potholes
an amazing subterranean world

Languedoc-Roussillon is the richest caving and potholing region of France. The ground beneath this region is like a Gruyère cheese: full of caves and potholes. About 15 of them have been made accessible to the public. They contain extraordinary limestone formations, amazing colours, narrow galleries and huge chambers. Over time the action of water on stone has created incredible shapes. In the Grotte de Trabuc, there is a battalion of soldiers to greet you, a Virgin and Child in the Grotte des Demoiselles and a Medusa at Clamouse. Now all you have to do is find the formation in the shape of Napoleon's hat!

Exploring the underground cathedrals

Languedoc-Roussillon is the birthplace of speleology, the study and exploration of the underground world. Édouard-Alfred Martel (1859–1938) and his successors, Robert de Joly, Norbert Casteret and Michel Siffre, explored the region which became a favourite with speleologists, geologists and climbers, as well as those who simply love the wonders of nature, especially unusual rock formations such as the cirques de Navacelles Mourèze and the caves of Limousis, Dargilan, les Demoiselles, etc.

For more information, contact the Secretariat of the Association Nationale des Grottes Touristiques de France (town hall, 38390 La-Balme-les-Grottes, ☎ 04 74 90 60 49).

The work of five million years

There is limestone all over Languedoc, from the *Grands Causses* to the slopes of the Montagne Noire, from the *garrigues* to Conflent. Rainwater does not circulate, but gradually seeps through the limestone rocks. Rainwater contains carbonic acid which dissolves the lime content of calcareous rock, chalk and limestone, creating small circular depressions called 'dolines'. When the water infiltrates more deeply through fissures in the calcareous substrate, the digging and dissolving of rock creates a natural well or abyss,

in other words, a pothole. Gradually the potholes get bigger and became interconnected through underground galleries and enlarge into caves.

The formation of stalactites and stalagmites

As the water cirulates underground it deposits the limestone which it collected as it penetrated the ground from above. It is these deposits which form the mysterious shapes you can see if you venture below – the stalactites and stalagmites and strange formations resembling pyramids, cones, columns and drapery. As every schoolchild knows, stalactites hold tight to the roof and stalagmites might just grow to join them. Before a drip actually falls it deposits a little of the calcite with which it is laden.

This forms a deposit along which other droplets come and deposit their calcite. As for stalagmites, the water droplets constantly falling in the same place deposit their calcite like a build-up of wax around a wick to make a candle. When a stalactite and a stalagmite join they form a column. It takes a century to form ¼ in (1 cm) of deposit.

Stalactites and stalagmites

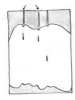 

*R*ainwater infiltrates the caves after seeping through the layers *of limestone. During the course of its flow, the water becomes charged with carbonate of lime. As it drips from the ceiling of the cave, the water forms stalactites in which it deposits part of its mineral salts. Immediately below, stalagmites form, constituted by an accumulation of the contents of the droplets. Over time, stalactites and stalagmites join up and form columns.*

Cave formation

*A*s it filters through the soil, rainwater, which is slightly acidic, *dislocates the layers of limestone, which it partially dissolves. The surface subsides. Rainwater collects in the depression and increases its destructive activity on the subsoil where it gouges out potholes and wells. As it rushes through the cavities, the water continues to excavate and erode the rock to create caves which are sometimes linked by subterranean passages.*

Canal boating

The Canal du Midi and the Canal de la Robine, the Canal du Rhône at Sète and the Petit Rhône all make it possible to explore the region from a different angle. Thanks to its 187½ miles (300 km) of waterways, there are wonderful sights to see as you glide along amid the pink flamingoes and Camargue bulls, past lagoons and pretty fishing ports. If you feel so inclined, take a break in the historic cities of Saint-Gilles, Narbonne, Carcassonne, Aigues-Mortes or Beaucaire or relax and soak up the atmosphere of ancient towns such as Montpellier, Sète or Béziers, and the landscape edged with cypress, plane trees, vines, orchards or fields of sunflowers.

There's more than one canal

Boat hire at Narbonne: Connoisseur Cruisers (7, Quai d'Alsace, ☎ 04 68 65 14 55), Nicols (36, Quai Vallière, ☎ 04 68 32 47 24).
Whenever navigable waterways in Languedoc-Roussillon are mentioned, one thinks first of the Canal du Midi. But there are others – the Canal de la Robine, for instance. This is the former course of the river Aude, which was

diverted in 1686 to link it to Narbonne via a canal, which was inaugurated in 1787. The Canal de la Robine is 18¾ miles (30 km) long from its starting point at Sallèles-d'Aude to its mouth at Port-la-Nouvelle. This is a short journey but a delightful one. A boat can be hired at Narbonne marina at the Promenade des Barques beside the cathedral. You can row or sail under the Pont des Marchands, which is lined with 14th-C houses. After Narbonne, maritime

influences become stronger as the canal passes through the lagoons of Bages and Sigean

and beside the protected island of Sainte-Lucie, ending at Port-la-Nouvelle, a seaside resort with vast expanses of beach.

The Canal du Rhône at Sète and the Petit Rhône

From Sète, the canal skirts the foot of Mont Saint-Clair between the Thau lagoon and the Mediterranean until it reaches Beaucaire, on the banks of the Rhône. It then runs along parallel to the sea through lagoons and the Sansouïre water-meadows, to join the white expanses of the salt marshes of the Petite Camargue. You can stop and

taste locally caught fish and the oysters of Bouzigues washed down with a *vin des sables*. You can admire the flight of the pink flamingoes and the herds of black bulls, discover Romanesque Saint-Gilles and Aigues-Mortes with its Crusader fortress. After Saint-Gilles, you will be sailing on the Petit Rhône through a canopy of forest to the Rhône delta, in a typical wild Camargue landscape.

Navigation

It is amazingly easy to navigate the canals. There is a speed limit of 3¾–5 mph (6–8 kmh) to prevent damage to the natural banks. You do not need a licence to take the tille and when you arrive,

someone will teach you the basics of navigation (mooring, passing through locks, etc.). Anyone can sail on the Canal du Midi and the Robine from March to November (except on the five public holidays).

You are only restricted by the times at which the locks open (8am-noon and 1.30-7.30pm). Some locks are still operated manually so try out your French and chat to the lockkeeper and enjoy the slow pace of life on the canal. There are plenty of moorings for pleasure-boats to enable you to explore villages, monuments, wine-cellars and restaurants, and if you feel like stretching your legs, the towpath is there for walking or bicycling.

How a lock works

Upstream

Downstream

When a boat arrives from upstream and waits outside the lock, the downstream lock-gate is closed and the lock is filled with water. As soon as the lock reaches the downstream level, the upstream lock-gate is opened. The boat enters the lock and the lock-gate is closed behind it. The downstream reach is then emptied. When the level of the lock drops to the level of the canal downstream, the lock-gate is opened for the boat to pass through.

The Canal du Midi

The Canal du Midi (p. 200) was the 17th C. brainchild of Riquet, a minor official in the taxation department. 150 miles (240 km) long, this impressive feat of engineering is spanned by 350 locks and bridges, and edged with a towpath lined with 300-year-old trees. This historic 17th-C. waterway links the Atlantic with the Mediterranean.

'Riquet's ditch'

It was the Romans who first considered linking the Atlantic to the Mediterranean, but it was not until the 17th C. that an obscure tax collector from Béziers named Pierre-Paul Riquet was so persistent that he got his plan approved by Louis XIV. Colbert, who was involved in all the king's major building projects, scoffed at first at this 'salt-tax collector who has taken an interest in land-levelling', but the king took the 'ditch' proposed by his tax-collector seriously. After all, work had begun on the port of Sète. The canal would be yet another asset for the port and a ready-made trading outlet, so Colbert was forced to concede.

A monumental job

For 15 years, from 1666 to 1681, 12,000 men wielded shovels and woven reed baskets to move the earth. Riquet became an engineer, geologist and hydraulics expert. He invented a device with which to feed the canal from five streams in the Montagne Noire, of which the furthest was 50 miles (80 km) away. He created the first utilitarian artificial lake in France – the 210 acres (85 ha) of the Saint-Ferréol reservoir – to feed his canal which was threatened by the summer drought of the Lauragais.

A dream costing 15 million pounds

Louis XIV soon found himself short of the money needed to finance this grandiose project. Versailles was swallowing up money, as were the wars of the 1670s. The canal was put on the back-burner. Riquet spent his own money on it, then his wife's money.

Sète, even though they were plagued by dust in summer and became stuck in the mud in winter. Inns and chapels were built at important stops along the canal. The post-boat was an early 19th-C. attraction that took five days to travel from Toulouse to Sète, pulled by three horses. Travellers were attracted by the atmosphere on board, which sometimes included women of easy virtue who were summarily jettisoned if they tried to ply their trade among the passengers. The boat disappeared when it was supplanted by the railway.

Everything went – houses, furniture, crockery. In total, the Canal du Midi was to cost 15 million gold pounds. In 1680, Riquet, ill and exhausted, retired to his property and died there a few weeks later without having seen his life's work completed.

The Genoese in Toulouse

In 1681, the superintendent of Languedoc-Roussillon was finally able to ride on horse-back from Béziers to Toulouse, along the bed of the canal which was filled with water shortly thereafter. The Atlantic and the Mediter-ranean were finally linked, and trade in Lower Languedoc experienced an enormous increase. The Catalan and Genoese coasters which sailed into Sète, laden with wood, oil and wine, could now take the canal to Toulouse. Later, barges took over – either sail-ing barges driven by the wind, or those towed by horses. The canal was deep enough to allow 80 ft (24 m) boats weighing 120 tonnes to pass through its 150 miles (240 km) and 64 locks. Coal, wood, wine, wheat and olives from the Levant and poultry from the southwest were carried on 'Riquet's ditch' for 200 years.

Water-bus and postal boat

Very soon, high society and fashionable ladies took the water-bus from Toulouse to

FROM WATER-BUS TO HOUSE-BOAT

Information: CRT (20, Rue de la République, 34000 Montpellier, ☎ 04 67 22 81 00). Nowadays, the only commercial traffic on the canal is the occa-sional barge loaded with wine. Tourism has given new impetus to this 300-year-old water course. This is the best way to discover the local foods, such as *cassoulet* and *confit*, and wines such as the Minervois, Corbières or La Clape. House-boats are available for hire at various rental centres (see above). They are easy to manoeuvre and a great way to explore the region.

Beaches, water parks & spas

Whether you want to cool off in the sea, relax in a spa or hot spring, or spend the day riding the flumes, the choice is yours!

Beaches

1. Canet-Plage
   p. 140.
2. Argelès-Plage
   p. 145.
3. Cap Béar
   p. 146.
4. Saint-Cyprien
   p. 142.
5. Banyuls-sur-Mer
   p. 147.
6. Collioure
   p. 148.
7. Narbonne-Plage
   p. 184.
8. Gruissan
   p. 186.
9. Sigean
   p. 188.
10. Leucate and Port-Leucate
    pp. 190 and 191.
11. Cap-d'Agde
    pp. 214 and 215.
12. Frontignan
    p. 217.
13. La Grande-Motte
    pp. 230 and 231.
14. Palavas-les-Flots
    pp. 232 and 233.
15. Le Grau-du-Roi
    pp. 266 and 267.

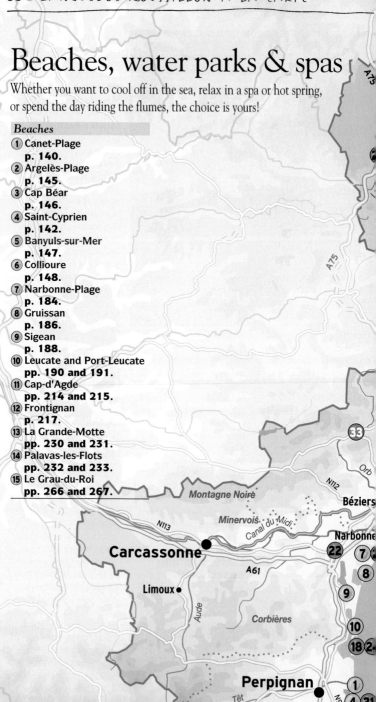

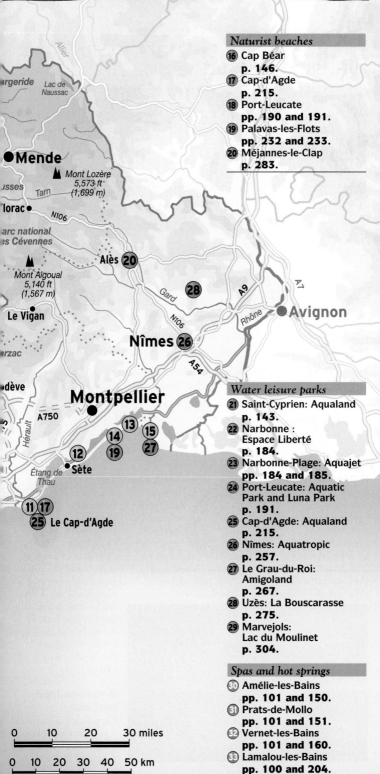

Naturist beaches

16 Cap Béar
   p. 146.
17 Cap-d'Agde
   p. 215.
18 Port-Leucate
   pp. 190 and 191.
19 Palavas-les-Flots
   pp. 232 and 233.
20 Méjannes-le-Clap
   p. 283.

Water leisure parks

21 Saint-Cyprien: Aqualand
   p. 143.
22 Narbonne :
   Espace Liberté
   p. 184.
23 Narbonne-Plage: Aquajet
   pp. 184 and 185.
24 Port-Leucate: Aquatic
   Park and Luna Park
   p. 191.
25 Cap-d'Agde: Aqualand
   p. 215.
26 Nîmes: Aquatropic
   p. 257.
27 Le Grau-du-Roi:
   Amigoland
   p. 267.
28 Uzès: La Bouscarasse
   p. 275.
29 Marvejols:
   Lac du Moulinet
   p. 304.

Spas and hot springs

30 Amélie-les-Bains
   pp. 101 and 150.
31 Prats-de-Mollo
   pp. 101 and 151.
32 Vernet-les-Bains
   pp. 101 and 160.
33 Lamalou-les-Bains
   pp. 100 and 204.

Beaches
sun, sand and surf

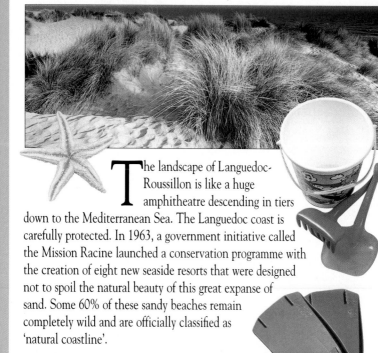

The landscape of Languedoc-Roussillon is like a huge amphitheatre descending in tiers down to the Mediterranean Sea. The Languedoc coast is carefully protected. In 1963, a government initiative called the Mission Racine launched a conservation programme with the creation of eight new seaside resorts that were designed not to spoil the natural beauty of this great expanse of sand. Some 60% of these sandy beaches remain completely wild and are officially classified as 'natural coastline'.

A varied coast

Languedoc's sandy coastline reaches right to the frontier with Spain. The vast beaches extend for 134 miles (214 km) from the mirror-like waters of the Camargue marshes to the Côte Vermeille (Vermillion coast). The coastline has been an inexhaustible source of inspiration for painters as it abuts the majestic landscape of solitary peaks such as Canigou and Ventoux.

The hinterland behind the beaches is extraordinarily diverse, ranging from wild and flat in the Camargue, volcanic around Agde, limestone at Mont Saint-Clair de Sète and La Clape, fringed with the lagoons of Thau, Or, Sigean, Leucate and Barcarès or rocky at Collioure, Port-Vendres, Banyuls and Cerbère.

Between land and sea

The coastline of Languedoc is a constant interaction of land and sea, low-lying and punctuated by dried-up or

drained lagoons. Areas of higher ground lead to the formation of bays, which over time can become cut off from the sea by narrow banks. These sand-bars, or lidos, growing to link what were once coastal islands, are formed by sand and silt from the Rhône delta and the little rivers loaded with alluvial soil which rise in the Massif Central and the Pyrenees. The bay becomes cut off from the sea and so the coastline is constantly shifting. It is thus possible to see a landscape changing and forming almost before your eyes, a ceaseless interplay between land, sea and human activity.

A protected coast

The Conservatoire du Littoral, a coastal conservancy body, and the local authorities are anxious to preserve the exceptional environment of the French Mediterranean coast. They safeguard some 40 sites of special scientific interest covering 16,480 acres (6,670 ha), as well as the cleanliness of beaches, of which 54 miles (87 km) are up to standard. Their efforts have been rewarded. In 1996, Languedoc-Roussillon was awarded the largest number of blue flags by the EU (30% of all French flags) for the quality, cleanliness and safety of its beaches, recycling of waste-water and town-planning.

NATURISM

The warm, sunny climate and diversity of the beaches makes Languedoc-Roussillon a true paradise and for this reason it is the premier naturist region of France. There are 22 centres and clubs, most beside the sea but some tucked away in the countryside, to which 400,000 naturists, French and foreign visitors, flock every year. To stay in a naturist club or holiday centre, you need to be a member of the Naturist Federation in your own country, and thus have a licence or a naturist passport. The average price is 120 F. For more information when in France contact the Fédération Française de Naturisme, (65, Rue de Tocqueville, 75017 Paris, ☎ 01 47 64 32 82). 'Naturism is a way of living in harmony with nature, characterised by the practice of nudity in a communal setting, the aim of which is to foster self-respect, respect for others and respect for the environment.' That is the official definition of naturism. It should not be confused with nudism, which is considered by some to be a form of exhibitionism. A few years ago, naturism was considered to be a sociological curiosity but today it has become a lifestyle which is practised extensively, especially in France, Germany, the Netherlands and Scandinavia.

Creation of the coastline

Bays can become cut off from the open sea and a coastal strip or 'lido' forms, consisting of alluvial soil and sand. A narrow strait is left which connects the sea with the gulf, but with time, this strait silts up, thus isolating a new area of water from the sea. The sandbar is planted with trees, the coastal strip is stabilised and the new coastline permanently fixed in place.

Spa resorts in the sun

L anguedoc-Roussillon has the second-largest number of visitors in France, many of whom come for the curative waters. There are 12 such resorts in Languedoc-Roussillon, in addition to numerous sea-water treatment centres and health farms. Hot springs and spas are favoured by patients for their natural appeal, and a thermal cure is considered to have both preventative and healing benefits.

Spa treatments

In a mud-bath, therapeutic mud is applied in layers of varying thickness all over the body, except on the face. The patient is then wrapped in a sheet and blanket to encourage sweating. The mud is washed off with a high-pressure hose. In under-water shower treatments the patient lies in a bath at a temperature of 98.6 °F (37 °C) and jets of water are directed at damaged joints. There are also gymnastics or exercises in a swimming bath.

Les-Fumades-les-Bains

☎ 04 66 24 80 24.
Cold water containing sulphur, bicarbonates and calcium make this small spa a specialist

centre for treating skin diseases and respiratory ailments. A Baroque villa on a hilltop was built for the German crown prince who came here for his sinusitis in 1914.

Bagnols-les-Bains

☎ 04 66 47 60 02.
This hot spring at the foot of Mont Lozère, 13 miles

(21 km) from Mende, at an altitude of 3,000 ft (900 m), has water which emerges from the mountain at a temperature of 107°F (41.5°C). It contains sulphur and fluoride, mineral salts and rare gases and is recommended for respiratory and rheumatic problems. Water from the 'cold spring' outside the spa has diuretic and digestive properties.

La Chaldette

Centre Thermal, Brion,
☎ 04 66 31 68 00.
This is a new spa on the Aubrac plateau, at an altitude of 3,333 ft (1,000 m). The water temperature is 96 °F (35.6 °C), and contains sodium bicarbonate. It has a sedative effect and is an ideal decongestant for respiratory and intestinal problems.

Lamalou-les-Bains

Thermes, 5, Av. Georges-Clemenceau,
☎ 04 67 23 31 40.
One of the most southerly spas whose metal-rich waters containing iron are used to

treat pain and nervous diseases. The spring was found in 1634 and the first bath officially opened in 1709.

Balaruc-les-Bains

Maison du Thermalisme, Pavillon Sévigné,
☎ **04 67 46 81 46.**
Open. 9am-noon and 2-7pm.
Every year, 34,000 people come here to the Étang de Thau to take the hot water cure. The water temperature is 122 °F (49.8 °C) and mineralised, containing about ½ oz (12–15 g) of salt per 1¼ pt (1 l). It contains trace elements of sulphates, calcium and magnesium which alleviate rheumatic pain.

Avène

Établissement Thermal,
☎ **04 67 23 41 87.**
These cosmetics are made from the waters of Sainte-Odile's spring, which is alleged to be calming and de-sensitising. The resort is a leading centre for the treatment of skin diseases and burns.

Molitg-les-Bains

4 miles (7 km) from Prades,
☎ **04 68 05 00 50.**
This is another resort that treats skin diseases, as well as respiratory and rheumatological diseases. It is in a lovely green setting beside a lake. The plankton from its springs is used by the Biotherm brand.

Amélie-les-Bains

☎ **04 68 87 99 00.**
This is one of the leading spas in France whose sodium and sulphur springs have been venerated since prehistoric times. The Roman baths, with their huge vaulted ceiling, are 80 ft (24 m) long by 40 ft (12 m) wide and 40 ft (12 m) high, showing their importance at the time. Rheumatism and respiratory diseases are treated here.

La Preste

Prats-de-Mollo
☎ **04 68 87 55 00.**
This ancient city on the Spanish border was fortified by Vauban in 1683. The sulphurous, radioactive springs led to the development of a spa here in the 19th C. It stands 3,766 ft (1,130 m) above sea level, in a magnificent setting dominated by the Costabonne at 8,220 ft (2,465 m).

Vernet-les-Bains

☎ **04 68 05 52 84.**
ENT infections and rheumatism are treated in this lively town (if you come in the third week in May you can attend the Belle Époque Festival and in October there is the Chestnut Festival).

Alet-les-Bains

☎ **04 68 69 90 27.**
'Planted like a basket of flowers in a delightful valley', this lovely little resort is in a pretty medieval village and has a particularly favourable microclimate. The hot springs are used to feed an on-site swimming-pool. Problems of the digestive system and metabolism are treated here.

Rennes-les-Bains

☎ **04 68 74 71 00.**
The Romans installed very popular baths in this lush green valley surrounded by mountains. The present name of 'Bains de la Reine' (the queen's baths) is due to the fact that Queen Blanche of Castille often came here for treatment. The waters are pleasantly warm, containing sulphates, calcium and chlorides, and are used mainly to treat rheumatic pains and several other diseases of the joints.

Taking the Cure

In France, these cures can still be taken under the French national health service, upon a doctor's recommendation. Foreigners are very welcome at the spas and hot springs, and many come simply for rest and relaxation. All have a 'health farm' style programme for those who merely wish to lose weight or relax away from the stress of everyday life. Bookings can be made directly with the resort.

Sports

There should be enough on offer here to keep sporty types occupied.
For hiking and walking, see the map on pp 80–81.

Water-sports

1. Saint-Cyprien: sailing, windsurfing.
   p. 143.
2. Port-Vendres: scuba-diving, sea-kayaking.
   p. 146.
3. Banyuls-sur-Mer: yachting.
   p. 147.
4. Collioure: sailing, windsurfing, scuba-diving.
   p. 149.
5. Les Angles (Lake Matemale): sailing, windsurfing.
   pp. 164-165.
6. Chalabre (Lake Montbel): fishing, swimming, various sports.
   p. 175.
7. Gruissan: sailing, windsurfing, funboarding.
   pp. 186 to 187.
8. Leucate and Port-Leucate: sailing, yachting.
   p. 190.
9. Lake Jouarres: sailing.
   p. 199.
10. Cap-d'Agde: sailing, windsurfing.
    p. 215.
11. Lake Barrou: sailing, windsurfing, funboarding.
    p. 217.
12. La Grande-Motte: scuba-diving, windsurfing, sailing, waterskiing.
    p. 230.
13. Palavas: windsurfing.
    p. 233.
14. Naussac (watersports centre): sailing, windsurfing.
    p. 309.

Gliding, hang-gliding

15. Céret
    p. 153.
16. Blandas
    p. 241.

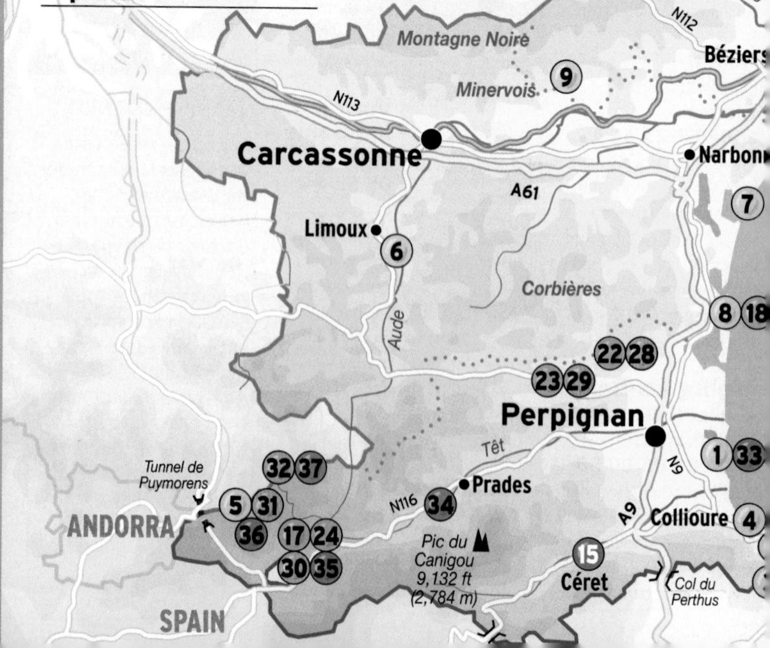

Montagne Noire

Minervois ⑨

N112

Béziers

N113

Carcassonne ●

A61

Narbonne ●

Limoux ●
⑥

Corbières

Orb

⑦

⑧ ⑱

㉒ ㉘
㉓ ㉙

Perpignan ●

Tunnel de Puymorens

㉜ ㉗
⑤ ㉛
㊱ ⑰ ㉔
㉚ ㉟

ANDORRA

N116 ㉞ ● Prades

Pic du Canigou
9,132 ft
(2,784 m)

Têt

A9

N9

Collioure ④
① ㉝

Col du Perthus

⑮ Céret

SPAIN

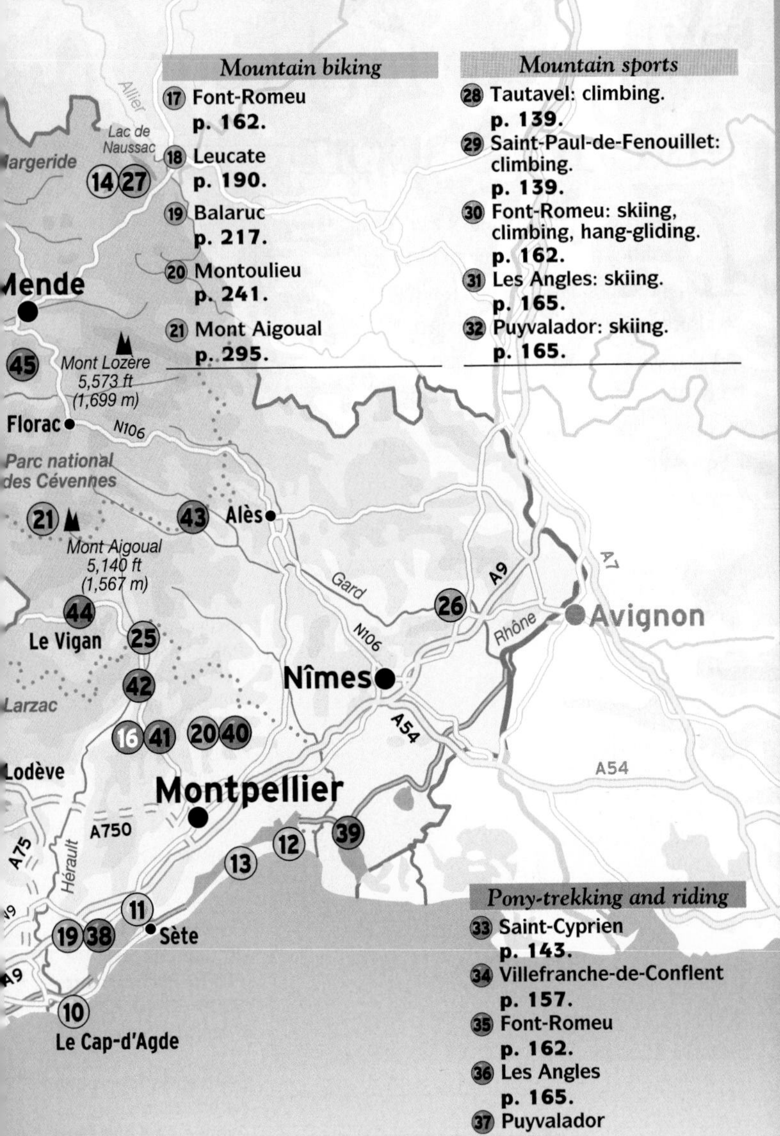

Mountain biking

17 Font-Romeu
p. 162.

18 Leucate
p. 190.

19 Balaruc
p. 217.

20 Montoulieu
p. 241.

21 Mont Aigoual
p. 295.

Mountain sports

28 Tautavel: climbing.
p. 139.

29 Saint-Paul-de-Fenouillet:
climbing.
p. 139.

30 Font-Romeu: skiing,
climbing, hang-gliding.
p. 162.

31 Les Angles: skiing.
p. 165.

32 Puyvalador: skiing.
p. 165.

Lac de
Naussac

Margeride

14 27

Mende

45 Mont Lozère
5,573 ft
(1,699 m)

Florac ●   N106

Parc national
des Cévennes

21 Mont Aigoual
5,140 ft
(1,567 m)

43   Alès ●

44

Le Vigan   25

42

16 41   20 40

Lodève

Montpellier

A750

13   12

11

Sète

19 38

A9

10

Le Cap-d'Agde

Gard

N106

26   A9

Rhône   Avignon

A7

Nîmes ●

A54

A54

39

Larzac

Héraut

Freshwater sports

22 Tautavel: rafting
p.139

23 Saint-Paul-de-Fenouillet:
rafting.
p. 139.

24 Font-Romeu:
canoeing and kayaking.
p. 162.

25 Ganges: kayaking.
p. 247.

26 Pont du Gard:
canoeing and kayaking.
p. 269.

27 Naussac:
canyoning, rafting.
p. 309.

Pony-trekking and riding

33 Saint-Cyprien
p. 143.

34 Villefranche-de-Conflent
p. 157.

35 Font-Romeu
p. 162.

36 Les Angles
p. 165.

37 Puyvalador
p. 165.

38 Balaruc
p. 241.

39 Aigues-Mortes
p. 265.

40 Montoulieu
p. 241.

41 Blandas
p. 247.

42 Saint-Bauzille-de-Putois
p. 247 (+ watersports)

43 Les Falguières
p. 292.

44 Le Vigan
p. 287.

45 Champerboux
p. 299.

Where to find your favourite sport

L anguedoc-Roussillon has excellent sports facilities of all types due to its varied landscapes. Water-sports (sailing, windsurfing, scuba-diving) can be enjoyed in the Golfe du Lion. There is also pony-trekking, canoeing and kayaking, cycling, hiking and winter sports – a very wide range of activities, to suit all levels.

For sky-diving, see p. 153 and 241

(See the index under the 'sports' entry.)

Sailing and windsurfing

Regional and departmental committees and correspondents of the Fédération Française de Voile can provide information as well as a list of the affiliated clubs and service-providers:

Aude
☎ 04 68 40 92 07,

Gard
☎ 04 66 53 11 06,
Hérault
☎ 04 67 41 78 35,
Pyrénées orientales
☎ 04 68 35 50 49.

You can also contact the Ligue Languedoc-Roussillon de Voile:
☎ 04 67 41 78 35,
(Maison Départementale des Sports, 200, Av. Père-Soulas, 34094 Montpellier cedex 05).

Our selection

Gruissan Windsurf-Pascal Maka, 11430 Gruissan,
Open all year round (p. 187).
The best places in the region for wind-powered sports, are those at Les Chalets (☎ 04 68 49 33 33) and Mateille (seawater lake and reservoir ☎ 04 68 49 88 31).

Cercle de Voile du Cap Leucate, BP 26, 11370 Port-Leucate,
☎ 04 68 40 72 66.
Open all year round.

Centre Méditerranéen du Nautisme, Avenue La Coudalère, 66420 Le Barcarès,
☎ 04 68 86 07 28.

Centre UCPA,
Avenue du Centurion,
30240 Le Grau-du-Roi,
☎ 04 66 51 47 92.
Open all year round.

Cercle Nautique de
Palavas, Boulevard
Maréchal-Foch,
34250 Palavas-les-Flots,
☎ 04 67 68 97 38.
Open all year round.

Espaces Nautiques
d'Agde et du Cap,
Avenue du Passeur-
Challiès,
Plage Richelieu-Est,
34300 Le Cap-d'Agde,

☎ 04 67 01 46 43.
Open all year round.

Yacht Club de
Banyuls-sur-Mer,
Laboratoire Arago,
66650 Banyuls-
sur-Mer,
☎ 04 68 88 00 62.
*Open from 1 June to
30 Sept.*

UDSIST
Saint-Cyprien,
BP 33,
Quai Jules-Vernes,
66755 Saint-Cyprien,
☎ 04 68 21 11 53.
Open all year round.

Scuba-diving

The Comité Interrégional de
la Fédération Française
d'Études et Sports Sous-
marins can send you a list of
diving clubs:
☎ 05 61 73 86 46.
(26, Place Marnae,
31520, Ramonville-
Saint-Agne).

Our selection

Centre de Plongée
Atlantis, 6, Rue
Becquerel, BP 19,
66755 Saint-Cyprien
Cedex,
☎ 04 68 95 89 49.

Horizon Plongée,
Résidence Le Tribord,
Quai du Ponant, BP 13,
11430 Gruissan,
☎ 04 68 49 10 23.

Espace Mer,
Port de Pêche,
30240 Le Grau-du-Roi,
☎ 04 66 51 75 25.

Centre International de
Plongée, 15, Rue de la
Tour, 66190 Collioure,
☎ 04 68 82 07 16.

Kayaking

The Ligue Régionale de
Canoë-kayak can give you
information:

Maison Départementale
des Sports,
200, Avenue Père-
Soulas,
34000 Montpellier,
☎ 04 67 41 78 40.

Our selection

Kayak Vert,
30210 Collias,
☎ 04 66 22 88 78.
(p. 269)
Exploring the Gardon Gorges.
Kayaking as far as the Pont du
Gard (Roman Bridge).

Le Moulin, BP 14,
34190 Saint-Bauzille-
de-Putois,

☎ 04 67 73 30 73.
Open from April to Sept.

L'Échappée Verte,
259, Rue Mas-d'Aussel,
34730 Prades-le-Lez,
☎ 04 67 59 63 95.
(p. 258)
Kayaking on the lagoons of
the Petite Camargue.

Les Aigles de Rivière,
5, Chemin des Pousets,
48000 Mende,
☎ 04 66 49 18 19.

Sud Rafting,
refuge de Tirounève,
Route de Galamus,
66220 Saint-Paul-
de-Fenouillet,
☎ 04 68 59 24 80.
(p. 139)

Skiing

The Comité Régional de Ski
des Pyrénées-Est will give you
up-to-date information about
all the ski resorts and the
affiliated clubs within the
region:

1, Bd Beaurepos,
31000 Toulouse,
☎ 05 61 63 10 11.

Our selection

Centre UCPA du
Mont-Lozère,
48190 Le Bleymard,
☎ 04 66 48 62 81.

École de Ski Français
(downhill skiing),
66210 Les Angles,
☎ 04 68 04 47 82.

Centre Guy-Malé
(cross-country skiing),
66210 Les Angles,
☎ 04 68 04 31 05.

UDSIST Centre de
Montagne,
Route du Pla-del-Mir,
66210 Les Angles,
☎ 04 68 04 31 05.

UDSIST Centre Évasion,
66210 Puyvalador,
☎ 04 68 04 30 95.

École de Ski Français,
Les Airelles,
66120 Font-Romeu,
☎ 04 68 30 21 29
and 04 68 30 21 29.

École de Ski
Internationale,
Les Airelles, BP 33,
66121 Font-Romeu
Cedex,
☎ 04 68 30 22 77.

Pony-trekking

ATECREL (Association
Régionale pour le Tourisme
Équestre en Cévennes-
Languedoc-Roussillon), the
local branch of the
Délégation Nationale au

Tourisme Équestre, will supply a list of all the affiliated riding centres in the region as well as the addresses of all the departmental representatives:

14, Rue des Logis,
Loupian,
34140 Mèze,
☎ 04 67 43 82 50.

Our selection

Goutarende
'Village du Cheval',
11390 Cuxac-Cabardès,
☎ 04 68 26 62 09.

Équipage du Lozet,
30400 Villeneuve-
lès-Avignon,
☎ 04 90 25 38 97.

Centre Équestre de
l'Orégon,
Quartier de Grézac,
30700 Uzès,
☎ 04 66 22 16 25.

Le Fer à Cheval,
Route de
Villeveyrac,
34140 Mèze,
☎ 04 67 43 61 11.

Centre Équestre
La Périgouse,
48210 Sainte-Énimie,
☎ 04 66 48 53 71.
(see p. 299)

Centre Équestre of the
Aigoual,
Pradines,
48150 Meyrues,
☎ 04 66 45 66 66.

Centre Équestre La
Boulène, Aspres,
48000 Mende,
☎ 04 66 49 23 37.
Centre Équestre
Can de Loste,
66740 Montesquieu,
☎ 04 68 89 85 20.

Cycling holidays

There are a multitude of cycling and mountain-biking facilities. The Fédération Française de Cyclotourisme advises you to contact its local representative for information and addresses.

Claude Parra,
Rue des Oliviers,
66720 Montner,
☎ 04 68 29 07 61.

Rambling and hiking

There are unlimited opportunities. For information, contact the French ramblers association, the Fédération Française de la Randonnée Pédestre, which will give you advice about routes and can also offer literature in English.

Gard
☎ 04 66 85 17 94,
Hérault
☎ 04 657 41 78 58,
Pyrénées-Orientales
☎ 04 68 66 04 13.

Rugby mania

French rugby fanaticism follows the Béziers-Narbonne-Toulouse-Lourdes routes. Precisely when the game caught on in France and why it should have become so popular there remains something of a mystery. However, support for the national teams is fanatical. Who would have thought this was the invention of an English public school?

Brief history

In 1823, William Webbs Ellis disobeyed the rules of football and picked up the ball, running with it to the opponent's goal and thus created the game of rugby. Since then, the game has been a combination of kicking and carrying the ball. The first French rugby club, Le Havre Athlétique, was founded in 1872.

A few rules

There are 59 rules of the game, the most important being that the player can catch the ball, run with it and pass it to someone on the same side behind him. The scrum shows the ability of a team to keep the ball for as long as possible. The rugby ball is oval to make it easier to hold. There are 15 men on a side, including forwards, halves, three-quarters and backs.

How it is played

Rugby is played on a pitch 333 ft (100 m) long (466 ft/140 m with the goalposts) and 230 ft (69 m)

wide. There are goal posts at each end of the pitch and a goal is scored by shooting the ball over the crossbar. The two teams compete for two halves, lasting 40 minutes each (half-time lasts 5 minutes). Up to seven substitutes are allowed. A referee, assisted by two linesmen, runs the match.

Some vocabulary

Try: action by a player who touches the ball down behind the opposing goal line.
Drop: after a touchdown, the player kicks the ball over the opponents' goalpost. This is also called converting a try.
Penalty: If the referee stops the game

because the rules have been broken, the side which did not break the rules is entitled to try and score a goal.

Rugby organisations

The International Board, which consists of members of various nations, manages world rugby, and organises competitions such as the World Cup.

Members of the **IARF** (International Amateur Rugby Federation) include all those countries currently developing the sport, including France.
The French Federation participates in international competitions and organises matches at all levels.

Major events

The most famous event is the Rugby World Cup which is held every four years. Sixteen nations take part. The Five Nations tournament has been held since 1910 and involves England, Scotland, France, Ireland and Wales. The challenge is to attain a Grand Slam – that is, to beat all the other four teams. A recent addition to the competition scene is the European Cup, in which the best French, Welsh, Italian, Romanian and English clubs compete against each other.

A French special

First division French Championship: this is a competition involving the 40 best teams divided into two groups. The champion is awarded the Brennus Shield by the President of the French Republic.
Le Stade Toulousain has won the French championship 13 times and AS Béziers has won it 11 times. The **Yves-du-Manoir Challenge Cup** is the French rugby football cup. The most representative first division teams take part. Many other rugby championships and competitions are organised at regional level throughout the rugby season.

Festivals and traditions

There is a strong tradition of festivals in thsi region. If you get the opportunity to experience one, you will take away an unforgettable memory.

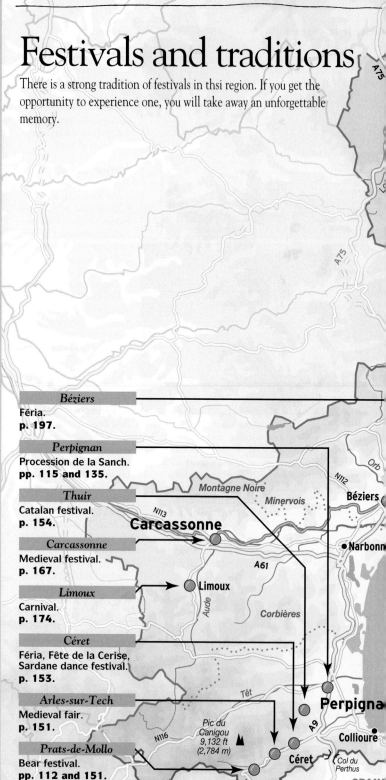

Béziers
Féria.
p. 197.

Perpignan
Procession de la Sanch.
pp. 115 and 135.

Thuir
Catalan festival.
p. 154.

Carcassonne
Medieval festival.
p. 167.

Limoux
Carnival.
p. 174.

Céret
Féria, Fête de la Cerise,
Sardane dance festival.
p. 153.

Arles-sur-Tech
Medieval fair.
p. 151.

Prats-de-Mollo
Bear festival.
pp. 112 and 151.

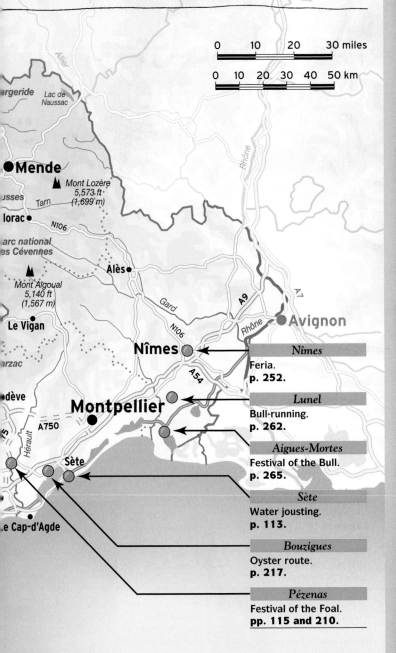

Nîmes
Feria.
p. 252.

Lunel
Bull-running.
p. 262.

Aigues-Mortes
Festival of the Bull.
p. 265.

Sète
Water jousting.
p. 113.

Bouzigues
Oyster route.
p. 217.

Pézenas
Festival of the Foal.
pp. 115 and 210.

Festivals and traditions
carnivals and water jousting

The Sanch procession in Perpignan

L anguedoc-Roussillon, an ancient land, shaped over the centuries by its inhabitants of various origins, is rich in tradition. Religious festivals of thanksgiving enrich daily life with colourful celebrations. In some cases the origin of these seasonal rites, celebrated to mark the end of plagues and other threats, has long been forgotten but they are still celebrated with great gusto.

Prats-de-Mollo

Festival of the Bear

First Sun. of the February holidays, followed by 3 days of carnival.

Bear and man have had a very close but ambiguous relationship throughout history. They have inhabited the same environment since prehistoric times, fighting for the same caves, and even the same prey. A curious medieval legend lies behind the Festa de l'Os, as it is called in Catalan, at Prats-de-Mollo

(p. 151). It is said that a shepherdess was kidnapped by a bear. The young girl's cries attracted the attention of woodcutters working nearby and who came to her rescue. The legend is re-enacted during the festival when, after a meal of grilled meat accompanied by plenty of wine, two men disguise themselves as bears by putting on sheepskins and fur hats, and cover their hands and faces with oil and

soot. Armed with heavy clubs, they dash into the village and pursue the villagers in order to smear them with soot. Hunters pursue the 'bears' pretending to over-

come them. At the end of the day some white 'bears' capture them and shave the two 'bears' to turn them back into men. The day ends with a dance and stories and legends are told about the terrifying habits of bears.

Limoux
Festival of Fécos
For 10 weeks, every Sun. from Jan. to March.
The Limoux Carnival (p. 174) traces its origins back to the 14th and 15th C.

WATER JOUSTING

In towns and cities all along the coast, in harbours and on canals, ceremonial water jousting is held. The most famous jousts take place in Sète. They date back to the Middle Ages, and consist of a ritual fight between married men and bachelors. The jousting (p. 218) takes place on 25 August, St. Louis' Day, before an enthusiastic crowd. The winner becomes a feared and respected celebrity for a year. This is in memory of Aubenque the Terrible who in 1749 anchored his lance firmly

against the solid wooden bridge of the Grand Canal of Sète, thus stopping his rowers who were unable to move. The jousting takes place throughout the summer, from June to September.

During this period, the flour trade made the city into one of the most prosperous in the Languedoc. The millers were rich individuals and paid an annual tithe to the Monastery of Prouille. They celebrated the tithing day lavishly, running through the streets distributing sugared almonds. The procession of the millers continues in the Place de la République, which is famous for its medieval arcades. Fécos (masked bands of leaders of the carnival) prepare themselves in secret. They emerge three times a day at 11am, 5pm and 10pm, and each time the costumes change. The first time they appear they are inspired by a current topic of interest, but in the carnival spirit. In the afternoon, they adopt traditional fancy dress, such as pierrot and harlequin costumes. Their last and most important appearance is in the evening, under the light of burning torches. The carnival dancers perform a slow march to the sound of brass and percussion. On the last evening, the local wine, the Blanquette de Limoux, runs freely and the carnival prince is chosen. The proceedings end with a long farandole which is danced throughout the town.

Gruissan

Festival of Saint-Pierre

29 June in the morning. The fisherman's festival takes place in Aude on St. Peter's Day. At Gruissan (p. 186), the church fills with a crowd following an effigy of St. Peter carried on a platform. Each fisherman holds a little model boat on a stick in one hand and a lighted candle in the other, and proceeds up the nave to meet his patron saint. The fishermen walk in procession with a rolling step to simulate a ship on the waves, to musical accompaniment. This ceremony calls upon the saint, the patron saint of fishermen, to protect seafarers. At noon,

BRINGING OUT THE TOTEMS

There are about 20 animals in the legendary bestiary of the Hérault, from the camel to the snail, via the ox and the caterpillar. Some are connected with sacred events, others pay homage to familiar animals, such as the donkey, the foal, ox, goat or pig. They are paraded at the following times: An ox heads a procession in Mèze in mid-August; Gignac parades its donkey on Ascension Day. Loupian shows its wolf on the 2nd Sunday in August. Roujan celebrates its hedgehog twice, for the April fair and 14th July fair. Béziers celebrates its camel on St. Aphrodise's day, at the end of April. Finally, Bessan parades with its donkey on both the 6th and 8th August.

when high mass is over, bread that has been blessed is distributed and the procession moves to the harbour where thousands of flowers are thrown in the water in memory of those who have been lost at sea. The fishing fleet and the nets are also blessed by the priest.

Fête du Poulain at Pézenas

Perpignan

Procession of the Sanch

Good Friday.
La Procession de la Sanch (Christ's blood) is a living reminder of popular Catalan faith. It takes place every year during Holy Week in an impressive ritual five centuries old in the streets of the ancient capital of the Kingdom of Majorca (p. 132). The *caparutxa*, the penitent's veil, has a dual significance. It is symbolic of the fisherman who covers his face and, more practically, it also evokes an ancient local organisation, *l'archiconfrérie*, or brotherhood, which aided prisoners who had been condemned to death. They surrounded the prisoner, dressed like him in a hood, to prevent the populace from stoning the condemned man on his way to the scaffold. Thus rendered anonymous, the prisoner escaped the wrath of the crowd. Today, the ceremony is organised by the Archiconfrèrie du Précieux Sang de Notre Seigneur Jésus-Christ, founded in 1416.

Pézenas

Festival of the Foal

The originality of the Carnival of Pézenas (p. 210) lies in the enormous wooden animal which leads the procession and which represents Louis VIII's foal. During one of his visits to the town in 1226, the king was forced to leave his favourite mare there because she had fallen ill. She was cared for by the populace and by the time the king returned, the animal was in excellent health and had given birth to a foal. The delighted monarch offered the town a wooden foal, which participated in all the public ceremonies. The carnival foal is made of hoops covered with a starry blue robe embroidered with the arms of the city. Its telescopic head can reach as far as the first floor of nearby buildings and it begs for alms for the poor to the sound of pipes, drums and tambourines. This lively procession lasts for at least three hours.

Bullfighting
a bloody spectacle

The bull has been a potent symbol for Mediterranean civilisations for centuries. The bullfighting tradition is in the blood of the southern people, who for generations have pitted their courage and agility against its strength in the tradition of the Camargue and Spain. The first bull-running dates from the royal celebrations held by King Alfonso II of Aragon. By the 13th C., the *mata-toro* (the man who kills bulls) was already an established figure.

A corrida

The *corrida* begins with the *paseo*, the preliminary processions in which two *alguaciles* (horsemen) salute the president. They are followed by three *matadors* and their *cuadrilla* (team of assistants). The *tercio* (first stage) begins. The bull enters the ring and is received by the *peones* (who draw the bull to the matador), then by the *maestro* who performs a series of passes with a small cape. Then come the *picadors* whose job it is to irritate the bull by sticking their pikes into it without weakening it. They are followed by the *tercio de banderilles*. The bullfighter or his *peones* stick pairs of these *bandarillas* into the bull's back. It is now the turn of the *tercio de muleta*. There is a trumpet fanfare and then the *torero* takes the *muleta*, the red cape, and approaches the presidential box to dedicate the bull to the president and ask for permission to fight it. The *faena* begins. The toreador makes several passes with his cape, all of which have names and include *pechos*, or statutory moves.

Finally, it is the moment of the *estocade*, when the bull is put to death. The matadors are awarded prizes, depending on their degree of skill. It may be one or two bull's ears, the tail being the supreme reward.

Bull-running in the Camargue

This ancient game is called the *course à la cocarde* or 'race for the rosette'. It is traditional in many villages in the *départements* of Gard and Hérault from May to October. Six bulls generally run in each race, each for 15 minutes. Men dressed in white try to remove the rosette attached to the horns and forehead of the bull. Style, agility and courage are the qualities looked for in these young men who are called *razeteurs*. In order to achieve their aim, they have to move in a circle, the *razet*. It is at this moment, when the beast meets the man, that the latter attempts to grab the red ribbon, and there is often a money prize. It is quite a dangerous game. Some of the bravest bulls have become so famous that statues have been erected to them, such as Sanglier, Clairon and Vovo. For more information about this festival, contact the Comité Départemental du Tourisme du Gard (3, Pl. des Arènes, 30000 Nîmes, ☎ 04 66 36 96 30).

The Nîmes festival

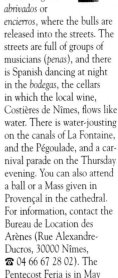

Every Pentecost (Whitsun) more than a million people visit Nîmes (p. 252) in order to attend the *feria*. It is a festival lasting for five days, during which people can either watch bullfights in the arenas or go to *abrivados* or *encierros*, where the bulls are released into the streets. The streets are full of groups of musicians (*penas*), and there is Spanish dancing at night in the *bodegas*, the cellars in which the local wine, Costières de Nîmes, flows like water. There is water-jousting on the canals of La Fontaine, and the Pégoulade, and a carnival parade on the Thursday evening. You can also attend a ball or a Mass given in Provençal in the cathedral. For information, contact the Bureau de Location des Arènes (Rue Alexandre-Ducros, 30000 Nîmes, ☎ 04 66 67 28 02). The Pentecost Feria is in May or early June. A number of other towns in the district hold their own smaller *ferias* at the same time of year. One of the most authentic is that of Béziers (p. 192).

Arts and cultural events

There is something for everyone here, whether French literature or cinema is your passion.

Festivals

Béziers

Festival de la Côte
Languedocienne
(music).
p. 197.

Bédarieux

Maison des Arts.
p. 204.

Collioure

L'Hostellerie des
Templiers.
p. 149.

Salses

Festival de la Mer.
p. 137.

Montolieu

The book town.
p. 173.

Perpignan

The Estivales (theatre)
Festival Méditerréen
(music).
Les Jeudis de Perpignan
(music and theatre).
p. 135.

Prades

Ciné-rencontres de Prades.
p. 159.
Journées Romanes.
p. 159.
Pablo Casals Festival
(classical music).
p. 159.

Céret

Musée d'Art Moderne.
p. 152.

Banyuls-sur-Mer

Mas Maillol.
p. 147.

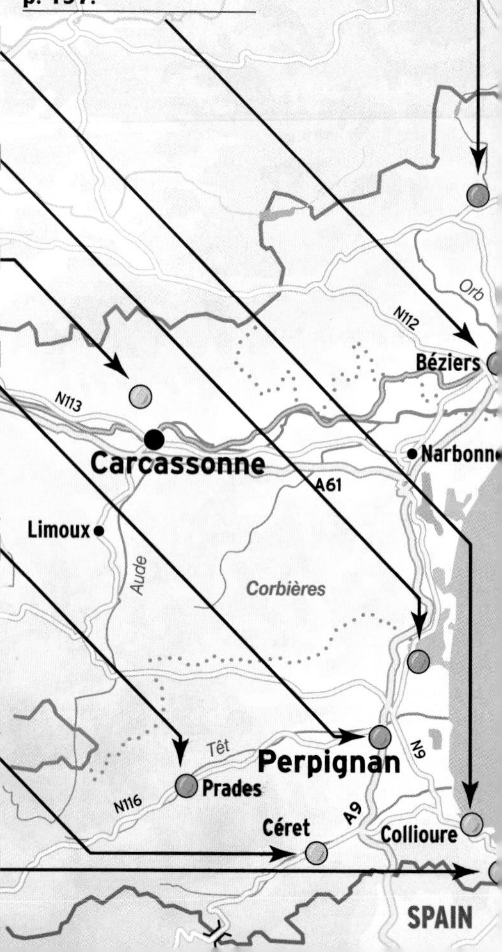

Carcassonne

Limoux

Béziers

Narbonne

Perpignan

Prades

Céret

Collioure

Corbières

SPAIN

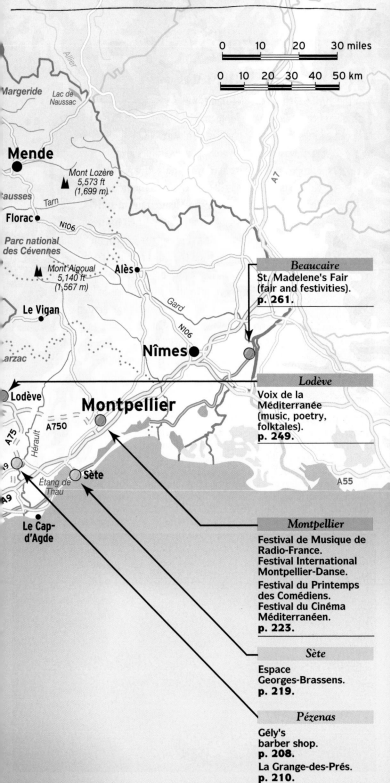

0   10   20   30 miles

0   10   20   30   40   50 km

Margeride

Lac de Naussac

Allier

Mende

Mont Lozère
5,573 ft
(1,699 m)

ausses

Tarn

Florac

N106

Parc national
des Cévennes

Mont Aigoual
5,140 ft
(1,567 m)

Alès

Gard

A7

N106

Le Vigan

arzac

Nîmes

Beaucaire
St. Madelene's Fair
(fair and festivities).
p. 261.

Lodève

Montpellier

Lodève
Voix de la
Méditerranée
(music, poetry,
folktales).
p. 249.

A75

A750

Hérault

A55

Sète

9

Étang de
Thau

A9

**Le Cap-
d'Agde**

Montpellier
**Festival de Musique de
Radio-France.
Festival International
Montpellier-Danse.**

**Festival du Printemps
des Comédiens.
Festival du Cinéma
Méditerranéen.
p. 223.**

Sète
**Espace
Georges-Brassens.
p. 219.**

Pézenas
**Gély's
barber shop.
p. 208.
La Grange-des-Prés.
p. 210.**

Parla català?
Do you speak Catalan?

In the 10th C., the counts of Barcelona threw off the yoke of vassaldom and in 1137 became kings of Aragon. The Catalan state of Aragon was one of the great powers in medieval Europe attaining its heyday in the 13th and 14th C. King Jaume I (1213–1276) expanded the frontiers of the kingdom throughout the Mediterranean and added the Seigniory of Montpellier. When his reign of economic and cultural prosperity ended, his son, Jaume II, inherited the Balearics, the counties of Roussillon, Conflent and Cerdagne, and the Seigniory of Montpellier (in 1262). But he was unable to withstand the greed of the French kings and the golden age of Catalan civilisation came to an end. The Treaty of the Pyrenees in 1659 turned Roussillon into the French heel of France and Catalan culture was not reborn until the 19th C.

The Catalan language

Catalan is a Latin language like Occitan, the language of southwest France. It is spoken from Salses in Roussillon to Valencia in Spain, throughout Andorra and at Capcir in the west. During the golden age of Catalonia, in the 13th C., it won its place in literature through the writer Raymond Lulle. Unfortunately, like Occitan, the *langue d'oc*, it suffered under the centralisation of the kingdom. In the 16th C., Philip II of Spain, forced Castilian on the population, to the detriment of the regional languages. Catalan remained the vernacular, however. It was not until the 19th C. that it was revived and contributed to the cultural identity of Roussillon. Today, there are some 7 million Catalan-speakers.

A taste of the Catalan sun

Catalan cuisine is a delicious mixture of foods from the sea and the mountains. The Pyrenees and the Mediterranean combine their resources to offer the finest natural ingredients. Based on these, simple but filling dishes are prepared, either baked or grilled on an open flame (*parrillada*) on an iron griddle (*planxa*). Catalonia is generous with its regional food containing all the exquisite aromas of the woods and fields – from olive oil, *aïoli* (garlic paste – *ail i oli* in Catalan) to anchovy paste (*anchoïade*) and pork products from

the Cerdagne, all a delight for the visitor's tastebuds.

Sins of gluttony

Here are a few Catalan specialities to give you an appetite: *escalivada*, an assortment of vegetables, including peppers, aubergines and onions, baked in the oven, then preserved in

olive oil and served as a cold or warm salad. *Bullinada pinyata* and *suquet* are traditional fishermen's dishes, based on eels or sea fish, with Banyuls wine. Depending on the season, you can eat *cargoladas* (*cargols* are snails), *petits gris* snails grilled over vine branches, or ceps (wild mushrooms) fried in olive oil as an accompaniment to partridge or wild rabbit. You will also be tempted by *crema catalana*, a delicious version of *crème brûlée* flavoured with cinnamon and accompanied by crunchy almond biscuits called *croquants de Saint-Paul* and a dessert wine from Banyuls. As the Catalans say, 'Bon profit!'

Dancing throughout the seasons

The Sardane is the traditional Catalan dance. Its origins are ancient and it probably comes from Crete. It is danced by the young and old. After a brief introductory step, the dance alternates eight short steps and 16 long steps. In the end, the participants join hands and move to the centre of the ring. The band or *cobla* comprises 11 musicians, whose instruments consist of the *flabiol* (a type of recorder played with one hand), the tambourine, two cornets, a *fiscorn* and two *tibles* (wind instruments) and the *tenora* (oboe). The latter instrument is the most symbolic of the Sardane. You'll find you are welcome to join in whenever it is danced in a Catalan village square. The popular Festival of the Sardane is held in late August in Céret (p. 152).

Regional identity

L'Occitanisme

Occitanism is an important facet of the Languedoc culture. Through the artistic and linguistic forms it has adopted, it has enabled the region to affirm its individualism at an early stage. Of course, the identity of the region is not limited to Occitanism, because many writers and artists who originate from Languedoc write in French. The language of expression is not all important. What is important are the influences of this very special part of the country.

The *langue d'oc*

The term *languedoc* first appeared in the 13th C. It was used by the king's officials to designate all of the lands in which the word for 'yes' was *oc*, as opposed to northern France where the word for 'yes' was *oui*. This linguistic divide between north and south very clearly reflects differences in French regional identities. The 'language of Oc' was used south of a line that ran across the country north of the Massif Central, so that Occitan in fact consisted of several dialects: Gascon, Limousin, Auvergnat, Provençal and the true Languedocien.

Courtly love of the troubadours

The language of Oc was first and foremost the language of the troubadours in the 12th and 13th C. The local lords surrounded themselves with these poets who were capable of 'finding' or inventing poems and songs in honour of their patrons. They often celebrated the love of a knight for his lady. A code of courtly love was established. Disputes between lovers were settled through a Court of Love, and a book of gallant jurisprudence was consulted on such occasions. Bernard de Ventadour (1147–1170), who was originally from Limousin

but who had settled at the court of Raymond V of Toulouse, was a renowned troubadour who had to flee from a viscountess and take refuge at the court of Eleanor of Aquitaine in England. The influence of this courtly poetry was such that Dante in Italy hesitated as to whether to write his *Divine Comedy* in Provençal or Tuscan.

The *coup de grâce*

With the crusade against the Albigensians (1209) and the troubles it brought in its wake for the south, the language of Oc began to decline. In 1323, the poets of Toulouse tried to rehabilitate it by introducing the Floral Games, poetic tournaments in the medieval tradition. The Edict of

Villers-Cotterêts in 1539 imposed the use of French as spoken in Paris for administrative documents. The creation of the kingdom of France dealt a fatal blow to the language of Oc and it was not until the 19th C. that the Occitan language began to experience a revival. The Escola Occitana, created in 1919, and the Institut d'Études Occitanes (established 1945) both had the mission of spreading the Oc language. The language is a linguistic treasure trove, with a vocabulary of 160,000 words, compared with 30,000 in French. Nearly 10 million people still speak it. Occitania covers 15 *départements* of France, or 23 if those that are in Provence are included in the list.

The Italian poet Dante Alighieri

Keeping the country alive

An attempt was made to involve the wider public. Before World War II, theatrical companies were created in Narbonne and Béziers. The carnival-style theatre often became a festival. Under the influence of militant Occitan nationalists, festivals that had died out were revived. In the late 1960s, Occitan singers emerged, such as Martin, Patrick and Marie Rouanet. 'Live in the country' – *viure al pais* – was the watchword at demonstrations in the region and Occitanism became confused with militant nationalism. Decentralisation did much to defuse the situation. However, there is still unfinished business, since the area's resources – once mining, now aeronautics, tourism and vineyards – are still in the hands of the 'colonists'.

Languedoc and the great writers

à boutique
de l' telier
...utenberg

DANIEL G. RIMBERT
Imprimeur typographe

The region of France which lies between Spain and Italy, between the Massif Central and the Mediterranean, has had a turbulent past. It has been invaded many times by different peoples, each bringing their own religion and cultural ideas. Great artists and writers have left their imprint on the region and there are even literary tours of the haunts of the writers of antiquity, such as the Greek writers Strabo and Polybius. The literature of Languedoc and Catalonia has also made some original contributions and many visitors and travellers have left their mark over the centuries. Let us follow in their footsteps.

The Cévennes in the company of Stevenson

Robert Louis Stevenson, a young Scotsman who was still unknown at the time, though he would later become famous as the author of *Treasure Island*, decided to cross the Cévennes on foot, accompanied by a female donkey. *Travels with a Donkey* has become a classic and is still a wonderful guide to this district. Stevenson was a precursor of the modern-day tourist, promoting all the pleasures associated with a walking tour – bathing in lakes and streams; sleeping under the stars; meeting interesting people. Many donkeys have since followed in the steps of Modestine, his pack donkey, and you can rent the services of one of her descendants and cross the highlands of the Lozère or the enchanting countryside of the Cévennes National Park stopping at *gîtes* or traditional inns (p. 291).

Pézenas, from Molière to Boby Lapointe

Between 1647 and 1657, Molière travelled through Languedoc, stopping at Pézenas where he was attracted by the magnificence of the court of the Prince de Conti. There are many stories about Molière's stay. His company of actors

New and second-hand bookshops and literary workshops crowd into Montolieu (p. 173)

performed in Gély's barbershop. In these stories,

Bust of Molière at Pézenas

Molière always played the role of the witty gentleman faced with the stupidity of others. According to tradition, *Le Médecin volant* (*The Thieving Physician*) was first played at the Hôtel d'Alfonse, on 9 November 1655. However, the next year Molière and his travelling players were banished from the town. You can still see Gély's shop in Place Gambetta, where Molière drew inspiration from the antics of Gély's customers (p. 208). Another frequenter of Pézenas was the French singer Boby Lapointe (1922–1972) who wrote poetic and clever lyrics. This singer, poet and humourist was born three centuries after Molière, and came to the notice of Georges Brassens with his 'Aragon et Castille'. He was the man who sung 'Avanie et Framboise' in François Truffaut's *Shoot the Piano-player*. Boby Lapointe's lyrics are still popular today and are good enough to be learned by heart, just like poetry.

Uzès, from Racine to Gide

Jean Racine, the great French playwright, was an orphan brought up by the nuns of Port-Royal, and became the pupil of the Solitaires. His teachers hoped to lure him away from the theatre and disrepute, so they sent him to live in Uzès in 1661 (p. 272) at the house of his uncle, Canon Sconin. Far from reconciling himself to ecclesiastical discipline, the 22 year-old became deeply involved in local life and was enthralled by the beauty of the countryside. He abandoned theology and upon returning to Paris, devoted himself completely to the theatre. His stay at Uzès lasted for just under a year but

Sewing the signatures of a book

the letters he sent to his friends in Paris from there are evidence of the strong impression the experience left upon him. It enabled him to discover a different world – the local customs, the sunny countryside, the temperament of the southerners – all exciting discoveries. According to local tradition, Racine wrote his first two tragedies, *La Thébaïde* and *Alexandre le Grand*, in the pavilion that bears his name. André Gide is another writer who spent summer holidays in Uzès with his grandmother. He wrote about it in *Si le grain ne meurt* (*If the seed does not die*).

Montolieu has become the 'city of the book' (p. 173)

Art and artists

When travelling through the region, it is easy to understand why so many painters were inspired by these landscapes. There is an abundance of natural life to be painted, a rich source of inspiration for the artist. The brilliant light of the Mediterranean shores, the ochres of the soil, coppery reds of the grapevines, the bluish-green of the evergreen oaks, sparkling sea and broken whites of the *garrigue* have inspired many a Cubist or Fauvist picture.

Collioure

Fauvism

In May 1905, Henri Matisse (1869–1954) discovered Collioure (p. 148). He was charmed by the light and the atmosphere of this little town of fishermen and winemakers. A month later, André Derain (1880–1954) met up with him there. Matisse was a relative novice when he settled in Collioure, at la Rosette, but it was at this time that he began to turn painting on its head, using the pure and arbitrary colours which gave birth to Fauvism, the movement that scandalised the public at the 1905 Autumn Exhibition. *La Fenêtre Ouverte* (1905) and the *Nu bleu* (1907) were both painted in Collioure. They are the 'inaugural' works

of this new movement in painting which many would follow. These include Derain, of course, who even painted the same subjects as Matisse, such as the belltower of Collioure. Until 1946, Matisse used to come to Collioure almost every year, living in various houses. But from 1906 onwards, he was no longer alone. Many artists followed in his footsteps including Raoul Dufy and Juan Gris, who came to seek the light and would immortalise the village, making Collioure into the town of painters. If you want to see their work, take the 'Fauvism Tour' (information at the

Tourist Office, p. 149). This tour includes reproductions of 20 paintings by Old Masters at the very spot in which these works were painted.

Céret
The Mecca of Cubism

Pablo Picasso (1881–1973), encouraged by the Catalan sculptor Manolo whose studio

was in Céret, lived for three consecutive summers in this little town on a mountainside (p. 152), between 1911 and 1913. His friend, Georges Braque (1882–1963), joined him in the first year. Others would follow, including Max Jacob, Moïse Kiling and Jean Marchand. He worked facing the Canigou and the Pyrenees. The newspaper *Le Perpignan* is used in certain canvases, figures and letters are applied in thick brush-strokes, a foretaste of their

later use in appliqué. The Convent of the Capucines, the Grand Café, and the arenas were the favourite haunts of the painters. Two other Cubists, Juan Gris and Auguste Herbin, went to Céret to work in 1913. André Salmon called the district 'the Mecca of Cubism' and it remained a pilgrimage for many artists who lived here later on, including Pierre Brune – who created a Museum of Modern Art which was opened in 1950, as well as Soutine and Chagall.

Banyuls-sur-Mer
Aristide Maillol

Aristide Maillol (1861–1944), born in Banyuls, is one of the great masters of the 20th C.

and the reviver of classic sculpture. Gauguin was one of his admirers and started a veritable Maillol cult. The sculptor came from a family of sailors and wine-makers and spent much of his career in Paris, but he remained deeply attached to his home town. Many of his models were the voluptuous local Catalan women who created an ideal of beauty that was both imposing and sensual. When Matisse came to Collioure in 1905, he knew that Maillol was working close by. The two men became friends and the painter would often visit the sculptor. Maillol is buried near Banyuls, where he died in an accident in 1944. One of his works, *La Méditerranée*, produced in 1902, has been placed on his tomb. As you wander through the town you will discover even more masterpieces by the artist. Do not miss a visit to his museum (p. 147).

The old port of Collioure

Languedoc-Roussillon in detail

The Uzège 272

The Biterrois coast 212

The Cévennes 280

The Montpellier district and the Lodévois 222

The Lozére 296

The Nemausais and the Lunellois 252

Languedoc-Roussillon in detail

On the following pages, you will find details of the most interesting places to visit in Languedoc-Roussillon. For your convenience, the region has been divided into zones. A colour code enables you to easily find the area you are looking for.

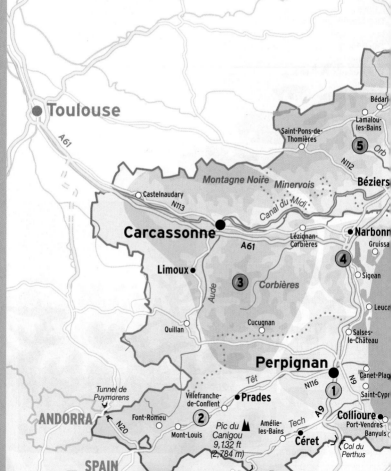

Perpignan

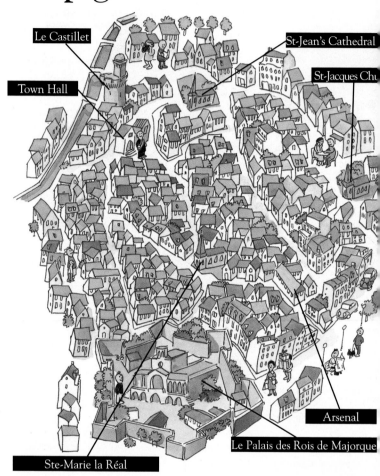

Le Castillet

St-Jean's Cathedral

St-Jacques Chu

Town Hall

Arsenal

Le Palais des Rois de Majorque

Ste-Marie la Réal

P*erpinyà* is first and foremost, a Catalan city. Nestling between mountain and sea, the economic and cultural capital of Roussillon owes its strategic position to a stormy history. The city was born of the meeting between Mediterranean civilisations and is today strongly influenced by Barcelona, capital of the new Catalonia. Its boisterous students, sunny palm-lined squares and good food and wine make it a delightful place to visit.

Le Palais des Rois de Majorque
Rue des Archers,
☎ 04 68 34 48 29.
Open daily 10am-6pm
(5pm in winter).

Admission charge.
The prestigious past of the city is linked to the expansion of the Catalan kingdom. Its economic prosperity was always dependent upon the

reign of the counts of Barcelona. The 12th–14th-C. Palace of the Kings of Majorca, is an imposing citadel that overlooks the town. However, only the gardens and the courtyard which are evidence of its former splendour are worth a visit. In the 15th C., King Juan II of Aragon granted Perpignan the title of 'Fidelissima' when the town sided with him against the king of France, Louis XI.

The Saint-Jean quarter and the cathedral

Place Gambetta.
Open 8-11.30am and 3-6.30pm.
With its 14th- and 15th-C. mansions and stately homes the Saint-Jean quarter is reminiscent of the prosperous past. Lose yourself in the network of narrow lanes, such as the Rue des Marchands, where the half-timbered façades are shaded with awnings. It leads to the Place de la Loge, the historic town centre. The Loge de la Mer, the former stock exchange, was also the seat of the Consulate of the Sea and the original weathervane in the shape of a ship remains on a corner of the building (1397). A statue by Maillol, Venus

with a Necklace, stands in the centre of the square. The elegant patio of the hôtel de ville, the former seat of the consuls, is an elegant combination of wrought iron, painted beams and heavily decorated Moorish ceilings evoking a brilliant past.

The Castillet-Casa Pairal

☎ 04 68 35 42 05.
Open daily except Tues.
15 June–15 Sept.,

Perpignan in carnival mood (p. 135)

9.30am-7pm; the rest of the year 9am-6pm. *Admission charge.* This 14th-C. brick château was once the town gate, then a prison. Its elongated machicolation and the pink dome of its belfry give it an Oriental look. Inside there is an excellent folklore museum, the

Musée d'Arts et Traditions Populaires du Roussillon, known popularly as the 'Casa Pairal'. From the terrace there is a wonderful view of the town and the plain of Roussillon, the sea and the imposing mass of Mont Canigou. The 14th–15th-C. Cathedral of Saint-Jean (open 7.30am-noon and 3-7pm) is an outstanding

Spotcheck
C6

Pyrénées-Orientales

Things to do
Visit a chocolate factory
Jardin de Saint-Vicens
Festivals and festivities

Within easy reach
Le Vallespir, 25km S, p. 150,
Céret, 29km S, p. 152,
Les Aspres, 15km SW, p. 154.

Tourist Office
Perpignan: ☎ 04 68 34 29 94

Reredos in the Cathedral of Saint-Jean

example of southern French Gothic architecture. The apses and chapels of the nave, which are 160 ft (48 m) long, are appropriate settings for the altarpieces of extraordinary beauty. Take a few moments to observe the details of the painting and sculpture. Continue on your way to the 14th-C. **Campo Santo Saint-Jean** in the Place Gambetta, the sole example in France of a cemetery-cloister with arcaded marble galleries. The family tombs are cut into the walls and bear the arms of the leading families of the city. Back in the land of the living, the **Saint-Jacques quarter** a maze of narrow streets and buildings. The *Jaumets*, as the St. Jacques residents are called, include

The Castillet tower

communities of gypsies and North Africans. Savour the atmosphere of the district, by drinking mint tea at one of the cafés. In the **Place Cassanyes** (open Tues., Thurs., Sat. and Sun.), there is a lively market. Items for sale include snails, local ham and herbs. Behind the 13th–14th-C. Church of Saint-Jacques, the **Jardin de la Miranda** (open 3-6.30pm) is a delightful garden in which to rest. It is small and carefully tended, like a curate's garden, and is right behind a buttress of Saint-Jacques with its delicate brick parapets and rounded stones. Sub-tropical and tropical plants exude their fragrances. It is a charming place from which to contemplate the city and the banks of the river Têt. The Saint-Jacques quarter was traditionally inhabited by the market gardeners who cultivated the *horta perpignanaise*, an agricultural area which can still be seen on the plain.

Sweet delights for gourmet travellers

There are two good places in which to enjoy the local chocolates and sweets. The **Chocolaterie Cantalou** (Route de Thuir, 2980, Avenue Julien-Panchot, ☎ 04 68 56 35 35. Guided tour in Jul.–Aug. daily am; Mon.–Fri., 2-5.45pm; the rest of the year on Wed. am). A visit will teach you all you need to know about the history of chocolate, the

cocoa bean and the drink which was once a royal privilege. You will be given chocolate flavoured, orange-flower water, said to be good for the nerves, and with almonds for curing irritability. Any excuse is good enough! The **Biscuiterie-Confiserie Lor** (85, Rue Pascal-Agasse, ☎ 04 68 85 65 00. Open Mon.–Fri. all year round, 9am-noon and 2-6pm). You will be shown a video and offered a free tasting of *rousquilles*, *amandines*, soft and hard nougat, and learn all about its manufacture.

Escargots du Roussillon

9, Place de la République, ☎ 04 68 34 47 65. Open Tues.–Sun., 8am-noon.

If you feel tempted to make the snail dish called *cargolade* (p. 36) at home, come and buy your snails at wholesale prices here (about 30 F for 100 *petits gris*). You can also purchase the herbs and a grill on which to lay them on the barbecue.

Jardin de Sant-Vicens, arts and crafts centre

Rue Sant-Vicens, ☎ 04 68 50 02 18. Open daily, phone for opening hours. *Free admission.* Created by the philanthropist Firmin Bauby in 1950, the garden was designed around a

aditional local farmhouse. here are orange trees, leanders, prickly ear cactuses and gaves (century plant), evocative of rab gardens, as well s beds of seasonal owers such as mpatiens, geraniums nd daffodils. Concerts re held in summer nd there is a perma-ent exhibition and sale f ceramics and textiles.

or information about this estaurant which serves Catalan uisine, see pp. 32–33

Maison Quinta

, Rue Grande-des-'abriques,
☎ **04 68 34 41 62.**
Open daily except Sun. nd Mon. morning, .30am-noon and .30-7pm.

This is the place to go in 'erpignan for elegant house-old goods. The shop is on wo floors of a former grand nansion. Not only does it

have the best decorative items, including local pottery and crockery but also fabrics – see Fabrics of the Sun (p. 55). Cloth is sold by the metre (40 in) as well as household linen and table linen. Huge choice and good taste guaranteed.

Festivals and festivities

Information at the Tourist Office

Do not miss the Procession de la Sanch, on Good Friday, a manifestation of Catalan faith (p. 115). The **Estivales**, a theatre festival, is held in June and July. The theme changes every year. The **Festival Méditerranéen**, a music festival, is held in July and August. The **Jeudis de Perpignan** are street perform-ances held on a Thursday.

Since 1750, the garnet has been the precious stone symbolic of the Catalans. The making of garnet jewellery goes back to the 17th C. when these semi-precious stones were extracted from the mines of Estagel in the Pyrenees. The garnet is only part of the jewellery making process. The jeweller has to create the gold mount, giving it the special convex back to hold the gem correctly. Then he inserts the garnet. The craft has survived thanks to the skill of the jewellers. Many families possess several gems which have been religiously handed down from generation to genera-tion. Here are a few addresses of jewellers who are members of the Grenat de Perpignan association: Gil et Jean Barate (5, Rue Louis-Blanc, ☎ 04 68 34 37 68). Michel Gourgot (4 and 6 Rue des Cardeurs, ☎ 04 68 34 67 79). Jacques Creuzet-Romeu (9, Rue Fontfroide, ☎ 04 68 34 16 94). Jean Paulignan (19, Rue des Augustins, ☎ 04 68 34 74 83).

Salses
watersports and wine

S alses is on the border between Roussillon and Languedoc. Occupying a strategic position, it was fortified from an early stage. Its pink brick and stone château is a model of military architecture. The nearby Étang de Leucate combines the pleasures of angling with those of water-sports. After having braved the winds and done some brisk exercise, it is time to relax and enjoy a dozen oysters washed down with the delicious local white wine. *Bon appetit!*

The creation of the lagoons

The waters of the Mediterranean reached the current level 3,000 years ago. The Golfe du Lion was lined with deep indentations. The surf and alluvial deposits from the coastal rivers combined to create sand-bars across the bay, called 'lidos'. Their formation caused the separation of huge expanses of water from the sea. These lagoons used to have an opening to the sea, but the sand-bars closed the gap and the fresh water from rivers and creeks gradually replaced the salt water. The lagoons expanded and passages to the sea opened up, called *graus* in Occitan. Man was wary, however, of settling on these temporary shores.

The lagoon of Salses and Leucate

The lagoon is 9 miles (15 km) long by 2 to 3 miles (3 to 5 km) wide and covers 17,300 acres (7,000 ha) marking the border between Roussillon and Languedoc. It has been famous since antiquity for its mullet and in the Middle Ages it developed fisheries which were dependent on the Abbey of Lagrasse. There are still some thatched huts on the Île des Pêcheurs and flat-bottomed boats for fishing in these shallow waters. Several modern fish-farms now cultivate sea-trout, sea-perch and salmon. In the northern part

f the lagoon, there are oyster-beds operated by the oyster-farmers of Leucate. The lagoon is rich in animal and plant life but it is seriously threatened as a resting-place for migrating birds. A **Festival de la Mer and de l'Étang** (festival of the sea and the lagoon), is held every April–May to enable people to get to know this natural environment better through exhibitions, displays and lectures (information at Port-Barcarès, ☎ 04 68 86 11 64).

❧ RIVESALTES, AN ANCIENT MUSCAT

Three miles (5 km) from Salses, take a detour via Rivesaltes and the Domaine Cazes (4, Rue Ferrer, ☎ 04 68 64 08 26), to this great producer of Muscat which has been operating for seven centuries (p. 48). Other makers include Henri Desbœufs (Espira-de-l'Agli, ☎ 04 68 64 11 73); Domaine Sarda-Malet (12, Ch. de Sainte-Barbe, Perpignan, ☎ 04 68 56 72 38).

Salses-le-Château

☎ 04 68 38 60 13.
Open June–Sept., 9.30am-6.30pm; out of season flexible opening hours.

Admission charge.

The town owes its name to two saline springs which emerge from the ground nearby. The Spanish Catholic King Ferdinand built a powerful **fortress** at Salses. Roussillon was owned by Spain until the Treaty of the Pyrenees in 1659. The fortress was built between 1497 and 1506, a time when fortresses had to be adapted to advances in artillery, and its walls are between 20 and 33 ft (6 to 10 m) thick,

Spotcheck
C6

Pyrénées-Orientales

Things to do

Sample some Muscat wine
Festival de la Mer
and de l'Étang
Salses-le-Château

Within easy reach

Sigean 26 km N, p. 188,
Leucate 20 km N, p. 190.

Tourist Office

Salses: ☎ 04 68 38 66 13

enabling them to withstand numerous sieges. After 1659, the strategic role of the château was no longer valid and it was converted into a prison. The military engineer Vauban restored it in 1691. There is a wonderful view from the terrace of the dungeon. You can see from Mont Canigou right to the Mediterranean Sea.

Salses-le-Château

Tautavel

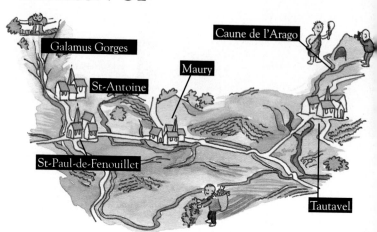

I n the course of your travels through Languedoc and Roussillon, you are sure to come across the Tautavel man. He is something of a local celebrity, like Tartartin of de Tarascon. However, Tautavel man is no raven-haired hearthrob – he lived 450,000 years ago! All that remains of him today are his bones and the cave in which he lived. It is nevertheless worthwhile visiting this ancient European – he may well be one of your ancestors!

Tautavel
13th-C. château and local food

Between sea and mountain, below the foothills of the Pyrenees, 18¾ miles (30 km) from Perpignan, lies

Tautavel, below the foothills of the Pyrenees

the village of Tautavel in the Corbières. Prehistoric man chose this area as a hunting-ground; it is now covered with vines. After a little tour of the remains of the 13th-C. **feudal château** you may have the pleasure of tasting the local foods. In July and August, a prehistoric meal is served, featuring bison and roebuck (☎ 04 68 29 07 76).

❀ Musée de la Préhistoire
☎ **04 68 29 07 76.**
Open Apr.–June
10am-6pm; Jul.–Aug.
9am-9pm; Sept. 10am-6pm and Oct–March
10am-noon and 2-6pm.
Admission charge.
Recently, 36 human bones, about 800,000 years old, were discovered in Spain, thus

depriving Tautavel man of his title as 'Oldest European'. He lived virtually next door, in the cave of La Caune de l'Arago, where his skull was unearthed in 1971. In fact Tautavel man was a mere stripling compared with the Spanish find as he was judged to be only 450,000 years old. The Museum of Prehistory has interactive terminals to tell the story of man thousands of years ago.

MASTER WINE-MAKERS OF TAUTAVEL

4, Av. Jean-Badia,
☎ 04 68 29 12 03.
Open daily 8am-noon and 2-6pm.

Free admission. An exhibition shows you how a wine-maker's work varies with the seasons. There are ancient tools, traditions and displays about the work of the vineyard. There are also tastings of Muscats and Rivesaltes with fruity and floral aromas, and the Côtes-du-Roussillon with its dark ruby colour. Wine-lovers should also visit Maury, in the direction of Saint-Paul-de-Fenouillet (p. 49). Visit the cooperative cellar, the Mas Amiel (☎ 04 68 29 01 02. Open daily 8am-6pm, Sat.–Sun. by appointment) or the Cave des Vignerons de Maury (128, Av. Jean-Jaurès, ☎ 04 68 59 00 95. Open daily 9.30am-noon and 2.30-7.30pm).

Écomusée de l'Abeille et du Miel

☎ 04 68 29 40 36.
Open daily June–Jul. and Sept.–Oct., 10am-noon and 3-7pm, Aug. 10am-8pm; Nov.–May school holidays 11am-noon and 3-6pm.
Admission charge.
This museum of apiculture was set up by an enthusiastic beekeeper, André Huguet. Six giant hives set out in a

botanical garden introduce the visitor to the fascinating art of beekeeping. Various types of honey are available for tasting. For an original gift, cast your eye over the range of apicultural products on offer.

The Torre del Far

If you need to lose a few calories, a climb along a stony path to the Torre del Far, a medieval signalling tower, will provide an unforgettable view of the Pyrenees and the sea. However, the walk might prove too strenuous in high summer, as there is no shade.

Arboretum and the cave

Before leaving Tautavel, visit the Gouleyrous arboretum (☎ 04 68 29 47 40), at the foot of the cave of La Caune de l'Arago (open in season from 9am-7pm), which has pathways running through a Mediterranean plantation of trees and shrubs.

Le Fenouillèdes
Wild landscapes

The Fenouillèdes, east of Tautavel, is a wild landscape of limestone escarpments, forests and mountain streams. The Galamus Gorges, 3 miles (5 km) from Saint-Paul-de-Fenouillet, are incomparably beautiful. The hermitage of Saint-Antoine nestles on the side of the rocky slope. One way to explore the cliffs is by whitewater rafting on the Agly (Sud Rafting: ☎ 04 68 20 53 73) or rock climbing.

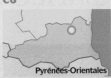

Sampling biscuits

Biscuiterie Brosseau,
7, Ch. de Lesquerde,
66100 Saint-Paul-de-Fenouillet,
☎ 04 68 59 01 62.
Open from Mon.–Sat., 9am-noon and 2-6.30pm.
All types of biscuits are available here, including *rousquilles*, *croquants* and almond rusks. If you are passing through Saint-Paul-de-Fenouillet, stop at this biscuit factory. Since 1890, five generations of the Brosseau family have used traditional recipes to produce these delicacies which you will want to take home.

Canet-Plage

Canet is the favourite seaside resort of the inhabitants of Perpignan. It lies on the Roussillon coast and has a lagoon with wild shores which is colonised by pink flamingoes and migrating coots. The extensive beach is wonderful for water-sports and the marina is an ideal departure point for pleasant sea-trips. Canet's museums include the aquarium, with Amazonian piranha fish and sharks, which are almost hypnotic as they swim by impassively.

Canet-en-Roussillon
A village full of history

The 16th-C. **Church of Saint-Jacques** is dominated by an imposing belltower. Visit the picturesque ruins of the

The Church of Saint-Martin at Canet-en-Roussillon

ancient **Château Vicomtal** (11th–14th C.) and the Romanesque **Church of Saint-Martin** (11th–12th C.). You can also visit the 17th-C. ice-well close by. In summer, there is a little train or tram (for which there is a charge)

Belltower of the Church of Canet-en-Roussillon

linking the village to the seafront. Information at the Tourist Office.

Canet-Plage
Going for a stroll

The resort flourished between the 1920s and 1940s but much of it was destroyed in World War II. Canet-Plage extends from the mouth of the Têt river to the lido of the lagoon, a distance of some $2\frac{1}{2}$ miles (4 km). Take a walk through the yacht harbour. You can also take boat trips – ask at the Tourist Office.

Musée de l'Auto

Les Balcons du Front de Mer (Canet S), ☎ **04 68 73 12 43.** Open 1 Jul.–31 Aug. daily, 2-8pm; 1 Sept.–30 June, 2-6pm and closed on Tues. Closed from end of Dec. to beginning of Feb. holidays. *Admission charge combined with admission to the Musée du Bateau.* This is a rare museum, run by enthusiasts, which traces the history of the motor car from 1908 to the 1970s. The most important makes are

Clemenceau, the boat museum is a delight for anyone interested in model ships and marine antiques. You will also learn about the pioneers of the oceans. A modelling workshop has also been opened.

Fire-engine at the Musée de l'Auto in Canet-Plage

represented. Choose a Citroën or an old Delage to take you to the beach!

❄ Musée du Bateau

Les Balcons du Front de Mer (Canet S),
☎ 04 68 73 12 43.
Open 1 Jul.–31 Aug. daily, 2-8pm; 1 Sept.–30 June, 2-6pm and closed on Tues. Closed from end of Dec. to beginning of Feb. holidays.
Admission charge, together with the Musée de l'Auto.
From the royal barge of the pharaoh Cheops to vast transatlantic liners, from the Catalan rowing-boat to the aircraft-carrier

❄ Musée du Jouet

Pl. de la Méditerranée,
☎ 04 68 73 20 29.
Open 1 Jul.–31 Aug. daily, 2-8pm; 1 Sept.–30 June, 2-6pm and closed on Tues.
Admission charge.
More than 3,500 toys from all over the world have been collected here.

Spotcheck
C6

Pyrénées-Orientales

Things to do
Musée d'l'Auto (Car Museum)
Musée du Bateau (Boat Museum)
The aquarium
Walk around the Canet lagoon

With children
Musée du Jouet (Toy Museum)

Within easy reach
Leucate approx. 25 km N, p. 190.

Tourist Office
Canet-en-Roussillon:
☎ 04 68 73 61 04
Canet-Plage:
☎ 04 68 73 12 43

This is the place to become re-acquainted with electric trains, lead soldiers, dolls and automata. Very possibly, Santa Claus's favourite museum!

❄ The aquarium

Bd de la Jetée,
☎ 04 68 80 49 64.
Open 1st Jul.–31 Aug., 10am-8pm; 1 Sept.–30 June, 10am-noon and 2-6pm, except Tues.
Admission charge.

Three hundred species of aquatic life from five continents are displayed here in tanks. From pretty corals to scary piranhas, from flamboyant tropical fish to the smooth glide of dangerous sharks, the aquarium is an opportunity to take a trip through a surprising, exotic and fascinating world.

A WALK ROUND THE CANET LAGOON

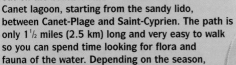

Information at the Scerem, Capitainerie du Port, ☎ 04 68 73 58 73. A hiking trail has been laid out on the banks of the Canet lagoon, starting from the sandy lido, between Canet-Plage and Saint-Cyprien. The path is only 1½ miles (2.5 km) long and very easy to walk so you can spend time looking for flora and fauna of the water. Depending on the season,

you can watch a multitude of birds in the reed-beds – grebes, black-headed gulls, cormorants and wading birds. Huts of thin rush have been built along the shores. To complete the visit, go to the Mas Roussillon, 5 miles (8 km) from Canet to see an olive grove, a bamboo grove and an exotic garden.

Saint-Cyprien
a family resort

This is one seaside resort that is real value for money. Saint-Cyprien has received the accolade of 'Station Kid', indicating its suitability for children. The environment, level of service and entertainment make it an ideal place for children aged between three and 16. Michel Platini and Yannick Noah founded the Grand Stade, now one of the stops on the yachting Tour de France, and there is an international golf course which offers lessons all year round. After all that exertion, find peace and calm in Saint-Cyprien village and in the Cloister of Elne…

Vous êtes dans une Station KID

Vous y trouverez :
un environnement, un accueil,
des activités et des aménagements
adaptés aux vacances de vos enfants.

The old village

Situated at about 2 miles (3 km) from the sea, the old village is surrounded by vineyards. The painter François Desnoyer (1894–1972) often stayed in Saint-Cyprien and he left a legacy to create the **Fondation François-Desnoyer**, Rue Émile-Zola (☎ 04 68 21 06 96. Open daily except Tues., 3-7pm in Jul. and Aug., and 3-6pm the rest of the year. Admission charge). There are paintings by Gauguin, Miró, Cézanne, Matisse, Braque and Picasso and statuettes by Bourdelle and Maillol. The **Centre d'Art Contemporain** (☎ 04 68 21 32 07, the same opening hours as the foundation) holds temporary exhibitions. A free shuttle bus (in summer, and twice a week out of season) as well as a footpath link the village to the beach.

Saint-Cyprien-Plage

Boat and train trip

Designed at the end of the 1960s, Saint-Cyprien became one of the leading seaside resorts. The Étang des Capellans has a large pleasure-boat harbour with 2,200 berths; a shuttle boat takes passengers around the lake, starting from the Quai de la Pêche at the Fontaine Marina.

There are also sea-trips along the coast of Roussillon from the pleasure-boat harbour. ☎ 04 68 21 44 91, Quai C; or for a day's sea-fishing,

Quetzal, ☎ 04 68 37 10 34 or ☎ 06 09 54 78 12, tickets at Quai H. A little train takes you round the resort on a guided tour of Saint-Cyprien.

SPORTS

A huge sandy beach stretches for 2 miles (3 km). All types of water-sports, from catamaran sailing to windsurfing and surfing are available at Hawaii Surfing, Route du Golf (☎ 04 68 21 08 34) which welcomes children aged five and six years; the Udsist sports centre, Quai Jules-Verne (☎ 04 68 21 11 53), offers yachting lessons for all levels, both with and without accommodation. These courses can be combined with horse riding. There is a pony club at the stables of the Mas des Angles (☎ 04 68 21 15 87, open all year round). South of Saint-Cyprien, at the Mas Bertrand, there is a naturist resort, as well as a huge sports complex, Le Grand Stade. Four racket sports are played here: squash, tennis (les Capellans, ☎ 04 68 37 32 00), badminton and ping-pong (table tennis).

Departure from the tourist office: Quai Arthur-Rimbaud, northern car park in the port, ☎ 04 68 21 01 33.

Aqualand
Rte d'Argelès,
☎ 08 36 68 66 13.
Open from 7 June–7 Sept. from 10am-7pm.
Admission charge, except for children under 40 in (1 m) tall.
Sail down the river, comfortably sitting on a buoy; speed down the flume, taking tight turns, and slip down dizzying depths in the dark Big-Eight tunnel. Aqualand, the largest aquatic centre in the region, also has musical parades and clowns.

Elne
A glorious past
This little village is enclosed behind **ramparts** and perched on the slopes amid vines and fruit trees. The Emperor Constantine named the town after his mother, the Empress Helena, hence the name 'Elna'. Elna was the capital of Roman Roussillon

Spotcheck
C6

Pyrénées-Orientales

Things to do
Visit the old village
Sea-fishing trips
Water-sports
Visit Elne and its cathedral

With children
Aqualand

Within easy reach
Le Vallespir, p. 150,
Les Aspres, p. 154.

Tourist office
Saint-Cyprien:
☎ 04 68 21 01 33

and a bishopric from the 6th to the 17th C. It has retained its lovely Romanesque cloister (open daily in summer, 9.30am-6.45pm, ☎ 04 68 22 70 90, admission charge). The cloister stands next to the **cathedral**, a remarkable Romanesque edifice built in the 11th C., whose crenellated façade makes it look like a fortress, not surprising in those troubled times before the Treaty of the Pyrenees. Before leaving Elne, take a walk along the ramparts from which there is a lovely view of the peach and apricot trees that cover the hillside.

La Côte Vermeille

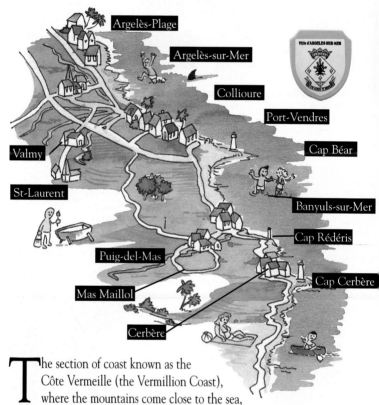

Argelès-Plage

Argelès-sur-Mer

Collioure

Port-Vendres

Cap Béar

Valmy

St-Laurent

Banyuls-sur-Mer

Cap Rédéris

Puig-del-Mas

Mas Maillol

Cap Cerbère

Cerbère

The section of coast known as the Côte Vermeille (the Vermillion Coast), where the mountains come close to the sea, is punctuated with deep bays which became fishing harbours. On the coast between Argelès and Cerbère, the shale rocks turn purple-red at sunset, hence the name Côte Vermeille which it was given in the 19th C. Fauvist and Cubist painters painted these brilliantly coloured landscapes. These old-fashioned Catalan ports, which have retained their maritime traditions, such as fishing for lampreys and the fish auction, invite you to linger. Take a seat on a shaded café terrace, order a sweet Banyuls wine, and drink in the atmosphere.

Argelès-sur-Mer

Catalan atmosphere

The old Catalan village of Argelès-Village is animated all year round with its colourful markets and games of *pétanque* (bowls) under the plane trees; on Mondays, from June to September, the Sardane is danced (p. 121). The 14th-C. Gothic **Church of Notre-Dame-del-Prat** has an atmosphere that makes it seem a thousand miles from the beach, which is really only 1¼ miles (2 km) away. To get to Argelès-Plage, between June and September, there is a little train or shuttle bus (tarif).

Casa des Albères

4, Plaça dels Castellans,
☎ 04 68 81 42 74.
Open. Mon.–Sat.
9am-noon and 3-6pm.
Admission charge.
This museum about **country life and ancient crafts** is near Argelès. There are displays showing working in the fields and vineyards, making whips and espadrilles, as well as wine bottle corks.

FLIGHT OF EAGLES AT THE CHÂTEAU DE VALMY

1¼ miles (2 km) from Argelès,
☎ 04 68 81 67 32.
Open March to mid-Nov., daily (2 to 3 shows per afternoon).
Admission charge.
In a magnificent wooded setting at the foot of the Albères peaks, you can watch the impressive sight of the free flight of eagles, kites and vultures. It is exceptional to see these huge birds of prey fly from handlers as if they were hawks or kestrels.

Argelès-Plage

The difference between winter and summer is like that between night and day. There are 7,000 residents in winter and 200,000 holidaymakers in summer. The area has over 60 camp sites, and a dozen beach and sailing clubs. The boats moored at the jetties of the marina at the mouth of the Massane tempt you to make a sea trip. Why not take a sailing trip in a Catalan yacht (☎ 04 68 81 20 21)? There

Spotcheck
C6-D6-D7

Pyrénées-Orientales

Things to do

Sea trips
Visit Mas Maillol
'Customs' officers' walks
La réserve et aquarium du laboratoire Arago

With children

Eagles at Château de Valmy

Within easy reach

Le Vallespir, p. 150,
Les Aspres, p. 154.

Tourist Office

Argelès-sur-Mer:
☎ 04 68 81 15 85
Port-Vendres:
☎ 04 68 82 07 54
Banyuls-sur-Mer:
☎ 04 68 88 31 58

are trips three times per afternoon in summer along the coast between the bay of Collioure (p. 148) and the Pointe du **Cap Béar** (information at the Tourist Office, Pl. de l'Europe, ☎ 04 68 81 15 85).

Sorède

A craft revived

Les Micocouliers,
4, Rue des Fabriques,
☎ 04 68 89 04 50.
Open daily, 9.30-11.30am, 2-4.30pm.

For more than a century Sorède was the centre of an industry which centered around the **nettle tree**, a typically Mediterranean tree, very flexible and heavy whose wood consists of long, malleable fibres; after soaking, it becomes very tough and does not rot. It was used for making the so-called 'Perpignan' whips and riding-whips, but the craft had completely died out by the 1970s (due to a decline in demand). Since May 1981, however, the CAT workshops have revived the ancient craft by altering the products slightly. The circus ring-master's whip is now made as well as walking sticks. The workshop can be visited.

Port-Vendres
A millennium site

Wrecks discovered at the entrance to the port show that the site was known as early as the 7th C. BC. Greek navigators sailed between Agde and Rosas on the Costa Brava where they would shelter from

storms. The Romans built a temple here, dedicated to Venus, hence the port's original name of Portus Veneris. Port-Vendres remained attached to Collioure (linked by a little train, p. 148) until the mid-17th C. under Spanish rule. When Roussillon became part of France in 1659, Port-Vendres became a naval harbour fortified by Vauban. Louis XVI had a wet dock constructed, and a pink marble obelisk was erected in one of the squares in his honour. After a period of brisk trade with Algeria, until the latter gained independence in 1962, Port-Vendres had to find a new commercial activity and now the movement of the pleasure-boats combines with that of the lamprey fishermen. The fish auction (the trawlers return from Mon. to Fri. from 4pm) is only open to the trade, but you might be able to smuggle yourself in to watch.

Sea and sun

There are pebble beaches all along this rocky coast as well as a number of little inlets which are difficult to reach

on foot. There is a little bay near Cap Béar which is popular with naturists (access by a footpath after the semaphore beacon). **Cap Béar** is the last spur of the rocky chain of the Albères, and has a sheer drop to the sea. The cliffs are about 200 ft (60 m) high and are edged with a little path leading to the semaphore signal, then on to the lighthouse. The best way to get to these inlets is to rent a sea-kayak which will also mean you can swim in peace. If you want to explore under water there are scuba-diving clubs offering instruction. Information at the Tourist Office, 3, Quai Pierre-Forgas.

The farmhouse walk

This is an easy, three-hour walk which will take you to the *mas*, mountain farmhouses which were once inhabited by people who earned their

living from farming, animal husbandry and the resources of the forest. Pass through a wood of chestnut and hazelnut trees and visit the hermitage of Notre-Dame-de-

Vie and the little Romanesque Church of Saint-Laurent-du-Mont just by a mimosa grove. Information at the Tourist Office: Rambles in Argelès-sur-Mer (brochure 15 F).

you make arrangements
through Cap Cerbère,
☎ 04 68 88 41 00.

Mas Maillol

**Vallée de la Roume,
approx. 2¹/₂ miles
(4 km) SW from Banyuls**
Open daily except Tues.
and public holidays,
10am-noon and 2-5pm
out of season; 10am-
noon and 4-7pm, May–
Sept. *Admission charge.*
Aristide Maillol, one of the
greatest sculptors of the late
19th and early 20th C.
(p. 127), spent the first and
last years of his life here at
this small farmhouse. Maillol
was born in Banyuls in 1861,
but spent most of his adult life
in Paris. He would come back
every autumn to sculpt in his
workshop in his home town.
Maillol died in 1944, after a
car accident, and was buried
at the Mas. *La Méditerranée*, a
monumental sculpture, deco-
rates his tomb.

Cerbère

Gourmet detour

This quiet and pleasant little
village is situated 2¹/₂ miles
(4 km) from the Spanish border. It is known for its pebble
beaches, its small creeks and
and its frontier post. La
Roumaguère at Cerbère is an
excellent place in which to
stock up on local wines, jam
made from prickly pears,
Cerbère honey or Catalan
charcuterie (cold meats).
La Roumaguère (☎ 04 68 88
41 72).

Banyuls-sur-Mer

Wine and sea

Banyuls is famous for its sweet
wine (p. 49) but it is also a
peaceful seaside resort beside
a lovely bay, above which rise
terraces, retained by low shale
walls. Wheat and olives were
once grown in this valley
and cattle were reared.
Honey was collected in
abundance. Today, the little
town is an interesting place
to explore on foot. There
is dancing in the **Place
Paul-Reig** in the shade
of the plane trees. Take
a detour to the pic-
turesque **Quartier de la
Pointe de l'Houne** with
its multicoloured
houses. The **Île Grosse**
offers walkers a magnifi-
cent view and the
village of **Puig-del-Mas**,
on a nearby slope, is charming. If you want to take a
yacht trip, contact the Tourist
Office, Av. de la République.
Wine tastings: Robert
Doutres, **Cave Coopérative
l'Étoile:** Domaines du Mas
Blanc, Domane de La Retoris,
Hospices de Banyuls, Cellier
des Templiers (Rte du Mas de
Reig, ☎ 04 68 98 36 70.
Open daily 9.30am-noon and
2-6pm).

La réserve et aquarium du laboratoire Arago

☎ 04 68 88 73 39.
Open daily 9am-noon

and 2-6.30pm and in
summer until 10pm.
Admission charge.
This marine nature reserve
covers a rocky coastline
1,606 acres (650 ha) long
from the Île Grosse to Cap
Peyrefitte. It is unique in
France. Here 25 researchers
from the CNRS, the
National Scientific
Research Centre, 10
instructors and 65
engineers carry out
research in a
natural environ-
ment. The best way
of finding out about
the wildlife that
inhabits the bays
and creeks is to
visit the aquarium
of the Arago
Laboratory. Here,
without having to
don flippers, you
will be able to see groupers,
octopus, anemones, corals
and rascasse fish which live
in the 36 tanks. You can
also scuba-dive in the part
of the reserve where diving
is permitted, as long as

Collioure

Collioure is a delightful little resort nestling in a bay beside the Mediterranean, overlooked by Mont Albères. Many artists have been inspired by the picturesque landscape, including Matisse and Derain, who painted this pretty little Catalan port with its vibrant colours. It is a real pleasure to wander through the narrow lanes with their brightly coloured shops. In the evening sample some *tapas*, the appetising southern hors-d'œuvres, which always include grilled vegetables and marinated anchovies.

A port since antiquity

In antiquity Cocoliberis was a port of call for seafarers of the great civilisations of the Mediterranean basin. After incursions by the Visigoths and Saracens, it was fortified under the Carolingians. From the 12th to the 17th C., Collioure was annexed in quick succession to the kingdoms of Arragon, Majorca and France. The town was finally restored to France in 1659, under the Treaty of the

Pyrenees. Many forts and towers are evidence of the town's eventful military past. There are special **walks** signposted in blue and white which will take you to see them (information at the Tourist Office, Pl. du 18-Juin). Collioure has always lived from fishing, and has large **anchovy** processing facilities (p. 37). Nowadays, a few small companies continue the tradition. Visit the Société Roque, 19, Route d'Argelès (☎ 04 68 82 04 99. Open daily, except weekends. Closed 20 Dec.–20 Jan.) and buy some of these salty delicacies. Paintings by the Fauvists and Cubists (p. 50) immortalised the brightly coloured sailing boats of the fishermen.

Château Royal

☎ 04 68 82 06 43. Open out of season, 9am-4.15pm, in season, 10am-5.15pm. Closed on public holidays. *Admission charge.*

This château, built on the site of the Roman occupation, was the residence of the kings of Majorca from 1276 to 1344. Visitors can go down to the dungeons, cross the parade ground, the courtyard and the ramparts. The rooms of the former château are used by the Fondation de Collioure which holds exhibitions there throughout the year. The Hostellerie des Templiers (*see opposite*) stands at the foot of the castle.

The old town

The **Church of Notre-Dame-des-Anges** (7.30am-noon and 2-5.30pm) is famous for its 17th- and 18th-C. altarpieces, wonderful examples of Catalan art, which decorate

SCUBA-DIVING AND SAILING

**CIP de Collioure,
15, Rue de la Tour,
☎ 04 68 82 07 16.**
This international scuba-diving club offers two types of training course, one lasting one week, the other for two days. Those who have passed the first level examinations will be able to scuba-dive to watch the underwater wildlife or explore the wrecks of ships sunk during World War II. The CIP also offers courses in windsurfing and in sailing a Catalan sailing ship. Overnight accommodation is also available at the centre.

the side-chapels and main altar. St. Vincent is the patron saint of Collioure and festivities are held in his honour from 14 to 18 August. A **pilgrimage** is organised to Notre-Dame-de-la-Consolation, and there is a *corrida* (bullfight) on 16 August and fireworks in the evening (*La Festa Major*), which attracts holidaymakers. From June to September, Collioure always has something to celebrate. There are Catalan boat-races, sardine festivals, concerts, exhibitions, Sardane competitions and fireworks on St. John's night (information, ☎ 04 68 82 15 47 or 04 68 82 05 66).

L'Hostellerie des Templiers

**12, Quai de l'Amirauté,
opposite castle,
☎ 04 68 98 31 10.**
Closed on Sun.–Mon. out of season, 1 week in Nov. and in Jan.

L'Hostellerie des Templiers

To find out more about Collioure's glorious past, visit Jojo Pous, an art lover and owner of this hotel-restaurant-museum. Jojo's father, René Pous, welcomed his friends, the painters and sculptors, and offered them accommodation in exchange for a painting or drawing. His illustrious guests included Matisse, Maillol, Dali, Picasso and Dufy. Ask his son to show you the guest book, filled with drawings and watercolours by the artists. The walls of the house are covered from cellar to attic with 2,000 original works of art. If you can't tear yourself away, you can stay the night.

Going for a swim

The **beaches** are small but numerous, so overcrowding is rare. There is the Saint-Vincent beach in the north near the church, the Plage Boramar, between the church and the château; the Port-d'Avall and Boutigué beaches on the town side, not forgetting the **creeks** of the Ouille and the Balette.

Boat or train trip

You can take a trip around the bay from the port. Information is available from Saint-Laurent, ☎ 04 68 82 00 28 and the Albatros, ☎ 04 68 82 56 77. Both offer trips every day in season along the rocky coast. In the town centre, board the little train which runs all year round between 10am and 10pm, ☎ 04 68 81 16 96 (admission charge). It calls at Fort Saint-Elme along the vineyard route in the mountains and returns to the coast at Port-Vendres; the return journey is along the seafront to Collioure (approx. 50 min). When you arrive, make for the wonderful Maison de la Vigne, Place du 18-Juin (☎ 04 68 82 49 00), and sample the fine Collioure wines. Taste to your heart's content before you decide what to buy.

Vallespir

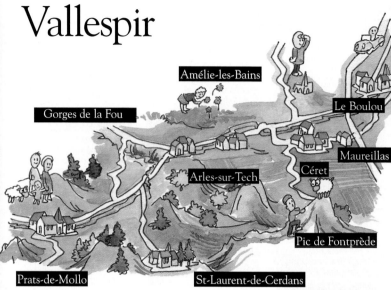

Amélie-les-Bains

Le Boulou

Gorges de la Fou

Maureillas

Céret

Arles-sur-Tech

Pic de Fontprède

Prats-de-Mollo

St-Laurent-de-Cerdans

Feel in need of a change? At Vallespir you can live life at a more natural pace. The spa resorts of Preste and Le Boulou (p. 54), in a sunny valley planted with cork-oaks and evergreen oaks, await you. As you ascend the mountain, the cool mountain air fills the lungs, and orchards and crops give way to chestnut trees and pastures. The beauties of nature abound in this classic Catalan setting.

Amélie-les-Bains
Health springs

The sulphurous hot springs at Amélie were worshipped even in Roman times. Today the town is one of the leading spas in France. The remains of the huge vaulted Roman baths have been incorporated into the spa complex. Treatment is offered here for **rheumatism** and **respiratory diseases**. (Thermes d'Amélie-les-Bains: ☎ 04 68 87 99 00).

To satisfy the pangs of hunger that may be brought on by the cure, there is a wonderful *pâtisserie* and confectioner who offers a wide choice of Catalan delicacies. There are *galets du Tech* (made of chocolate and almonds), nougat, almond biscuits, apricot and cherrry bars, Céret candied cherries, and a host of other sweets, cakes and biscuits. **Antoine Alaminos**, Rue des Thermes (open 7am-1pm and 3.30-7.30pm in summer).

Saint-Laurent-de-Cerdans
Fabrics of the Sun

This town has a long history of Catalan textile mills (p. 55), and traditional espadrilles are still made here. There is even a **Musée de l'Espadrille** (Rue Joseph-Nivet, ☎ 04 68 39 55 75. Open May–Sept. daily 9am-

ARLES-SUR-TECH: CATALAN TRADITIONS

Arles maintains its lively Catalan traditions through numerous religious or secular festivals throughout the year. Its Medieval Fair is a wonderful street spectacle. So is that of its two patron saints, Abdon and Sennen (Procession de la Rodella on 30 July. Information from the Tourist Office).
The Church of Sainte-Marie was founded in 778 by Charlemagne. Its 13th-C. Gothic cloister has an austere elegance. A 4th-C. sarcophagus here is supposed to be an inexhaustible supply of fresh water. The International Basketball Centre has a complete infrastructure adapted to the sport. A fascinating old Catalan weaving mill is also open to visitors (see p. 55).

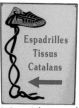

noon, 3-7pm, Oct.–Apr. Mon–Fri. 9am-noon and 2-6pm. Admission charge). This shows you how the classic espadrille of jute and hemp with a rope sole, is made. There is a video about the history of the village and of the espadrille. At **Aux Toiles du Soleil** (Le Village, ☎ 04 68 39 50 02. Open Mon.–Fri., 9am-noon and 2.30-7pm), true Catalan cloth in the traditional colours of red and yellow (blood and

gold) is made. There is table linen in 6 ft (1.80 m) lengths, for blinds or deck-chairs, curtains and *razzeteurs* (handmade espadrilles with rope soles and laces, about 300 F a pair). Many shops in the Pyrenees-Orientales sell this high-quality brand.

Prats-de-Mollo

Walks and festivities

At 2,470 ft (740 m) above sea level, Prats-de-Mollo is a pretty town, whose fortifications were built by Vauban. It is famous for its Bear Festival (**Fête de l'Ours**, p. 112) in February, followed by three days of **carnival** (information at the Tourist Office) and its **hot springs** (p. 100). In 1984, 5,913 acres (2,393 ha) of mountain ecosystems in the foothills of Canigou were classified as a nature reserve. Rhododendrons, gentians and Turk's cap lily can be found here at the right season. There are lots of signposted hiking trails, including a **botanical path**, starting from the Chalet de las Conques and lasting one and a half hours. From the Preste, you can climb the **Costabone** 8,217 ft

Spotcheck
B7-C7

Pyrénées-Orientales

Things to do
Arles-sur-Tech Medieval Fair
Musée de l'Espadrille
Visit the health springs
Gorges de la Fou (caves)

Within easy reach
Perpignan, p. 132,
Saint-Cyprien, p. 142.
La côte Vermeille, p. 144,
Collioure, p. 148.

Tourist office
Arles-sur-Tech:
☎ 04 68 39 11 99
Prats-de-Mollo:
☎ 04 68 39 70 83

(2,465 m), an eight-hour hike. It is 9 miles (15 km) by car from Spain along the Col d'Ares. At the fortress there is quite a show, with canons being fired and demonstrations of horsemanship and gymnastics. (open daily in Jul.–Aug. at 2.30pm and 4pm except Sat., in June and Sept. at 3.30pm except Sat.).

Gorges de la Fou
☎ 04 68 39 16 21.
Open Apr.–end Sept., 10am-6pm.
Admission charge.
In places there is a sheer 670 ft (200 m) drop. These are the narrowest gorges in the world; 5,000 ft (1,500 m) of footbridges takes you through a series of caves and waterfalls.

Cloister in the Church of Sainte-Marie at Arles-sur-Tech

Céret

Céret, in the heart of Vallespir (p.150), in the foothills of the Catalan Pyrenees, can claim to be the cherry tree and still life capital of France! With 310 days of sunshine a year it produces the earliest fruiting cherry in France. The sun was also what drew Picasso to the village in the early 20th C. He fell under the spell of the village and brought all his friends here, including

Braque, Masson and Dufy, which made it the Mecca of Cubism. Céret is a treasure-trove of curiosities. Here you can visit a museum, go hang-gliding and dance the Sardane!

The Musée d'Art Moderne

8, Bd du Maréchal-Joffre,
☎ 04 68 87 27 76.

Open daily Jul.–Sept., 10am-7pm; Oct.–June, 10am-6pm; Oct.–Apr. 10am-6pm, closed on Tues.
Admission charge.
This extraordinary little museum was opened in 1950 in a small convent by the painter Pierre Brune. Many painters, including the greatest masters of the

20th C., lived in the Céret region, and many of them – Cocteau, Dalì, Mirò, Picasso – donated original paintings when the museum was opened. The walls are also hung with paintings by Juan Gris, Tapiés, Max Jacob and Matisse as well as a collection of 28 little terracotta cups painted by Picasso.

Métiers d'Art Saint-Roch

4, Bd de La Fayette,
☎ 04 68 87 04 38.
Open in winter, 10am-noon and 2-6pm, except Sun.–Mon. morning; in summer, daily 10am-noon and 3-8pm.
This building was once a school run by nuns, but since 1967 it has been used as workshops by a few craftsmen who run a **regional arts and crafts centre**. About 15 craftspeople work on ceramics, wood, jewellery, weaving, glass, leather and painted

SOCIETE DES ARENES DE CERET

Spotcheck
C7

Pyrénées-Orientales

Things to do
Musée d'Art Moderne
Crafts at the Métiers d'Art
Saint-Roch
Festivals, carnivals and *féria*

Within easy reach
*Perpignan, 29km N,
p. 132,
La côte Vermeille, 25km E,
p. 144.*

Tourist office
Céret: ☎ 04 68 87 00 53

silk. Some craftsmen hold classes in their workshops. To learn to make models, pouring liquid clay into moulds, using a potter's wheel, firing and glazing, contact Pierre Devis or Marc Delattre.

In festive mood
There is always something happening in Céret. There are the **Feux de la Saint-Jean** (23 June, midsummer's eve), **Saint-Ferréol** (18 September), when you can compete in a 12½ mile (20 km) race, **the Carnival** in February, the great **Sardane festival** (p. 121) on Easter Monday, the **Fête de la Cerise** (cherry festival) at Pentecost, and the **Festival de Musique Méditerranée** in mid-September. The highlight of the year is the **Féria** in July with its traditional bullfights in the arenas, which Picasso loved to attend. For three days, wine flows in the *bodegas* and there are fireworks every night. On Saturday, visit the market which has lots of regional produce (information from the Tourist Office).

Pop the cork!
According to legend, it was in Roussillon that Dom Pérignon discovered a type of cork strong enough to contain his lively wine called champagne. In truth, the cork-oak does grow wild all over Roussillon, covering thousands of acres. The cork was a very important crop until the 1950s, when competition from Spain and Portugal was too strong and the plantations were abandoned. An increase in demand revived the crop. **Sabaté corks**, Espace Tech, Oulrich, ☎ 04 68 87 20 20. Free guided tour (Mon.–Fri.) Reservations required.

✿ On land and in the air
Céret is a favourite site for freefall parachuting and hang-gliding; and for those who love exciting sensations, deltaplaning can be practised at the **Pic Fontfrède** at a height of 3,440 ft (1,031 m) from a springboard. Local contact: Delta Club (ODPO, ☎ 04 68 87 25 54, see coupon at the end of the guide) or M. Delseny, (☎ 04 68 87 34 15). If you prefer terra firma, the Tourist Office can supply leaflets about signposted hiking and rambling paths. There is an interesting walk to the hermitage of Saint-Ferréol, two hours walk from the 14th-C. **Pont de Céret** (path marked in orange) or the Pic de Fontfrède from Les Capucins, a 4½ hour walk, signposted in blue. There is a beech-grove and a heath with a view over the **Canigou**.

Les Aspres

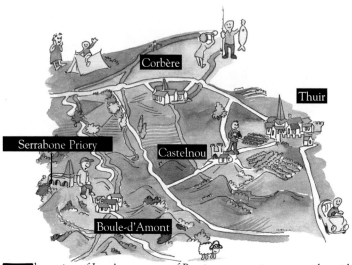

The region of Les Aspres, west of Perpignan, owes its name to the aridity of its stony ground. The Serrabone Priory, with its remarkable medieval bestiary, stands in the midst of the fragrant, stony *garrigue* (scrubland). Little hilltop villages, scorched by the sun, are enhanced by a Romanesque church or the ruins of a castle. Byrrh, sweet and aromatic, a favourite French apéritif, is also made right here.

Thuir

'Tuïr la Catalana'
Information
☎ 04 68 84 67 67.
This is a Catalan folklore festival with exhibitions, conferences and performances. A colourful parade accompanied by musicians opens the festival. The festivities continue for a whole week in July.

Byrrh cellars
6, Bd Violet,
☎ 04 68 53 05 42.
Open Apr. (except Sun.) May, June, Sept. daily 9-11.45am and 2.30-5.45pm; in Oct. (except Sat.), Jul.–Aug., daily 10-11.45am and 2-6.45pm. Closed first two weeks of Jan.
Free 45-min guided tour.

Thuir is the capital of the region and famous mainly for the apéritif called byrrh. Seven of the plants in this fortified wine are present in medicinal wines used as digestive aids, stimulants and tonics; cocoa and orange zest give it a pleasant aroma. A visit to the cellars reveals the history of the Violet brothers who invented this sweet wine with a quinine base in the 19th C. The company was bought by Pernod-Ricard in the 1970s.

The cellars produce several other apéritifs, including Cinzano and Dubonnet.

Castelnou

Serrabone Priory
☎ 04 68 84 09 30.
Open daily 10am-5.45pm, closed 25 Dec.-1 Jan., 1 May and 1 Nov.
Admission charge.
A little road runs along the mountainside through the forest of evergreen oaks and bright heather to the priory. Serrabone Priory stands in a remote spot in the mountains and is one of the marvels of Romanesque architecture in Roussillon. It was built in the 12th C., and has been lived in for nearly 200 years. The priory is remarkable for its pink marble carved with

intertwined floral motifs and extraordinary monsters. These elegant refinements stand in stark contrast to the austerity of the church and the overall architectural design, typical of medieval monastic buildings, where decoration was equated with worldliness.

GOOD FOOD AT CASTELNOU

Leave Thuir in the direction of Castelnou Open 10am-8pm, in summer.

The château is one of the loveliest historic sites in the region *(photo below right)*. The golden stone of the houses of the village and fine restaurants make it a good place to stop for a meal. At l'Hostal (p. 32), 13, Carrer de na Patora or Patio, 9, Carrer del Mig, you will appreciate the generous cuisine of Roussillon, washed down with robust wines. Dishes include *cargolades* (snails), meat grilled on vine twigs, stuffed squid, game and wild mushrooms. Castelnou has a picturesque market (Tues. from 9am-7pm, from mid-June to mid-Sept.).

A nature ramble

When you leave the church, take the little nature walk which gives you the opportunity to admire the local wild flowers. These include artemisia (wormwood), rock-rose and nettle trees... A small vineyard containing about 500 grape vines produces a local wine called Cuvée de Serrabone. A regional **fruit tree conservation area** (including fig trees and peach trees) and an arboretum of forest species complete this interesting view of the plant-life of the lower slopes of the Pyrenees.

Boule-d'Amont

Relais de Serrabone

☎ 04 68 84 26 24. Open daily except Tues. Easter–end Oct., in summer daily, 11am-7pm. On the way back, stop to shop for food in the magnificent setting of the valley of Boulès. Farmers have got together to offer delicious produce for sale direct to the public, including duck, foie gras, goat's cheeses, honeys, jams, aromatic herbs, wines and other local delicacies.

A holiday blessed by the gods

Auberge du Val d'Amont, ☎ 04 68 84 76 76.

Spotcheck
C6

Pyrénées-Orientales

Things to do
Tuïr la Catalana Festival
Visit the Byrrh cellars
Serrabone Priory

Within easy reach
Perpignan, p. 132,
Les Fenouillèdes, p. 138,
Saint-Cyprien, p. 142,
Côte Vermeille, p. 144.

Tourist Office
Thuir: ☎ 04 68 53 45 86

Weekly or nightly accommodation. Closed in Jan. Les Aspres means 'bitter' in French but there is not the slightest trace of bitterness in this delightful and hospitable place. The little church has brightly coloured Baroque altarpieces (there is even a *son et lumière* performance for 10 F). From the inn, it takes 1½ hours to walk to the Serrabone, or take the 2-hour sanctuary path (mountain bikes can be hired).

The Château of Castelnou has stood here since the Middle Ages

Villefranche-de-Conflent

Conflent runs from Mont-Louis to Prades and is part of the Têt valley. It is a point at which several rivers meet, hence its name, 'confluence'. From the coastal plain to the mountain villages of Canigou and Madres, the landscape changes from market gardens and vines at Vinça and peach trees at Prades to apple trees in the Rotja valley. The middle and high mountains have lush pastures which are grazed by cattle and sheep.

Villefranche, fortified city

Villefranche controls the Têt valley and its tributaries. It was a stronghold from early times and as you approach all you see are its ramparts and fortifications, created by Louis XIV's military engineer, Vauban, in the 17th C. Vauban also built **Fort Libéria**, which overlooks the river gorges in the valley. The 12th-C. **Church of Saint-Jacques** at Villefranche has a Romanesque pink marble façade. It stands amid medieval lanes with wrought iron shop signs tempting you to browse. Some of the old doors have a large thistle fixed to them which serves as a barometer.

The Yellow Train, 'métro of the Pyrenees'

Information at the Villefranche SNCF station,

☎ 04 68 96 56 62.
The train runs all year round. In summer it makes seven round trips daily; the journey will take five hours in each direction if you go right to the terminus at Latour-

Fort Libéria at Villefranche-de-Conflent

CONFLENT
ON HORSEBACK

Contact: Éric Loux,
La Cavale, 66360
Mantet,
☎ 04 68 05 57 59.
Only one road leads to and
ends at Mantet, an isolated
spot in a splendid mountain
setting. It is the departure
point for a gentle pony-trek
along almost forgotten paths.
There is shade and light, and the
forest echoes to a symphony of
noises, betraying the presence of many
wild creatures. Much of the flora is unique and
birds of prey, such as eagles, vultures and sparrow-
hawks, can be glimpsed as they soar in the deep-
blue skies. Pony-trekking is a wonderful way of
discovering Conflent. A 'breath of fresh air' weekend with accommodation in *gîtes* costs from 650 F.

de-Carol (186 F return). The
round trip is 40 miles (63 km)
and the average speed is
about 19 miles per hour (30
km/h). It is a lovely ride, both
because of the countryside,
with little villages clinging to
rocks, narrow passes, valleys
and rushing streams, and
because of the engineering
feat which the line represents.
The train passes through the
highest station in France,
5,000 ft (1,500 m) above sea
level, and there are various
viaducts and bridges. The
Yellow Train is also used by
the local inhabitants to get
to work, especially in winter
when there is black ice on the
roads. Do not miss a delightful trip on this winding
railway track that conquered
the Cerdagne!

Le Conflent

Small and large
Canalettes
On the Route de
Vernet,
☎ 04 68 96 23 11.
Open 10am-6pm in sum-
mer, by appointment in
winter. *Admission charge.*
The Canalettes are caves
between 30 and 400
million years old with
amazing stalactites
and stalagmites.
Dress warmly
so as not to
be turned
into a

stalagmite yourself – the
temperature is only 57 F°
(14 C°) on average!

✿ A trek through
Upper Conflent
Starting from Olette, the trek
goes through villages clinging
to the steep slopes of the
valley such as Thuir-d'Evol
and Escaro. This is a five- or
six-day hike along well-
signposted paths through
nature reserves
such as Mantet
(see voucher
at the end of
the guide)
and Jujols,
where there
are 'bird
ecology'
courses
(☎ 04 68 97
00 34). It is also
available to horse-
back riders (informa-
tion at the Adeco,
Olette,
☎ 04 68 97
08 09).

The ramparts of Villefranche-de-Conflent

Prades

Prades, surrounded by orchards, is a town of 7,000 inhabitants. It offers a wide variety of activities, and there is much to see and do. Prades is also a good starting point for

excursions into the Massif du Canigou. There is a Catalan summer university where Catalans can learn all about their heritage and culture. Film fans will love the film festival, with its attendant lectures and seminars. Most famously, Prades is the home of the Pablo Casals Festival, a chamber music festival. The abbey of Saint-Michel-de-Cuxa is a magnificent example of Romanesque art.

The Church of Saint-Pierre

This church is the main monument in the town. It was rebuilt in the 17th C. place of the Romanesque building. The 12th-C. marble and granite belltower is one of the vestiges of the older building. The interior decoration of the church is well worth seeing, particularly

the 17th-C. **Baroque reredos**, the largest in France, the work of Joseph Sunyer.

Musée Pablo-Casals

4, Rue Victor-Hugo, ☎ 04 68 05 41 02. Open in winter Mon.–Fri., 9am-noon and 2-5pm; in summer, Mon.–Sat. and Sun. morning 9am-noon and 2-6pm. *Free admission.* The Rue du Palais-de-Justice, with its pink marble pavements, streams and old Catalan houses, with their fine doorways and wrought-iron locks, leads to the Musée Pablo Casals. It is a modest homage to the great cellist. On the

first floor, there are rooms containing a permanent archaeological display and a reconstruction of an old-fashioned Catalan kitchen. The museum shares the premises of the Tourist Office (☎ 04 68 05 41 02), which organises guided tours

SUMMER FESTIVALS

In 1939, the famous Spanish cellist Pablo Casals went into voluntary exile, fleeing from Franco's regime. He settled in Prades, giving concerts that drew a Europe-wide audience and the profits from which went to refugee artists. Casals refused to play in Spain until democracy was restored. In 1950, Casals founded the Bach Festival here. He died in Puerto Rico in 1973.

The Pablo Casals Festival is now dedicated to chamber music. It takes place between 26 July and 13 August and attracts the most renowned performers as well as major ensembles, ☎ 04 68 96 33 07.

Catalan Summer University: there are courses for beginners and advanced students in Catalan, lectures, workshops and a free performance in the Place de l'Église (from 15 to 24 August, ☎ 04 68 96 41 02).

Ciné-rencontres de Prades: this centres around a particular film theme and is run by an expert. There are showings of feature films and documentaries, attended by directors, actors and camera operators, as well as colloquiums, discussions and analyses of videos (third week of July, ☎ 04 68 05 20 47).

Journées Romanes: lectures and guided tours about Romanesque art in Catalonia (first two weeks of July: Abbey of Saint-Michel-de-Cuxa, ☎ 04 68 34 41 02).

of the town on Wednesday mornings. You can also obtain information here on exploring the Massif du Canigou (p. 160). Ask about mountain shelters, guides, routes, and hiring mountain-bikes and four-by-four vehicles and ordinance survey maps. Information about potholing, canyoning and whitewater rafting is also available.

Saint-Michel-de-Cuxa Abbey
1 mile (3 km) south of Prades, via the D 27. ☎ 04 68 96 15 35. Open daily, except Sun.

morning, 9.30am-11.50 am, 2pm-5pm (6pm in summer). *Admission charge.* This was a prestigious monastery between the 9th and 17th C., but it was destroyed during the Revolution and left in ruins. It was subsequently pillaged by unscrupulous art dealers (part of the cloister is now in New York!).

Much of the abbey has been restored. The 12th-C. **cloister** is a work of art whose pink marble capitals are carved with flowers and animals. A Benedictine community from Montserrat in Catalonia inhabits the monastery now.

Cloister of the Abbey of Saint-Michel-de-Cuxa

Canigou

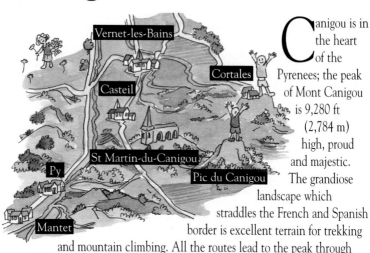

Vernet-les-Bains

Cortales

Casteil

St Martin-du-Canigou

Py

Pic du Canigou

Mantet

Canigou is in the heart of the Pyrenees; the peak of Mont Canigou is 9,280 ft (2,784 m) high, proud and majestic. The grandiose landscape which straddles the French and Spanish border is excellent terrain for trekking and mountain climbing. All the routes lead to the peak through woodland, moorland, bogs and mountain pastures. There are two nature reserves as well as the magnificent Saint-Martin Abbey.

Le Canigou

Sacred mountain of the Catalans

In the 18th C. cartographers believed Mont Canigou to be the highest peak in the Pyrenees, or even in Europe. It inspired numerous legends, fuelled by various air disasters which gave it the reputation of swallowing up aeroplanes. Since then, the mystery has been solved. The strong concentration of manganese and iron in the rocks makes them act like a magnet. The

mythical mountain of the Catalans is the focus of traditions dating back thousands of years. On midsummer's eve, the feast of St. John, French and Spanish Catalans welcome the flame of St. John on the summit of Mont Canigou and use it to light bonfires throughout the surrounding countryside. Wreaths of St. John's wort, verbena and walnut leaves are assembled in the form of a cross; and are said to bring good luck to all homes and families.

Climbing

The climb is quite easy from mountain refuges, which are on the GR 10 route from Mariailles

(☎ 04 68 96 22 90) or Les Cortalets (☎ 04 68 96 36 19 and ☎ 04 68 05 63 57). Off-road vehicles will take you to the Chalet des Cortalets, which a coach or other vehicle would find hard to negotiate. From Vernet-les-Bains: Transport Taurigna, ☎ 04 68 05 63 06 or 04 68 05 54 39; station taxi ☎ 04 68 05 62 28. Guides Association: ☎ 04 68 05 31 42 or 04 68 05 71 42.

Vernet-les-Bains

Getting into shape

This spa treats those suffering from **rheumatism** and **respiratory infections**. The writer Rudyard Kipling used to come here for a cure. There is also a health farm using the hot springs where you can relax after mountain-climbing. On the first Sunday of August, the town organises the Course du Canigou, a running race which is open to anyone. Before you go off into the mountains, find out where to sleep and eat by contacting the Vernet-les-Bains Tourist Office (practical information is contained in two brochures).

Saint-Martin-du-Canigou Abbey

After Vernet-les-Bains, on the D 116 to the village of Casteil. A pedestrian ramp leads to the abbey in 30 min. Jeep Service at the Garage Villacèque, ☎ 04 68 05 51 14 and 04 68 05 50 03.

Guided tour at 10am, noon (11.30am and 12.30pm Sun. and public holidays), 2pm, 3pm, 4pm and 5pm in summer; 15 Sept.–14 June: 10am, noon, 2.30pm, 3.30pm and 4.30pm. Closed on Tues., from 1 Oct. at Easter.

Admission charge.
The crenelated belltower of Saint-Martin-du-Canigou was built in 1007. In 1428 the abbey was hit by an earthquake which damaged the building and the whole structure had to be rebuilt. The influence of the abbey later waned; it was abandoned and pillaged and eventually fell into ruin. In 1952, Saint-Martin, perched like an eagle's nest on a peak at an altitude of 3,633 ft (1,090 m) once more found its spiritual vocation with the arrival of the community of the Beatitudes. The pink and white marble capitals of the cloister are beautifully carved and the setting is magnificent.

Spotcheck
B7

Pyrénées-Orientales

Things to do

Climbing Mont Canigou
Saint-Martin Abbey

With children

Casteil animal park

Tourist office

Vernet-les-Bains:
☎ 04 68 05 55 35

Casteil animal park

Open daily in summer, 1-7pm; winter, 8am-4pm.
☎ 04 68 05 54 08.
Free admission.
This 7-acre (3-ha) park contains many animals – lions, bears, monkeys, emus, llamas, chickens, etc. All the animals have been donated or 'loaned'. Children can learn about the Pyrenean bear.

❀ NATURE RESERVES OF PY AND MANTET

These two nature reserves are very diverse (see the coupon at the end of the guide for the Mantet Reserve). They lie on the northwest slopes of Mont Canigou, between an altitude of 3,333 and 9,000 ft (1,000 and 2,700 m). There are birch, hazelnut, beech and fir trees and meadows with large expanses of fescue-grass and spikenard. This variety of plant life is matched by the diversity of wild animals, including foxes, wild boar, martens, squirrels, badgers, wildcats and Pyrenean chamois. The royal eagle and large grouse also frequent the area. Four signposted paths leave from the Mantet village square and the Py parking area.

The Cerdagne

T he Cerdagne is a high plateau in the western part of Roussillon, 4,000 ft (1,200 m) above sea level, which opens into valleys of meadows and cultivated fields. It is surrounded by granite peaks, is covered in pines and is a haven of fresh air. It also has maximum exposure to the sun, which is why a huge solar furnace has been installed here. In this remote environment edelweiss and angelica flourish, and wildlife abounds; sightings of shy marmot and mouflon are possible.

Font-Romeu

A sporting paradise

This sun-drenched ski resort at an altitude of 6,000 ft (1,800 m) is also a base for innumerable hikes in the mountains through forests as well as a health resort which specialises in treating asthmatics. As for sports, there is so much to choose from: canoeing and kayaking, whitewater rafting, hang-gliding, parachuting, horse-riding, golf, rock-climbing, mountain-biking, ice-skating, skiing and snowboarding as well as rambles around Lac Pradella or the Roc de la Calme. Ask for the programme at the Tourist Office and Bureau des Guides et de la Montagne (☎ 04 68 30 23 08).

Odeillo solar furnace
2 miles (3 km) from Font-Romeu, ☎ 04 68 30 77 86. Guided tour 10am–12.30pm and 1.30–5.30pm (7.30pm, 1 Jul.–1 Sept.).

THE EYNE VALLEY AND NATURE RESERVE — SPORT AND DISCOVERY

The 2,900 acres (1,177 ha) of the nature reserve (☎ 04 68 04 77 07) begin at an altitude of 5,670 ft (1,700 m). It is rich in rare plants and is an excellent place to ramble and see the wildlife of the mountain range. It has enjoyed scientific renown since the 18th C., and is a paradise for botanists, particularly in the spring. In winter, the lovely little ski resort of Eyne 2600 operates on the slopes of the Cambras-d'Azé. Like Llo and Planes, nearby villages, the town has a lovely Romanesque church with Baroque altarpieces. The best place to stay in the area is Cal Paï, a comfortable *gîte* which has a range of open-air activities on offer. We tested it as a family and can vouch for the charm of the place and the very friendly welcome (☎ 04 68 04 06 96).

Admission charge.
Odeillo gets more sunshine than anywhere else in France, so in 1968 the largest solar furnace in the world was installed here. It is part of the CNRS research laboratory and is used for studying the behaviour of materials at high temperature. Its gigantic mirror is larger than the Arc de Triomphe and enables it to reach temperatures of 5,432 °F (3,000°C).

The village of Llo

Saillagouse

Musée-Charcuterie de la Cerdagne

6 miles (9 km) from Font-Romeu,
☎ 04 68 04 71 51.

Open all year round except Wed. and Sun. afternoon.
This museum explains how local pork products are made, particularly the Cerdan hams which have been famous since antiquity. The owner, Bernard Bonzom, an enthusiast, will show you around. The drying-room contains 700 hams and there are 70 'home-made' products to choose from to take home.

Spotcheck
B7

Pyrénées-Orientales

Things to do

Skiing, rambling, horse-riding
Visit the Odeillo solar furnace
Musée-Charcuterie de la Cerdagne
Musée de la Cerdagne

Tourist office

Font-Romeu:
☎ 04 68 30 68 30

Sainte-Léocadie

Musée de la Cerdagne

At 3 miles (5 km) from Bourg-Madame,
☎ 04 68 04 08 05.
Open in summer daily 10am-7pm; out of season, daily 10am-noon and 2-6pm except Tues. Closed mid-Nov.–mid-Dec. *Admission charge.*
This folklore museum is housed in the beautiful 18th-C. farm of Cal Mateu, and its collections illustrate life in the region. There are exhibits about shepherds and their flocks, farming, the slaughter of the pig, and the Yellow Train (p. 156). The varied landscape of shale, granite, pasture and frontiers is also explained. This is also the highest vineyard in France, at an altitude of more than 4,265 ft (1,300 m). More than 400 bottles of the wine is auctioned every year.

Capcir

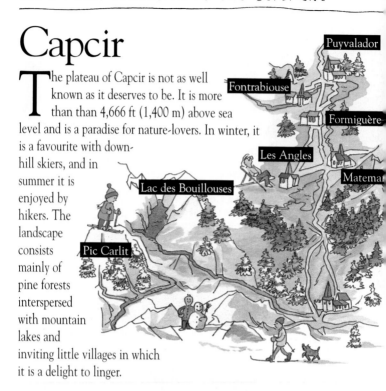

The plateau of Capcir is not as well known as it deserves to be. It is more than than 4,666 ft (1,400 m) above sea level and is a paradise for nature-lovers. In winter, it is a favourite with down-hill skiers, and in summer it is enjoyed by hikers. The landscape consists mainly of pine forests interspersed with mountain lakes and inviting little villages in which it is a delight to linger.

Puyvalador

Fontrabiouse

Formiguère

Les Angles

Matemal

Lac des Bouillouses

Pic Carlit

A high glacial valley

Capcir is an upper valley in the Aude, about 8 miles (13 km) square. From the Quillane peak, at 5,700 ft (1,714 m), to the village of Puyvalador, it takes the form of a glacial basin between the Carlit and Madrès ranges. It was once an area of forests and grazing, but local industry is now focused mainly on the **ski resorts** of Les Angles, Matemale, Puyvalador and Formiguères, and its many **hiking trails.**

Trekking round the Carlit

The circular trek ends at 8,090 ft (2,426 m). It can be done in four stages, with accommodation in shelters, starting from the Lac des Bouillouses. The route is well-signposted. The departure point is the **Refuge des Bonnes Heures** at the Lac des Bouillouses (6,800 ft/2,050 m, 66210 Mont-Louis ☎ 04 68 04 24 22). Half-board per person: 180 F in dormitory accommodation (end of Oct.–Nov.). **Rando**

Confort is another option for this trek. Information from Pyrénées-Roussillon, Perpignan, ☎ 04 68 67 53 35. **La Pastorale**, based at Porta in the Cerdagne, organises a 7-day pony trek, ☎ 04 68 04 83 92.

Les Angles

Sport or leisure?

Lake Matemale is 5,333 ft (1,600 m) above sea level on a plateau nicknamed 'Canada in miniature'. It is surrounded by a huge pine forest. Its water-sports centre has a well-maintained beach and offers

all types of sporting activities, including windsurfing, yachting and dinghy sailing (Club Nautique de l'Ourson, ☎ 04 68 04 30 77). In this magnificent setting, you can also go pony-trekking (Les Crinières Blondes, ☎ 04 68 04 43 71), some treks lasting several days (Équisud, ☎ 04 68 04 43 62). The lake of Balcère has trout fishing and offers angling holidays. In winter, this becomes a ski

PUYVALADOR CAPCIR ON A DONKEY

Rieutord, 4 miles (7 km) NW of Formiguères, ☎ 04 68 04 41 22. Open from June to Oct. Claudine and Bruno, the owners, offer all-day treks with a pack-donkey who will either carry packs or the kids. Trips of several days are also possible. You can also decide to leave your children with Claude and Bruno for a few days, to give you a real break. They will explore the mountains with other kids. The camp is approved by Jeunesse et Sport, the Ministry of Education supervisory body. In winter, there are also hikes on snow-shoes and skiing.

resort with a ski school: École de Ski Français: ☎ 04 68 04 47 82. Cross-country skiing: centre Guy-Malé, ☎ 04 68 04 31 05. Compagnie des Guides: ☎ 04 68 04 39 22).

The animal park

☎ 04 68 04 17 20. Open from June to August, 8am-7pm; in winter, 9am-7pm. *Admission charge.* In a natural setting at 6,000 ft (1,800 m), there are two hiking trails of 1 and 2 miles (1.5 and 3.5 km) respectively.

If you are lucky, you will encounter wild animals such as the isard (Pyrenean chamois), wild boar, mouflon, ibex and bear. There are even wolves in the area, though they tend to avoid humans.

Formiguères

A breath of fresh air

In the 13th and 14th C., the kings of Majorca had their summer residence in this village which is famous for its bracing air. Formiguères has wonderful historic sights including the Romanesque Church of Sainte-Marie (12th-C.)

Spotcheck
B6

Pyrénées-Orientales

Things to do

Trek round the Carlit
Water-sports and angling
Hiking in the animal park
Visit Formiguères

With children

Capcir on a donkey

Tourist office

Formiguères:
☎ 04 68 04 47 35

and the ruins of the 9th-C. **château,** where King Sancho of Majorca died in 1232. The Tourist Office organises a **tour of the works of art of the churches of Capcir.** West of Formiguères, the best hike is around the **Camporells lakes** at an altitude of 7,470 ft (2,240 m). Departure is from Formiguères, and the route can either be covered on foot (in 4 hours) or by ski lift.

The **Forest of the Matte,** planted by Colbert in the 17th C., is inhabited by deer and chamois and is a favourite with ramblers. The **Pic de Madrès** has some wonderful beauty spots. There is a stalactite cave in the area, the **Grotte de Fontrabiouse** (open 15 June–15 Sept., 10am-7pm. Admission charge). The ambient temperature is 43°F (6 °C), so take a sweater.

Carcassonne

The city's drawbridges, machicolations and 52 towers can be visited on foot, by train or in an open carriage. It was this fortified medieval city that provided Walt Disney with the inspiration for the castle in his version of *The Sleeping Beauty*. Carcassonne is world-famous and unique in terms of its architectural heritage. The lower town, with its lovely 13th-C. bastion, is also worthy of note. Thanks to the architect Viollet-le-Duc, who restored the town in the 19th C., the buildings are in excellent condition. The summer festival called *Cité en Scène* recreates life in the middle ages.

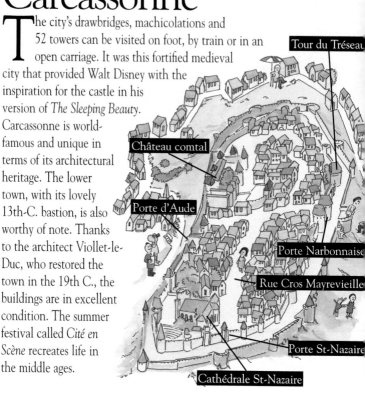

Tour du Tréseau

Château comtal

Porte d'Aude

Porte Narbonnaise

Rue Cros Mayrevieille

Porte St-Nazaire

Cathédrale St-Nazaire

At the crossroads

Two major routes used from the most ancient times happen to cross at Carcassonne. They are the east-west road from the Atlantic to the Mediterranean via the Seuil de Nabouze and the north-south route which links the Massif Central to Spain through the Aude and the foothills of the Pyrenees. Perpignan is on both the Canal du Midi and the Aude river, a rare privilege in this relatively arid land and a situation which helped shape its destiny. It is the *préfecture* of the Aude and has a population of 44,250. This thriving market town is a wine-trading centre with several industries.

More than 2,000 years of history

The origins of Carcassonne reach back as early as the 4th C. BC. Early traces can be found on the promontory on which the old city stands.

Spotcheck
B5

Aude

Things to do

The 'Cité en Scène' Medieval
Festival
The eagles of the citadel
Bicycle rides
Cathedral of Saint-Nazaire

Within easy reach

Le Minervois, p. 198.

Tourist office

Carcassonne:
☎ 04 68 10 24 30

In the 2nd C. BC this strategic outpost was fortified by the Romans, who gave it the name of Carcasso. The Visigoths succeeded the Romans in the 5th C. AD and overran Gaul. The fortified city was then conquered by the Visigoths and when they converted to Christianity, it became a bishopric. In the 8th C., the fortress fell to the Franks, who defended it against attacks by the Saracens.

The legend of Dame Carcass

In 795, the Emperor Charlemagne besieged the town, which was held by Dame Carcass, a Saracen princess. The only food left in the town at the end of the five-year siege was one little pig and measure of corn. Dame Carcass gave the little pig the measure of corn to eat and sent it out to the foot of the ramparts. Charlemagne raised the siege, since he thought that there was enough corn even to feed the pig. Before the Emperor left, Dame Carcass rang out the bells, making them sound the word 'Carcassonne'!

Crusade and troubadours

Under the Trencavel dynasty (1082–1209), viscounts of Béziers, Albi and Nîmes, the city flourished. The most famous troubadours lived in the castle, including Ramon de Miraval and Peire Vidal. Throughout this golden age, Catharism (p. 76) was developing to the detriment of Catholicism. Raymond Roger Trencavel tolerated and protected the heretics on his

RUE DU VICOMTE RAYMOND ROGER TRENCAVEL 1185-1209

lands. Thus, in 1209, the crusade led by Simon de Montfort was directed against him. The town was besieged and finally fell. Trencavel died in a hiding place. His young son tried in vain to recapture the town in 1240.

'CITÉ EN SCÈNE', THE MEDIEVAL FESTIVAL

First two weeks of August.
Every August, an event that is unique in Europe takes place in the setting of the most beautiful medieval city in the world. The spectator enters into the spirit of the festivities and is plunged into the Middle Ages when the city knew its finest hour. Jugglers, fire-eaters, tightrope walkers, jousters and troubadours animate the streets and there are also magnificent displays using all the modern techniques (laser, xenon, enhanced sound) to bring the city to life.

Decadence and Renaissance

In the hands of the French royal family, the fortified city grew. Its proximity to the Catalan border caused the French kings to reinforce the ramparts and enlarge the cathedral in the 13th and 14th C. Its strategic importance was to disappear with the signing of the Treaty of the Pyrenees in 1659, when Roussillon was restored to France; the city walls were no longer required nor maintained and the lower town

grew at the expense of the upper town. In the 19th C., Prosper Mérimée saved the

the 13th C., as were the gatehouse of the Porte Narbonnaise, the Tour du Trésau, the Tour de l'Inquisition and the Porte Saint-Nazaire.

The Cathedral of Saint-Nazaire

The cathedral was consecrated in 1096. It has a Romanesque nave which contrasts greatly with the Gothic transept and apse. Also of interest are the 13th- and 14th-C. stained-glass windows and 15th–16th-C. rose windows and statues.

THE EAGLES OF THE CITADEL

Colline de Pech-Mary, 900 yards (800 m) from the citadel
☎ **04 68 47 88 99.**
Open Easter-All Saint's Day, demonstrations in the afternoon.
Admission charge.
Large birds of prey are flown above your heads in the finest traditions of medieval falconry. Mind your head!

fortress and the architect Viollet-le-Duc restored it. Today, Carcassonne is a city with two faces, the modern lower town, which is the commercial and administrative centre, and the upper town or city, enclosed behind massive ramparts.

City of 52 towers

Two concentric rings of curtain walls, flanked by 26 towers, enclose the old city of Carcassonne. The ramparts cover a total of 2 miles (3 km). The vestiges of the inner wall remain from Roman times, but it was constantly rebuilt over the course of the centuries, though along the same outline. The second wall, separated from the first by the tilt-yards, was constructed in

By train or by carriage

There is a **little train** that tours the ramparts, departing from the Porte Narbonnaise (admission charge). The trip takes 20 min (May–Sept., 10am-7pm). You can also ride in a **carriage** to see the tilt-yards, which will give you an idea of the massiveness of the

...alls. The best time to visit the walls by carriage is at night, when the fortress is beautifully illuminated. From the Rue Cros-Mayrevieille, you can gain access to the château. If you are with the family, you can buy swords for your young knights to attack the castle. The street is full of shops and museums (the School Museum, the Medieval Museum which children will enjoy.

Regional speciality foods

1, Pl. du Château,
☎ 04 68 25 52 76.
Daily, 9.30am-noon and 2-7pm.
Free admission.
Behind an old-fashioned shop

window, the delicacies of the region are displayed for your delectation. They include *cabardises* (honey crunch), *grès de la cité* (almond, vanilla and caramel puff pastry), olives flavoured with herbs and home-made *cassoulet*. Do not forget to visit the lower town which dates back to the 13th C. It is built on a grid pattern and still has two lovely mansions from the time when it was a major cloth-weaving town. It also has an 18th-C. *halle aux grains* (corn exchange), a marble fountain and the Musée des Beaux-Arts which contains memorabilia of the poet André Chénier. There is also a lively **market** held every day of the week except Sunday.

The Arboretum

The arboretum stands on the hilltop of Pech Mary and covers an area of 247 acres (100 ha). This protected site is a favourite haunt of nature-lovers and a lovely place for a **picnic**.

Bicycle rides

Rental: L'Olive bleue,
☎ 04 68 24 03 03.
Ride along the banks of the Aude and towpaths of the Canal du Midi (p. 200), a pleasant trip for keen cyclists.

The Château Comtal

☎ 04 68 25 01 66.
Open daily 9am (or 10am)-12.30pm and 2-5pm (or 6pm or 7.30pm), last admission 30 min. before closing time. *Admission charge. Guided tour.*
Built at the end of the 12th C. by the viscounts of Carcassonne, this château has undergone many changes. It is a fortress within a fortress, backing on to the ramparts and surrounded by moats. Furthermore, it is reinforced by six 13th-C. towers. The interior, which contains medieval rooms, has a **lapidary museum** displaying artefacts from the city and the region from ancient times to the 17th C.

Lac de la Cavayère

1¾ miles (3 km) from Carcassonne.
This lake is a pleasant spot for a swim, as it has **beaches** and **games areas**. You could ramble around it for an hour or so or stroll back to Carcassonne along the GR 36, which is signposted in white and red; this will take approximately two hours. Horses can be hired at the lake from the **Centre équestre:** ☎ 04 68 71 05 03.

Castelnaudary

The quiet little town of Castelnaudary (population 12,000) nestles in a wide valley in the plain of Lauragais, surrounded by grain crops and market gardens. Thanks to its position between Toulouse and Carcassonne, it developed into a market town, and its trading status was enhanced by the opening of the Canal du Midi; it is now a favourite stop for river tourism, largely because of its reputation for good food, especially *cassoulet* (p. 38).

Collegiate Church of Saint-Michel

Whether you enter the town from the east or the west, the handsome building of the Collegiate Church of Saint-Michel, its 18th-C. belltower-porch topped with a little spire, which straddles the Rue de la Chanoinie, will be one of the first things you notice. The church was rebuilt after the Black Prince set fire to the town in 1355. It was abandoned after the Wars of Religion and restored in the 18th and 19th C. It is surprisingly large inside. Its regular shape is a good example of southern French Gothic. Note the 16th-C. cross in the fourth chapel on the right.

It has an 18th-C. **organ** which is played every Sunday.

The Old Town

Around the church there is a network of narrow streets, such as the rues Gauzy, Ménard, Latapie and Bataille lined with corbelled houses

RUE DU COLLEGE

and 18th-C. mansions, evidence of the past prosperity of the town. The Rue du Collège leads to the **Présidial** (☎ 04 68 23 05 73). The **old château** was besieged twice, first in 1212 by Simon de Montfort (p. 76) and again in in 1220 by Raymond VI, Count of Toulouse. It was torched in 1355 by the Black Prince, and was rebuilt the next year. In 1553, Catherine de Medici, Countess of Lauragais, made the county into a separate administrative area (*sénéchaussée*). The château became a court of law (*présidial*) and a prison. In summer, its courtyards and Renaissance façade are a lovely setting for concerts.

Le Grand Bassin

The Grand Bassin, on the other side of the Pont Saint-Roch is a 17-acre (7-ha) artificial lake and a pleasant place for a walk. The lake is formed by the Canal du Midi and feeds the locks of Saint-Roch. It is used as a yachting harbour and is very busy in summer (ramble from Port-Lauragais, ☎ 04 68 60 15 98). Follow the canal to the Place aux Herbes which is very attractive on Monday, market day, with its plane trees and fountains. A food fair, the **Foire au Gras** (Fat Fair), is held in December and attracts professional foodies from all over the world.

Cugarel mill

Guided tour daily 16 June–15 Sept. Other days the rest of the year. ☎ 04 68 23 05 73. *Admission charge.*
Before leaving the town, climb the Pech hill to see the Cugarel mill, the last survivor

Spotcheck

A5

Aude

Things to do

Visit the Grand Bassin
Visit the Cugarel mill
Water-sports at Ganguise lake

Tourist office

Castelnaudary:
☎ 04 68 23 05 73

accepts special commissions.
His customers include
Provençal nurseries and
ceramics collectors.

of the 32 mills which once
graced the town. There is a
lovely view over the plain, an
immense multicoloured
patchwork with the
Montagne Noire in the
background.

Ganguise lake
Belflou, 9 miles (15 km)
W of Castelnaudary.
This 670-acre (270-ha)
artificial lake is surrounded by
pine woods and used for all
types of water-sports. The
Ecole Française de Voile
runs sailing courses for
young people, and
there are windsurfing
boards, catamarans
and dinghies

(☎ 04 68 60 35 68. Open
daily all year round, except in
Dec. and Jan.). If you like the
area, you can stay here in one
of several camp sites nearby.

Summer with glazed terracotta
The town is also known for
its ceramics. If you want to
watch all the stages of
manufacture, from the potter's
wheel to firing and glazing,
visit the **Poterie du Castel**,
1, Rue de la Prairie (on RN
113 towards Carcassonne).
This potter may well have
been inspired by the Anduze
vases (p. 58). He makes
everything by hand and

EAT CASSOULET... THEN BUY IT

(See p. 38). At the
Hôtel de France, *cassoulet* made with preserved goose is sold in
terrines (210 F for four)
or in tins (46 F for
four), 2, Av. Frédéric-
Mistral
(☎ 04 68 23 10 18),
open daily. Other
places to eat it are the
Restaurant du Centre
et du Lauragais, 31,
Cours de la République
(☎ 04 68 23 25 95)
and Au Tirou 9, Av.
Monseigneur-de-l'Angle
(☎ 04 68 94 15 95).
If you want to take
some home for your
friends, another good
place to buy it is the
Maison Rivière where it
is vacuum-packed (45 F
for three people), ZI
d'En-Tourre, Av. Passy
(☎ 04 68 94 01 74).
The Conserverie
Esquines
126, Av. des Corbières,
11700 Douzens
(☎ 04 68 79 19 77) is
another canning factory
that makes *cassoulet*.

Montagne Noire

The Montagne Noire (black mountain) is at the southern end of the Cévennes. The highest point is the Pic de Nore at 4,033 ft (1,210 m). It gets its name from its thick, dark forests and the exposed rocks which have darkened with age. The area has been inhabited since prehistoric times.

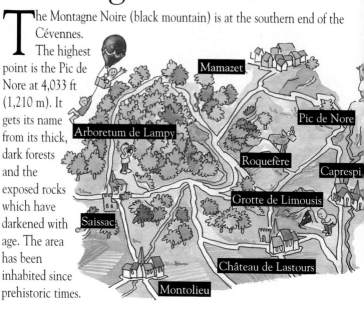

Mamazet

Pic de Nore

Arboretum de Lampy

Roquefère

Caprespi

Grotte de Limousis

Saissac

Château de Lastours

Montolieu

Lastours
A magical sight
☎ 04 68 77 56 02.
Open daily 9am–8pm Jul.–Sept.; 10am–6pm, May–June and Oct. Ask for more information concerning other months.
Admission charge.
The four castles of Lastours, 9 miles (15 km) north of Carcassonne, perched on a rocky outcrop, are evidence of the unstable period of the crusade against the Albigensians. In summer (Thursday and Sunday evenings, from 10pm, admission charge), a *son et lumière* show re-enacts Cathar resistance.

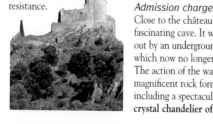

Grotte de Limousis
☎ 04 68 77 50 26.
Open daily 10am–6pm, Jul.–Aug. Out of season, telephone first.
Admission charge.
Close to the châteaux is a fascinating cave. It was carved out by an underground river, which now no longer flows. The action of the water left magnificent rock formations including a spectacular **crystal chandelier** of **aragonite** with a circumference of 33 ft (10 m) formed by the mineral accretions.

Roquefère
La Chèvrerie de la Cascade
Hameau de Saint-Julien
☎ 04 68 26 36 36.
Open daily June–Sept., 10am–7pm and during school holidays; otherwise Wed., Sat. and Sun. 10am–6pm.
This goat farm, in a magical setting amidst forests of sweet chestnut trees, beside one of the highest waterfalls in Europe, will delight young and old alike. You can also taste goat meat and cheeses.

Le pic de Nore

Rambling and pony-trekking

The highest peak of the Montagne Noire provides a **magnificent view** over the surrounding mountains. A 15½-mile (25-km) signposted walk along the GR 710 leads to the Château de Lastours and the Grotte de Limousis. It is also possible to pony-trek through the forests, criss-crossed by rivers and rivulets, the very waters which Riquet wanted to harness to feed the Canal du Midi (Domaine de l'Albejot, ☎ 04 68 24 44 03).

The giant Caprespine cave

☎ 04 68 26 14 22.

Open 1 Jul.–31 August, 10am-5pm ; 1 March– 30 June and 1 Sept.– 30 Nov., 10am-noon and 2pm-5.30 or 6pm. *Admission charge..* This is one of the most extraordinary caves in Europe. The visitor is greeted at the entrance by a huge stalacmite formation almost 434 ft (130 m) in size. The Devil's Balcony, 833 ft (250 m) above the cave floor, shows how vast it is (40-minute guided tour, ambiant temperature 59 °F/15 °C).

Saint-Papoul

The Benedictine abbey

☎ 04 68 94 97 75.
Open daily in Jul.–Aug. 10am-7pm, other opening hours for the rest of the year. Closed in Jan. *Admission charge.*

Things to do

The Castles of Lastours
Grotte de Limousis (cave)
Rambling and pony-trekking
The giant Caprespine cave
The Benedictine Abbey

Within easy reach

Minervois, p. 198.

Tourist office

Carcassonne:
☎ **04 68 10 24 30**

The village of Saint-Papoul owes its origin to the Benedictine abbey founded there in the reign of Charlemagne. The abbey has a lovely cloister and stone bell-tower. The village has wonderful ramparts and narrow streets, half-timbered, corbelled houses and an old market hall.

Saissac

The fantastic world of the forest

The **Lampy Arboretum**, 3 miles (5 km) from Saissac, is 2,333 ft (700 m) above sea level, facing a lake of the same name (one-hour guided tour; open daily from 9.30am-6pm, ☎ 04 68 24 46 07. Admission charge). The owners have covered 5 acres (2 ha) with more than 120 unusual species of tree. Afterwards, visit the **Réserve de Cerfs et Biches de Picarel-le-Haut** (½ mile (1 km) N of Saissac). This 148 acre (60 ha) park contains 250 deer which roam around freely. (One-hour guided tour; open in summer and school holidays 10am-noon and 2-7pm; Sun. from 2pm to dusk, ☎ 04 68 24 44 08. Admission charge.)

Limoux

Situated 16 miles (25 km) from Carcassonne, Limoux is deep in the fertile basin of the river Aude. This position has made it an important trading centre with Spain. Its wool-weaving industry, established in ancient times, has contributed to its prosperity. Limoux is an excellent starting point for an excursion into Cathar country.

More than 1,000 years of history

Limoux appears to have been founded around a Gallo-Roman villa on the estate of a certain Flassian. The town later fell into the hands of the counts of Carcassonne. During the crusade against the Albigensians, it surrendered to Simon de Montfort. It prospered in the 13th C. by exporting woollen cloth to Italy and the Levant. Fulling-mills, leather-dressing workshops and tanneries lined the banks of the Aude. The leather and clothing industry still survive, and the town is known for its shoes.

House with arcades, known as couverts, in Limoux

Walking under cover

You enter the town via the Porte de la Goutine and along the Rue du Marché, beside the old Augustinian convent, which was partially destroyed by fire in 1685. This brings you to the Place de la République, three sides of which are occupied by *couverts*. These **arcades** were originally made of wood and

are a stage for all types of carnival performances. Every Sunday, between January and March (p. 113), various masked carnival performers leave from here and wander through the town. (Information ☎ 04 68 31 11 82). The **Church of Saint-Martin** (11th–15th C.) nearby has an elegant spire.

Ville and *Petite Ville*

The lazy Aude divides the town into two parts, which were once surrounded by walls. The *ville* (town) is on the left bank while the *petite ville* (little town) is just across the bridge. **The old quarter** of the town is a mesh of narrow lanes, lined with tall houses with wide staircases and arcaded inner courtyards. Of particular interest are 12 Rue Toulzane, the Hôtel de Brignac; and 63, 59 and 13 Rue Blanquerie.

Church spire of Saint-Martin

Spotcheck
B5

Things to do
Stroll through the Ville and Petite Ville
Visit the Catharama
Musée des Dinosaures

Tourist office
Limoux: ☎ 04 68 31 11 82

Catharama
Mémoire de l'Aude, 47, Avenue Fabre-d'Églantine, ☎ 04 68 31 48 42. Open daily, Easter to 1 Jul., 10.30am-noon and 2-6pm: summer, 10.30am-7pm.
Admission charge.
What is Catharism (see p. 76)? Why was there an inquisition? What happened to the Cathar treasure? For answers to these questions and to experience this saga of religious faith, intrigue, war and mystery, visit Catharama, a show covering three screens which depicts the historic sites of the region.

For the gourmet
The soft nougat which is a speciality of the town (p. 40) can be sampled and purchased at **Labadie**, 37, Avenue Fabre-d'Églantine, ☎ 04 68 31 08 75. Open Mon. to Fri., 9am-noon, and 3-7pm or at **Chez Bor**, 23 *bis* Avenue Fabre-d'Églantine (☎ 04 68 31 02 15).

Espéraza

Musée des Dinosaures
Avenue de la Gare, 9 miles (15 km) S of Limoux via the D 118 ☎ 04 68 74 02 08. Open 10am-7pm daily in summer: 10am-noon and 2-6pm, Sept.–Jun.
Admission charge.
Lifesize skeletons, a video about the local excavations and a display shows you the types of dinosaur that inhabited the Aude valley 70 million years ago.

Chalabre

A picturesque bastide
About 7 miles (12 km) SW of Limoux
Chalabre is a picturesque village containing many corbelled houses from which there is a **lovely view** of the valley. You can swim and fish and enjoy many water-sports on the nearby **Montbel lake** (☎ 04 68 69 27 27).

LA BLANQUETTE DE LIMOUX WINE

Visit to the Coopérative Aimery Sieur d'Arques, Avenue du Mauzac, E of Limoux, ☎ 04 68 74 63 00.
Open daily 9-11am and 2-6pm.
Film on wine-making and free tasting.
The wines of Limoux have been famous since ancient times. In the Middle Ages, the wine-makers of Limousin, with its sunny, limestone slopes, defended the originality of their white wines. Three varieties of white grape are used to make Blanquette, the oldest sparkling wine in the world. They are Mauzac, Chardonnay and Chenin. The 'brut' version of Blanquette can be drunk with any kind of meal, but the 'demi-sec' version is particularly suitable for accompanying desserts and sweet foods.

Les Corbières

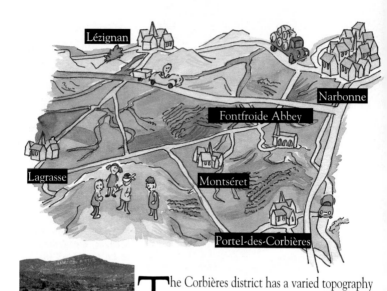

Portel-des-Corbières

The Corbières district has a varied topography of peaks and plateaux, gorges, valleys and mountain passes. It is an area of wild beauty which has been occupied successively by the Ligurians, Iberians and Romans who came to exploit its mineral wealth – (iron, copper, gold and silver), which were still being extracted in the 10th C. Corbières has retained much of its medieval heritage, in the form of impressive abbeys and fortresses in which the Cathars took refuge (p. 76).

The Corbières vineyard

The wines of Corbières have an AOC covering an area of 56,800 acres (23,000 ha). The reds have a superb body, a fruity, spicy nose and hints of cherry, raspberry and vanilla. They can be kept for about five years. The whites and rosés are pleasant. A few of the best names are Châteaux Aiguilloux, la Baronne Hélène, Lastours, Quéribus, Vauglas, Domaine de Villemajou and Domaine de la Voulte Gasparets.

Terra Vinea and Rocbère cellars

Ch. des Plâtrières, Portel-des-Corbières, ☎ 04 68 48 64 90. Open daily; 1 June– 30 Sept. 9.30am-6pm; Oct.–May 10am-noon and 2-4pm or 5pm. *Admission charge.* Terra Vinea is 266 ft (80 m) underground; a unique place. First take the **botanical path**, then go down into a cathedral-like vault of gypsum in which the wine casks form a guard of honour for the visitor. This is where Rocbère is aged. You are then told the history of the wine and shown the Gallo-Roman amphoras, goblets and the hot baths. Suddenly, an **underground lake** comes into view. You leave through an exit with a **panoramic view** over the *garrigue*, after tasting the

LAGRASSE BOTANICAL TRAIL

Information and booking at the Tourist Office.
Open Jul. and Aug.
Admission charge.
There is a tour led by an expert guide. In about three hours you will learn all about the flora and fauna of the Corbières. The walk takes you through groves of Aleppo pines and the *garrigues*, with their subtle perfumes of rosemary, lavender, juniper, pistachio, aphyllanthus and orchids.

best wines. To complete the visit, Lézignan has a **Musée de la Vigne et du Vin** (☎ 04 68 27 37 02. Open 9am-7pm. Admission charge).

Fontfroide
The Abbey and its rose-garden
☎ 04 68 45 11 08.
Open daily, 10 Jul.–31 Aug, 9.30am-6.30pm.
Guided tour every 30 min. (charge).
The Cistercian Abbey of Fontfroide nestles in the hills of Corbières surrounded by

cypress and arbutus. It was built in the 12th C. and embellished in the 17th–18th C., and is ideal for serene contemplation. Its high sandstone walls hide an elegant Romanesque church, a pink marble colonnaded cloister, a

dormitory designed to hold 100 to 200 postulants and thousands of roses.

Miellerie des Clauses Montseret
☎ 04 68 43 30 17.
Open daily.
Near Fontfroide Abbey, there is a bee-keeping cooperative which offers guided tours. The owners of these 900 or so hives have an infectious enthusiasm. You can leave with spice-bread flavoured with aniseed, honey flavoured with lemon and hazelnuts and pollen to see you through the winter.

Spotcheck
C5-C6

Aude

Things to do
Rocbère cellars
Visit a miellerie (honey farm)
Lagrasse Abbey

Within easy reach
Narbonne, p. 180,
Sigean, p. 188,
Le Minervois, p. 198.

Tourist office
Lagrasse: ☎ 04 68 43 11 56

Lagrasse
Lagrasse Abbey
☎ 04 68 58 11 58.
Open May–Sept., 10.30am-12.30pm and 2-6pm; Oct–1 Nov. and Easter–May, 2-5pm; closed from 1 Nov. to Easter.

Admission charge.
The wild and lonely landscape of the Corbières attracted monks. The village of Lagrasse stands in a semicircle of hills, the 133 ft (40 m) bell-tower of the Benedictine abbey dominating the houses, a reminder of the spiritual and temporal power exerted by this institution. The present monastery was heavily rebuilt in the 18th C. but still contains an 11th-C. chapel and the vestiges of the 14th-C. abbey. A little 12th-C. humpbacked bridge straddles the river Orbieu and links the abbey to the village, with its quaint half-timbered houses and market halls (1315) which are still used.

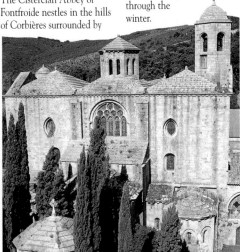

Fontfroide Abbey

The Cathar châteaux

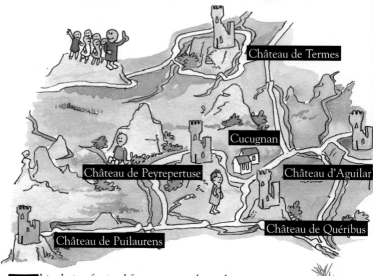

Château de Termes

Cucugnan

Château de Peyrepertuse

Château d'Aguilar

Château de Puilaurens

Château de Quéribus

This chain of ruined fortresses stands on the top of limestone outcrops and can barely be distinguished from the rocks to which they are anchored. They brave the high winds in the southern Corbières. These heroic strongholds overlook dizzying sheer drops amid the grandiose setting of the rosemary-scented *garrigues* and sun-drenched vines. You are invited to follow in the footsteps of the 'perfect ones'.

The five sons of Carcassonne

The area is at the crossroads of the major routes to Spain and Aquitaine. After the fall of the Roman Empire, this border area was occupied successively by the Visigoths, Saracens and

The Château de Quéribus

the Franks. The heights of the Corbières were thus soon covered with impregnable fortresses. Aguilar, Termes, Quéribus, Puilaurens and Peyrepertuse were outposts to protect the city of Carcassonne, hence their name 'the five sons'. For five centuries they housed royal garrisons, responsible for defending the new frontier with the Kingdom of Aragon. They became refuges for the Cathars resisting Simon de Montfort's crusade in 1209

(p. 76), and were destroyed and rebuilt several times. Their ruins still dominate the landscape.

Cucugnan, and its notorious curate

The Occitan legend of the curate who hurried through Midnight Mass to get home to his dinner, was adapted by Alphonse Daudet and it is quite surprising to discover that there really is such a place. Today, it is a tiny hamlet, set amid vineyards, whose ancient streets are lined with little shops and craft workshops. It no longer has a curate, but its church contains a pregnant Virgin! At the **Théâtre Achille-Mir**

(admission charge and times combined with the Château de Quéribus), you can listen to the sad story of the Abbot Marti who went to Paradise to find his parishioners but did not meet any of them. So he went down to hell where he discovered a 'spit on which all the villagers of Cucugnan were turning and roasting'!

EXCURSIONS ON FOOT OR ON HORSEBACK

The Terres d'Aventure agency organises week-long excursions into Cathar country (7 days 3,400 F/pers.). It follows in the footsteps of the 'Bonhommes', on foot or horseback, exploring the range of landscapes. There is also the chance to sample the local foods and wines. Like the 'perfect ones', the Cathars, you will criss-cross this magnificent landscape, searching for the eagles' nests, these hidden treasures of the history of the land of Occitan. Information available from the Terres d'Aventure, 6, Rue Saint-Victor 75005 Paris, ☎ 01 53 73 77 77.

Château de Quéribus

☎ 04 68 45 03 69.
Open daily in summer, 9am-8pm: Apr. and Oct. 10am-6pm: May, Jun. and Sept. 10am-7pm: in winter, weekends and school holidays 10am-5pm. Climb takes 10 min. *Admission charge coupled with the Achille-Mir theatre.*

The château was built between 11th and 15th C. on a forbidding spur of rock and was the last bastion of Cathar resistance; it fell in 1255. It subsequently became a royal fortress of the Marches of Spain until Roussillon once more became part of France in 1659. The polygonal keep,

The Château de Puilaurens

an excellent example of **military architecture**, is famous for its Gothic-style chamber whose ceiling rests on a circular pillar which spreads out like a palm tree. On a clear day, you will be able to see the Pyrenees and the sea.

Château de Peyrepertuse

☎ 04 68 45 03 26.
Open daily. Jul.–Aug 9.30am-8pm: Sept.– 11 Nov. 10am-7pm, 12 Nov.–Jun. 10am-6pm, closed Jan.

Spotcheck
B6-C6

Aude

Things to do

Cathar country and its castles

Within easy reach

Tautavel and the Fenouillèdes, p. 198.

Tourist office

Château de Quéribus:
☎ 04 68 45 03 69
Château de Peyrepertuse:
☎ 04 68 45 03 26

Admission charge.
After a stiff 20-minute climb up steep paths you reach the Château de Corbières. When it defended the frontiers, it was garrisoned by nine sergeants-at-arms, a watchman, a chaplain, a porter and a pack of hounds. It is the largest of the Cathar castles but it is believed to have been spared during the crusade against the Albigensians. From the top of the San Jordy rock, there is an **exceptional panoramic view** of the surrounding area.

Narbonne and district

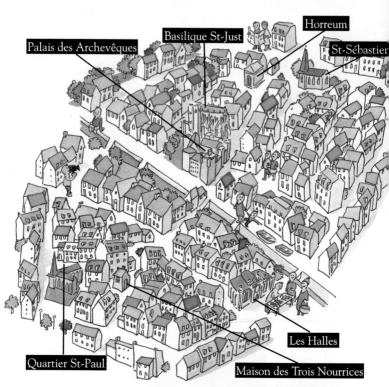

Palais des Archevêques
Basilique St-Just
Horreum
St-Sébastier
Quartier St-Paul
Les Halles
Maison des Trois Nourrices

Narbonne has a population larger than Carcassonne's, although the latter is the region's administrative centre, and also tends to be more prosperous. It is pleasant to wander around the town, with its historic remains, in the shade of the plane trees, through its narrow winding streets with their pink shadows and along the romantic banks of the Canal de la Robine. The French singer-composer Charles Trenet was a native of Narbonne

A long and eventful history

Narbonne was founded on the **Colline de Montlaurès** (2½ miles/4 km N of the town), which has been inhabited since the 7th C. BC. By the 2nd C. BC, the Roman city of Narbo had become one of the most important in southern Gaul. The Visigoths made it their capital when they invaded in the 6th C. AD. The decline began in the late 14th C., when the port silted up and the Hundred Years War and the Black Death took their toll. In the

Domaine de l'Hospitalet vineyard (p. 184)

Spotcheck
C5

Aude

Things to do

The Archbishops' Palace
Trip on the Canal de la Robine
Basilica of Saint-Just-et-Saint-Pasteur
The old district of Saint-Paul

With children

Espace Liberté
Aquajet, Narbonne-Plage

Within easy reach

*Les Corbières, p. 176,
Béziers, 23km NE, p192
Canal du Midi, p. 200*

Tourist office

Narbonne: ☎ 04 68 65 15 60

mid-19th C., the building of the railway and the expansion of the vineyards restored its vitality. Narbonne is now the largest city in the *département* with 47,000 inhabitants.

The city centre

The Place de l'Hôtel-de-Ville is the lively city centre. From here the recently discovered Via Domitia, a Roman road, leads to the **Archbishops' Palace** and the **Basilica of Saint-Just**. Note that there is one admission ticket which takes you to all the town's attractions, all of which have the same opening hours (open from 2 May–30 Sept., daily from 9.30am-12.15pm and from 2-6pm; from 1 Oct.–30 Apr., daily except Mon. from 10am-noon and from 2-5pm). The Tourist Office is in the Place Salengro. From 17 June–13 Sept., there are paid guided tours with licensed guides that start daily from the entrance of the town hall (10.30am-12.30pm, and 2.30-4.30pm, ☎ 04 68 90 30 66). From mid-June there is a **music festival and fairs** (information at the Tourist Office).

The Archbishops' Palace

The centuries have left their mark on these religious, military and civil buildings. The building is divided into the **Old Palace** (12th-C.) surrounding the Donjon de la Madeleine, a keep, and the Gothic **New Palace**, consisting of the 13th-C. Donjon de Gilles Aycelin and the Tour Saint-Martial. If you are brave enough to climb to the top of the **Donjon Aycelin** (162 steps) you will have a magnificent view over the Roman-tiled houses and out to the distant Pyrenees. The **Musée d'Art et d'Histoire** occupies the upper floors of the New Palace, in the former private apartments of the archbishops. If you want to get an idea of daily life in Narbonne in Roman times, take a look at the **Archaeological Museum** in the New Palace. Enter on tiptoe because a drunken Silenus is shamelessly chatting up cupid grape-harvesters.

Roman art in the Archaeological Museum

Now take the passage which runs between the Tour de la Madeleine and the Tour Saint-Martial. There is an old entrance marked by an ancient ship's anchor, the symbol of the feudal rights and privileges enjoyed by the archbishop over coastal navigation. This **Passage de l'Ancre** was once a fish market. It leads to the medieval Basilica of Saint-Just-et-Saint-Pasteur.

The Basilica of Saint-Just-et-Saint-Pasteur

The basilica was built between 1272 and 1354, and is the only **Gothic cathedral** in the Mediterranean that can rival those in the north. The outside wall of the choir has flying buttresses of wonderful delicacy 137 ft (41 m) high. The cathedral is part of a defensive system but remains unfinished and has

no nave. The choir contains magnificent canopy created by Jules Hardouin-Mansart in the 17th C. and a large number of 18th-C. choirstalls showing how important the chapter was prior to the French Revolution. The treasury has extraordinary accoustics and contains a 15th-C. tapestry depicting the Creation, illuminated manuscripts and reliquaries with ancient intaglios.

Before leaving, visit the 14th-C. cloister and walk through the Archbishop's Garden, a haven of peace where there is an excellent view of the complex. Upon leaving the cathedral, your eye will be drawn to a shop sign advertising **La maison de Lucille** (22, Rue Droite, ☎ 04 68 65 25 08). The shop sells Anduze pottery, Provençal cottons, fragrances and dried flowers. Take away a little packet of sunshine!

The suburbs

To escape from the stifling heat in the city, take the waterbus or the Tramontane at the foot of the Pont des Marchands

The Basilica of Saint-Just and the Archbishops' palace

and explore the **Canal de la Robine** which runs from Port-la-Nouvelle through the ponds and beside the Île Sainte-Lucie (Call M. Pajot for further information, ☎ 04 68 49 12 40). **Les Halles** is a lively market beside the canal which is busy every morning from 7am–1pm; the market-hall is 100 years old, an elegant wrought iron and glass structure that is a festival of colours, tastes and smells. Narbonne market is famous throughout Languedoc. The stalls offer a plethora of brightly coloured fruit and vegetables, fresh fish, cheese and local wines. Browse happily here and savour the atmosphere.

The old district of Saint-Paul

Then lose yourself in the streets of the old district of Saint-Paul, with its little

THE HORREUM

The Horreum is in the Rue Rouget-de-Lisle, and is the town's only Roman building. It consists of underground galleries which were used for storing goods and was situated beneath a market. A few sculptures and bas-reliefs are evocative of ancient civilisations. There is a strange atmosphere in these labyrinthine stone corridors and cellars. The strange name is based on the Latin word for 'loft'.

squares that are cooled by fountains. The Basilica of Saint-Paul-et-Saint-Serge is built over the tomb of the first missionary bishop and dates from the 3rd C. The basilica is large and elegantly furnished with Aubusson tapestries, altarpieces, a large organ and elaborate tombs. A stone frog sits on the edge of the font and inspired an amusing legend. He is supposed to have started croaking heretically during a mass, and as a punishment he was immediately turned to stone!

Patisserie Combot

30, Rue de l'Ancien-Courrier, ☎ 04 68 65 00 89. Open Mon.–Sun. morning, 8am-1pm and 2.30-7.30pm. *Galets de la Clape* (chocolate-covered almonds), *bouchons du Languedoc* (almond, honey

Beside the Canal de la Robine

and pine-nut rusks), and *olives de l'Aude* (chocolate and almonds) are just some of the delicious local *patisserie* and confectionery sold by this fine baker.

Open air leisure

If you are looking for outdoor sports, the **Espace Liberté** (RN 9, Rte de Perpignan, ☎ 04 68 42 17 89) has an outdoor Olympic swimming-pool, water-games, including a 283 ft (85 m) flume, a skating rink and a bowling alley. There are also cafés and restaurants, all enclosed beneath a glass pyramid.

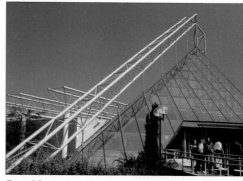
Espace Liberté

Around Narbonne

Domaine de l'Hospitalet

Leave the motorway at Narbonne-Est and make for Narbonne-Plage. ☎ 04 68 45 34 47. **Open March–Dec. daily 9am-noon and 2-6pm, weekends 2-7pm.** The Domaine de l'Hospitalet is a vineyard which is a real discovery. It lies in the heart of the La Clape range, in the *garrigue* (scrubland) planted with olive trees and truffle-oaks. Not only is it a vineyard and cellar but the visitor is offered plenty of other attractions including 16 museum exhibitions and two restaurants. The Musée de l'Automobile contains the Rolls Royce of an Indian maharajah and the Bentley of an emperor; there is also a Musée du Téléphone and a Musée des Fossiles. A gastronomic restaurant is attached to the Domaine. Specialities include red mullet in olive oil and wild strawberries.

Narbonne-Plage

6¼ miles (10 km) from Narbonne. This little resort developed at the foot of the Montagne de la Clape, on a strip of sand only 1,666 ft (500 m) wide.

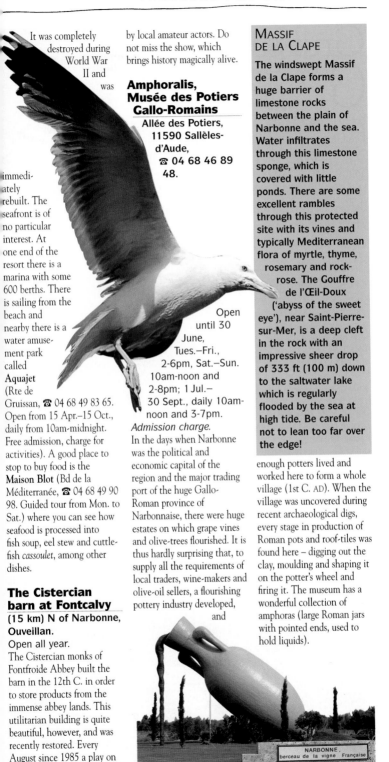

It was completely destroyed during World War II and was immediately rebuilt. The seafront is of no particular interest. At one end of the resort there is a marina with some 600 berths. There is sailing from the beach and nearby there is a water amusement park called **Aquajet** (Rte de Gruissan, ☎ 04 68 49 83 65. Open from 15 Apr.–15 Oct., daily from 10am-midnight. Free admission, charge for activities). A good place to stop to buy food is the **Maison Blot** (Bd de la Méditerranée, ☎ 04 68 49 90 98. Guided tour from Mon. to Sat.) where you can see how seafood is processed into fish soup, eel stew and cuttle-fish *cassoulet*, among other dishes.

The Cistercian barn at Fontcalvy

(15 km) N of Narbonne, Ouveillan.
Open all year.
The Cistercian monks of Fontfroide Abbey built the barn in the 12th C. in order to store products from the immense abbey lands. This utilitarian building is quite beautiful, however, and was recently restored. Every August since 1985 a play on a historic theme is performed by local amateur actors. Do not miss the show, which brings history magically alive.

Amphoralis, Musée des Potiers Gallo-Romains

Allée des Potiers, 11590 Sallèles-d'Aude, ☎ 04 68 46 89 48.

Open until 30 June, Tues.–Fri., 2-6pm, Sat.–Sun. 10am-noon and 2-8pm; 1 Jul.–30 Sept., daily 10am-noon and 3-7pm.
Admission charge.

In the days when Narbonne was the political and economic capital of the region and the major trading port of the huge Gallo-Roman province of Narbonnaise, there were huge estates on which grape vines and olive-trees flourished. It is thus hardly surprising that, to supply all the requirements of local traders, wine-makers and olive-oil sellers, a flourishing pottery industry developed, and enough potters lived and worked here to form a whole village (1st C. AD). When the village was uncovered during recent archaeological digs, every stage in production of Roman pots and roof-tiles was found here – digging out the clay, moulding and shaping it on the potter's wheel and firing it. The museum has a wonderful collection of amphoras (large Roman jars with pointed ends, used to hold liquids).

MASSIF DE LA CLAPE

The windswept Massif de la Clape forms a huge barrier of limestone rocks between the plain of Narbonne and the sea. Water infiltrates through this limestone sponge, which is covered with little ponds. There are some excellent rambles through this protected site with its vines and typically Mediterranean flora of myrtle, thyme, rosemary and rock-rose. The Gouffre de l'Œil-Doux ('abyss of the sweet eye'), near Saint-Pierre-sur-Mer, is a deep cleft in the rock with an impressive sheer drop of 333 ft (100 m) down to the saltwater lake which is regularly flooded by the sea at high tide. Be careful not to lean too far over the edge!

NARBONNE, berceau de la vigne Française

Gruissan

ruissan is a village, port and beach all rolled into one. It emerges like an island from the Étang de Bages, in a privileged position between sea, lake and mountain. The Festival of St. Peter, patron saint of seafarers, is celebrated here on 29 June each year (see p. 114, information at the Tourist Office). The port was built only recently, but it is lively with a friendly atmosphere. Along the beach are some of the strange chalets on piles which were used for location shots for the French film *37.2° le matin* (known as *Betty Blue* to English speakers). You can choose to sunbathe, or windsurf on the sea or the lake.

Gruissan-Village

This village is laid out like a spider's web. Its fishermen's and vine-growers' cottages wind in a spiral around the Tour Barberousse, the vestige of a 12th-C. château, dating from a time when there was brisk trade with Spain.

37.2° le matin

Even in high summer it doesn't actually get as hot as this (99°F). The chalets on Gruissan beach were simply used as the rather surrealist set for the film. They are simply beach huts, built in the late 19th C. for the use of holidaymakers from Narbonne. They are aligned to be protected from the wind. Unfortunately, some are rather dilapidated.

Port-Gruissan

This marina was built in the 1970s with the aim of 'enhancing the coast of Languedoc-Roussillon'. It is not one of the best examples of its kind, but in July and

August it is very busy, as are the restaurants and cafés. A thousand boats can berth in the various basins.

❀ **The home of funboarding**

Gruissan Windsurf,
Pascal Maka,
☎ 04 68 49 88 31.
Open all year round.

Here you can learn to wind-surf in the pond or improve your existing skills. The club was only built recently and offers every possible convenience. The more experienced can practise their skills in the sea, sail catamarans and, of course, go funboarding. Gruissan is actually the home of funboarding – on the beach called the Plage de la Vieille Nouvelle, which is swept by the wind of the Tramontane, the north wind, the first stage of the **French Funboard Championships** are held.

Sea fishing

If you have a desire to catch your own dinner yourself, then visit the Gruissan Thon-Club, Basin no. 1, Quai du Levant (☎ 04 68 49 14 41), or the Merry Fisher-Club (Résidence Amphitrite, Bd. de la Corderie ☎ 04 68 49 28 25).

Chapel of Notre-Dame-des-Auzils

2 ½ miles (4 km) from Gruissan,
Open 15 Jun.–15 Sept. daily 3-6pm: in spring and autumn, open Sun.
The Chemin de la Bonne-Mère, an avenue of pine trees edged with memorials to the sailors of Gruissan who were

lost at sea, leads to the Chapel. There are many votive offerings attached to the walls (paintings, models of ships and watercolours).
    There is also a nice view.

Campignol pond

Maison Saint-Louis, Route de Tournebelle, ☎ 04 68 49 12 12.
    The Ligue pour la Protection des Oiseaux, the French ornithological protection organisation, has a

branch here. This pond is close to the Camargue, and is one of the most popular with migrating birds. A little exhibition explains their movements throughout the year. Depending on the season, you can watch snipe, redshank, reed-buntings, bitterns, black kites, windhovers and white storks in action.

Spotcheck

C5

Aude

Things to do

Stroll through Gruissan-Village
Funboarding, windsurfing
Sea fishing

Tourist office

Gruissan: ☎ 04 68 49 03 25

SEAFOOD

**La Perle Gruissanaise,
Robert Rozek,
6–7, Avenue
de la Clape,
☎ 04 68 49 23 24.
This is an excellent
place to eat fresh
oysters and deep-sea
mussels. At the
Fumeries Occitanes,
Zone Artisanale des
Chalets (☎ 04 68 49
05 00), various local
fish, mainly tuna,
salmon, eels and
swordfish, are salted,
dried and then smoked
over beech-wood.**

The Chapel of Notre-Dame-des-Auzils

Sigean

The kingdom of pink flamingoes, egrets and seagulls, the Bages and Sigean lake cover an area of 13,600 acres (5,500 ha). This remarkable natural expanse of

water is trapped between dunes and marshes, the sea and the plain. It is held in place by an uneven and tenuous shoreline and has been changing its shape for centuries, depending on the winds, the streams that feed it and the tides. In this extraordinary and unique environment, the calls of cormorants, coots and terns mix with those of the crested cranes, lions and gnus of Sigean. Bring binoculars and explore this protected site at leisure.

A unique lagoon environment

The huge Bages and Sigean lake was once a lagoon that was wide open to the sea. In Roman times, merchant vessels would moor in the trading port of Narbonne. A sand-bar, the lido, gradually enclosed the lagoon over the centuries, thus denying the town an outlet to the sea and closing its port. This did not stop the little villages of Sigean, Peyriac-de-Mer and Bages from developing on the shores of the lake, thriving on fishing and exploiting the salt-pans. Local industry is now concentrated more on tourism and the vineyards which cover the lower foothills of the Corbières.

Sigean
A fortified village

Sigean is about 1½ miles (2.5 km) from the lake It looks like a little Italian town with its narrow lanes and central drains. The Église des Pénitents has a lovely belfry and there is the Musée des Corbières in the Place de la Libération. (Open 10am–noon and 2–6pm Jun.–Sept., admission charge, ☎ 04 68 48 14 81). The museum is housed in a 17th-C. stately home and it contains a wide range of archaeological finds as well as exhibits about trade in the Middle

A narrow lane in Sigean

Ages. There are also displays about everyday contemporary life, harvesting salt and fishing. Take a few moments to see the exhibit about the birds of Corbières which live in the *garrigues* and lagoons.

WAPITIS, WISTITIS AND THE LIKE

The Sigean African Reserve,
☎ **04 68 48 20 20.**
Open daily fron 9am.
Admission charge.
The reserve lies close to the coast, in an area of lakes and scrubland covering 645 acres (261 ha). It contains more than 3,100 animals from the five continents. The visit includes a 3-mile (5-km) car journey through an area frequented by lions, bears, white rhinoceros, eland and ostriches. The walking tour lasts at least 2 hours, during which you can spend time with nandus, wallabies, macaws, ibises and pelicans. More than 2 tonnes of food are distributed to the animals daily.
Don't miss feeding time for the cheetahs and lynxes at about 5pm. A word of advice: get here early in the morning before the reserve gets full.

Spotcheck
C5

Aude

Things to do

Musée de Corbières in Sigean
Visit the Port-la-Nouvelle
Trip to the Île Sainte-Lucie

With children

The Sigean African Reserve

Within easy reach

*Les Corbières, p. 176,
Salses, 25km S, p. 136.*

Tourist office

Sigean: ☎ **04 68 48 14 81**

They include herons, long-legged plovers, common scoters and shelduck.

Port-la-Nouvelle

An important trading port

Since Roman times, ships heading for the port of Narbonne had to pass through here. Gradually, thanks to its important straits which linked the lake to the sea through the sand-bar, Port-la-Nouvelle took over from Narbonne, which had been completely silted up by 1787. The Canal de la Robine linked the Mediterranean directly with the Canal du Midi. The fishermen's village thus became an important trading port. During World War II, Port-la-Nouvelle was completely destroyed, but was later rebuilt. A cemetery, grain silos and an oil terminal were added. Today, Port-la-Nouvelle is the third-largest commercial port in France on the Mediterreanean coast. Of course, it is still a fishing village, and from Monday to Friday at 4pm when the boats come back, there is a fish auction and sale on the quay-side, at the far end of the sea wall. If you want to take trips out to sea or fancy an excursion to the Île Sainte-Lucie, which is owned by the Conservatoire du Littoral, or would like to see the skeleton of a beached whale which arrived in 1989, you can get information from the Tourist Office, Place Paul-Valéry, ☎ 04 68 48 00 51.

Leucate to Barcarès

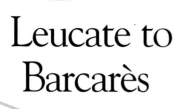

I n the early 1960s, the French government offered developers the 1,850-acre (750-ha) lido separating the Salses-Leucate lake from the sea. Barcarès, Port-Barcarès and Port-Leucate thus sprang out of nowhere in the space of a few years. The architect Georges Candilis coordinated the project. The coastal plain between the Pyrénées-Orientales and the Aude is a paradise for holidaymakers, offering a huge range of sporting and leisure activities. Yachts have gradually replaced the berths for fishing-boats and numerous improvements have enabled summer visitors to taste the pleasures of the sea. You can choose between scuba-diving, water-skiing, minigolf, seawater therapy or casinos…

Leucate and Port-Leucate

The old village

The old village lies 1¼ miles (2 km) from the beach and is dominated by the ruins of the fortified castle built in 1036, which stands on a promontory from which there is a **magnificent view** of Les Corbières, the Salses lake, Mont Canigou and the roofs of the village. Leucate is said to have been founded by the Phoenicians, who reputedly named it after the white cliffs of its coast (*leukas* means 'white' in Greek). **Cap Leucate** is where hikers meet mountain-bikers. It is a landmark for seamen and a stop for migrating birds. There is a signposted walk for all abilities lasting 1¼ hours along the clifftop at Leucate (information from the Tourist Office, Avenue Jean-Jaurès). Leucate is about 7½ miles (12 km) from Port-Leucate. Between the two, three naturist villages, Ulysse, Aphrodite and Oasis, are popular resorts for those for whom freedom also means release from having to wear clothes.

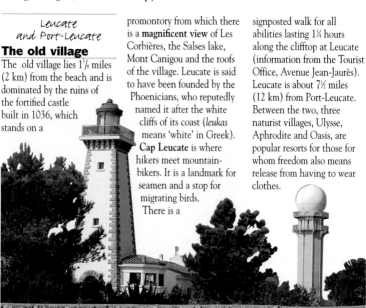

The Cap Leucate lighthouse

DISCO-CASINO ON BOARD A STEAMER

Open daily in summer, Fri. and Sat. out of season.
☎ 04 68 86 07 35.
The *Lydia* is the top attraction in Port-Barcarès. It is a 300-ft (90-m) long steamer built in the shipyards of Copenhagen in 1931 and bought in 1966 by the *département* of Pyrénées-Orientales. It has become the symbol of the resort. Dutch experts dug a 2,000-ft (600-m) channel which made it possible for a tug to tow the steamer into the port in June 1967. The channel was then closed, imprisoning the *Lydia* forever behind sand banks. It has been converted into a casino and discotheque and is the haunt of night-hawks and revellers. In summer a Miss Lydia is elected every fortnight.

The resort

Port-Leucate is divided into little villages of pedestrianised streets edged with tamarisks and oleanders. The 1,000-berth yacht harbour in the heart of the resort is lively at any time of the day or night. The resort is very much oriented towards **yachting and sailing**. A fine sandy beach stretches as far as the eye can see. **Aquatic Parc** (☎ 04 68 40 29 98; open Jul.–Aug., 10am-7pm. Admission charge) has a slide and corkscrew flume, so there is much splashing and

shouting. In July and August, a little train will take you to the **Luna Park** (Avenue du Roussillon, open 8pm-midnight), where there is a ferris wheel and a big dipper, so fasten your seatbelts!

Barcarès and Port-Barcarès

Lakeside town

The little port of Barcarès once served felluccas and other Mediterranean sailing ships which carried Rivesaltes wine and Salanque pottery to Sète or Marseille. Port-Barcarès has a fine sandy **beach** 5 miles (8 km) long, from which the reddish hills of the Corbières and Canigou can be seen in the distance. It lies between the sea and the Salses-Leucate pond; in summer the lakeside town swells to 70,000 residents. **Port-Saint-Ange**, linked to

Spotcheck
C6

Aude et Pyrénées-Orientales

Things to do

Water sports
Rambling to Cap Leucate
Disco-casino on a steamer

Things to do with children

Aquatic Parc; Luna Park

Within easy reach

Perpignan, 25km SW, p. 132,
Salses, 20km SW, p. 136,
Canet-Plage, 15km S, p. 140.

Tourist office

Leucate: ☎ 04 68 40 04 73

the pond by a channel, is a harbour for yachts and fishing boats (fish auction between 7-8am). The resort offers water-skiing (☎ 04 68 86 23 45).

The Leucate pond

Béziers

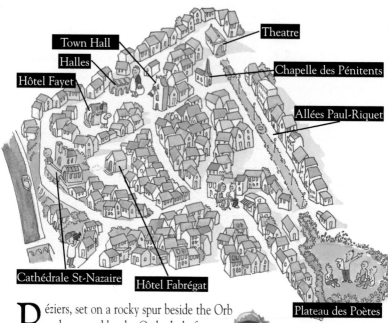

Town Hall
Halles
Hôtel Fayet
Theatre
Chapelle des Pénitents
Allées Paul-Riquet
Cathédrale St-Nazaire
Hôtel Fabrégat
Plateau des Poètes

Béziers, set on a rocky spur beside the Orb and crowned by the Cathedral of Saint-Nazaire, overlooks the great plain of the Hérault . Thanks to its unusual strategic location, it flourished and soon established a reputation for wine production. The city has known wealth and ruin in turn, but has always managed to recover from misfortune. The lavish food and traditional festivals of Saint-Aphrodise (end of April) and the Féria (around 15 August) give it a Spanish flavour. Not forgetting its devotion to the oval ball (p. 108) which excites the city on certain evenings, and its guardianship of huge vineyards and châteaux, tangible signs of the former prosperity of the Biterrois, as the district is known.

In the beginning, there was wine...

The city and wine have always been linked together and this has affected both the economy and local attitudes. Among Bézier's exceptional advantages were its strategic position, the ability to control the road network, the proximity of the Greek fort settlement of Agde, and the outlet

Spotcheck
D5

Hérault

Things to do
Cathedral of Saint-Nazaire
Jardin du Plateau des Poètes
Paul-Riquet Avenues
Festival de la Côte
Languedocienne

Within easy reach
Narbonne, 23km SW, p. 180
Agde, 22km E, p. 212.
Étang de Thau, 25km E,
p. 216.

Tourist office
Béziers: ☎ 04 67 76 47 00

to the Mediterranean through the Vendres lagoon. This attracted successive masters to Béziers. A 'fortified town', according to the Greek geographer Strabo, as well as a ford and cross-roads, it soon made its reputation through viti-culture. The wine of Béziers has been prized since antiquity, 'its reputation speaks with authority among the Gauls'. And it was the wine-makers who invented the amphora, the vessel best shaped to carry wine in a ship's hold. Bézier became a Roman colony in 36 BC, and was an important staging-post on the Domitian Way (p. 72).

The Phoenix rises from the ashes

In the 13th C., Saracens and Franks set fire to the city thus repulsing the invading barbar-ians; it was not revived until the days of Charlemagne. The viscount and the bishop ruled the city and from 1131 it also had a consul. At the height of the Middle Ages, the tragedy of the Albigensian persecu-tions made the streets run with blood. The sack of Béziers in 1209 (p. 76) was terrible. All the inhabitants were put to the sword, whether or not they were Cathars. The city soon recov-ered; churches and convents were built, but these were attacked in 1562, when the reformers took the city. In the 17th and 18th C., the middle classes grew wealthy from trading in wine, wheat and oil grown on their estates. Distilleries, potters and gold-smiths were everywhere in the town. The Friday market, which flourishes to this day, harks back to this period of prosperity.

Viticulture in crisis

In the 19th C., Béziers prospered again. The railway came and capital flooded into the area to

lit by the setting sun, which shines through a **rose window** 33-ft (10-m) in diameter. The wide, cool and airy nave contains vestiges of the original church. The carved capitals of the crossing harmonise with the coloured frescoes of the side chapels. Visit the **14th-C. cloister** (open 9am-noon and 2-6pm) which contains remarkable sculptures, including a pair of lovers. From here, go to the **Bishops' garden**, a verdant haven of peace from which there is a magnificent view over the Orb, the old bridge and the roofs of the town.

modernise the farms. Wealthy merchants sponsored performances in the arena. When phylloxera of the vine reached the region in 1878, wine production was hardly affected. The real crisis came in 1907 from over-production. Violent demonstrations forced the government to regulate the markets. Today, the town's main industry is still connected with the wine trade but also includes transport, thanks to its position on the main route between Italy and Spain.

Panorama

On arrival in the city, make directly for the concourse in front of the cathedral to take in the landscape. Vines stretch to the horizon and not far off are the **blue mountains of Caroux and the Espinousse**, the first foothills of the Massif Central to the north. The **Orb**, a fast-flowing river brimming with clean water and full of fish, runs at your feet. It contains pike, carp and pike-perch, renowned for their very delicate flesh.

The Cathedral of Saint-Nazaire

Open 9am-noon and 2-7pm.
The **cathedral**, with its 160-ft (48-m) spire, has a harmonious structure and was built over the course of three centuries (13th–15th C.). The façade is

The museums

From there, make for the Place de la Révolution, with its 14th-C. fountain near the courthouse, installed in the former bishops' palace (17th-C.), and visit the **Musée des Beaux-Arts**, in the Hôtel Fabrégat (☎ 04 67 28 38 78. Open 9am-noon and 2-6pm, from Tue.–Sat., Sun. 2-6pm. Closed Mon. A ticket for one museum gives access to the others.) This museum has collections of paintings and sculptures from the 15th C. to the present day, including some important works such as *The Garden of Love* by Rubens, *Suzanne* by Géricault and a landscape by Corot. The rich Jean Moulin bequest adds a contemporary touch. Jean Moulin,

a famous Résistance fighter, was a native of Béziers, and during the German occupation he posed as an art dealer. To complete the visit, go to the **Musée Fayet**, an annexe in a delightful 17th-C. mansion (9, Rue du Capus, ☎ 04 67 49 04 66. Open from Tue. to Fri. 9am-noon and 2-6pm). The setting, with its ornate ceilings and high fireplaces as well as the indoor garden, is a delight.

Le Jardin du Plateau des Poètes

Down below, the avenues extend into a huge garden. The **Plateau des Poètes** is a huge belvedere which was part of a late 19th-C. redevelopment project created by the landscape gardener Bühler. Its naturalistic layout has been preserved, so that railway travellers can reach the city centre through a pleasant park. Injalabert, a local sculptor, produced an enormous *Titan* and *Child with a Fish*. The carefully angled winding avenues, the moss-covered fountains, expanses of still water and rare species of trees are a delight for lovers and casual strollers.

Throughout the summer, the **Théâtre de Verdure**, an open-air theatre, offers a variety of performances, concerts and drama in this lovely setting (information at the Tourist Office). You can continue walking along the **Promenade des Belvédères** looking over the kitchen gardens that reach right down to the Orb; from each balcony you can watch *pétanque* players, children at play or lovers, depending on the time of day.

The old town

The winding lanes with their southern charm are a good place to get lost, but make a little detour to the **Halles**. The **market** is held here every morning except Monday, and is famous for its local foods. The **Place Pépézut** contains the statue of a Roman emperor found during archaeological excavations, but it was named after Pépézut, a legendary hero and defender of the town. Once you have reached this point, and after visiting the shopping streets, you can admire the **handsome mansions** and the 17th-C. well in the courtyard at 7, Rue Mairan and the 18th-C. Hôtel du Lac in the Rue du 4 Septembre. If you take the Rue du Quatre, you will find yourself

aiming for the Avenues Paul-Riquet, first passing the 15th-C. **Église des Pénitents** with its flamboyant façade.

A new Eldorado

During the second half of the 19th C., the Biterrois region, which had hitherto been focused on grain, olives and vines, became converted exclusively to vineyards. The opening of the railway line

Delicious Biterrois chocolate
(see p. 41)

from Bordeaux to Sète in 1857 gave new impetus to commerce. Fortunes were made and the first châteaux emerged in what was to become an ocean of vines – 'the Eldorado of wine'. This golden age can be read in the landscape, since within a radius of only 19 miles (30 km) there are a good hundred such opulent mansions. Suddenly, in a region where sobriety and discretion were the rule, this **architectural exuberance** flourished, reaching its peak

RUGBY PLAYER: THE TOTAL LOOK

If you want to bring home a gift for your little nephew who dreams of becoming a champion rugby player, then buy him the whole kit (or part of it) of a player on the Béziers team. The strip can be bought direct from the ASB Rugby Club House next to the Stadium (Avenue des Olympiades, ☎ 04 67 11 80 93) or at Géant Casino, (ZAC Montimaran, ☎ 04 67 62 52 75, shorts, 90 F, shirt, 290 F).

under the Second Empire. (late 19th C.). There was a passion for luxury and pleasure but also for culture and fine art. The new rich bourgeoisie now sought to join the nobility. The houses therefore seek an imagery borrowed from the past, using neo-medieval (Rouïere, Libouriac and Grezan), neo-Renaissance (La Tour, Le Contrôle and

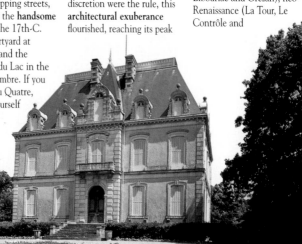

Sériège) and Neo-classical (Luch and Saint-Martin-de-Grave) styles, alongside the contemporary Napoleon III architecture of La Tour and Saint-Pierre.

Life in the châteaux

The châteaux were designed as country seats and advertised the social importance of their owners. Marble, precious woods, wrought iron and stained glass were thus *de rigueur*. The **Château de Belle-Île** houses the largest private auditorium in France. The grounds with their English gardens are adorned with statues, fountains, waterfalls and ornamental lakes. The taste for château building died on the eve of World War I, in about 1910. Even though the French soldiers of the 1914–1918 war had quite a taste for wine, which increased local production, the world was changing. Cosy villas, which were more comfortable and required fewer servants, became the fashion. But the extraordinary châteaux are still here, some of them still occupied by the descendants of the original families. To visit the stately homes of the region, ask at the Béziers Tourist Office (p. 193) for the brochure about the châteaux. During the **Festival des Jardins** (from May to October), these private homes are open to the public. Some are even open permanently and offer **tastings of their wines** (such as the Château de Raissac, ☎ 04 67 49 17 60).

Biterrois is a cake of almonds and macerated raisins (details pp. 40–41)

Béziers celebrates

Night and day, for a whole week, around 15 August, Béziers is alight with the full force of the Féria. In Spain, the **féria** is a fair and festival of the bull. In Béziers, it is also the festival of the horse, the cinema, wine and music. There are bullfights, displays of horsemanship, parades of floats and bull-running; something is happening every day. On the closing day there are fireworks in the arenas

as the signal for 'the night of madness'. **The Festival de la Côte Languedocienne** (Languedoc Coast Festival) is one of the oldest music festivals in the Mediterranean, and has been held in Béziers since 1968. It lasts for a week in July. It is a way of appreciating through music the various historic or artistic settings in which the concerts are held. The programme is divided between classical and contemporary composers. Information at the Tourist Office, Palais des Congrès, 29, Avenue Saint-Saëns, which is inside a delightful 17th-C. mansion (p. 193).

La Cataroise de Béziers or 'the gold of the vine'

Long before it was a wine-growing capital, Béziers was a place where **spirits** from all over the world were drunk. This tradition has almost disappeared though the Cataroise de Béziers has survived. The village women are said to have taken a little glass of this spirit at about 5pm and the husbands claim that it loosened their tongues, hence its name 'magpie wine'! A few producers in western Hérault continue to make it. The word Cataroise comes from the Greek word for 'pure' because it is 100% natural, and is made from the best grapes. If you are lucky enough to come across a bottle of Cataroise, buy it – it truly is sunshine in a bottle.

Le Minervois

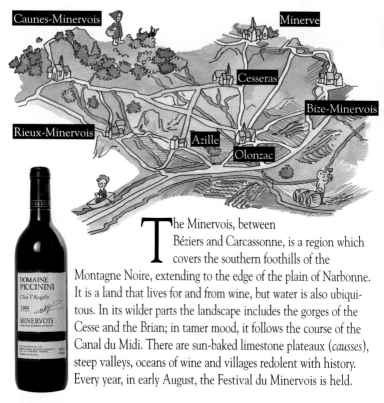

The Minervois, between Béziers and Carcassonne, is a region which covers the southern foothills of the Montagne Noire, extending to the edge of the plain of Narbonne. It is a land that lives for and from wine, but water is also ubiquitous. In its wilder parts the landscape includes the gorges of the Cesse and the Brian; in tamer mood, it follows the course of the Canal du Midi. There are sun-baked limestone plateaux (*causses*), steep valleys, oceans of wine and villages redolent with history. Every year, in early August, the Festival du Minervois is held.

Minervois vineyards

Vines extending over 44,478 acres (18,000 ha) cover hillsides and terraces. A signposted wine route enables you to discover this delightful AOC wine.There are the reds of Causse, Argent-Double, Petit Causse and Mourels, all of which can be kept for five or six years; the whites and the strawberry-coloured rosés are dry and fruity and should be drunk young (at less than five years). Don't forget the **Muscat de Saint-Jean-de-Minervois**, a jewel of a vineyard. Visit the cooperative (☎ 04 67 38 03 24) or the Domaine de Barroubio (☎ 04 67 38 14 06).

Minerve

Town on a rock

This little town must be visited on foot (it is crowded with tourists in summer). It overlooks the abysses of the Cesse and the Brian and was built in the 11th C. It retains its medieval look, with its ruins and the frontages of many of the houses. The white marble altarpiece on the main altar in the **Church of Saint-Étienne**, was commissioned by Bishop Rustique in 456.

Musée Hurepel
☎ 04 68 91 12 26.
Open Apr.–Oct.,
10.30am-12.30pm
and 2-6pm.
The Cathar epic has been
reconstructed with figurines
by a *santon*-maker named
Philippe Assier. The scenes
are extremely authentic.

Bize-Minervois

L'Oulibo
☎ 04 68 41 88 88.
Open all year
round, 9am-
noon,
2-7pm.
This
dynamic olive oil cooperative
was founded in 1942. It makes
a very fruity **olive oil** at its
oil-mill, the last in the
département. The most exotic
of olives with the most

delicate flavour are also cured
here; they are the green *lucques*
olives, which are the shape of
an elongated crescent.

Jouarres

Water sports
½ mile (1 km)
from Olonzac,
☎ 04 68 91 10 35.
The lake covers 296 acres
(120 ha) and is very
close to the
Canal du Midi.
It is a
reservoir
which
contains 141,260,000 cu ft
(4 million m^3) of water. Amid
pine trees and vines, you can
sail in a dinghy or catamaran
or ride a pedalo. The **beach**
has a lifeguard.

Olonzac and Azille

The origins of the wine
These two villages are
surrounded by vines.
Veterans of the legions of

A LOCAL DISH
Frejinat
takes its
name
from the
Occitan
word for
'fried', and is
typical of the
Minervois. It is made of
a neck of pork which is
diced and fried with
garlic and then sprin-
kled with Minervois
white wine. It is served
with fried potatoes and
garlic. Follow it with
lavender-flavoured ice
cream for a truly
traditional meal.

Spotcheck
C5

Hérault

Things to do
Visit the Minervois vineyards
Musée Hurepel
Jouarres water sports centre

Within easy reach
*Carcassonne, 25km SW,
p. 166,
La Montagne Noire,
p. 172,
Les Corbières, p. 176.*

Tourist Office
Minerve: ☎ 04 68 91 83 43

The Church of Rieux-Minervois

Julius Caesar apparently
founded the wine industry
here. Visit the cooperative
Les Celliers d'Onairac
(☎ 04 68 91 20 20). And for
spiritual nourishment, visit
the lovely 12th-C. **Chapel of
Saint-Étienne-de-Vaissière**,
near Azille.

Rieux-Minervois

12th-C. Church
The village stands amid vineyards beside the Argent-
Double and contains some old
houses as well as an important
12th-C church. It is a rare,
seven-sided building and its
ambulatory has 14 carved
capitals, one of which features
the Annunciation.

The Canal du Midi

Avignonet-Lauragais
Laredorte
Olonzac
Capestang
Béziers
Agde
Bram
Trèbes
Le Somail
Le Grau-d'Agde
Villeneuve-les-Béziers
Castelnaudary
Pexiora
Carcassonne
Cap-d'Agde

The Canal du Midi has been classified by UNESCO as a World Heritage Site. It is also the best way of exploring the region, along with its food specialities, vineyards and the Minervois, Corbières and Clape districts. The serenity and tranquillity are incomparable and magnificent sights can be seen along the waterway or very close to it, many preserved for the benefit of modern travellers along the canal (see p. 94).

From Lauragais to the Mediterranean

It takes about ten days to cross Languedoc from Port-Lauragais to the Étang de Thau, during which, time seems to stand still. At **Port-Lauragais**, there is a new attraction which combines a motorway rest area, a canal port and an exhibition of photographs and documents tracing the history of the building of the canal. A **museum of rugby**, the region's favourite sport, has recently been added. The **Seuil de Naurouze** is the 630-ft (189-m) basin in which the waters are divided between the Atlantic and the Mediterranean and is an essential stop along the canal. This is where the canal is fed

Spotcheck

ABCD-5

Tourist office

Castelnaudary:
☎ 04 68 23 05 73
Carcassonne:
☎ 04 68 10 24 30
Béziers:
☎ 04 67 76 47 00
Agde:
☎ 04 67 94 29 68
Sète:
☎ 04 67 74 71 71

by the feeder stream which carries water for 50 miles (80 km) from the Montagne Noire. The site is dominated by an obelisk erected in 1825 in memory of Pierre-Paul Riquet. A picnic area beneath the 300-year-old trees invites you to stop and think about taking a side-trip to the Montagne Noire. From here, the canal follows a sandy course, lined with plane and pine trees. The approach to the sea is nearby. The Mediterranean sights and smells become stronger and the buzzing of crickets louder.

Castelnaudary
See also p. 170.
After the 17th-C. hump-backed Pont-Vieux, the port of Castelnaudary, called **Le Grand Bassin**, opens up before you. The old town

and its monuments are reflected in the waters of this little lake which is closed by the **Saint-Roch lock**, created by four twinned basins which enables boats to navigate a 32-ft (9.5-m) drop. The

section between here and Carcassonne involves negotiating a series of locks and little bridges, modest masterpieces of 17th-C. architecture. You pass through the villages of Lasbordes and Bram, the

latter built on a circular plan, Pexiora and its cemetery with Celtic crosses and Villesequelande, in which a huge elm tree planted in Sully's time still provides shade in the Place de l'Église.

Carcassonne
See also p. 166.
As you pass through, you can admire the Lower Town, founded in the 13th C., the 18th-C. mansions, fountains and the 15th-C. church. After Carcassonne, the canal

The Canal du Midi at Somail

runs through the Aude valley to the **Aqueduc du Fresquel**. This three-arched canal-bridge, built in the early 19th C., allows the canal to flow alongside the road over the aqueduct.

Trèbes

The **Aqueduc d'Orbiel** is another three-arched aqueduct enabling the canal to cross the Orbiel. It was built according to Vauban's plans in 1688. Further on, the triple **Écluse de Trèbes** is partially cut into the rock. Beside the lock entrance there is a mill which dates from 1700. From here onwards, the traveller has

a whole 6¼ miles (10 km) of straight run, perhaps the nicest part of the canal. The banks of this reach are lined with plane trees and cypresses which are reflected in streams, crossed by 18th-C. aqueducts. There are plenty of **pretty villages** in which to stop: Marseillette, Blomac, Saint-Couat and Puichéric, all with fine Romanesque churches; the old streets of Laredorte, the château of the Knights of Malta at Homps, Argens perched on a little hill and the hilltop ruins of Montrabech. The **Aqueduc de Répudre** was built by Riquet in 1676, and is the

oldest on the canal. It was the first aqueduct ever built in France and is the second-oldest in the world.

Somail

The little port of Somail is evidence of the importance of the canal for the economy of the region, since it is surrounded by wharves. The village has attractive 17th-C. houses, a church on a bridge, inns and a remarkable ice-house. The canal then follows the curves of the hills of the Minervois, and the traveller has a **lovely view** of the Abbey of Capestang (13th–14th C.), the Cistercian barn at Fontcalvy and in the distance Narbonne cathedral.

The Malpas tunnel

After the delightful village of **Poilhès**, where there is a tiny statue of Riquet beneath an arch, comes the most impressive engineering feat of the canal, the **Malpas tunnel**. The tunnel runs through the Ensérune hill, on the crest of which there are the remains of a Roman settlement dating from the 6th C. BC (there is an excellent museum). Instead of skirting round the hill, Riquet tunnelled out 577 ft (173 m) of it and

The Orb quayside and the Cathedral of Saint-Nazaire at Béziers

A RIVER GUIDE TO SAFE STEERING AND NAVIGATION

Les Editions du Breil have brought out a very practical guide to river navigation in France and we recommend buying it before you leave (90 F; in French). It contains detailed maps and useful addresses of restaurants and shops. You will learn to calculate your distances in kilometres and hours, understand how a lock works and how to dispose of waste in the most ecologically friendly way! The way to get an angling licence for the canal, whose waters teem with fish, is also explained. You will need a holiday licence which is valid for 15 days between June and September for the whole family, and is available from fishing tackle shops for 120 F. Éditions du Breil: 'Midi-Camargue-Aquitaine', guide fluvial n° 7, Le Breil, 11400 Castelnaudary, ☎ and fax: 04 68 23 51 35.

the canal passes through it. The soil is sandstone tufa. You come out at the upper end of the valley of the Orb, facing Béziers.

The locks of Fontséranes

To get down to the level of the plain, 83 ft (25 m) below, Riquet designed a series of nine locks, an extraordinary feat which graphically illustrates the genius of this former tax-collector. A modern water-slide now runs alongside this system of locks to make it quicker to move through them. About ½ mile (1 km) from Fontséranes, there is the longest aqueduct on the canal, the **Aqueduc de l'Orb** (1854). It is a seven-arched bridge topped by a series of smaller arches, enabling the waters of the Orb to flow over it, a distance of 633 ft (190 m).

From Béziers to Agde

Béziers is the wine-trading capital of the region (see p. 92), and an unmissable sight for tourists, with its Poets' Garden, the Cathedral of Saint-Nazaire (13th C.), its

museums and mansions. From here the route passes beneath a canopy of plane trees and crosses the villages of **Villeneuve** (11th-C. Romanesque belltower) and **Portiragnes** (14th-C. church built of black lava). After passing through **Libron** and its amazing series of overflow channels which would isolate the canal if the river flooded, you have finally reached the level of the coastal plain and after the black lava church at Vias, Agde cathedral comes into view. Another of Riquet's spectacular engineering achievements still awaits, a round, three-door lock with a turntable connecting this canal to the Canal de Béziers, which runs between Agde and the Hérault.

Cathedral of Saint-Étienne at Agde

From Agde to the Étang de Thau

This 2,000-year-old town, founded by the Greeks, has many treasures. They include the 18th-C. **La Recette**, mansions and a chapel. The nearby Grau-d'Agde has fishing boats and there is the **Cap-d'Agde** resort and its **Ephebe** (p. 214). After Agde, you glide through the **marshes** and **old salt marshes** beside the nature reserve of the Étang du Bagnas, before reaching the **Étang de Thau aux Onglous** and the noisy bustling port of **Sète** where the canal ends.

Lamalou-les-Bains

and the Upper Languedoc Nature Park

The wooded region around this spa town at the gates of Upper Languedoc is an ideal setting for those who wish to combine tourism with the cure. Between the turn of the 19th–20th C. and the 1930s, Lamalou was the place where the crowned heads of Europe and high society met.

Lamalou-les-Bains

The hot springs

The hot waters of the Usclade spring (125.6 °F/52 °C) and the warm waters of the Vernière spring (82.4 °F/28 °C), containing a mixture of bicarbonates, gases and trace elements, made the resort's name (p. 100).

The charm of the Belle Époque

The Rue Foch and the Avenue Charcot contain handsome examples of 19th-C. architecture, just right for staging operettas, and in fact for more than a century an operetta festival has been held in the charming Italianate theatre. A company of 90 musicians, singers, dancers and technicians create the performances, which are attended by audiences of more than 10,000. There is a pleasant health walk in the Parc de l'Usclade.

The casino

The casino was built in 1895 by architects of the Italian Escuola and is typical of spa architecture of the period. The grounds (admission charge) are very pleasant. From the terrace of the neighbouring theatre you can listen to an afternoon concert and other performances.

Bédarieux

Mines and arts

Bédarieux was a mining town in the 19th C. but now makes woollens and has a leather industry. Walk along the dyke known as the Perspective (prospect) from which there is a view of the 37-arch viaduct which crosses the valley. At the **Maison des Arts** in the former Hospice Saint-Louis (☎ 04 67 95 16 62, Jul.-Sept., 10am-noon and 2-6pm), you can meet two local celebrities, the poet Ferdinand Fabre and the painter Pierre-Auguste Cot. Rock and jazz concerts and dance and drama performances are held here in July and August. The Salon Floris, a trade show for Mediterranean horticulturalists which is held every two years in May or June, organises botanical forays.

L'Oustal des Abeilles

La Falette, Soumartre, 5½ miles (9 km) from Bédarieux, ☎ 04 67 23 05 94. Open Jul.–Sept., daily except Mon. 10am-1pm and 4-8pm; or on Wed., Sat. and Sun., 10am-noon and 3-7pm. *Free admission.* Everything you need to know about bee-keeping as well as a botanical path and traditional hive activity (watched from

THE HÉREPIAN BELL FOUNDRY

Av. de la Gare,
☎ 04 67 95 07 96.
Open Jul.–Aug., daily except Sun., 10am-noon and 2-6pm; or by appointment.
Bells have been made here for four centuries and still ring out, from , Nîmes to Beirut. You will learn that 435 vibrations are required to produce a C note, no more no less, and there is only a 10th of a millimetre in it! The foundry produces bells for churches, as well as hand-bells and other types of bells and percussion instruments.

behind glass!) is here, as well as honey tastings. There are 400 portable hives producing a variety of honeys: acacia, rosemary, lavender, linden and arbutus (from 42 to 60 F for $2^1/_4$ lb/1 kg).

Pic du Tantajo

An $8^1/_4$-mile (14-km) excursion which begins at the signposted path in Bédarieux in front of the Campotel, Avenue Jean-Moulin. Potsherds and Roman tiles found on the peak are evidence of early occupation. The Tantajo is 1,720 ft (516 m) high.

● The litte train through the Gorges d'Héric

☎ 04 67 97 70 98.
Admission charge.
This little tourist train runs on an old section of line from Bédarieux to Mons-la-Trivalle,

the entrance to the gorges. The route is along the Orb valley, at the foot of the Espinouse range, and through the Upper Languedoc Nature Park.

Gorges d'Héric

The road runs beside the Héric which cuts deep into the rock to a depth of $3^3/_4$ miles (6 km)! You can continue along the road on foot (a four-hour walk).

Saint-Pons-de-Thomière

Green tourism

Saint-Pons-de-Thomières is a town with a rich past and the headquarters of the regional park. It has all the facilities for green tourism, including a Campotel, a sports centre with solar-heated-pool, etc. The **Maison Traditionnelle du Pays d'Espinouse** (p. 67) displays traditional building methods in Jul.-Aug., 2.30-6.30pm; information, ☎ 04 67 97 38 22.

Hiking through the Upper Languedoc Nature Park

The Regional Nature Park (☎ 04 67 97 78 22 or 04 67 97 38 22) has wonderful native flora. The Mas de Riols (☎ 04 67 23 10 34), in the Carroux range, organises family walking tours. Llamas and donkeys are available to carry your packs.

Spotcheck
C4

Hérault

Things to do

Operetta festival
Visit to the Hérapian bell foundry
The little train through the Gorges d'Héric
Hiking through the Upper Languedoc Nature Park

Within easy reach

Lodève, approx. 30 km NE, p. 248.

Tourist office

Lamalou-les-Bains:
☎ 04 67 95 70 91

The Massif at Espinouse

Clermont-l'Hérault

The town was founded by the Phoceans in the 8th C. BC. It stands between plain and mountain at the foot of the ruined citadel of the lords of Guilhem. After wandering its steep, narrow lanes, you can windsurf on the Lac du Salagou or walk up to the bowl-shaped rock formation of the Cirque de Mourèze.

Medieval city

With its feudal castle, its 5,300 ft (1,600 m) of ramparts, its 15 towers (of which seven remain), its four gates with drawbridges, moats and fortified churches, this was one of the **strongholds** of Lower Languedoc. Its role as a look-out post meant that it was besieged many times.

The Collegiate Church of Saint-Paul

The church was built in the 13th and 14th C. and fortified during the Hundred Years' War, hence the machicolations and watchtowers. It is the most handsome **Gothic building** in the region. The austerity of the façade is softened by a delicate rose window and impressive flying buttresses.

An olive oil cooperative

13, Avenue du Président-Wilson, ☎ 04 67 96 10 36. Open daily except Sun. 8am-noon and 2-6pm. More than 2,000 growers bring their olives to the oil-press attached to the shop. The olives are sorted by quality to produce different types of oil. Try the **Clermontaise** (75 F for $1\frac{1}{4}$ pt/1 l), the local extra-virgin olive oil that has very little acidity. There are also olive wood items and olive oil soap.

Cave Coopérative de Cabrières

☎ 04 67 88 91 60. Open daily except Sun. 9am-noon and 2-6pm:

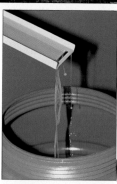

Sun afternoon in Jul.-Aug. You can taste the wine here, and visit the little museum which traces the history of the community and holds temporary exhibitions of work by local artists. AOC Cabrières red, rosé and white are made here. The oldest wine is the Estabel.

Things to do

Cave Coopérative de Cabrières (cooperative wine cellar)
Visit a woollen cloth mill
Hiking, mountain-biking, pony-trekking, rambling
Visit the Cirque de Mourèze
Lac du Salagou leisure centre

Within easy reach

Hérault Valley, 15km NE p. 244,
Lodève, 20 km NW, p. 248.

Tourist office

Clermont-l'Hérault:
☎ 04 67 96 23 86

Villeneuvette
Woollen cloth mill
2¼ miles (3½ km) from Clermont, by the D 908,
☎ 04 67 88 09 11 or 04 67 96 06 00.
The mill was founded on Colbert's initiative in 1673. It specialises in fine, light worsteds, sometimes dyed in bright colours. From 1677, it was patronised by Louis XIV and reached its zenith in the mid-18th C., but was finally closed in 1954. There are guided tours of the town throughout the year.

Cirque de Mourèze
A *cirque* is a rock formation in the shape of a bowl. This *cirque* is further along the D 908. The rocks have been strangely sculpted by erosion and have taken strange forms which have been given names such as The Young Girls, The Bear, The Shepherd and The Sphinx. The bowl is cut into the Liausson mountainside and covered in hiking trails. A reconstruction of a prehistoric dwelling has been

created in the **Parc des Courtinals** (open Apr.–Oct. daily 9.30am-7.30pm).

The salagou
Hiking trails
There are all types of hikes, rambles, mountain-bike trails and pony-treks. The Bureau du Pays d'Accueil du Salagou can give you the list of professional guides who will help you choose the route and tell you where to hire what you need. The guides will also show you the sights of interest in the region which you might not be able to find for yourself.

Flora and fauna
Perch-pike, perch, roach and carp have been introduced, while poplars, ash, willow and alders grow wild. Three interesting birds inhabit the region: the great crested grebe whose plumage is red in summer and grey in winter, the song-thrush which arrives in May from Gabon to nest in the Salagou, which it leaves in September, and the great cormorant which spends the winter here. The only

LAC DU SALAGOU

4½ miles (7 km) from Clermont. The banks of the lake are bright red, thanks to the ruff, a sort of sandstone, a nice contrast to the sky and water. The soil is covered with round lumps of lava because the lake is inside the crater of an extinct volcano. Anglers, windsurfers, campers and beach lovers will appreciate this 1,850-acre (750-ha) tranquil stretch of water, created by a dam (Leisure Centre, ☎ 04 67 96 05 17). Municipal campsite (☎ 04 67 96 06 18), Campotel (☎ 04 67 96 13 13).

problem is the zebra mussel. It is brought in by the birds in its larval state and covers the stones and rocks. The shell is very sharp and can cut quite badly. It is not an edible mussel so do not attempt to eat it.

The Cirque de Mourèze is an amazing geological formation, a natural crater with spectacular rock formations

Pézenas
and the Hérault

P ézenas stands in a fertile plain known as the 'Garden of the Hérault' between the beaches of the coast and the mountains of the hinterland. It was very prosperous in the 15th and 17th C., and contains some magnificent stately homes which have been very well restored. The Tourist Office provides a signposted two-hour walk to see them.

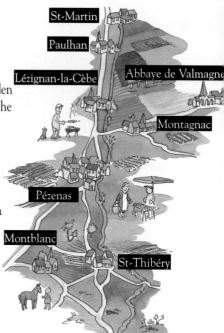

St-Martin

Paulhan

Lézignan-la-Cèbe

Abbaye de Valmagne

Montagnac

Pézenas

Montblanc

St-Thibéry

Hôtel de Lacoste
8, Rue François-Oustrin.
This magnificent 16th-C. mansion is now the local branch of the Société Générale de Banque. There is a grand staircase and stone balcony overlooking the well in the courtyard.

Gély's barber shop
This famous shop is now the Tourist Office. It is in the Place Gambetta, once the commercial and political centre of the town. The shop was a 'meeting-place for idlers, country bumpkins and loiterers'. Molière (p. 124) was a frequent visitor and delighted in noting the words and habits of his compatriots which he later used in his plays.

CRAFTS AND SWEETS

This is a delightful spot for setting up a workshop or shop. Among those who have done so are M.-P. Boniolk (L'Art du Feu, 16, Rue Mercière, ☎ 04 67 98 07 27), who specialises in Limoges enamels, and Francine Le Bon whose Atelier du Lumiphore sells bas-reliefs and lamp-holders made of pottery. La Maison des Métiers d'Art, in the former house of the consul, exists to help young craftspeople and artists. As for local food specialities, do not forget the candy-striped sticks (*berlingots*) and little pies (see p. 40) which can be bought all over the town. Visit M. Boudet's factory where he makes *berlingots*, Chemin de Saintistol (☎ 04 67 90 76 05).

Hôtel d'Alfonse
32, Rue de Conti,
☎ 04 67 98 10 38.
Open 15 June–15 Sept, Mon.–Sat., 10am-noon and 2-7pm; in winter by appointment.
This magnificent 17th-C. Italianate mansion has three floors of arcaded galleries. The apartments open on to the galleries which look out on an interior courtyard and a little garden. This is where Molière staged his play *Le Médecin volant* (*The Thieving Doctor*) for the first time.

Spotcheck
D4

Hérault

Things to do
The Pézenas Carnival and its famous foal
Visit the Marty flavourings distillery
Hiking in the Pézenas district

Within easy reach
Agde, p. 212,
Étang de Thau, 216.

Tourist office
Pézenas: ☎ 04 67 98 36 40

Cours Jean-Jaurès
This main avenue is lined with shady trees and magnificent houses. The detail of the doors, frontages, balconies and staircases of these handsome 17th-C. dwellings (Pastre, Mazuc, Landes de Saint-Palais, Grasset, Bazin-de-Bezons) draws the attention

and admiration of passers-by. This is also a shopping street.

Church of Saint-Jean

Go and visit this Romanesque church in the street of the same name, which was built as a chapel but became a parish church in the 14th C. Most of the present building dates from 1743. The marble interior (main altar, pulpit, baptismal fonts and the chapels of the Virgin and of Saint-Blaise, patron saint of the town) is remarkable. The House of the Commanders stands opposite the church.

Church of Sainte-Ursule

Note the fine late 17th-C. gilded wooden altarpiece, and visit the chapel on the right which contains a legendary wooden statue of the Black Madonna. It is believed either to have been washed up by the sea or brought back from Rhodes by a crusader. It is usually robed and all that is visible is the face.

Musée Vulliod-Saint-Germain

Rue des Alliés.
Open daily except Tues.
Jul.–Aug,
10am-noon
and 3-5pm or
7pm; Sun.
2-5pm.
The museum contains five Aubusson tapestries, a reconstruction of a typical Languedoc kitchen, collections of 18th-C. pottery and pharmacy jars made by the Royal Manufactory of Montpellier. And of course, there are souvenirs of Molière, a bust of the playwright and a copy of his armchair.

The Foal

This huge wooden horse, covered with a blue cloth patterned with gold fleur-de-lys, is paraded at the start of every event, especially the carnival (see p. 112). Information, ☎ 04 67 96 36 40.

Around Pézenas

The Marty flavourings distillery

5 miles (8 km) S from Pézenas, Rte de Montblanc, Saint-Thibéry,
☎ 04 67 77 75 94.
Open Jul.–Aug., Mon.–Fri. 9am-noon and 3-8pm. Out of season and Sat.
Guided tour.
This is where spirits, syrups and essential oils are distilled. A tour reveals which plants are used and the various stages of production, including distillation and maceration. Purchases include Languedoc brandy or an apéritif made with lime juice and mulberry syrup (free tasting).

La Grange-des-Prés

On the road to Montagnac (where the largest wine cellar in Europe is open in season on Friday, 10am-noon), the Prince de Conti attracted Molière and his Illustre Théâtre company to the princely residence of his provincial court in 1650,

HIKING IN THE PÉZENAS AREA

There is nothing easier than taking the Mourguettes footpath (Mourguette is the local name for a type of snail) from Cazouls-d'Hérault, for a two-and-a-half hour walk. The Cami Ferrat walk leaves from the Nizas town centre and lasts about 6 hours, following an old Roman road once used by shepherds. The route then leads through the Capitelles, past the lime kiln which was once used to make mortar and fertiliser. The landscape also consists of *garrigue* (scrubland) and woodland.

1653 and 1657. This inspired Marcel Pagnol to remark 'Jean-Baptiste Poquelin was born in Paris, but Molière was born in Pézenas.'

Valmagne Abbey
Villveyrac
☎ **04 67 78 06 09.**
Open 15 June–30 Sept., daily 10am-noon and 2-6pm; or daily 2.30-6.30pm.
The abbey is 9 miles (15 km) from Pézenas, and between the 12th–14th C. was one of the richest in southern France. After the Revolution, it became the Valmagne wine store (it has the perfect conditions of darkness and coolness) which saved it from destruction.

Paulhan
The Central Hérault region is slightly off the beaten track. This village is one of the 90 circular villages of Languedoc, built according to a plan in which development occurs in concentric rings. It is spectacular from the air, as many postcards prove. Go to the **Miellerie Rouquette** (9 *bis*, Rte de Saint-Martin, ☎ 04 67 25 04 40) where for more than 30 years father and son have been making aromatic honeys.

Lézignan-la-Cèbe
Cèbe in the local language means 'onion'. Onions have been grown here for many years, and they are particularly mild in flavour. They can be eaten cooked of course, but are preferably eaten raw in a salad, combined with slices of tomato and a sprig of basil. They will keep in the refrigerator for several days. The 17th-C. **château** can be visited from July to October from 2.30-6pm, except on Mondays (☎ 04 67 98 23 80).

Valmagne Abbey was only saved from destruction during the Revolution by becoming a wine store

Agde

Agathê, means 'the beautiful' in Greek. The town stands on top of an extinct volcano so most of the buildings are built of basalt, hence its nickname 'the Black Pearl'. It was a busy port in the 17th C., but it is now devoted mainly to tourism, its access to the sea being via Cap d'Agde. Park your car in a car park and wander the streets on foot to get a true feel of the little crooked houses.

The Cathedral of Saint-Étienne

The cathedral is shut when there is no service. It is one of the loveliest fortified churches in the region and was built in the 12th C. The basalt walls act as ramparts. It should be viewed from the opposite bank of the Hérault. The interior is rather austere apart from the Baroque reredos on the main altar. When you leave, take a look at the surrounding houses which are also built of basalt, with their interesting staircases and 16th- and 17th-C. doorways.

La Glacière

This district is enclosed by ramparts (its other boundaries

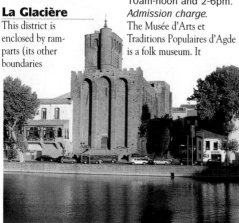

are the Hérault, the Rue du 4-Septembre and the Rue Jean-Roger) and is the oldest in the town. In the 17th C., in a square of the same name, an underground ice-house made it possible to store ice, which was brought from outside the town in winter and preserved in straw.

Musée Agathois

Rue de la Fraternité, ☎ 04 67 94 82 51. Open 6 Sept.–14 Jun. daily except Tue., 10am-noon and 2-6pm. 5 Jun–15 Sept. daily, 10am-noon and 2-6pm. *Admission charge.*
The Musée d'Arts et Traditions Populaires d'Agde is a folk museum. It

explains the mail-coach route to Béziers and exhibits regional costumes including

the *sarret*, a lace headdress, instruments of navigation and 19th-C. votive offerings.

Around Agde

Étangs du Bagnas Nature Reserve

Domaine du Grand Clavelet, RN 112, ☎ 04 67 01 60 23. Telephone first, because the hours vary depending on the activity. *Admission charge.*
This nature reserve covers 1,384 acres (560 ha) of marsh, heath, dunes, water-meadows and salt marsh and is used by 200 species of migrating birds including pink flamingoes, white long-legged plover, purple herons and more. The Société de Protection de la

Nature organises guided tours. Boots or sturdy walking shoes are recommended.

Grau-d'Agde

The road runs besides the banks of the Hérault for 2.5 miles (4 km) and leads to this old fishing village which is now a family resort with a fine sandy beach. The sister resort of La Tamarissière faces it from the opposite bank of the river. If you feel like it, walk to the beach at Cap d'Agde, about 3 miles (5 km) away.

Mont Saint-Loup
Route du Cap d'Agde.

The walk over the three hills which are the remains of a 740,000-year-old volcano is spectacular. The volcano supplied the lava used for

building 'The Black Pearl'. The hills are planted with pines and cedars and command a magnificent view over the Golfe du Lion.

La Maison des Pays d'Agde
Route Saint-Thibéry, Bessan,
☎ 04 67 77 41 12.
Open 1 Jul.–30 Sept.; Mon.–Fri., 10am-6pm and weekend 9am-7pm. A few miles from Agde at the exit from the A9 motorway, the route covers 94 miles (150 km) of the wine-makers and fishermen's road. A little newspaper gives details of the itinerary. Rooms in hotels, *gîtes* or camp sites can be reserved.

Along the Canal du Midi

Ride along the towpath on a mountain bike to Béziers, 12½ miles (20 km) away, or to Marseillan, 5 miles (8 km) away. The bikes can be rented at La Cadotière Garage, Place Jean-Jaurès (☎ 04 67 94 42 92). You can also take a boat; the canal is refreshingly cool. If you do, take a cruise with the Bateaux du

Soleil (☎ 04 67 94 08 79) or rent a barge or river boat from EURL Leveque- Nautic (☎ 04 67 94 78 93).

Cap-d'Agde

This seaside resort, created in 1963, has 100,000 beds and is a paradise for night owls as well as being the European capital of naturism. This does not stop you from dressing up to wander through the port or seek entertainment on the Île des Loisirs.

Musée de l'Éphèbe
**Mas de la Clape,
☎ 04 67 94 69 60.**
Open daily June–Sept.
9.30am-12.30pm and
2.30-6.30pm;
daily Oct.–May
9am-noon and
2-6pm; closed
on Sun.
morning.
*Admission
charge.*
The museum is
devoted to the
history of navi-
gation from
antiquity to the
present day and
to underwater
archaeology.
Don't miss the
bronze statue
which was found
about 30 years
ago in the bottom of the
Hérault and which gave its
name to this museum of
Hellenistic archaeology.

La Conque
Wait for a stormy day to
admire this wild spot where
the sailors of old once moored
their craft. Get there along
the **Rue des Tamaris**, along
the clifftop. These cliffs of
volcanic rocks have been
deeply eroded and there is a
black sandy beach at the
foot. Return to La Plagette
and the Richelieu quay to
come back via the quayside.

❀ Aquarium marin
**11, Rue des Deux-
Frères,
☎ 04 67 26 14 21.**
Open Apr.–Sept.,
10am-11pm; Oct–
March,2-6pm.
*Admission
charge.*
Life under
water in the
Mediterranean
and tropical seas
in 30 tanks,
each with its
own special
theme.

Fort Brescou
Open 15 June–15
Sept., 10.30am-noon
and 2.30-5.15pm.

Vauban, the military engineer,
was responsible for this fort
built in the late 16th C. on
an island of basalt rock with
a circumference of 950 ft
(285 m). It was converted
into a state prison in the
17th C., but no longer houses
convicts.

Port de la Clape
The wide quay-
side is paved with
basalt, of course. A
wander round the docks is
always interesting. The
little streets and squares
leading off from it, such as
the Rue de la Hune, are full
of shops and cafés.

BOAT TRIPS TO THE MEDITERRANEAN

For a lovely outing in a single-hulled pleasure-boat or catamaran, contact Sud Croisière, 18, Quai Di-Dominico (☎ 04 67 26 83 34); Aventure Organisation, Cap 2000 (☎ 04 67 26 37 15); Bleu Marine Plaisance (☎ 04 67 26 77 67) or Compagnie À Bord (☎ 04 67 26 96 96). The last two are in the Base de Loisirs Nautiques. Les Bateaux Oranges, Quai Jean-Miquel, Centre-Port (☎ 04 67 26 92 44), shuttles between the Cap d'Agde, the Grau d'Agde and Agde and has excursions to Fort Brescou, along the coast and up the Hérault river. Les Bateaux Blancs et Bleus, same address (☎ 04 67 26 28 41), also sails to Sète every Wednesday morning (market day).

Aqualand

Av. des Îles-d'Amérique, ☎ 04 67 26 71 09. Open 5 June–11 Sept., 10am-6.30pm
Admission charge.
Young and old will have plenty of fun here with a huge water toboggan, bubbling pools, a wave pool and Oliver's Water Show

in which divers perform the most hair-raising feats and there are other water-based performances.

The underwater path

SPN Agde-Vias-Portiragnes
☎ 04 67 01 60 23.
Leaving from the Grande-Conche beaches of the Môle, or from the Fortin car park, this underwater route is free and signposted. Features include caves, flat rocks, little clefts and scree. You can rent a mask, snorkel, wetsuit, flippers and a guide with the SPN.

The water-bus

You board the bus at Quai Jean-Miquel, Port-Dauphin (☎ 04 67 26 38 81) and use it for a trip round the harbour (40 min), to go to the beach (buses about once every half hour) during the day or, in the evening, to go to the Île des Loisirs (every 10 min).

The Île des Loisirs and the Marinas

Casino (black-jack, roulette, baccara and 140 one-armed bandits), Luna Park, night-clubs, Dino Park and its dinosaurs and a children's playground – a drain on the wallet! The Île des Loisirs (leisure island) can be reached on foot or by bicycle from the Richelieu beach which is the largest beach at the resort.

Spotcheck
D5

Hérault

Things to do
Aquarium marin (Marine Aquarium)
The underwater path
Boat trips
Windsurfing and sea-fishing

Things to do with children
Aqualand

Within easy reach
Béziers, 26 km W, p. 192,

Tourist Office
Cap d'Agde: ☎ 04 67 01 04 04

Windsurfing or fishing?

If you want to take a lesson or course of lessons or to rent a **sailboard**, try the following places: Bounty, Plage de la Roquill, (☎ 04 67 01 27 71); Capao-Plage, Hôtel Capao, Plage Richelieu-Est (☎ 04 67 26 99 44); Neway Centre, parking du Temps-Libre, Île des Loisirs (☎ 04 67 26 24 47).
For sea-fishing, try Bateaux Oranges (in the daytime, the catch can be anything, but at night it is conger eel) or the Bateaux Blancs et Bleus (addresses and ☎ above). D'Acunto (Quai du Commandant-Méric, le Grau-d'Agde, ☎ 04 67 21 38 72) organises fishing competitions.

Naturism

East of the access channel of Port-Ambonne, more than 30,000 people take their clothes off in summer (be warned, it is very busy from 14 July to 15 August!). The Centre Héliomarin Oltra (☎ 04 67 01 06 36) has room for 2,400 at its seaside camp sites. You can also rent caravans, mobile homes or chalets.

The Étang de Thau

This lagoon is 11 miles (18 km) long by 3 miles (5 km) wide and is more like an inland sea. In the 17th C. it was crossed by sailing ship or rowing-boat. In the 19th C. steam tug-boats took over. Today, it is easy to cross the Thau except during high winds.

Marseillan

Noilly Prat cellars

1, Rue Noilly,
☎ 04 67 77 20 15.
Open daily 1 Mar.–31 Dec., 10am-noon and 2.30-6pm; in winter on appointment.
Free guided visit.
This apéritif, which was created in 1810, is based on the light white wines of Languedoc which is then aged in oak casks to give it its aroma and body. It is then exposed to the air in barrels.

La halle aux Oiseaux

Place du 14-Juillet,
☎ 04 67 01 74 20.
Open Jul.–Aug. daily, 9am-noon and 3-7pm; in winter closed Sun. and Mon.
Admission charge.
On the first floor of the beautifully restored market halls, M. Bort exhibits his private collection of more than 400 species of stuffed birds from all over the world.

Pomérols

Guy Bouzigues chocolates

Grand-Rue,
☎ 04 67 77 04 99.
Open daily, by appointment.
This little village produces an excellent **white wine**, but it is also worth a detour to visit Guy Bouzigues, whose speciality is **chocolate**. *Lou Picpoul* (a chocolate stuffed with brandy fondant) and the *Pavé* (a dark chocolate liqueur) received the European Golden Laurels in 1996.

Balaruc

The old fortified village

The fortress-church of Saint-Maurice dates from the 14th C. A game called *'balle au tambourin'* is played here in a stadium. Two teams hit a ball made of very hard rubber. A little train will take you on a 1¼-hour trip around the medieval village and a **'tour of the Jules Bouzigues oyster-beds'**, including tastings of oysters (Wed. at 10.30am and Fri. at 5.30pm).

DOMAINE DES ARESQUIERS

The Conservatoire du Llittoral has managed to save this 370-acre (150-ha) woodland on either side of the Rhône to Sète canal. It includes the pinewoods of La Fontaine, the only coastal forest in the region and a swampy lido as well as 494 acres (200 ha) of salt marsh which is being made into a bird sanctuary.

bottles a year (p. 18). Note the portal of the Church of the Conversion-of-Saint-Paul (12th-C.), with its frieze of fish and ships. Then go to the seaside resort which has a huge sandy beach.

Lac du Barrou
Yachting centre
☎ 04 67 53 55 24.
Open all year round, Mon.–Sat., 9am-noon and 2-6pm.
The lake is exposed to the fierce north wind, the Tramontane, so there is a sailing club here which offers

visit. Oysters and mussels are farmed here; tastings cost 40 F. If you just want to eat oysters, go to La Tchèpe (Av Louis-Tudesq, ☎ 04 67 78 33 19) where oysters cost 46 F a dozen.

Le Massif de la Gardiole

Between Balaruc-le-Vieux and Fabrègues, there are more than 9,885 acres (4,000 ha) of woods, scrub and heath (and the ruined **Abbey of Saint-Félix-de-Montceau**). They are crisscrossed by 25 miles (40 km) of **signposted paths** which can be covered on foot, on horseback or on a mountain bike (Information, ☎ 04 67 48 25 25).

Frontignan
Muscat and beach
Take a tour round the co-operative of the famous **Muscat** wine (14, Avenue du Muscat. Open daily ☎ 04 67 48 12 26) which produces almost 2 million

beginners or advanced courses in various types of sailing craft, including dinghies and catamarans, as well as wind-surfing and funboarding. Some years it takes part in the **Fête du Barrou**, in the old fishermen's district, and organises regattas.

Bouzigues
The oyster route
This little port dominated by the Church of Saint-Jacques, has given its name to the local oysters. The **Musée de l'Étang de Thau** (Place du Port-de-Pêche, 10am-noon, 2-5pm or 7pm depending on the season, ☎ 04 67 78 33 57) explains the various tasks involved in farming oysters. The Oyster Route is about 37 miles (60 km) long and takes you to the oyster-beds. The **Établissements Jean-Pierre Molina** (Chemin de la Catonnière, ☎ 04 67 43 84 50. Open daily) is a good place to

Mèze
Lagoon Centre
☎ 04 67 46 64 80.
Open daily, Jul.–Aug. 10am-7.30pm;
Sept.– Jun., 2-6pm;
15 Nov.–5 Feb. closed on Sat.
Admission charge.
This research centre includes a commercial fish-farm which is unique in Europe. Some of the species of fish raised are exotic.

Sète

port and seaside resort

The city stands on a hill dominating the landscape between the Étang de Thau and the Mediterranean. It has a distinctive character, full of atmosphere, light and fragrance. Sète is the largest port on the French Mediterranean coast, and a seaside resort with almost 7 miles (11 km) of fine sand. It is also the town of Paul Valéry, Georges Brassens and Jean Vilar.

The fishing port

Wander along the quays with their exotic names of La Consigne, Licciardi, Maroc and Alger or la République with their intense activity. At about 5pm, the fishermen unload sole, bass, gilt-head bream, mackerel and rascasse and there is a fish auction. Trawlers and tuna-boats wait for the right time to leave. A few old sea-dogs repair nets and sell shellfish and starfish.

La Marine

Quai Général-Durand.
The old trading port is known as 'La Marine'. In the course of time, it has been used by Catalan and Moorish sailing ships, feluccas, cattle-boats, three-masters, schooners, and tug-boats. Although it is cluttered with fish-boxes, barrels, casks and fishing nets it is the best place to discover the trading past of the town with its 18th-C. façades and Art Deco buildings.

It is also the ideal place to eat fish soup, *bourride*, octopus, squid and stuffed mussels in one of the many restaurants.

The trading port

Unfortunately, this port is closed to the public for security reasons. The **ninth-largest French port** has some 247 acres (100 ha) of docks and more than 6¼ miles (10 km) of quays. The average annual throughput is 4 million tonnes. Cargoes include exotic woods from Africa, cattle, minerals, grain and oils. There is room to store more than a million hectolitres of wine.

Musée Paul-Valéry
**Rue François-Desnoyer,
☎ 04 67 46 20 98.**
Open daily except Tue.
10am-noon and 2-6pm.
Thanks to its glass construction, the museum commands a view of the sea, across the naval cemetery. It is dedicated to the history of Sète and the nautical jousts (p. 115) and has classic paintings by Courbet and Monticelli among others, as well as contemporary works. One room is dedicated to the poet and thinker Paul Valéry.

Espace Georges-Brassens
**67, Boulevard Camille-Blanc,
☎ 04 67 53 32 77.**
Open 10am-noon and 2-6pm or 7pm except Mon. in winter.
Admission charge.
The singer and poet was born here (in 1921) and was buried here (in 1981). In this very successful, lively but intimate environment, headphones in each room allow visitors to hear Brassens tell the story of his life, his work and his songs. An absolute delight for his fans everywhere. In the Le Py cemetery opposite, the artist's grave is always covered with a range of floral tributes to his memory.

La Pointe-Courte
This district (which gave its name to Agnès Varda's first film in 1956) is like a little fishing village. The navvies lived here during the building

of the railways and made it into a separate enclave. On the Quai du Mistral, nets are laid out to dry; on the shores of the lake, small craft and fishermen's tools merely add

LA TIELLE, A LOCAL DELICACY

**Patimer, 35, Rue de la Révolution,
☎ 04 67 53 65 33.**
Open daily except Mon. and Sun. afternoon, 8.30am-1pm, 5.30-8pm.
Buy one or more slices of *tielle*, a pie made with a bread dough and filled with baby octopus in a spicy tomato sauce. (A whole pie costs 45 F for 6 pers.). Also: l'Île singulière, 16 Rue de Provence, ☎ 04 67 51 59 65.

atmosphere to the delightful surroundings.

Le Mont Saint-Clair

This spur of limestone 607 ft (182 m) high offers a spectacular view not only over the lower town of Sète but also the Étang de Thau, the Cévennes to the Pyrenees and even as far as the Pointe de l'Espiguette... The path has many flights of steps and there is an orientation map at the top. The footpaths wind among the pines.

La Croix Saint-Clair

This huge illuminated cross commemorates the bonfire lit by the people of Sète on 12 July to celebrate the saint who gave her name to the mount.

The Chapel of Notre-Dame-de-la-Salette

This low, dark chapel is decorated with **frescoes by Bringuier**, and commemorates an appearance of the Virgin Mary on 19 September 1866, at Salette (Isère).

The white stones

According to legend the seven daughters of the king of the Thau Basin, who were extremely beautiful, were tired of the young men of Sète who came to admire their beauty and turned them into white stones! The forest contains more than 700 plant species some of which were brought in cargoes from South America, Africa or the Middle East. There is a **nice view** over the lido.

The deaconate Church of Saint-Louis

This church was built in 1702 in honour of the patron saint of Sète. The style is pure and

THE FISH AUCTION

The Sète fish market opened in March 1969, and was also the first fish auction in France to be computerised. It is in the heart of the fishing port. Every evening at 5pm, the fishermen unload sole, bream, gilthead bream, mackerel and other fish which are sold to fish merchants. You can also see the ice tower which produces 28 tonnes of ice cubes daily to keep the fish fresh. This is a local sight that should definitely not be missed.

sober and the building is topped with a **statue of the Virgin** protecting the town. Three clocks and **magnificent stained glass** (1892) have been added to the oldest church in the city, which contains an organ built by Moitessier in 1843.

The little train

Departure in front of the Tourist Office, Quai Général-Durand,

☎ 04 67 51 27 37. Telephone for the opening hours.

There are guided tours of the town, visits on a theme, a tour of the mountain (town, ports, Étang de Thau) or a souvenir walk through the town, seafront, Le Py and Espace Georges-Brassens. You have plenty of choice.

Les Bateaux Rouges

Quai de la Marine, Quai du Général-Durand,
Open Jul.–Aug., Mon., Wed., Thur., and Sat. Book 2 days in advance.
☎ 04 67 46 00 46.

These boats have glass bottoms so you can look at the sights underwater. They visit the fishing ports or the Étang de Thau. You can also take them sea fishing or cruise to Aigues-Mortes with a stop to visit the medieval city, and the Sardine Festival off the coast of Sète.

Espace Fortant-de-France

278, Avenue du Maréchal-Juin,
☎ 04 67 46 70 12.
Open 1 Jul.–31 Aug., daily, 10am-7pm:
1 Sept.–30 Jun., closed Sun.

This is the place to learn all about the wines of the Pays d'Oc in a new type of wine cellar. There are vineyards, a modern bottling plant (14,000 bottles ph), tastings, a shop and contemporary art (Combas, Di Rosa).

The naval cemetery

The cemetery, which overlooks the sea, was immortalised by Paul Valéry and contains his tomb. Notice that in the upper part of the cemetery the names are mainly French, Belgian and Swiss, whereas in the lower part, where Jean Vilar is buried, the names tend to sound Italian.

Montpellier

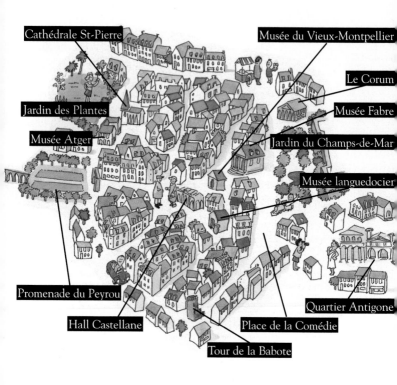

Cathédrale St-Pierre
Musée du Vieux-Montpellier
Le Corum
Jardin des Plantes
Musée Fabre
Musée Atger
Jardin du Champs-de-Mar
Musée languedocier
Promenade du Peyrou
Quartier Antigone
Hall Castellane
Place de la Comédie
Tour de la Babote

This regional capital is so multifaceted that it is impossible to describe concisely. The average age of the population is the lowest in France due to the huge number of students –

some 60,000 of them – who make up one quarter of the inhabitants.

The city is friendly and picturesque with lanes, passages, little squares and mansions dating from the 17th and 18th C. The historic centre has been pedestrianised, so it is a pleasant place linger. The city is lively in the evening, thanks to the theatres, cinemas, operas and other performances. Altogether a great place to stay.

Festivals and festivities

The **Festival de Musique de Radio-France** in July is a festival of French popular music which revives old favourites and introduces new material. The **Festival International Montpellier-Danse** (June–July) is a world-famous dance festival, which focuses on choreography. The **Festival du Printemps des Comédiens** (June), a drama festival, ensures that there are performances in all the towns of the *département*. The **Festival du Cinéma Méditerranéen** and the **Foire de la Vigne et du Vin**, both in October, end the season.

Place de la Comédie

This is the true centre of Montpellier, a place that is impossible to miss. Like the rest of the town centre, the area called the **Écusson** is pedestrianised (there is adjacent underground parking). The huge square was laid out in the 18th C., like the theatre on one of its sides (which was restored in the 19th C. due to a fire). It is surrounded by handsome buildings with balustraded balconies and stone

Place de la Comédie

swags, and in the centre stands the Fountain of the Three Graces. Stop and have a drink in one of the numerous cafés here and reflect on the fact that even Montpellier is not immune to the craze for fast food.

Fountain in the Place de la Comédie

The Charles-de-Gaulle Esplanade

The **walk** between the Place de la Comédie and the Corum is shaded by plane trees and enlivened by fountains, games areas and park benches.

On the right, the **Jardin Champ-de-Mars** is an extension of the esplanade. To the south, in the Allée Jules-Milhaud there is the little station of Palavas whose train takes the people of Montpellier to the seaside. The **Corum** is a building made of concrete and pink granite which houses the opera and a conference centre (guided tours on Sat., 2-7pm. Free admission). Apart from the opera auditorium itself, it looks very much like the concourse of a modern train terminal.

Rue de la Loge

This road runs between the Place de la Comédie and the old town centre and is one of the busiest shopping streets in the city. It is lined by beautiful houses so try to tear yourself away from the shop windows to look at them. A little market is held every

'MIDI LIBRE'

Pl. de la Comédie,
☎ **04 67 07 67 17.**
Open Mon.–Fri., 10.30pm-12.30am
Free admission.

This daily paper began publication in 1944 and has a circulation of 220,000. It is 'put to bed' in the evening. It is interesting to see how a French newspaper is put together. This one publishes articles by more than 150 journalists and 1,250 local correspondents. No less than 35 tonnes of paper a day are used – all so that people can find out how many dogs were run over that day in Languedoc-Roussillon! A fascinating tour.

morning in the **Place Jean-Jaurès** where cafés and restaurants vie for custom. Many young people prefer to gather here rather than in the Place de la Comédie. The **Halle Castellane**, on the corner of the Rue de l'Aiguillerie, is a modern metal structure which contains a large market.

Musée Languedocien

7, Rue Jacques-Cœur,
☎ 04 67 52 93 03.
Open daily except Sun. and public holidays, 2-5pm; Jul.–Aug. and Sept.–Oct., 3-6pm

The Corum

except Sun. and public holidays.
Admission charge.
The museum is housed in the 17th-C. **Hôtel des Trésoriers de France** and is one of the best art and history museums in France. The treasures of the Société Archéologique are displayed in 20 rooms. There are Greek vases with 18th-C. glazes (including the Montpellier vase to which a room is dedicated), Gallo-Roman and Roman art, and folk art of the region.

The Cathedral of Saint-Pierre

Pl. Saint-Pierre,
Open 9am-noon and 2.30-7pm, except Sun. afternoon.
This black fortress of a building was built in the 14th C. and restored in the 17th C. It is famous for its

Façade of the Cathedral of Saint-Pierre

unusual **porch**, consisting of two huge rocket-shaped pillars supporting a stone canopy which protects the entrance. The impression is one of clumsiness. The cathedral is next door to the famous Faculty of Medicine, one of the best in France.

Jardin des Plantes

163, Rue Auguste-Broussonet,
☎ **04 67 63 43 22.**
Open daily except Mon., 10am-5pm (7pm, Apr.–Sept.)

'In order to place there all sorts of plants, both foreign and domestic...'
Thus Henri IV gave the order in 1593 to create this botanical garden, the oldest in France. It was only opened to the public in 1841, and has attracted many researchers. Visit the magnificent tropical plan houses, the very old

trees and the 3,000 or so plants. They are part of the 'systematic school' devised by de Candolle in the 19th C. for studying the classification of plants. Other attractions are the orangery, ponds, statues of botanists and Anduze vases.

Antigone

The modern architect Ricardo Bofill gave this new district a classical name because the spirit of the place is impregnated with Graeco-Roman antiquity. The style of the flats, offices and shops is reminiscent of the set of *Ben Hur*, despite the absence of chariots and the presence of green spaces. You get to it through the Polygone shopping centre which contains all the big stores, from Galeries Lafayette to Naf-Naf.

Around the Tour de la Babote

Bd Victor-Hugo.
This is one of the 25 towers of the medieval fortifications. It was altered in the 18th C. when an astronomical observatory was built on the top. The building is now the headquarters of the **Société Astronomique** de l'Hérault. Note the architecture of the Municipal Tourist Office (6, Rue Maguelone), which

is housed in the former Paris-Montpellier department store. If you leave by train, you will see the station whose facade is the colonnaded peristyle of the former embarkation hall, to which the pediment and clock were added in 1870.

Musées Vieux-Montpellier and Le Fougau

2, Pl. Pétrarque,
☎ **04 67 66 02 94.**

Open daily except Sun. and Mon., 9.30am-noon and 1.30-5pm.
Free admission.
The Museum of Old Montpellier is housed on the first floor of the Hôtel de Varennes. The city's history is displayed through pictures, old maps and contemporary furniture. The Fougau Museum on the floor above, which is only open Wed–Thurs., 3-6.30pm, is dedicated

The Quartier Antigone by Ricardo Bofill

Babote Tower

to domestic life of the past, with 19th-C. interiors and traditional costumes, old sewing machines, Christmas cribs and old postcards and newspapers.

Musée Fabre

39, Bd Sarrail,
☎ **04 67 14 83 00.**
Open daily except Mon., 9am-5.30pm, 5pm Sat., Sun. and public holidays.
Admission charge.
In 1825, François-Xavier Fabre, who was himself a painter but mainly a great collector, donated 224 paintings, drawings, engravings, bronzes and thousands of other works to the city. Right up until his death in 1835, he continued to add to the collection. Other donors also gave or bequeathed art to the museum. The museum, housed in a former Jesuit college built in the 15th and 16th C., now has one of the best collections in France of

paintings by Italian, Flemish and French Old Masters (Raphael, Veronese, Poussin, Greuze, Courbet). Frédéric Bazille and other local artists are represented.

Musée de la Faculté de Pharmacie

15, Av. Charles-Flahault,
☎ **04 67 54 80 62.**
Open Tues. and Fri. 10am-noon.
Admission charge.
Herbals, jars, pots, documents, instruments and preparation equipment are all here to teach you about the history of pharmacy, medicine and surgery. Two pharmacies have been reconstructed, originally from the 19th C. and the early 20th C., as well as an unusual 18th-C. Korean pharmacy.

Musée Atger

2, Rue de l'École-de-Médecine,
☎ **04 67 66 27 77.**

Open 10am-6pm except Sat., Sun. and university holidays.

LUNARET ZOOLOGICAL PARK

50, Av. Agropolis,
☎ **04 67 63 27 63.**
Open daily 8am-7pm (5pm or 6pm in the winter).
Free admission.
5¹/₂ miles (9 km) of roads run through the 198 acres (80 ha) of the park inhabited by more than 700 animals. The natural enclosures are bounded by ditches making it possible to watch the gibbons, panthers and chimpanzees... Do not miss the huge tropical greenhouse and the otter pool. Otters are an endangered species and have been protected in France for 20 years.

Free admission.
This museum is inside the Faculty of Medicine, between the library and the Anatomy Museum, and bears the name of its first donor. It contains some excellent exhibits from the archives of the Faculty of Medicine, including more than 1,000 drawings from the French,

Italian, German, Flemish and Dutch schools of the 16th to 18th C. There are landscapes, cartoons, pencil drawings and aquatints by Tiepolo, Rubens, Rigaud and Fragonard among others. Only part of the collection is on show.

✿ Agropolis
951, Av. Agropolis,
☎ 04 67 04 75 04.
Open daily except Tues.,
2-6pm.
Admission charge.
Peasants and landscapes, food and nutrition. These are the two themes developed over the 16,000 sq. ft (5,000 m²) of this museum dedicated to the **food chain**, 'from soil

cultivation to the food we eat' in the modern world. Scientists present their agricultural research here. The general public, on the other hand, continues to ask itself the vital question: what shall we eat tomorrow?

Guided tour of centre
The Tourist Office (Pl. de la Comédie, ☎ 04 67 60 60 60) organises a guided tour of the town centre on foot. The tour lasts two hours, taking in interesting streets and façades, and a visit inside one of the mansions normally closed to the public. Themed tours are also organised on subjects such as history, monuments, culture, etc. There is a light rail train which leaves from the Esplanade Charles-de-Gaulle and runs through the town centre and Antigone

A HELICOPTER RIDE

Aéro 34, Aéroport de Montpellier, Mauguio, ☎ 04 67 65 18 55. If you want to see the region from another perspective, consider taking a ride in a helicopter. There are two options. You can either fly over the Camargue to Aigues-Mortes or over the foothills of the Cévennes to Pic Saint-Loup. Both of these rides last about 20 minutes and cost around 760 F for two people – a little expensive but quite unforgettable. You can also choose which route you take.

(from 10am in summer and 2pm in winter, ticket required).

Promenade du Peyrou
This long promenade is where open-air festivals were held in the days of Louis XIV. Access is via a triumphal arch, which has replaced the former Porte du Peyrou, designed by a pupil of Mansart. A statue of the mounted Sun King has stood in the centre of the promenade since 1718; he is

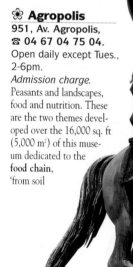

Louis XIV, at the beginning of the Promenade du Peyrou

Triumphal arch, the entrance to the Promenade du Peyrou

looking towards the town. The promenade ends in a sort of temple decorated with sculptures inspired by marine themes. From here there is a lovely view over the town and to the Cévennes. In the distance, the Saint-Clément aqueduct, dubbed 'les Arceaux', which brings water to the town, is a miniature version of the Pont du Gard.

Sweet things

How about something sweet? Here are a few addresses: **Guy Auzier**, 3, Rue du Courreau, ☎ 04 67 92 63 35, daily except Sun. and Mon. 9am-noon and 2-6pm: who specialises in sugared almonds, gums and liquorice. **Robert Valgalier**, 18, Rue du Fbg-Saint-Jaumes, ☎ 04 67 63 30 61, daily except Mon. morning, 6am-1pm and 2.30-7.45pm: this master *patissier-chocolatier* won first prize in the Hérault Gourmand competition for his white nougat (16 F for 3¹/₂ oz/100 g); he also makes Écussons de Montpellier. **Chez Deleuze**, 39, Route de Toulouse, ☎ 04 67 42 50 68, daily except Sun., 8.30am-noon and 2-7pm, closed 20 Aug.–10 Sept. This

family business opened in 1889. The shop sells the best marshmallows in the world, flavoured with violets or orange-flower water (5 F each) and its famous liquorice (90 F for 2¹/₄ lb/1 kg). Visit **Godiva**, 5, Rue de la Loge, ☎ 04 67 66 16 21, to taste the *grisettes* (see p. 40).

Le Jardin des Glaces
25, Bd Sarrailh,
☎ **04 67 66 01 07.**
Open1 March–30 Oct. daily, 11am-2 pm. You must visit this ice-cream parlour, with its 250 seats overlooking the esplanade. Everything is natural 'no powders or colour-

ings', and it is hard to choose from among the 40 flavours: mango, lychee, tea, papaya and coconut.

La Grande-Motte

This seaside resort was created from a wilderness of water, sand and lagoons, one of the most ambitious projects of the 1960s. Its 'pyramids' have been decried as often as they have been admired. Be that as it may, they are now part of the landscape in which green spaces play such as important part. The sandy beach is extensive and there is a marina and a host of leisure activities.

The solar pyramids
When work began on the port and access roads to the resort in 1965, the architect **Jean Balladur** used the pyramid as the basic shape for his apartment blocks, because 'it made it possible to arrange recessed terracing on each level'. From the sea, the buildings seem to float on the horizon. They have given the town a unique identity.

Nature at La Grande-Motte
Almost one third of the resort consists of green areas, planted with 30,000 trees. There are 9½ miles (15 km) of avenues along the coast and across the lawns that separate the buildings. To protect the chain of dunes, the Conservatoire du Littoral, the coastal preservation authority, acquired 865 acres (350 ha) of land on the Petit Travers and the Grand Travers on the lido.

Water-sports
Water-sports, yachting (1,400 berths in the port and 130 temporary moorings) and sea angling – there is plenty to do on the water. There is also a swimming pool at the **Espace**

Grand-Bleu which is in the middle of a pine forest and has a giant flume, rivers, a sports pool and aquagym. (195, Rue Saint-Louis, ☎ 04 67 56 28 23. Admission charge).

The beaches
The Plage de l'Epi or Plage de l'Est beside the Ponant strait is ¾ mile (1 km) long but is not safe for bathing. The west beach, 3¾ miles (6 km) long, is full of holidaymakers and people from Montpellier who are very fond of the dunes of the Grand Travers. In summer, every square inch of the beach is jealously guarded. If you want peace and quiet come early in the morning or late in the afternoon.

Spotcheck
E4

Hérault

Things to do

Water-sports and fishing
Panoramic aquarium
La Grande-Motte golf courses
Trip in a junk

Things to do with children

L'Éspace Grand-Bleu

Within easy reach

*Lunel, 17 km N, p. 262,
Aigues-Mortes, 14 km NE,
p. 264,
Le Grau-du-Roi, 6 km E,
p. 266.*

Tourist office

La Grande-Motte:
☎ 04 67 56 00 61

The real Grande-Motte

This was the **highest dune on the coast**, more than 20 ft (5 m) high, and it was this that gave the resort the name 'Grande Motte'. It was also the first resort centre, known as 'Point zéro' but it is a little

neglected and only symbolic nowadays. You can get there from the Casino beach along a promenade lined with cafés.

Porte Saint-Jean

This architectural curiosity stands at the entrance to the town on an internal road. On St. John's Day (midsummer day) at noon, when the sun is at its highest, the rays penetrate the opening pierced at the top of the building and project a perfect circle onto the table of the bridge.

TRIP IN A JUNK

To navigate the waters in the Chinese fashion, take a trip on the most exotic boat at La Grande-Motte. The wooden junk *Suwansan* will take you out every day to swim in the waters or simply enjoy the cruise, which lasts 2–4 hours. Contact: Croisières Éole (Quai d'Honneur, ☎ 04 67 56 19 36).

The panoramic Aquarium

Esplanade de la Capitainerie,
☎ 04 67 56 85 23.
Open daily, mid-Jun. to mid-Sept., 10am-noon and 2.30-7.30pm and 8.45am-11.30pm. Call first out of season.
Fish large and small from the French coasts and further afield can be seen in the 50 tanks containing some 300 species. They include turtles, murex and sharks.

La Grande-Motte golf courses

The two 18-hole courses were designed by the famous Robert Trent Jones and cover 250 acres (100 ha). The Pink Flamingo course is 6,888 yards (6,200 m) long and has quite

a few obstacles, such as fast greens and bunkers. The Seagull course is shorter and very good for perfecting your swing. The six-hole course, beside the pine grove, called the Herring-gull, is perfect for beginners (☎ 04 67 56 05 00).
Beginner's lessons are one hour and cost 240 F.

Pony-trekking

Manade Gre, Domaine de la Loua, Route de la Petite-Camargue, ☎ 04 67 56 71 16. Open all year round.
Visit the bull-rearing facility on horseback. If there has been a birth at the stud, you can spend the day watching the branding of the new animals, as well as see the ear clips being attached to the young bull, which enables an owner to recognise his own animal at a glance.

Palavas-les-Flots

When the fashion for sea-bathing started in around 1850, this little fishing village became the favourite beach of the residents of Montpellier. It was once linked to the city by a quaint little train, which inspired the cartoonist Dubout, and now extends as far as Carnon-Plage. It has a huge sandy beach, a pretty fishing harbour and a busy quayside, making it one of the most pleasant resorts on the coast.

The town by the sea

The town is split in two by the river Lez, the two halves being linked by two bridges. The strangest attraction in this seaside town is a **cable car** designed like a ski-lift with individual chairs, strung across the channel at its mouth. There are no buildings of special interest but the lively quayside is lined with

souvenir shops and cafés and ice-cream parlours and the atmosphere is pleasant, especially on summer evenings.

Musée Dubout

Redoute de Ballestras, Île du Levant,
☎ **04 67 68 56 41.**

Open Jul.–Aug., daily, 4pm-midnight; daily except Mon. 2-6pm in winter and public holidays.
Admission charge.
Hundreds of drawings and objects that belonged to the cartoonist Dubout are housed in this 18th-C. museum. It can be reached by free shuttle boat which is an attraction in itself.

The Cathedral of Maguelone

Open 9am-6pm.
The cathedral stands on an islet and is the remains of a 6th-C. bishopric. It stands in a landscape of changing colours. The building was fought over by Catholics and Protestants during the Wars of Religion and was dismantled on the orders of Richelieu in 1622. It was restored in the 19th C., and has lost its crenelations and machicolations but retained a handsome **sculpted pediment** over the Romanesque entrance. It is a delightful place, and a **Music Festival** is held here in July (☎ 04 67 66 73 89).

Plage de Maguelone

The beach can be reached by car from Palavas (parking charge) or from Villeneuve-lès-Maguelone. Near the car park there are showers,

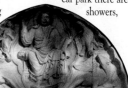

Spotcheck
E4

Hérault

Things to do

Musée Dubout
Beaches and watersports
Exploring the lagoons area
The little train

Within easy reach

Sète, p. 218,
Aigues-Mortes , p. 264,
Le Grau-du-Roi , p. 266.

Tourist office

Palavas:
☎ 04 67 07 73 34

a snack-bar and funboard and jet-ski facilities. The beach is long but there is no lifeguard. Its unspoilt look attracts naturists who go there to sunbathe as soon as the sun rises. A little train runs from the car park to the beach.

EXPLORING THE POND AREA

Information at the Tourist Office.
There are three signposted routes around the lagoons of Prévost, Le Grec and Méjean. The longest of these is 6¼ miles (10 km) and takes 2½–3½ hours. The first (blue) route centres on Maguelone cathedral; the second (yellow) takes you through the narrow strip of land separating the lagoons of Méjean and Le Grec; and the green signposts lead to Pérols. You will see oyster-catchers, plovers, seagulls, egrets, avocets and pink flamingoes along the way.

Carnon-Plage

This is a small, modern resort about 3 miles (5 km) from Palavas. Apart from the beach, you can visit the protected dunes of the **Petit and Grand Travers** (owned by the Conservatoire du Littoral which has thus prevented Carnon and La Grande-Motte from becoming one huge strip). There are narrow access roads for cars, but you should take time to explore the area on foot and with binoculars or camera in hand, to see the wildlife.

The other beaches

The beaches to the left of the canal are gently sloping and of fine sand, ideal for children. They adjoin Carnon-Plage 2¼ miles (3.5 km) away. To the right of the canal the beaches are steeper, more exposed and ideal

for sporting activites (windsurfing, beach volley-ball); they adjoin Frontignan 9½ miles (15 km) away. As everywhere, there are clubs for children and pedalo, lilo and beach umbrella hire. The many camp sites are quite crowded in July and August.

The little train

☎ 04 67 07 73 34.
Open daily, 4pm to midnight, every half hour. *Admission charge.*
The head of the driver pops out of the twisted, spitting funnel. The open carriages are painted blue, yellow and bright red and on the roof, a little man in a striped tee-shirt is fishing in a goldfish bowl; behind there is a very fat lady. To discover Palavas, take this little train based on Dubout's cartoons. Once a week it runs as far as Maguelone.

The Étangs du Montpelliérain

Mauguio, Pérols, Méjean and Vic

These lagoons lying just off the coast, near Montpellier provide a haven for bird life. They are separated from the sea by a coastal chain of sand dunes. Take the time to hike or ramble through the area. You will enjoy the wonderful colours of the landscape, the cries of the thousands of birds and the relative tranquillity of the villages.

The plant life

This depends on the degree of salinity of the soil. The *sansouire*, a meadow temporarily flooded by salt water, is covered in samphire, which concentrates the salt in its reddish shoots. Saladella prefers to expel the salt in tiny crystals which cover its branches. This plant is sometimes called 'sea lavender' because in August it smothers the dried-out lagoons in a wave of mauve flowers. Sand camomile, maram-grass and sea-holly grow on the dunes.

Samphire

Étang de Mauguio or Étang de l'Or

The fourth of the coastal lagoons covers more than 7,413 acres (3,000 ha). Its shores are often marshy and unsafe. They lie beside pastures or former salt-ponds frequented by birds, especially pink flamingoes. The commune of Mauguio, which is very close to Montpellier-Fréjorgues airport, is notable for its attractive Place de la Mairie.

Pond fever

This disease of the marshes is known locally as *malaïgue*, meaning 'bad water'. The phenomenon occurs when the summer is particularly hot. The water becomes putrid and turns reddish, and may cause plants and animals to die. This is because oxygen levels drop and, poisonous fermentation increases, giving off a sulphurous smell. Bacteria develop, consuming

Spotcheck

E4

Hérault

Things to do

Birdwatching at Étang
de L'Estagnol
Maison des Vins du
Languedoc at Lattes

Within easy reach

*Étang de Thau, p. 216,
Sète, p. 218,
Aigues-Mortes, p. 264,
La Grau-du-Roi, p. 268.*

Tourist Office

Vic-la-Gardiole:
☎ 04 67 78 94 43
Montpellier: ☎ 04 67 60 60 60

the detritus and regenerating the water, but turning it red. It is proof of how delicate the balance of nature is here.

Pérols

This is the smallest of the lagoonside communities with a lively bullfighting tradition. Unfortunately, the large wine-growing estates have been replaced by commercial activities, mainly the Montpellier fairground and exhibition halls.

Lattes

This was the port of Montpellier in the Middle Ages. It was abandoned when the delta became blocked by sand dunes. If you are interested in the history of the region, visit the **Musée Archéologique** (Open daily except Tue., 10am-5.30pm, or 10am-noon and 2-5.30pm). It is housed in an elegant farmhouse which belonged to the Impressionist painter Frédéric Bazille, and contains Gallo-Roman artefacts and finds from local excavations. The Syndicat des Coteaux-du-Languedoc (Mas de Saporta, ☎ 04 67 06 04 44. Open daily except Sun.) runs a **Maison des Vins du Languedoc** which is installed in a late 17th- and early 18th-C. farmhouse of a winemaker. There is a restaurant serving local food, a retail outlet selling wines and local foods and a *gustarium* which will teach you all about the local wines.

Étang de L'Estagnol

This lagoon is near Villeneuve-lès-Maguelonne and is slightly salty due to its salt springs. It is edged with reed-beds, which between October and March are inhabited by thousands of birds, ducks, teal, coots and purple herons. The miniature hills that surround the lagoon and the marsh make it easier to watch the ducks which are even more numerous during the hunting season.

❀ Étang de Vic and Vic-la-Gardiole

The belfry and machicolations of the **fortified Church of Sainte-Léocadie** of Vic-la-Gardiole are built of fossil limestone (that is to say agglomerates of fossilised oysters and other shells) and dominate the ponds. A subway at the entrance to the church leads to the Domaine de Maureilhan, some 2,500 ft (750 m) away. The **Cave Viticole de Rabelais** (☎ 04 67 78 15 59) will enable you to buy Muscat et Vin de Pays des Collines de la Moure (the Mireval vineyard). You can also buy from Jean-Pierre Maraval, at the Domaine de La Capelle (☎ 04 67 78 15 14). If you want to walk all or some of the 31 miles (50 km) of **signposted paths**, you should contact the Tourist Office of Vic-la-Gardiole (☎ 04 67 78 94 43).

LAGOON FISH

The lagoons are full of sea-fish including sea-perch (which remains there from Apr. to Nov.), gilthead bream (which eats shellfish), grey mullet and eel (which lives here for about ten years before making for the open sea). In the rock-pools there are mussels, crabs and prawns.

The Montpelliérain châteaux

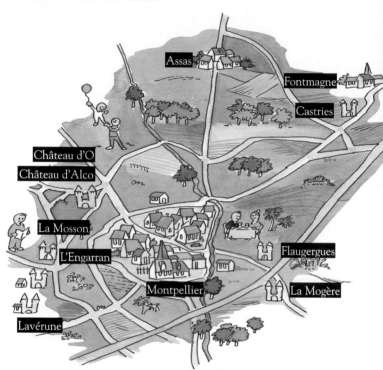

E legant marquesses would have felt at home in these 18th-C. follies on the outskirts of Montpellier. They are supposed to have been so called because of the foliage (*folium* meaning 'leaf' in Latin) which obscures them. However, the more likely explanation is that their design and construction, a madly extravagant caprice, defied all reason. Whether privately or publicly owned, these châteaux and their grounds are now open to the public.

Château de Flaugergues

RARE PLANTS

Another of the beauties of the châteaux is the number of rare trees which the local nobility imported from the ends of the earth to grace their parks. They include the *Ginkgo biloba*, which was only cultivated in the gardens of the Imperial Palace in China. Linnaeus gave it this scientific name because the leaves have double lobes, which turn a luminous yellow in the autumn. It is also known as the forty écu tree, because this was the price of a cutting under the Ancien Régime, a vast sum, and several years' wages for a gardener. The first ginkgo introduced into France was planted in 1788 in Montpellier at 3, Rue du Carré-du-Roi (where it continues to flourish!)

❀ Flaugergues
1744, Avenue Albert-Einstein,
☎ 04 67 65 51 72.
Open Jul.–Aug., daily except Mon., 2.30-6.30pm, or on appointment.
Admission charge.
This **folly** was built in 1690 in an Italianate style. Note the extraordinary staircase with its vaulted hanging keys which rises through three storeys without any support. A **formal garden** and grounds containing bamboos, blue cedars, parasol pines, white oaks and arbutus complete the ensemble. In the cellar you can taste and buy wine made here.

Spotcheck
E4

Things to do
Flaugergues and its gardens
Nuits de Castries
The Domaine de Grammont

Within easy reach
Étang de Thau, p. 216,
Lunel, p. 262,
Aigues-Mortes, p. 264.

Tourist office
Montpellier:
☎ 04 67 60 60 60

La Mogère
Route de Vauguières,
☎ 04 67 65 72 01.
Open Whitsun–1 Oct., daily, 2.30-6.30pm.
Admission charge.

This château, next to that of Flaugergues, dates from 1716. It is surrounded by huge grounds. The former kitchen

Staircase of the Château de Flaugergues (1690). The property has been in the ownwership of the same family ever since it was built and is a good example of a traditional local wine-producing estate.

garden, with its monumental fountain decorated with shells, rockery, mosaics and laughing cherubs, is impressive. The Vicomte de Saporta, who still lives on his estate, often receives visitors himself.

The Château d'Alco and the Château d'O

These two châteaux once belonged to the General Council of the Hérault. L'Alco, Avenue des Moulins, is a handsome residence in the Languedoc style, surrounded by formal gardens (open to the public), which is now a seat of local government, with a very smart restaurant. The **Château d'O**, in the same avenue opens its grounds on Saturdays and Sundays (8am-6pm). The gardens and the huge fountain dominated by a stone tribune were laid out in 1762.

Château d'Alco

The Château de la Piscine

This château is right in town on the Avenue de Lodèbe (between the *gendarmerie* and the Super Monoprix). It is a mysterious **folly** but it is not open to the public. Only the park may be visited and only by appointment (☎ 04 67 75 73 56). The name of the estate comes from the old *Mas de la Peyssine* (fishpond) which was built here in

Château d'Alco

The Domaine de Grammont

This château is now owned by the city of Montpellier and has reception rooms and auditoriums. It hosts many cultural and sporting events in the middle of the superb **park** (free visit). The building is flanked by a neo-gothic chapel and has an entrance consisting of a peristyle flanked by two staircases. Botanists came to set their plants here from the 16th to the 18th C. Today there is a horticultural centre which specialises in growing the red canna lily, the city's symbol.

1435. A huge lawn runs down to the groves. There are monumental vases, statues of the Seasons, and a classic fountain set on a huge lawn.

Fountain at the Château d'O

The Château de la Mosson

Between Celleneuve and Juvignac,
Open daily, 8am-7pm.
All that remains of this folly is the castle, deprived of its woodwork, grilles, sculptures, paintings, mirrors and statues. Only the music room with its elegant plasterwork has been restored. The garden is now a huge field of weeds and even the pool has lost its decor of statues and shells. Yet the place has an inscrutable charm and, even before restoration, it is worth a visit.

The Château de l'Engarran

Towards Lavérune,
☎ 04 67 47 00 02.
Park visit by appointment but wine sales daily, noon-7pm.
Little museum is free.
This is a residence with rounded corners and geometrical flowerbeds. Three masks of life (youth, maturity and

Château de Grammont

old age) in a female face adorn the rear façade and there is a dilapidated pool. A very wise folly, in fact.

Lavérune
In the village centre.
Park open daily,
24 hours.
Free admission.
Visit the Italianate **Music Room**, decorated with plasterwork and built on the model of that of Mosson (information at the Town Hall, ☎ 04 67 27 59 54). A monumental, exuberantly decorated portal hides the machicolations and arrow-slits which defend access to the residence. The **Musée Hofer-Burry** (open Sat.–Sun., 3-6pm, admission charge) in the grounds of the château exhibits paintings and sculptures by contemporary artists from the region.

Castries
Rue du Cantonat (by the N 113 and N 110),
☎ 04 67 70 68 66.
Open 1 Apr.–15 Dec., daily except Mon., 2.30-5pm; Jan.–Apr., Sat. and Sun., 2.30-5pm.
Admission charge.
This Renaissance building contains a gallery 106½ ft (32 m) long in which the États généraux du Languedoc used to meet. It still contains paintings from the school of Boucher, family portraits and lovely furniture. An **aqueduct** 4½ miles (7 km) long waters the gardens designed by Le Nôtre, who created those of Versailles. In 1985, the château was bequeathed to the Académie Française, which meets here annually.
Every July, the **Nuits de Castries** are held

here. This is a music, theatre and dance festival (information, ☎ 04 67 06 84 84).

Assas
7½ miles (12 km) N from the town,
☎ 04 67 59 62 45.
Open 1 May–1 Nov., Sun and bank holidays, 2-6pm.
Admission charge.
This folly has a slightly medieval air, its thick walls flanked by round towers. An elegant balustrade conceals the roof. The reception rooms overlook the garden and in the summer are used for recitals of **classical and Baroque music** (there is a wonderful 18th-C. clavicord which was has been used to make many recordings), as well as concerts of contemporary music (information from the château).

Castries aqueduct

The Montpellier *garrigue*

and Pic Saint-Loup

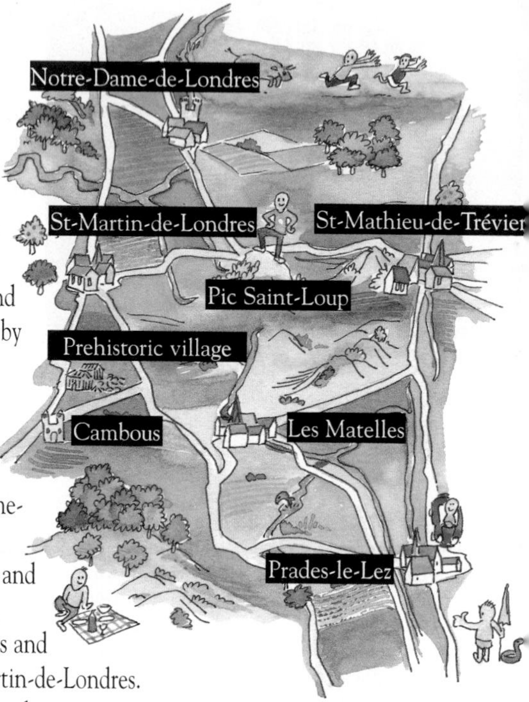

As soon as you leave Montpellier, you enter the fragrant *garrigues* (scrubland), with its deep gorges and steep cliffs dominated by the Séranne and the Pic Saint-Loup, high hills from which there is an almost limitless view. This limestone ridge is 2½ miles (4 km) long, and 2,193 ft (658 m) high, overlooking the Hortus and the basin of Saint-Martin-de-Londres. It is well worth taking a day to see it.

Notre-Dame-de-Londres

St-Martin-de-Londres

St-Mathieu-de-Trévier

Pic Saint-Loup

Prehistoric village

Cambous

Les Matelles

Prades-le-Lez

Prades-le-Lez

Domaine de Restinclières

☎ 04 67 10 39 40.
Open daily 9am-noon and 2-5pm.
Free admission.

This 18th-C. château, which now houses the environmental office of the *département*, stands in grounds of 530 acres (215 ha) at the entrance to the *garrigue*. It is bounded by the rivers Lez and Liron and has a lovely formal garden with geometric flowerbeds. Many pleasant walks on various themes and several picnic areas are to be enjoyed in this tranquil place.

Les Matelles

Fortified village

This village beside the Liron is one of the oldest inhabited sites in the *garrigue*. The well-restored houses and little squares give it its charm.

Cambous prehistoric village

The **Musée préhistorique** (☎ 04 67 84 30 23; open 15 June–15 Sept daily except Tues. and Fri.; 3-6pm; the rest of the year Fri. and Sun. same opening hours. Admission charge) has an interesting collection.

Viols-en-Laval
Cambous prehistoric village

Open 1 Jul.–15 Sept., 9am-noon and 2-6pm, daily except Tues.; the rest of the year, Sat.–Sun. same opening hours. *Admission charge.*

This is **the oldest village in France**. It was discovered in 1967 and dates from about 2,000 BC. The buildings are amazingly well preserved. There were four hamlets of eight to 10 huts, one of which has been reconstructed. The walls were about $6\frac{1}{2}$ ft (2 m) thick and the roof was thatched or made of soft limestone, cut into thin flat tiles. There is proof of a civilisation of peasants and shepherds (granite grinding-stones and flints) and there are menhir-statues. This extraordinary complex has not been fully excavated.

ON FOOT, HORSE-BACK, MOUNTAIN BIKE — OR FLYING?

If you want to look for fossils, it is best to go on foot, but you can also take a mountain bike or go on horseback. Inquire at Tashunka, Route de Montoulieu, Saint-Bauzille (☎ 04 67 73 76 67). You could also go gliding, (Info. at the Mas de Londres ☎ 04 67 55 01 42), or parachuting with the Ecole de Montoulieu (☎ 04 67 73 73 48).

Le Pic Saint-Loup
Climbing

The Pic Saint-Loup is part of the hill country, with its high plateaux (*causses*), narrow valleys and sinks. The sign-posted climbing path starts $10\frac{1}{2}$ miles (17 km) from Ganges (p. 246). The round trip takes about 2½ hours. Try to avoid the hottest time of the day, especially at the summit. The **view from the top** is over the Hortus escarpment, Saint-Martin-de-Londres and the plain of Languedoc.

Spotcheck
D4-E4

Hérault

Things to do

Domaine de Restinclières
Rambling, mountain-biking and riding
Crambous prehistoric village

Within easy reach

*La vallée de l'Hérault, p. 244,
Ganges, p. 246.*

Tourist office

Montpellier:
☎ 04 67 60 60 60

According to legend, in the Middle Ages, three men, Guiral, Loup and Clair, were in love with the same woman. She sent them off to war to prove their valour but when they returned she was gone. Mad with grief they became hermits, each occupying a hill which has taken their name (Aigoual, Saint-Loup and Saint-Clair).

Le ravin des Arcs
Rambling

This is a **canyon** $6\frac{1}{4}$ miles (10 km) long. There is a fine view from Véziers. The D 1 then passes through the breach cut between the Hortus and the Pic. You reach Montpellier via Saint-Mathieu-de-Tréviers.

Sommières

Sommières, close to Nîmes, stands between the Causses and the Languedoc coast. The old town developed around a Roman bridge, built over the Vidourle during the reign of Tiberius. The vestiges of the Château des Bermond dominate the medieval town which, with its shady lanes, arcaded squares and overhanging houses, has kept its ancient character.

Lawrence Durrell and Sommières

The author of *The Alexandria Quartet* spent the end of his life at Sommières (he died in 1990). This is what he wrote about it to friends: 'I must confess I have never seen anywhere as lovely as Sommières. Sommières is extremely amusing, deeply marked by the spirit of Raimu and of Fernandel… The local stories are really hilarious. Naturally, the deviant world of mopeds and hairdressing salons with television have begun to invade the region…' (*Spirit of Place*).

Château fort

This 11th-C. fortress was built in a strategic location, overlooking the Roman bridge, the only crossing-point on the Vidourle between the Cévennes and the sea. All that remains is a tower 80 ft (25 m) high. Take the time to climb the 74 steps when the weather is fine. From here you will be able to see the Pic Saint-Loup and the hill on which Villevieille is built.

Tour de l'Horloge

The clocktower stands beside the Roman bridge and is carved with the arms of the city which include the river, the bridge and its two towers (the tower facing the clock-tower was destroyed in the 18th C.). The bell, installed in 1657, weighs nearly 3,000 lb (1,323 kg).

Place des Docteurs-Dax and Place Jean-Jaurès

The Place des Docteurs-Dax is the **marketplace** (the market is held every Saturday morning). It is surrounded by picturesque arcades of various shapes and sizes which form a homogenous ensemble. Note the **Passage de Reilhe** leading to Rue Marx-Dormoy and the

SOMMIÈRES EARTH

Sepiolite (meerschaum) was first extracted near Salinelles. The first deposit of magnesite was found in 1815; in 1875, Émilien Dumas performed the first geological surveys from a drill-hole dug 20 years before. This mineral has the unique property of being able to absorb grease, and it was used for washing raw wool. It is still today used as a stain-remover. In Morocco, it was known as Fez soap, and was used for washing hair. In France, is is known as '*pierre de taches*' or '*terre de Sommières*'. It was once used for making the bowls of pipes and is still used as a building material.

steps cut into the thickness of the pillars linking the houses of the Rue du Pont to the Place du Marché. The Place Jean-Jaurès is the site of the old **corn market**, and now the commercial centre of the village.

La Rue de la Taillade

The name indicates that the street was cut into the cliff to enable the Roman road to pass over the bridge. It is lined with shops and 17th- and 18th-C. town houses which are tall and narrow due to lack of space. But behind these modest frontages there are grand staircases, vast halls and elegant wrought iron work. Note the **Ruelle Bombe-Cul** between no. 38 and no. 40, an old vaulted passage.

Around Sommières

Le Château de Villevieille

**About 1 mile (1.5 km) N, ☎ 04 66 80 01 62.
Open Jun.–Oct. 3-7pm, or by appointment.
*Admission charge.***
The village depends on its castle, the ramparts of one being attached to the wall of the other. It consists of a forbidding 11th-C. castle keep and three main buildings around an inner courtyard. The medieval architecture is enhanced by a delicate Renaissance frontage. Inside,

Spotcheck
E3

Gard

Things to do

Le Château de Villevieille

Within easy reach

*Nîmes, 28 km NE, p. 252,
Lunel, 13 km S, p. 262.*

Tourist Office

Sommières:
☎ 04 66 80 99 30

Passage dit de BOMBE CUL

one of the rooms is lined with Cordoba leather and there is a superb collection of china. In August, concerts are held in the courtyard.

Excursions with local guides

Associations des Terres de Sommières,
☎ 04 66 80 32 00.
If you take time to hire an enthusiastic local guide, you will learn all about the historic, cultural and natural peculiarities of the region. You can also take a tour on a particular theme, such as wine and the vineyards, Sommières or its surroundings, the *garrigue* or the olive trees. Guides also offer night-time excursions.

Château de Villevieille

The Hérault valley

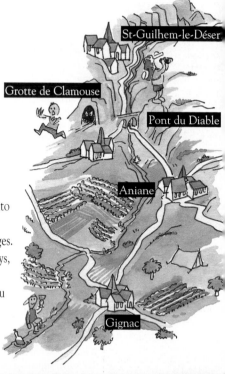

St-Guilhem-le-Déser

Grotte de Clamouse

Pont du Diable

Aniane

Gignac

The river has cut deep into the limestone *garrigues*, creating passes and gorges. It irrigates the cultivated valleys, finally emerging into the Languedoc plain at the Pont du Diable, a meandering 43-mile (69-km) course. Follow its route for a great day out.

The Gorges of Hérault

After crossing a desolate landscape of limestone escarpments and boulders, you enter the gorges, which are quite wide up to Saint-Guilhem, then very narrow. There are a few terraced vineyards, a little meadow and two or three olive trees. The sun-drenched wilderness is quite grandiose.

Saint-Guilhem-le-Désert

'A rose in the heart of the mountains'

This is what ancient travellers called this oasis of greenery in the midst of the wilderness. The *sauta-rocs* (rock-jumpers), as the villagers are called, like to gather in the **Place de la Liberté**, in the shade of a giant plane tree, 18 ft 3 in (5.5 m) in diameter, which was planted in 1848. There are several easy **walks** you can take from the village. The walk around the Vallée du Bout-du-Monde, or the Cirque de l'Infernet, starts at the ramparts. You can walk up the course of the Verdus to its source which is in a magnificent setting (a 1-hour round trip). From the Rue du Bout-du-Monde, a road on the right leads to the gate in the city walls from Cap de la Croux; a footpath on the right will take you to the ruins of the castle.

Romanesque Abbey of Saint-Guilhem-le-Desert

The **view** of the village from the castle is magnificent.

Abbey of Saint-Guilhem

Open 8.30am-noon and 2.30-6.30pm.

This is one of the best examples of Languedoc **Romanesque architecture** on the route to St. James of Compostella. It was built in the 11th C. in a white stone which contrasts with the blue sky. The tall narrow nave, 60 x 20 ft (18 x 6 m), the porch-belfry and sculpted portal are of particular interest. Unfortunately, the cloisters were sold bit by bit and reconstituted at The Cloisters, a branch of the Metropolitan Museum of Art in New York!

Le Pont du Diable

Benedictine monks built the so-called Devil's Bridge in the 11th C. The Devil had demanded the soul of the first creature to cross the bridge. It was a dog, with saucepans attached to his tail (and behind him came the priests, blessing the bridge). There is a modern bridge now which offers a view of the gorges.

Grotte de Clamouse

Between Saint-Guilhem-le-Désert and Saint-Jean-de-Fos,
☎ 04 67 57 71 05.

Open daily, 10am-5pm, 6pm or 7pm depending on the season.

The name of this cave means 'howler' in Languedoc. It is almost a **Museum of Minerals** and was discovered in 1945 after a bad drought. There are chambers on two levels linked by passages. The Porch Room and the White Corridor, lined with rivulets of aragonite, are the most beautiful.

THE GÉOSPACE OBSERVATORY

☎ 04 67 03 49 49.
Open Jul.–Aug., Tues.–Sun., 10am-noon and 2-5pm.
The seven cupolas of the Géospace observatory stand in the midst of a fragrant *garrigue*. 'See to know' is the maxim shared by geologists, astronomers and botanists who have created a research area here where one can learn about their fields of expertise. On some evenings, you can even watch the stars from here, and the resident astronomers will help you make out the constellations.

Saint-Jean-de-Fos

Orjolerii

3, Route d'Aniane,
☎ 04 67 57 77 25.

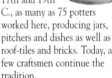

There have been potteries in this village since the 15th C., thanks to its clay deposits. Between the 17th and 19th C., as many as 75 potters worked here, producing jars, pitchers and dishes as well as roof-tiles and bricks. Today, a few craftsmen continue the tradition.

Gignac

La Maison du Fleuve Hérault

Barrage de la Meuse,
☎ 04 67 57 99 00.

This museum explains all there is to know about the Hérault from where it rises on the slopes of Mont Aigoual to the mouth of the river at Grau-d'Agde.

Ganges
and the Vis gorges

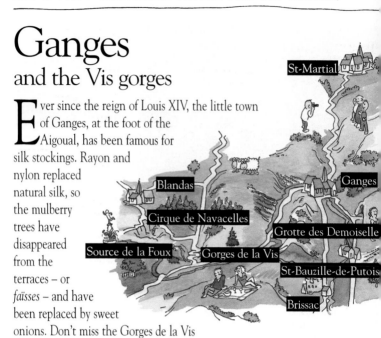

Ever since the reign of Louis XIV, the little town of Ganges, at the foot of the Aigoual, has been famous for silk stockings. Rayon and nylon replaced natural silk, so the mulberry trees have disappeared from the terraces – or *faïsses* – and have been replaced by sweet onions. Don't miss the Gorges de la Vis and the Cirque de Navacelles, major tourist attractions.

St-Martial

Blandas

Cirque de Navacelles

Source de la Foux

Gorges de la Vis

Ganges

Grotte des Demoiselle

St-Bauzille-de-Putois

Brissac

Ganges
Former silk capital

The huge ruined buildings beside the Hérault and the Vis are reminders of the rich industrial past of the silk stocking capital of France. In the late 18th C. the town was producing more than 80,000 pairs a year. The old town centre with its labyrinthine streets boasts lovely 16th- and 17th-C. mansions, little squares with fountains and vaulted passages. It is said that it was here that the Protestants who rebelled between 1702 and 1704

Saint-Maurice-de-Navacelles

acquired the nickname of *camisard*, because they looted a shirt factory.

Saint-Martial
L'Artisan du Cachemire
Avenue Cabanevieille,
☎ 04 67 81 35 83.
Open Wed., Fri.and Sat. 2-7pm, Sun. 2-6pm, every afternoon in summer.
Patrick Ducros is a native of the Cévennes and in order to stay in the area he has worked hard and has created a small

factory which specialises in cashmere knitwear. There are 87 colourways for his tailor-made models. The prices are to match, from 1,400 F to 2,000 F.

Saint-Bauzille-de-Putois
La Grotte des Demoiselles
☎ 04 67 73 70 02.
Open daily in summer 9.30-6.15; rest of the year 9.30-noon and 2-4.15pm.
Admission charge.
This cave beneath the plain of Thaurac was first explored

SAINT-BAUZILLE-DE-PUTOIS WHITE-WATER CANOEING

After the Grotte des Demoiselles, continue on to Saint-Bauzille-de-Putois, where you can rent kayaks and paddle them for 2, 8³/₄ or 10¹/₂ miles (3, 14 or 17 km) (return trip by minibus). Contact (from Apr. to Sept.) Canoë Le Moulin (☎ 04 67 73 30 73), or the Centre Les Lutins Cévenols (☎ 04 67 73 70 30) which also offer accommodation in rooms or dormitories.

in 1780. Since 1928, a tunnel containing a funicular railway accesses the 'cathedral of the abysses' in which there is a Virgin and Child. You can walk right around the rock formation thanks to a placed walkway. Stone medusas are frozen in a motionless ballet.

through a grandiose, savage countryside over a distance of 16.9 miles (27 km). It runs through Alzon before disappearing into the limestone depths, re-emerging at La Foux where it has gouged out its masterpiece, a sort of giant funnel.

The gorges of the Vis
Wild countryside

The Vis has cut a channel 1,000 ft (300 m) deep and 2,667 ft (800 m) wide into the limestone rock. It meanders

Blandas
A healthy walk

On the D 113, ¹/₂ a mile (1 km) from the village of Blandas, a 'healthy' walk has been laid out in the forest of black Austrian pine. There are two circuits of 4,000 and 8,667 ft (1,200 and 2,600 m) with 14 special exercises to perform. You can also cover the route by mountain-bike.

Pony-trekking

Joëlle Grazioli,
Open all year round.
Booking only.
☎ 04 67 81 53 50.
You can ride for periods ranging from two hours to the whole day along the ridge to

Spotcheck
D3

Hérault

Things to do

Canoeing on the Vis
Hiking, rambling in the wild countryside

Within easy reach

Le Vigan, 17 km NW,
p. 286.

Tourist office

Ganges: ☎ 04 67 73 85 03

the Cirque de Navacelles, through the Fontaret pine forest and the arid, wild plateau (*causse*) fragrant with thyme, boxwood and lavender.

The Cirque de Navacelles
A magnificent sight

This geological formation, unique in Europe, is a huge bowl 1,000 ft (300 m) deep. The lookout post on the D 713 on the bank of the Gard or directly above the Baume-Auriol farm on the Hérault side are the places to view this amazing sight. If you are lucky, you may see a bird of prey (a black kite or buzzard) floating overhead in spring or autumn. Or you may see a swift, a swallow or, in winter, the alpine accentor which migrates from the area in the spring.

Lodève and the Larzac

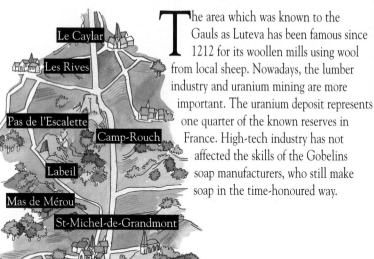

The area which was known to the Gauls as Luteva has been famous since 1212 for its woollen mills using wool from local sheep. Nowadays, the lumber industry and uranium mining are more important. The uranium deposit represents one quarter of the known reserves in France. High-tech industry has not affected the skills of the Gobelins soap manufacturers, who still make soap in the time-honoured way.

Lodève
Saint-Fulcran
Open daily, 9am-6pm.
Free admission.
Saint Fulcran was a wealthy bishop who lived in the 10th C. He fed the poor, cared for the sick and, as a good soldier,

built fortresses. The original cathedral was sacked by the Huguenots in 1573, but it still has a 13th-C. **Gothic tower** and part of its **fortifications**. The final resting-place of the 84 former bishops of Lodève is located in one of the chapels.

Spotcheck
D3-D4

Hérault

Things to do
Festivals and fairs
Trout fishing
Grotte de Labeil (Labeil cave)

Within easy reach
Bédarieux approx. 30 km SW, p. 204.

Tourist office
Lodève: ☎ 04 67 73 85 03

Musée Fleury
Square Georges-Auric,
☎ 04 67 88 86 10.
Open daily except Mon.
9.30am-noon and
2-8pm.
The museum is dedicated to the prehistory of Lodève and the region and is housed in a lovely 16th–17th-C. mansion. There is also an exhibit about the silk industry and the work of a local artist, Paul Dardé, who died in 1963. There is a museum of Dardé's works, the **Halle-Dardé**, in the square of the same name, which holds exhibitions of other painters, such as Utrillo, in 1997, and Albert Marquet, in 1998.

FESTIVAL AND FAIRS
IN LODÈVE
**Les Voix de la
Méditerranée is a
festival, first held in
July 1998, which brings
together singers, poets
and storytellers.
Traditional fairs are
held on 13 February,
25 August and
8 November, and
there are other fairs
of itinerant stall-
holders and peddlars.**

The merchant quarter
It starts at the Mazel, the Occitan word for the shambles, the butchers' shop, near the **Church of Saint-Pierre**. There are Romanesque and 14th-C. buildings in the Rue Neuve-des-Marchés and the Grand-Rue which leads up to the cathedral. In the Rue de la Cavalerie, the **Hôtel des Hospitaliers** has a 15th-C. square tower. The **Maison des Métiers d'Art du Lodévois** is a craft centre whose craftsmen include a wood-carver, a stonecutter, a marble-polisher, ceramicists and a wrought iron smith (open daily except Monday).

RUE NEUVE DES MARCHÉS

Gobelins carpets
☎ 04 67 96 40 40.
Open Tues., Wed. and Thur., 2-5pm,
by appointment.
The visiting hours are few and far between but this unique annexe of the National Carpet Workshop is fascinating. Identical copies of antique Gobelin carpet patterns are made for official buildings, such as ministries, embassies and important state-owned buildings. This weaving mill was opened in 1964 to employ the wives of lumberjacks working in the forests of the region.

Barri de Montbrun
This suburb on a hill on the opposite bank of the Soulondre is reached via a gate. It once had its own oven, well and church and was an over-crowded working-class district where the textile workers lived. Wander through its stepped streets with their medieval doors and 14th- and 16th-C. windows.

Melting with pleasure
Marc Frères, Avenue de la République,
☎ 04 67 44 01 34.
Open Tues.–Sat.,
8.30am-1pm and 3-8pm., Sun. 7am-8pm.
If you have a sweet tooth, visit Paul Marc, who has a bakery in which he makes his own cakes, as well as choco-lates, confectionery and ice cream (at least 20 different flavours). Taste his specialities which include the *lodévois*, a cake made with meringue and almonds and Mère Cande's nut tart.

Around Lodève

The Priory of Saint-Michel-de-Grandmont

Soumont, 5 miles
(8 km) from Lodève,
☎ 04 67 44 09 31.
Visits Jul.–Aug. daily,
10.30am., 3pm., 4pm.
and 5pm.; Jun., Sept.
and Oct. daily 10.30am,
3.15pm and 4pm.; 1
Nov.–15 Dec., weekend
and bank holidays
3.10pm and 4pm; 8
Feb.–31 May daily, 3pm.
Admission charge.
The Romanesque cloister,
church and chapter-house all
date from the 11th and 12th
C. and are intact. The park
contains dolmens, menhirs
and Gallo-Roman sarcophagi
covering 5,000 years of
civilisation.

Trout fishing

From Lodève, on the D
35 towards Lunas. Stop
at the Mas de Mérou,
☎ 04 67 44 03 41.
It would be difficult not to
catch anything because farmed

trout are regularly thrown into
this stream that runs through
the farmyard. Another good
place to fish is at the
Pisciculture de Gravezon,
Route de Joncels, Lunas
(☎ 04 67 23 88 98. Open
March to 30 Sept., daily 9am-
8pm). Here you pay for what
you catch (35 F per 2¼ lb/1 kg
of trout). You can also enjoy a
picnic in the shade. Don't
forget to apply for a fishing
licence beforehand – the
penalties for not having one
are severe.

Le Pélardon du Haut Languedoc

Coopérative Agricole,
ZI du Capitoul,
☎ 04 67 96 43 00.
Open Mon.–Fri.,
8am-noon and 2-6pm.
Thirteen goat farms in the
Hérault got together to
produce this soft, fine, smooth
cheese which is eaten fresh,
mature, dry or even warm
in a salad or on garlic
bread with a bunch
of grapes
and a glass
of wine. The raw
milk is curdled on
the goat-farm.
Moulding and the
other processes are
performed using traditional

methods. There is a shop at
which the cheese can be
tasted before buying.

Grotte de Labeil
On the D 151, N from Lodève,
☎ 04 67 96 49 47.
Open 15 March–1 Oct., daily 11am-5pm; Jul.–Aug., daily 10am-7pm.
Admission charge.
The guided tour of this 1,000-ft (300-m) cave takes three quarters of an hour. The cave is fed by underground springs and rivers and it has multicoloured rock formations. Afterwards, you can lunch in a beautiful room with a vaulted ceiling.

Le Pas de l'Escalette and Les Rives
This is one of the **entrances to the Larzac** which can be reached by the N 9 or the A 75 and is at an altitude of 2,420 ft (726 m). It is a fairly easy climb because steps have been cut into the rocky footpath, hence the name 'Escalette'. Then take the D 155 to the fortified village of **Les Rives**. Further on, along the D 151, note the **Ferme de Combefère** whose architecture is typical of the Causse.

Le Caylar
About 12 miles (19 km) from Lodève.
The countryside around this rock consists of arid plateaus and green plains. The rock itself is dominated by crags that look like impregnable ramparts. There are narrow passageways and houses with 14th- and 15th-C. detailing. The church contains a lovely altarpiece depicting the life of the Virgin Mary.

Chaos de Camp-Rouch
3¾ miles (6 km) S of Caylar by the D 155.
This rock formation is the result of erosion and looks like a succession of ruins of all kinds: arches, massive Egyptian monuments and rounded rocks. Of the numerous caves, the best known, the Trou de la Baume, was once used by highwaymen as their lair.

Le Larzac
The southern part of the limestone plateau covering 386 sq miles (1,000 km²) is in the *département* of Hérault. The air is fresh here, 2,334 ft (700 m) above sea level, and the wind blows hard. The climate is severe and the almost bare land is grazed by sheep and goats. It is much easier to

LE JARDIN DU PUECH
On the D 148, S from Lodève,
☎ 04 67 44 10 28.
Open Mon.–Sat. 10am-7pm, Sun. 2-7pm.
Admission charge.
On 12.4 acres (5 ha) of the red soil which border Lac Salagou is the last botanical garden to be created in Hérault. Numerous guided itineraries take you through the ancient fruit trees and holm oaks and past 65 species of rose laurel, medicinal plants, irises, mulberry bushes and pistachio trees.

reach the area since the RN 9 has been built but Larzac remains a remote spot.

Gardarem 'Lou Larzac'
This was the slogan shouted by the 103 peasants, heavily reinforced with tractors and herds of sheep, who came to protest in Paris in 1981 and met under the Arc de Triomphe. They were trying to prevent the army camp in the area being extended – it was to be enlarged from 7,413 to 42,000 acres (3,000 to 17,000 ha). This was also a demonstration of the determination of the Caussenard, his patience and strong will.

Nîmes

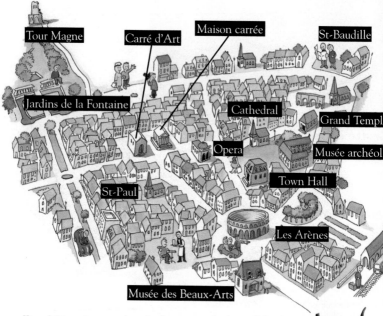

Tour Magne

Carré d'Art

Maison carrée

St-Baudille

Jardins de la Fontaine

Cathedral

Grand Templ

Opera

Musée archéol

Town Hall

St-Paul

Les Arènes

Musée des Beaux-Arts

Nîmes is a sun-drenched town in which rainfall is low and the hot summers are torrid, yet it is built on water, with streams and rivulets that sometimes overflow. A city of paradoxes; Protestant and austere by day, it turns pagan and wild by night; the pink hue of its houses gives it a refined appearance, but in its passion for bullfighting it is violent, especially during the *férias* at Whitsun (Pentecost) and in September and February (p. 117). In this town, tradition and the avant-garde are combined, drawing both artists and tourists alike.

Maison Carrée

Place de la Maison-Carrée,
☎ **04 66 36 26 76.**
Open 9am-noon and
7pm (6pm in winter).
Admission charge.
This famous Roman building
was erected in the year AD 5
and was dedicated to Caïus
and Lucius Caesar, son and
grandson of the Emperor
Augustus. It is one of the
best-preserved temples in the

JARDINS DE LA FONTAINE

Open daily until dusk
These were the first public parks in the history of France and were created in 1750. They cover the south face of the Mont Cavalier at top of which stands the **Tour Magne** (open 9am-7pm in summer, 10am-noon and 1.30-6pm in winter. The view from the top is magnificent). The formal gardens with their long avenues, lines of flowerbeds and stone balustrades have statues in the lower part. The upper part is a landscaped garden with little pathways and a cottage garden look. A stream is dedicated to Nemausus, genie of water and god protector of the city.

The Tour Magne at the top of Mont Cavalier dominates the city. It is 107 ft (32 m) high and was built in 15 BC. Its austerity and simplicity are typical of Roman monuments in Languedoc.

Roman world. It was used as a council chamber for consuls in the Middle Ages, as stables in the 17th C., as an archive after the Revolution and today **a small museum** and **bookshop** are installed in its one room.

Musée Archéologique

13, Boulevard de l'Amiral-Courbet,
☎ 04 66 67 25 57.
Open daily except Mon. and bank holidays, 11am-6pm.
The Archaeological Museum, housed in a former Jesuit college, is the most popular museum in the town. It contains many pieces found here and in the area, especially on the Domitian Way. They include ancient coins, vases, sculptures, mosaics, funerary items, stone lintels, inscriptions, tools and a huge variety of instruments from chisels and tongs to weights and scales. A wonderful insight into Roman daily life in the area and a truly essential part of any visit to Nîmes.

Carré d'Art

Place de la Maison-Carrée,
☎ 04 66 76 35 80.
Open 10am-6pm, except Mon.
Admission charge.
Sir Norman Foster designed this area of nearly 139,900 sq ft (13,000 m²) which houses a media library, library, workshops and a **Museum of Contemporary Art** which was opened in 1993. The museum contains about 300 works from the 1960s to free figuration based on three themes: art in France; Mediterranean sensitivity to art and art in the English-speaking world. The artists represented include Boltanski, Claude Viallat, Penone, Polke and Schnabel.

Le Musée des Beaux-Arts

Rue Cité-Foulc,
☎ 04 66 67 38 21.

Spotcheck
E3-F3

Gard

Things to do

Musée Archéologique
(Archaeological Museum)
Jardins de la Fontaine
(Fontaine Gardens)
Les Arènes
Maison Carée
Planétarium du Mont-Duplan

With children

Aquatropic

Within easy reach

*Sommières, p. 242,
Pont-du-Gard, p. 268,
Uzès, p. 272.*

Tourist office

Nîmes: ☎ 04 66 67 29 11

Open 11am-6pm, closed on Mon.
Admission charge.
The museum was built in the early 19th C. and reconstructed by J.-M. Wilmotte in 1986–87. A large Roman mosaic embedded in the ground floor depicts the marriage of Admetus. On the upper floors, the museum contains a huge collection of French, Italian, Flemish, Dutch and regional paintings. These include *Suzannah and the Elders* by Jacopo Bassano (1685), a Flemish triptych of *The Virgin and Child* and the *Portrait of Marcelliano de Barea* by Rubens.

Musée du Vieux-Nîmes

Place aux Herbes,
☎ 04 66 36 00 64.
Open 10am-6pm, except Mon.
Admission charge.
The museum is in a 17th-C. former bishops' palace and contains a remarkable collection of local art from past centuries, including everyday objects and artefacts, ceramics, shawls (copies can be bought at the shop), furniture and games. There are reconstructions of an interior and a garment workshop.

PLANÉTARIUM DU MONT-DUPLAN

Avenue du Mont-Duplan,
☎ 04 66 67 60 94.
Open all year round, Wed. and Sat., at 3pm and 6.30pm, at 9pm on Fri. night and 4pm on Sun.
On Wednesdays there is an introduction to astronomy. On Saturdays and Sundays, the sessions are based on a theme such as galaxies, the history of astronomy and all the other major fields of astronomy. On Friday evening, the current night sky is displayed and you are taught how to observe it. There is also a special programme designed for children.

The Cathedral of Notre-Dame-and-Saint-Castor

Place aux Herbes.
The Romanesque cathedral was destroyed and rebuilt in the 17th C. On the façade, a sculpted frieze represents the story of Adam and Eve, the sacrifice of Cain and Abel and the death of Abel, a masterpiece of **Provençal Romanesque art**. The choir and nave are neo-Medieval and were only built in the 19th C.

Les Arènes

Place des Arènes,
☎ 04 66 76 72 77.
Open 9am-6pm in summer; in winter 9am-noon and 2-5pm.
Admission charge.
This, one of the best-preserved amphitheatres in the Roman world, was inspired by the Coliseum in Rome. It can hold 20,000 spectators and is in constant use for **bullfights, musical shows, sporting**

events and **concerts**. It measures 444 x 337 ft (133 x 101 m), has 34 tiers of seating and two storeys of vaulted arches containing five concentric galleries. There are 126 internal staircases used for entrances and exits. From October to April, a movable, inflatable cover is erected over the amphitheatre, which means that it can be used in the winter. In one of the arches of the amphitheatre, there is a shop called La Boutique des Arènes (☎ 04 66 21 80 52. Open daily, 9am-noon and 2-6.30pm) where you can buy reproductions of shawls, oil lamps or antique Roman coins, really unusual souvenirs.

Classical Nîmes

Around the Hôtel de Ville (town hall) most of the houses date from the 17th and 18th C., a prosperous period during which there was a great deal of construction. The **Rue de l'Aspic** and the **Rue Dorée** are lined with handsome mansions such as Fontfroide, Meynier-de-Salinelles, Démians, d'Aubais, de Villard and de Cabrières. The doors, windows, embellishments and stone staircases are all extremely elegant.

Contemporary Nîmes

As regards architecture, Jean Nouvel (designer of the Institut du Monde Arabe in

Sculpture by Martial Rayssein in the Place d'Assas

Paris) built the HLM which looks like a cross between a spaceship and a beetle. Martial Raysse redesigned the Place d'Assas according to the Golden Section. Norman Foster produced a mediatheque opposite the Maison Carrée, a glass cube with metal columns and grills. Three huge paintings by Julian Schnabel are displayed inside the Maison Carrée. The designer Philippe Starck built a bus shelter in dark marble, representing the crocodile and the palm tree, emblems of the city.

The designer Philippe Starck designed these city bus shelters for Nîmes

JUST THE TICKET

REDUCTIONS MUSÉES & MONUMENTS

TRIANGLE D'OR

ARLES AVIGNON NÎMES

Depending on how much time you have at your disposal, you have a choice between an all-in ticket for Les Arènes and the Tour Magne; a three-day pass for all the monuments and museums; a 'Golden Triangle' card which gives you reductions at all the monuments in Nîmes, Arles and Avignon; a carriage ride (45 min, from the Esplanade, daily, 3-9pm); a taxi ride (60 min, rather expensive, ☎ 04 66 29 40 11, with commentary on cassette) and a ride in a little train (May–Oct., 40 min, departure from the esplanade every hour, 10am-1pm) or a bike tour (2 hours, Apr.–Sept., departure from Place d'Assas at 8.30pm, ☎ 04 66 22 76 72). Finally, bus no. 8 runs along all the main boulevards for a really inexpensive tour.

Jean-Michel Wilmotte renovated the town hall, the market halls, the tourist office, the theatre and the famous Hôtel Cheval-Blanc.

Indienne fabrics

The fabrics sold under the brand names of Souleïado, Les Olivades and Valdrome are from Nîmes and are known as *indiennes de Nîmes de Mistral*. They are **hand-printed cotton,** made by a technique invented in China 2,000 years ago,

which came to India via the Silk Route, hence the name of *Indienne*. Marseille, a port that traded with the Orient, first dealt in these fabrics, then developed its own thanks to Colbert. From the 17th C. onwards, these printed **cottons** took on a local style. Despite the crisis which hit the textile industry from the 1950s onwards, the town has continued to operate textile mills and there are still many that belong to world-famous ready-to-wear couturiers such as Cacharel and Éminence.

And blue jeans were born...

In the early 20th C., the town's merchants prospered by exporting to the United States a type of heavy cotton **sailcloth** that was used to make sails for ships, tarpaulins and workmen's trousers. In 1870, a Bavarian immigrant named Levi Strauss used this 'serge de Nîmes' to make trousers for the conquerors of the Wild West. From Genoa

(pronounced 'Jean'), the place where the cloth was actually made, came the word 'jeans'. Blue jeans were born, made of denim ('de Nîmes') sailcloth. However the *gardians*, the cowboys of the Camargue, refuse to wear jeans, favouring the traditional moleskin trousers for horse-riding.

Taillerie de Nîmes

212, Impasse Vincent-d'Indy, ☎ 04 66 27 00 74. Visits by appointment. Learn all about gemstones from their geological formation until they are cut. Stones are treated

Good things to eat
Raymond, 34, Rue Nationale,
☎ 04 66 67 20 47.
Open daily, 8am-noon and 2-6pm.
La Bonbonnière, 24, Rue de la Madeleine,
☎ 04 66 67 89 57.
Open daily except Sun., 9am-noon and 2-7pm.
Raymond is a firm that has been going for 100 years and specialises in **brandade de Nîmes** (creamed salt cod; the Nîmes version has no puréed potatoes), either the classic or the old fashioned version (in which the salt cod is not puréed). They also sell *tapenade* (olive paste), anchovy paste, aubergine caviar and potted beef. La Bonbonnière is an Ali Baba's cave of **confectionery.** Every sort of sweetmeat from the region is found here, from traditional pastries to crunchy ground almond biscuits (p. 40). If you are particularly fond of olives (p. 21) don't forget to visit **Daniel,** Halles Centrales de Nîmes (☎ 04 66 26 68 08), which stocks 18 different varieties and the **Castelnau-Sablier,** Impasse Miraman (☎ 04 66 27 12 02), which is particularly famous for its *tapenade.*

differently depending on whether they are precious, semi-precious or decorative and this is explained and demonstrated. In the exhibition hall you can admire a range of gemstones of various origins, including opals, multi-coloured jasper, moonstones and sapphires – and let yourself be tempted.

Aquatropic
39, Chemin de l'Hôtellerie,
☎ 04 66 38 31 00.
Admission charge.
This is an ideal place to relax if you want to spend a day without touring. This **aquatic park** has every attraction for young and old alike: wave pools, flumes and river rapids, waterfalls and a spa and whirlpool baths, picnic areas and a children's play area. If the weather is cloudy Aquatropic is an attractive prospect, especially if you have children. There is even an on-site bar and restaurant.

The Petite Camargue
bulls and pink flamingoes

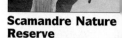

The Petite Camargue, a patchwork of lakes and marshes, vineyards and asparagus-beds, with its typical villages is probably more easily accessible than its big sister. When you encounter herds of bulls and flights of pink flamingoes, take your time; watch them in this garden wilderness .

Exploring the lakes by canoe or kayak

L'Échappée verte,
☎ 04 67 59 63 95 or 06 13 07 04 03.

Explore the *étangs*, the numerous freshwater lakes and lagoons, with an expert kayaker and guide who is also a naturalist. You can leave either early in the morning or in the late afternoon, the latter time being the best in high summer, because birds and other wildlife only emerge at dusk. You can picnic beside the fishermen's huts.

Vauvert

Going to the devil

Au diable Vauvert, meaning to celebrate wildly, has been a French expression since the Middle Ages. Pilgrims came here to celebrate the *diableries*, in which the devil was mocked. Today the old town is still picturesque with its narrow lanes such as Rue des Juifs and Rue des Bonnets-Carrés.

RUE DES BONNETS CARRÉS

Scamandre Nature Reserve

Rte des Isles-Gallician,
☎ 04 66 73 52 05.
Guided tour Wed. booking only.
This 544-acre (220-ha) nature reserve was created in 1993 and is a mosaic of marshes, pastures, lakes, reed-beds and salt marshes. More than a hundred migratory or nesting birds stay here, including the purple heron, snipe and grey curlew. There is a path about ½ mile (1 km) long and a hide.

❀ Perrier spring

On the D 139, N of Vauvert, les Bouillens, Vergèze,
☎ 04 66 87 61 01.
Open daily during the week in summer 9.30-10.30am and 1-6pm; winter 9.30-10.30am and 1.30-4pm; weekend 10am-4pm.
Admission charge.
The Perrier bottling plant organises an industrial exhibit, which explains the process of extracting water from the spring, bottling it and bringing it to the table (see p. 28), as well as how the bottles are made. You can taste the water which contains 50 million bubbles per litre (1¼ pt).

Le Cailar
The Church of Saint-Étienne

Le Cailar, the capital of the Petite Camargue, stands at the confluence of the Petit Rhône and the Vistre. It is a bull-rearing centre with a lovely Romanesque church. Note the windswept tomb topped with the effigy of a bull. It belongs to Le Sanglier, the fiercest bullfighter in the history of the Camargue who died in 1933, at the age of 17.

use as a base because, although close to the sea, it is not over-crowded like the resorts.

Saint-Gilles
Gateway to the Camargue

Saint-Gilles is in the middle of a vast plain, a patchwork of canals and orchards, paddy-fields and vineyards. Its **abbey** is a masterpiece of Languedoc Romanesque, begun in 1116 but only completed in the early 14th C. The tall build-ing is perfectly proportioned with pure lines and has a façade with three sculpted portals. The sarcophagus of St Gilles lies in the crypt. Saint-Gilles is a nice place to

Musée de la Tonnellerie

Château de Générac,
On the D 14, N of Saint-Gilles
☎ 04 66 01 85 06.
Open every morning except Mon. and Tues.; Sat. 2-6pm; by appoint-ment other days.
For centuries, this community was an important cooperage centre, producing barrels from chestnut wood from the Isère, in sizes ranging from 5 1/4 pt (3 l), a *barral*, to more than 877 pt (500 l), the *demi-muid*. In the 1950s, the invasion of plastic wiped out the indus-try forever. Many tools are displayed.

Gallician-Montcalm
Cooperative cellar

Av. Costières,
☎ 04 66 73 31 65.
This cooperative cellar is the place to taste Costières-de-Nîmes (the soil of the marshes is warm

Spotcheck
E4-F4

Gard

Things to do

Canoeing on the lakes
Scamandre Nature Reserve
Visiting the Perrier spring
Boat trip

Within easy reach

*La Grande-Motte, p. 230,
The ponds of
Montpelliérains, p. 234.*

Tourist office

Vauvert: ☎ 04 66 88 28 52
Saint-Gilles:
☎ 04 66 87 33 75

BOAT TRIP

A trip on the Rhône to Sète canal between Saint-Gilles and Aigues-Mortes is a good way to explore the secret reaches of the Camargue. Boats can be hired for several days: inquire at 'Fleuve Trotter' (☎ 06 09 52 47 15), a hotel-barge where you can stay moored in one place, or take a weekend trip (1,500 F) or a full week from Gallician to Sète (4,000 F per person, including bicycle hire).

and stony). The D 779 leads to Montcalm where a few farmhouses shelter behind umbrella pines. The imposing castle is in ruins, but the cellars are still used for wine storage.

Beaucaire

From the Middle Ages to the end of the 18th C., Beaucaire has owed its fame and prosperity to St. Madeleine's Fair. Today, it is a popular stop for pleasure-boats on the Rhône to Sète canal. It is worth taking a long walk around the town to see its many lovely mansions and other interesting relics.

Hôtel de Ville

The town hall, in classic style, was built between 1679 and 1683. Note the double royal sun on the façade, topped with the town's motto, which translated means 'Famous for its fair, illustrious for its loyalty'.

Château Royal

Open all year round; 1 Apr.–31 Aug., daily, 10am-7pm; 1 Nov.– 31 March, Wed., weekend and school holidays, 10am-12.30pm and 1.30-6pm. This 11th-C. citadel was built on a hill overlooking the Rhône to protect the town from the Mistral. There is an imposing 14th-C. wall and a large triangular tower. The grounds, which were laid out in the 19th C. and are now a listed monument, are open to the public. There is a pine grove with winding paths and stone steps.

The eagles of Beaucaire

Château de Beaucaire, ☎ 04 66 59 26 72. Open from Easter to All Saints' Day, every morning except Wed.; Jul.– Aug daily, Four morning sessions with one hour intervals (2-5pm March– June, 3-6pm Jul.–Aug.). *Admission charge.* This medieval costumed spectacle shows off birds of prey, including falcons, buzzards, vultures and kites in flight performing aerial acrobatics.

Around Beaucaire

Living like the Romans

Mas des Tourelles, 4294, Rte de Bellegarde (2$^1/_2$ miles (4 km) from Beaucaire), ☎ 04 66 59 19 72, fax: 04 66 59 50 80. Open from Easter to All Saints' Day, 2-7pm, Jul.–Aug., 10am-noon and 2-7pm. *Admission charge.* In a delightful Provençale farmhouse, Diane and Hervé Durand invite you to discover how the Romans lived. At the site of a 1st-C. Gallo-Roman villa, you can see the reconstitution of how vineyards were tended, kilns for firing amphoras, a cellar with a fulling-mill, press and *dolia* (wine jars with a capacity of

Summer fêtes

The ancient **St. Madeleine's Fair** is celebrated on 21 July and is the occasion for an historic parade. It is followed by week-long festivities, including exhibitions, flea-markets, craft markets, a wine festival, street theatre, concerts, bull-running and various types of bullfighting. Information ☎ 04 66 59 08 48.

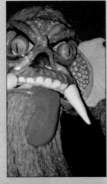

Spotcheck
F3

Gard

Things to do
Les Estivales (St Madeleine's Fair)
The eagles of Beaucaire
Living like the Romans
The Vieux Mas (Old Farmhouse)
Château Royal

Within easy reach
Pont du Gard, p. 268, Villeneuve-lès-Avignon, p. 270.

Tourist office
Beaucaire: ☎ 04 66 59 26 57

2,105 pt/1,200 l). Drinks served in the tavern include *mulsum* (red wine flavoured with honey and spices), *turriculae* (white wine flavoured with walnut) and flavoured grape juices.

Equestrian Centre
Saint-Denis-d'Argence (on the D 15, towards Fourques), ☎ 04 66 59 17 71.
This bull-rearing and equestrian centre also has an excellent bistro and restaurant. Depending on the time of year, there are brandings, rounding up of bulls and bull-fighting courses (*courses camarguaises*).

Saint-Roman Abbey
3 miles (5 km) by the D 999, towards Nîmes, ☎ 04 66 59 04 73.
Open 1 Oct.–31 March, Sat.–Sun. and school holidays, 2-5pm; 1 Apr.–30 Sept., daily except Mon., 10am-6pm.
Admission charge.
This monastery was cut out of the rock in the 5th C. The **sculpted seat** cut into the limestone is unique in France. The **view** over the Rhône valley, with the ramparts of Avignon in the distance, is magnificent.

The Vieux Mas
Mas de Végère, at 3¾ miles (6 km) on road leading to Fourques

☎ 04 66 59 60 13.
Open daily except Jan., 10am-7pm.
Admission charge.
It's as if you were there! This is what life was like on an old Provençal farmhouse between 1900–1950. There are demonstrations of traditional crafts, such as blacksmithing and clog-making.

Vallabrègues
3¾ miles (6 km) N from Beaucaire.
This little town on the east bank of the Rhône was once a flourishing centre like Beaucaire. **Basketry** is celebrated here at the **Musée de la Vannerie** (☎ 04 66 59 23 41), in the **basketry workshop** (☎ 04 66 59 62 08) and during the **Grande Fête de la Vannerie**, in August (Information at the Beaucaire Tourist Office).

Lunel
Muscat wine and medieval relics

L unel is alleged to have been founded by Jews expelled from Jericho by Vespasian in AD 68. This would explain why in the 12th C. it became a centre of Jewish culture and a prosperous trading town. Today, this little town, with its many medieval relics, is surrounded by a vineyard which produces a delicious Muscat (p. 19), the sweet aperitif or dessert wine, which was served at the table of Frederick II of Prussia.

The old town

Wander through the little streets of the centre, especially the vaulted Passage des Caladons (meaning 'large flagstones') which dates from 1240. The Hôtel de Bernis in the Rue Alphonse-Ménard, contains the remains of the 13th-C. Jewish medical school. Visit the Church of Notre-Dame-du-Lac, whose belfry tops the old watchtower. For a few days in August, Lunel renews its ties with the Middle Ages through street theatre.

Les Arènes

Many shows are held here in the arenas, including bullfights and bull-running for which the Pescalune Trophy is awarded. Pescalune is the name given to the local inhabitants and means 'moon fishermen'.

Wine with a taste of the sun

Cave de Vérargues, Route de Lunel-Viel, ☎ 04 67 86 00 09, 9am-noon and 2-6pm except Sun. And at the **Mas de Bellevue**, Route de Sommières, Lunel, ☎ 04 67 83 24 83, daily except Sun., 9am-8pm. Wine tasting and purchase.

Stone carver

Christian Poujol, **Avenue du Vidourle**, ☎ **04 67 71 97 93.** Open daily, 2-6.30pm. If you are impressed by the life-size carving of a bull which has adorned one of the town squares since 1991 visit this unusual **craftsman.**

The Belfry of Notre-Dame-du-Lac

Ambrussum: the Roman bridge over the Vidourle

Spotcheck
E4

Hérault

Things to do

Bullfights and bull-running
in Les Arènes
Visit a *manade* (bull herd)

Within easy reach

*Montpellier, 24 km SW,
p. 222,
La Grande-Motte,
17 km S, p. 230,
Sommières, 13 km N,
p. 242.*

Tourist office

Lunel: ☎ 04 67 71 01 37

Note in particular the extraordinary mantelpieces, in classical or contemporary style which can take the shape of a woman's torso! Commissions from 30,000 F.

Lunel Gardians
**Rue des Caladons,
☎ 04 67 71 30 46.
Open Tues.–Sat., 9am-noon and 3-7pm: Sun. 9am-noon.**
If you want to dress like a Camargue cow-boy, you will find all the gear right here. All the tack is here too: typical saddles, trident, Camargue cross and racing hook.

Aux environs
Ambrussum
2½ miles (4 km) N from Lunel.
Those who love ancient stones will find an exceptional archaeological site here, which was first occupied in the 3rd C. BC. There is a signposted path.

Marsillargues
The village is surrounded by ancient plane trees and has an imposing **castle** built c. 1305 by Guillaume de Nogaret, to whom the king had granted the town. It was rebuilt in the 17th C. (open Jul.–Aug., Tues.–Sat. 3-6pm., ☎ 04 67 83 52 10). Visit the restored dining room, the billiard room decorated with

ornate plasterwork and a parade room. Within the castle walls, there is also a small **folklore museum**.

Rhôny-Vidourle
This canton consists of eight small communes which are close to each other but very different in character. They are Aimargues, Codognan, Gallargues-le-Montueux, Le Cailar, Mus, Uchaud, Vergèze and Vestric. They are definitely worth visiting.

Aimargues
This is where the Éminence underclothes are made, one of the most popular French brands (the factory is not open to the public). Instead, go and see the **Château de Teillan** (☎ 04 66 88 02 38. Open 15 Jun.–15 Sept. except Mon., 2-6pm.).The Richelieu Room is an historic monument, as is the boudoir, which was decorated in 1805 for Pauline Bonaparte. The park contains the largest chain-pump in Languedoc. The **pigeon-loft** was used to breed carrier-pigeons for Aigues-Mortes.

DETOUR TO A *MANADE*

Manade Jean Lafon, Mas du Grès, Saint-Nazaire-de-Pezan, ☎ 04 67 71 31 42, fax: 04 67 71 20 89. Telephone in the morning between 10am-noon to find out what is happening on the day you want to visit.
A *manade* means a herd as well as the land on which it grazes. There are Camargue bulls here and little white horses who gambol in this delightful setting. In the cool shade of an authentic reed hut, Jean Lafon will welcome you and let you celebrate with him. He will also let you into the secrets of branding and Camargue folklore, culture and cuisine.

Aigues-Mortes

This medieval walled town seems to be stranded in the centre of the Petite Camargue, 3¾ miles (6 km) from the sea and is symbolic of human obstinacy when confronted with a port that is sanding and silting. It has become the salt capital of the Camargue and it also attracts more than 130,000 tourists a year.

and various medieval and historic performances take place. There are feasts, tournaments of knights, gymkhanas and concerts.

The ramparts

The 5,333 ft (1,600 m) fawn stone ramparts enclose this typical medieval Languedoc town in a perfect rectangle, pierced by ten fortified gates and defended by towers. The town is laid out on the grid pattern of the medieval *bastides* (fortified towns) with streets at right angles to each other. It is almost like being on the set of a period film into which a few modern shops have accidentally strayed. Cars, fortunately, have to be left outside the ramparts, even though parking is expensive.

Louis IX's town

In 1248, 40,000 crusaders followed Louis IX (Saint Louis) on his First Crusade. For the Second Crusade, in 1270, more than 100,000 went with him. Saint Louis never returned, dying of typhus in Tunis, but the king had wanted to give the kingdom of France a Mediterranean port and was able to produce the plans for the walled city. On St. Louis' Day, 25 August, week-long celebrations, including an historic parade

Tour Constance

Open 1 May –30 Sept. 9.30am-7pm, 1 Oct–31 March 10am-4pm, Apr. 10am-5pm

The Tour Constance defended the town – the walls are up to 20 ft (6 m) thick – before becoming a prison in which knights templar and protestants were held. There is a wonderful view from the top.

Place Saint-Louis

A statue of Louis IX, in his crusader's armour stands in the centre of the square. He seems oblivious to the sight of all the lively cafés

and souvenir shops. After a refreshing pause here, visit the Chapels of the Pénitents-Gris and Pénitents-Blancs or the Church of Notre-Dame-des-Sablons, whose interior is very dilapidated.

Tour Carbonnière

As you leave Aigues-Mortes by the D 46, you cannot miss this tower which stands in isolation in the middle of the marshes. It was one of the forward defences of the town. Climb up to the top for a **view** over the **landscape**, the salt marshes, the town and the Petite Camargue. Further along the road, there are the ruins of the

THE MIDI SALT MARSHES

Information at the Tourist Office. Guided tour 1 May–31 Aug., Wed.
In the middle of the

19th C. the Compagnie des Salins du Midi (p. 26) was formed. It still has 34,594 acres (14,000 ha) of salt marshes producing 450,000 tonnes of salt each year in the traditional way. There is a 2-hour coach tour with a stop beside the sea.

Benedictine Abbey of Psalmody which are well worth a visit.

✾ Domaine Listel

☎ 04 66 51 17 00. Open from Apr. to Sept. daily, 10am-6.30pm; From Oct. to March from Mon. to Fri., 9.30-11.30pm and 2-5.30pm. This vineyard grows on deep sand, carried on the wind

from the coast. The wines produced are fine and light and low in acidity. The best known of these *vins de sable* is the Gris de Gris. There are mainly whites and rosés, but a robust red has been made here since the 1960s. The wine-cellar dates from 1870, and the press is 16th-C. Tastings are available.

✾ Pony-trekking

Pony Ranch, Ch. de Vireventre, ☎ 07 07 43 10 29 or 04 66 53 86 89. Open all year round. Take the kids for a pony-ride along the Rhône to Sète canal, between pine forests and marshes, accompanied by a guide. You

Spotcheck
E4

Gard

Things to do

The ramparts
Visiting the Midi salt marshes
Pony-trekking along the Canal

Within easy reach

La Grande-Motte, 14 km SW, p. 230
Palavas, 26 km SE, p. 232.

Tourist office

Aigues-Mortes:
☎ 04 66 53 73 00

may be lucky enough to see some of the local wildlife, such as grey herons, nutria, etc. You can ride the horses and even stay on a ranch overnight or for several days.

Viva el toro!

In the second week of October, after the salt and grapes have been harvested, there is a week-long **votive festival**. There are bull-running displays, *abrivados*, bandidos (when the *gardians* take the bulls from the arena to their pastures) and various other events involving bulls which will delight both novices and bull-fighting aficionados.

Le Grau-du-Roi and Port-Camargue

Le Grau-du-Roi is a fishing village which has kept all its original charm, with a lively harbour, an old lighthouse and long, sandy beaches stretching as far as the Boucanet district. Port-Camargue is a gigantic, modern marina whose low houses and stretches of water are all designed for water-sports and leisure. Both are extremely popular with holidaymakers in the height of summer.

Le Grau-du-Roi

Fishing and beach

A *grau* is a 'breech' or channel open through the line of coastal dunes which separates the lagoon from the sea. This is one of the main tourist resorts in the region, thanks to its 11¼ miles (18 km) of fine sandy beaches which are very popular in summer. It is also the second-largest trawling port in the Mediterranean, with an annual catch of between 5,000 and 6,000 tonnes a year. All that remains of the old fishing village is a few houses in the pedestrianised area where the shops and cafés are to be found.

Centre Méditerranéen des Vins

Domaine de l'Espiguette, ☎ 04 66 53 07 52. Open daily, 9am-noon and 3-7pm (8pm in summer) On returning from the beach at l'Espiguette, stop to fill your basket with bottles. All the local

vintages are stocked from Costières-de-Nîmes to Côtes-du-Rhône, Vins de Sables, Corbières, Coteaux-d'Aix and Cassis. Regional foods, books and local crafts are also on sale.

A sea trip

Quai Colbert.
The *Picardie* is a sailing catamaran which plies between Grau-du-Roi and Port-Camargue (☎ 04 66 51 45 96)

and takes 79 passengers. It was built for fishing on the high seas but has been beautifully converted and will give you an hour of pleasure. On the same quay, *Le Météore* (☎ 04 66 53 55 20) and *La Providence* (☎ 04 66 51 48 08) also offer sea trips.

Port-Camargue

The largest pleasure port in Europe

This is a world of marinas, canals and small buildings. If you like beautiful yachts go and see the *Freedom*, which won the Americas Cup in the 1980s. It has been restored by local craftsmen after it was abandoned. It now stands proudly in its new navy blue coat of paint.

The beaches

Espiguette beach (parking charge) is huge but has no lifeguard. It is popular with families and, further along, with naturists. Renée Lamouroux has had dinghies at the South Beach since 1974.

Spotcheck

E4

Gard

Things to do

Seaquarium
Sea trips
Fishing and beaches

With children

Amigoland

Within easy reach

*La Grande-Motte, 6 km W,
p. 230*
*Palavas, 20 km SE,
p. 232.*

Tourist office

Le Grau-du-Roi:
☎ 04 67 71 01 37

Nowadays, Renée also rents windsurfing boards, catamarans and pedalos and runs the beach efficiently.

Plage du Boucanet

This beach stretches westwards towards La Grande-Motte. It is a wide beach nearly 2 miles (3 km) long. However, developments and camp sites have sprung up rather haphazardly and have invaded the shore. Lilos and umbrellas can be rented as well as pedalos, and other water-sports are available.

Amigoland

Rond-point de l'Espiguette.
Open daily, from 8.30pm, 1 Jul.–10 Sept. *Charges for the attractions; free parking.*
This is an amusement park halfway between Le Grau-du-Roi and Port-Camargue, which has a big dipper, waterchute, turbojet, flying carpet, roundabouts and all kinds of rides which should

please those who like thrills and outdoor entertainment. Perfect for the children.

Poissons d'Argent

Facing the camp site, La Petite Camargue,
☎ 04 66 51 51 28.
Open Easter to end Sept., daily 8am-7pm. This fish-farm sells sea-bream, sea-bass and prawns. Sea-fishing trips are offered for 70 F. You are loaned rods and bait and can take your catch home. Organised fishing trips are also available (you pay for what you catch, by weight) and there is also a snackbar and

rides which should

SEAQUARIUM

Palais de la Mer
☎ 04 66 51 57 57.
Open daily, 10am-7pm or midnight depending on the season.
Admission charge.
The most spectacular sight is the shark tank, containing nurse sharks, black point and lemon sharks. The tank contains 875,000 gallons (400,000 l) of water, all above your head because you are in a 67-ft (20-m) long tunnel below it which is protected by thick glass. Thrills are guaranteed.

tastings of various fresh shellfish to complete the pleasure of the day.

Espiguette lighthouse

Pont du Gard

More than a million visitors come every year to gasp with delight at this extraordinary feat of Roman art, architecture and engineering. This incredibly photogenic Roman bridge is actually an aqueduct. One can't help but be fascinated by the know-how and skill of its architects and builders. 'If only I had been born a Roman,' cried Jean-Jacques Rousseau, an avid admirer of 'the art of this simple and noble work', which is set in a beautiful landscape of rock-roses, juniper trees and kermes (evergreen) oaks.

A capricious river

The Romans wanted to supply Nîmes with the water of a spring captured near Uzès, so they built an aqueduct (*aquae ductus* in Latin means 'water carrier') over 30 miles (50 km) long. The Romans adapted the line of the aqueduct to the lie of the land. It circumvents

obstacles that are too difficult, passes through a tunnel of soft rocks and bridges the valleys. The **Pont du Gard** is the best preserved and most spectacular of the whole project. One of the main hazards of the gorges of the Gardon is the autumn *gardonnades* – catastrophic floods that cause the

river to rise from a trickle to a throughput of 88,300 cu ft (2,500 m^3) a second! One of the secrets of the longevity of the bridge is its lateral construction as a series of arches. This allows it quite a lot of movement.

The Romans, first stonemasons of the West

The Roman citizen, whether in Rome or in the provinces, consumed ten times more water than the modern European. In the cities of antiquity, the gardens needed to be watered, the dyers' vats needed filling, the latrines flushed, and lots of water was

ON FOOT OR BY CANOE

Walk along the road leading to the top part of the bridge to see the limestone deposits which reduced the width of the channel and, in a few places, the coating which made the structure waterproof. It was a sort of concrete made of lime, sand and ground brick, covered with red paint and made flexible by adding fig-tree sap. The Pont du Gard Tourist Office is only about 5 minutes walk from the bridge on the right bank if you are coming from Nîmes on the N 86, after the car park (☎ 04 66 37 00 02. Open Jun.–Sept.). You can explore the Pont du Gard in a canoe-kayak with the Association Kayak vert (open March–Oct., ☎ 04 66 22 84 83, p.106), at Collias, which offers several routes, depending on the water level.

Spotcheck
F3

Gard

Things to do

The Pont du Gard by canoe

Within easy reach

*Nîmes, 23 km SW, p. 252,
Beaucaire, 21 km SE, p. 262.*

Tourist office

Pont du Gard :
☎ 04 66 37 00 02

needed for the baths and fountains. The need to control the water supply has left amazing works of engineering from water collection to water towers, but the **Nîmes Aqueduct** – an example of technical prowess which is evidence of the ancient art of masonry – and the Pont du Gard, the bridge built in the 1st C. AD, required an extensive knowledge of the topography. It is more than 160 ft (48 m) high and 917 ft (275 m) long. It consists of a double tier of very wide arches, from 50 to 80 ft

(15 to 24 m) wide and a third tier of smaller arches 2.7 ft (0.80 m) wide which carries the water. The material used is Vers stone, a fossil limestone extracted from nearby quarries. Some blocks weigh nearly 6 tonnes and are laid dry. In the days when apprentice masons had to tour France and the Pont du Gard was a necessary stop for them, many of them engraved their names, places of origin and a typical masonry tool on the pilings.

Viaduct or aqueduct?

The gradient between the Eure spring, near Uzès, and Nîmes was only 57 ft (17 m), making an average gradient of 13½ in (34 cm) per km (⅝ mile). There was no

The protruding blocks on the bridge pilings were used to attach scaffolding while the bridge was being repaired

margin of error and parts of the route even slope upwards! Yet the aqueduct was in use right up to the end of Roman domination. It then fell into disrepair and gradually became blocked by limestone deposits. It finally stopped working in the 9th C. It could clearly be turned into a bridge and this was done during the Middle Ages by cutting back the stone on the second tier. In the 18th C. the stones were restored and a road bridge was added next to the old bridge (between 1743 and 1747). In the 19th C., the structure was shored up and closed to road traffic.

Villeneuve-lès-Avignon

The Rhône separates it from Avignon but despite its name, Villeneuve is not a suburb of Avignon. It is a city in its own right with a flourishing art scene and a magnificent palace, in which life goes along at a gentle pace. It contains the largest charterhouse, or Carthusian monastery, in France with more than 6 acres (2.4 ha) of buildings. Its narrow streets are best viewed on foot.

Tour Philippe-le-Bel

Avenue Gabriel-Péri, Route d'Avignon.
Open daily except Tues., 10am-noon and 3-5pm or 7pm depending on the season.
Admission charge.
The tower was built in 1307, and overlooks the bridge of Avignon on which people dance, according to the famous nursery rhyme (actually the Saint-Bénézet Bridge). From the terrace on the top floor, reached by a spiral staircase, there is a **lovely view**.

The Collegiate Church of Notre-Dame

Open daily except Tues., 10am-noon and 3-5.30pm or 7pm, depending on the

season; closed in Feb.
Admission charge.
Arnaud de Via, a nephew of Pope John XXII, built this church in the 14th C. Its large square tower blocks it off from the road. See a **copy of the Villeneuve Pietà,** the original of which is in the Louvre.

La Chartreuse du Val de Bénédiction

Rue de la République,
☎ **04 90 15 24 24.**
Open daily, 9am-5pm or 6.30pm depending on the season.
Admission charge.
The largest charterhouse in France was founded by Pope Innocent VI in 1356. It covers more than 6 acres (2.5 ha) of buildings. It now houses the Centre National des Écritures du Spectacle. The cloisters, bursar's garden, cells, chapterhouse and laundry are open to the public.

The Coronation of the Virgin, painting in the Musée Pierre-de-Luxembourg.

Musée Pierre-de-Luxembourg

Rue de la République,
☎ 04 90 27 49 66.
Open daily, 10am-noon and 3-5.30pm or 7pm depending on the season: closed Mon. 16 Sept.–14 Jun.

The museum contains masterpieces of Western medieval art, including a superb 14th-C. Virgin in ivory, the Coronation of the Virgin by Enguerrand Quarton and a panorama of 17th- and 18th-C. Provençal painting.

The Gardens of the Saint-André Abbey

☎ 04 90 25 55 95.
Open daily, 10am-noon and 2-5pm or 6pm, depending on the season.

MARK, PATRON SAINT OF VINE-GROWERS

St. Mark's Day, 25 April, is celebrated in the square that bears his name. After mass, a dancer holding a beribboned vine plant performs a dance. In the evening the plant is put on a bonfire but is not allowed to burn. Rejoicing and libations of the local wines are the order of the day.

This garden was created in the early 20th C. on the site of a large Benedictine abbey. It contains oleanders, cypress, judas trees, umbrella pines, roses and typically Mediterranean flora around the ruins of two churches.

Leisurely trips

It is a nice idea to tour the town in a carriage. Information and reservations ☎ 04 90 25 74 55. Open Easter–15 Jun., Sat. and Sun., 9.30am-1pm (leave from Place Jean-Jaurès) and 2.30-7pm (leave from the Tourist Office); 15 Jun.–15 Sept., open daily except Thur. Or you may prefer to take the little train in the historic centre (☎ 04 90 25 37 56).

Fort Saint-André

☎ 04 90 25 45 35.
Open 10am-noon and 2-5pm or 6pm.
Admission charge.
The fortified centre was built in the 14th C. on the orders of Jean le Bon to guard Avignon and protect the little town which had existed for four centuries previously. From the platform of the crenellated twin towers, there is a lovely view over Avignon and the Mont Ventoux.

The Cloister of Saint-Jean in the Chartreuse du Val de Bénédiction

Spotcheck
F3

Gard

Things to do

La Chartreuse du Val de Bénédiction
Parc du Soleil and du Cosmos
St. Mark's Day Festival

Within easy reach

Beaucaire, 26 km SW, p. 260.

Tourist office

Villeneuve-lès-Avignon:
☎ 04 90 25 61 33

Vaulted passage at Fort Saint-André

Around Villeneuve

The Parc du Soleil and du Cosmos

Les Angles (2 miles (3 km)), Avenue du Général-de-Gaulle,
☎ 04 90 25 66 82.
Open daily except Tues., 1 Apr.–15 Oct., 10.30am-noon and 2.30-4pm: or Sat. and Sun. morning.
The park has a model of the universe, including our galaxy, the planets, stars and other satellites. A route with commentary has been traced through the garrigue.

Uzès

This city of art and history, which was saved by André Malraux, can be seen from a great distance, its towers, proudly rising above the tiled roofs, giving it a strongly medieval appearance. The first duchy of France was established here in the 18th C., hence the numerous mansions. This major village on the Mediterranean is one of the loveliest in France and invites leisurely exploration.

Son et lumière at the Duché

☎ 04 66 22 18 96.
Open daily, Jun–14 Sept.. 10am-1pm and 2.30-6.30pm: 15 Sept.–May 10am-noon and 2-6pm.
Admission charge.

This superb complex stands on the site of a Roman fortress. It consists of a large square tower, the Tour Bermonde (11th-C.) and a château with a lovely façade beside a 15th C. chapel which is emblazoned with the motto of the dukes of Uzès: *Ferro non auro* ('By iron, not by gold'). A *son et lumière* performance with about 60 characters recreates the marriage of Simone d'Uzès and the Comte de Crussol in 1486.

Glazed tiles depicting the arms on the roof of the Duchy of Uzès

The three towers

They represent the three powers which caused so many conflicts of interest and authority between the Middle Ages and the French Revolution – the bishop, the king and the duke. The Tour du Roi is a massive 17th-C. square tower on which there are machicolations. The Tour de l'Évêque (in the Rue Entre-les-Tours) was part of the original château. The duchy tower is the Tour Bermonde.

The Cathedral of Saint-Théodorit and the Tour Fenestrelle

The cathedral, on the Rue de l'Évêché, was built in the 17th C. but has a strange 19th-C. façade attached to the original which was judged not to be grand enough. Inside there is a 17th-

Cathedral of Saint-Théodorit and the Tour Fenestrelle

Tympanum of the Cathedral of Saint-Théodorit

Spotcheck
F3

Gard

Things to do

Musée 1900 and Musée
du Train et du Jouet
The Haribo Museum
Uzès Garlic Fair
Place aux Herbes

With children

La Bouscarasse

Within easy reach

Nîmes, 25 km S, p. 252,
Alès, 33 km NW, p. 280.

Tourist office

Uzès: ☎ 04 66 22 68 88

C. organ, restored in 1964. The tower housing the cathedral belfry is a gem of Romanesque art. It is 140 ft (42 m) high and is the only round tower with windows in France.

A walk under the sweet chestnuts

This is a romantic spot in the autumn. The Promenade Jean-Racine, favoured by *pétanque* players, contains the Pavillon Racine built on the remains of a tower which was part of the fortifications, 25 years after Racine visited the town in 1661. The balustrade runs parallel to the severe buildings of the former bishopric. The Parc du Duché is now a recreation ground with tennis courts, a swimming pool and even a camp ground.

THE TRUFFLE MARKET

From November to March a truffle market is held every Saturday, in the Place aux Herbes. Most of the truffles are sold to wholesalers but anyone can buy from the growers. On the third Sunday in January, you can also buy tree seedlings implanted with truffle spores. For enthusiasts try the: Syndicat des Producteurs de Truffes du Gard, 24, Avenue de la Gare (☎ 04 66 22 58 36. Open in the morning 8am-noon). Note that there are guided tours of the truffle-groves with tastings and sales. Truffières du Soleil, Mas du Moulin de la Flesque (☎ 04 66 22 08 41).

Place aux Herbes

The inhabitants of Uzès gather here to celebrate events, happy or sad. The square is ringed with arcades and medieval houses which were 'revised' in the 17th and 18th C. It is especially lively on Saturday mornings, market day. Note the turret on no. 5, the corner house, the Hôtel d'Aigaliers at no. 2 and the Hôtel de la Rochette at no. 26. There is also the Hôtel de Trinquelagues in which the writer André Gide, spent his childhood holidays with his grandmother (p. 125).

The Church of Saint-Étienne and the Quartier des Bourgades

The church was built in the 18th C. in the form of a Greek cross. It is an example of late Baroque and has a handsome façade. Inside, the gilded wooden altar is flanked by two paintings by Romanelli (17th-C.) brought from Rome. Leaving the church, behind the Caisse d'Épargne, you enter the 14th-C. Quartier des Bourgades.

Promontory with a view

Mount Castellas dominates the gorges on the left bank. The white, beige and blue of the hillside contrasts with the green of the *garrigue*. When the weather is fine, there is a good 360° view, with Mont

Bouquet in the north, Mont Ventoux in the east, the *garrigues* and the Cévennes in the northwest.

The beehives of Mas de Tessan
Rue Olivier-de-Serres,
☎ 04 66 22 65 42.
Open 8am-noon and 2-6pm.
The Boileau family of Uzès is a family of bee-keepers. For 30 years, they have been gathering different

types of honey: lavender, sweet chestnut, rosemary, acacia and *garrigue* (35 F to 58 F per 2¼ lb/1 kg). They also sell mead and nougat. You can also find them in the market on Wed. and Sat. morning.

Musée 1900, and Musée du Train et du Jouet
Arpaillargues, 1 mile (3 km) on the road to Anduze, Moulin de Chalier,

☎ 04 66 22 58 64.
Open daily, 9am-noon, 2pm-5pm; July and Aug. 9am-7pm. *Admission charge.*
The Gard is reconstituted in miniature here with its winding railway lines. Model trains and steam engines run on the track. There are also rocking horses and antique games, a player piano, cinema of the brothers Lumière and scenes from 1900.

Uzès Garlic Fair
This has been a tradition since the Middle Ages. The inhabitants of the neighbouring villages make a regular habit of attending the

spectacular **Foire à l'ail** on 24 June. It was once the Fair of St John the Baptist, established by letters patent from Charles IX in 1571. All the garlic growers from the region offer their white, pink or violet cloves.

Around Uzès

Saint-Quentin-la-Poterie
3 miles (5 km) from Uzès
A dozen workshops manufacture and sell earthenware, porcelain, glazed wares and decorative pottery. The **Maison de la Terre** contains a little museum, workshop

and the Terra Viva Gallery (☎ 04 66 22 48 78. Open May–Sept, daily from 10am-12.30pm and 2.30pm-7pm; closed Mon.). You can browse at your leisure and buy the wares. The *toupin* is a local speciality, a pot coated in a yellow glaze. In even years, in mid-July, the Terralha, a **potters' fair** is held in Uzès.

La Caracole

La Cantonade,
Saint-Florent-Auzonnet,
☎ 04 66 25 65 70.
July to end of Oct.,
Fri., Sat. and Sun., 3pm-
7pm; Nov.–June, Sun.
and Wed., 3pm-7pm.
This amusing ecomuseum,
10 miles (15 km) N of Uzès,
will give you a glimpse into
the world of the gastropods,
which are very popular in the
local cuisine (p. 36). At one
time they were also taken for
medicinal purposes.

Gorges of the Gardon

The river Gardon, which
lent its name to the *département*, can turn into a raging
torrent carrying hundreds of
cubic feet of water per second,
then trickle to 88,300 cu ft
(2,500 m³) per second.
This submerged the
bridge under 10 ft (3 m)
of floodwater.

HARIBO

Haribo,
Pont des Charrettes,
☎ 04 66 22 74 39.
Open daily except Mon.,
10am-7pm.
Admission charge.
Crocodiles, Dragibus,
Car-en-sac and the
mythical Tagada
strawberry. Let
anyone who has never
eaten a Haribo sweet cast
the first stone. To learn how they are made,
marvel over old boxes and advertisements, laugh
at Zigoto or Hari-Croco, and other characters and
finally taste the sweets themselves. This is a
delicious place to go.

❀ La Bouscarasse

On the D 981, at
5 miles (8 km),
☎ 04 66 22 50 25.
Open Jun.–Sept. daily,
10am-7pm: May and
Sept. Wed, weekend
and bank holidays,
10am-6pm.
Admission charge.
This aquatic park is in a
huge area shaded by
ancient evergreen oaks.
You can ride down the river
on buoys (for the youngsters)
or swim it. There are
minigolf, a snack bar and
various picnic areas.

though in summer it is a
stream. The river cut these
gorges 330–500 ft
(100–150 m) deep in the
Nîmes *garrigue* over an 18
mile (29 km) stretch between
Dions and the Pont du Gard.
No road runs beside them, so
the only way to see them is by
canoe or kayak. The *gardonnades* are terrible floods but
fortunately they are rare.
During the last one, in 1958,
the water rose at Dions from a

Collias

Collias was once popular with
the hippies in their heyday. In
high summer the beach below
the village gets overcrowded.
There is a path beside the
river. The film *Le salaire de la
peur* (The Wages of Fear) was
filmed on the corniche road a
little further along. If you feel
brave, walk down the valley
and climb up to the hermitage
of Notre-Dame-de-Laval (2.8
miles (4.5 km) round trip).

Bagnols-sur-Cèze

This quiet little provincial market town originally grew up around its Roman baths. It changed suddenly in the 1950s when the Marcoule atomic power station was built. The population quadrupled and a new town sprang up. The old part is still picturesque and pedestrianised and around 14 July, there is a jazz festival. If you stay here, visit the villages, forests, vineyards and beaches along the Cèze.

Place Mallet

This is the former market place and the town centre. There were once stalls in the arcades (now there are tourists) built to protect them from sun and rain. But it is a shame that cars are allowed to park in the centre of this little square – they spoil the look of it. The market is held on Wednesdays and spreads out from here into the neighbouring streets.

Musée Albert-André

Place Mallet,
☎ **04 66 50 50 56.**
Open Jul.–Aug. daily, 10am-noon and 3-7pm: or Tues.–Sun. 10am-noon and 2-6pm.
Admission charge.
This little museum on the second floor of the town hall contains 200 fine paintings by Renoir, Monet, Matisse, Signac and Picasso.

Beautiful mansions

The 17th- and 18th-C. mansions have beautiful façades and it is worth a little walk to see them. In the Place Mallet are the Hôtel de Luynes with its fluted columns, the Hôtel Mallet with its tower and crenellations and, in the Rue Rivarol, the birthplace of the pamphleteer of the same name. There are also the Hôtel de Gorce, Rue Fernand-Crémieux, and the home of Lord Melford.

How does nuclear energy work?

Centre Atomique de Marcoule, Cogema,
Open Jul.–Aug. and bank holidays, book at the Tourist Office. Book before Sat. at noon to visit on Wed. morning.
Free admission.
(15 years old minimum; ID required.).
This will help you understand the fuel cycle and how the Marcoule supergenerator works. There are two rooms, one devoted to nuclear power, the other about this power station, clearly explaining how tomorrow's power

LAVENDER ESSENCE

René Frach, Domaine de Vilgoutrès, Verfeuil, ☎ 04 66 79 02 17. Open Jul.–Aug., 9am-noon and 4-7.30pm; in the morning for the rest of the year.

You can buy flasks of lavender essence at this former wine-cellar set in the middle of lavender fields. It takes 2½ acres (1 ha) of lavender to obtain just 220 lb (100 kg) of essence. This essential oil has many useful healing properties. A few drops of lavender essence in an inhaler, for instance, will unblock the nose, help you sleep, and of course, delicately perfume your bath and linen.

supplies will be produced and distributed. From the look-out post, there is a lovely view of the Rhône and the plain of Nord-Vaucluse.

Around Bagnols

La Roque-sur-Cèze

This village on a steep hill can best be appreciated on foot. Nearby, go and visit the **Cascades du Sautadet** (waterfalls). The Cèze turns into a foaming torrent pouring into pools like deep bowls. You can walk on the rocks above but keep tight hold of children's hands as it can be dangerous. Downstream, there is a beach where swimming is permitted.

Goudargues

An **oasis of freshness** thanks to a channelled spring which winds through the village under the old plane trees and widens out into a lake. Local activities all take place along this canal to the shady square, where *pétanque* players gather. Visit the **abbey**.

Laudun

This large agricultural town stands on the limestone plateau on which Caesar established a camp (the archaeological site covers 44½ acres (18 ha)). In the centre, there is a handsome **Gothic church** dating from the

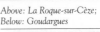

Above: La Roque-sur-Cèze; Below: Goudargues

14th C. The **house of Albert André** is here at 81, Rue de Boulogne. He was a friend of Renoir and became the curator of the museum at Bagnols-sur-Cèze in 1918, which is why the museum is so well endowed. The vast 3rd-C. **Château de Lascours**, 1¼ miles (2 km) away in the direction of Avignon has become a centre for artistic research (music and dance).

A refreshing stop at the Sautadet waterfalls, at the foot of La Roque-sur-Cèze village.

Pont-Saint-Esprit

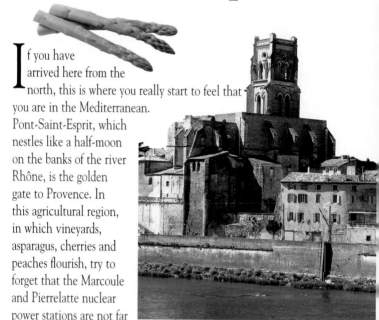

If you have arrived here from the north, this is where you really start to feel that you are in the Mediterranean. Pont-Saint-Esprit, which nestles like a half-moon on the banks of the river Rhône, is the golden gate to Provence. In this agricultural region, in which vineyards, asparagus, cherries and peaches flourish, try to forget that the Marcoule and Pierrelatte nuclear power stations are not far away and sit under the plane trees to drink a glass of wine, especially on Saturday morning, the big market day.

Pont Saint-Esprit

The bridge over the Rhône was built in the late 13th C., from money collected by donation. It is 3,062 ft (919 m) long and the road rests on 25 arches. Although in the 18th C. carts had to cross it empty so as not to topple it, today the heavy holiday traffic (single lane in each direction) proves just how solid it is. There is a lovely view of the town from the bridge.

Musée Paul-Raymond

Place de l'Ancienne-Mairie,
☎ 04 66 90 75 80.
Open daily except Tues. 10am-noon and 3-7pm Jul.–Sept. 10am-noon and 3-7pm Wed., Thur. and Sun., Oct.–May.

Apart from local prehistoric artefacts and religious art of Languedoc, the museum contains the hospital pharmacy including 247 17th- and 18th-C. chemist's jars and 15th-C. Hispano-Mauresque pottery.

CÔTES-DU-RHÔNE

This appellation (AOC) covers the triangle formed by Remoulins, Villeneuve-lès-Avignon and Pont-Saint-Esprit. Two wines are particularly well known: Tavel (king of the rosés and rosé of kings) and Lirac (which comes in white, red and rosé). But you should also try the village's appellations of Chusclan, Laudun and Saint-Gervais. There are many tasting cellars along the little roads such as the Cave des Vignerons de Saint-Gervais (☎ 04 66 82 77 05. Open Tues.–Sat. daily in summer, 8.30-noon, 2.30-6.30pm).

The Citadel

The fortifications were improved by Vauban but were dismantled after World War II. Enter through the Tourist Office to see the former hospital and collegiate church (built c. 1315) with its handsome Gothic portal. From the bridge, walk along the Quai de Luynes to the double flight of steps which leads to the Place Saint-Pierre.

Around Pont-Saint-Esprit

The Chartreuse de Valbonne

Saint-Paulet-de-Caisson, ☎ 04 66 90 41 24. Open daily, in summer 10am-1pm and 2-7pm, in winter 10am-noon and 2-6pm.

Admission charge.
Deep in the forest there is a charterhouse with curtain wall and glazed roof-tiles. You can visit the cells and the cloisters. The charterhouse was built in the 13th C. and converted into a sanatorium for tropical diseases in 1926 (mainly leprosy). It now produces a good Côtes-du-Rhône.

Valbonne forest

Leave the town and go for a walk in the magnificent 3,360-acre (1,400-ha) forest, mainly of evergreen oak. This huge **arboretum** is maintained and supervised by the ONF, the French forestry commission, which recently replanted it. It is one of the primeval Mediterranean forests, almost all of which have disappeared. Lovely **walks** along GR 42 which pass the Maison Forestière (information centre).

Things to do

Walks in the Valbonne forest
Tasting Côtes-du-Rhône wine
The citadel

Tourist office

Pont-Saint-Esprit:
☎ 04 66 39 44 45

Cornillon

This little village winds snail-like around the dismantled castle at the top of a 267-ft (80-m) hill. The benches against the façade are made from two antique columns. The houses are huddled together in narrow lanes as protection against the Mistral. Nice view of the valley.

Chartreuse de Valbonne

Alès

The very mention of coal mines conjures up a picture of a black town, slag-heaps, dust, sadness and desolation. At the Mine Témoin you can see mining conditions as they would have been in Zola's day. But this town, at the gateway to the Cévennes, deep in the valley beside the Gardon, has much that is of interest, especially as it endeavours to preserve the memory of its past in industrial tourism. Here is a different kind of identity, in amongst the *garrigues* and the grasshoppers.

Grotte de la Cocalière

Barjac

Château de Portes

St-Ambroix

Méjannes-le-Clap

Château de Rousson

Le Guidon du Bouquet

Alès

The Cathedral of Saint-Jean

This is a strange mixture of a Romanesque church, of which all that remains is a tiny piece of the façade hidden behind a 15th C. belfry, a Gothic nave, and a Renaissance choir rebuilt in the 18th C. In the **Chapel of the Virgin**, there is a painting by Mignard, *The Assumption of the Virgin*.

Fort Vauban and the Jardins du Bosquet

The fort was built in 1688 as protection against the Huguenots. It now contains the municipal archives and is not open to the public. The **public park** with its ancient trees that surrounds it contains exhibits of finds from archaeological digs. There is a nice view of the town.

Château du Colombier

☎ 04 66 86 30 40.
Open daily except Tues. and public holidays, June–Sept. 2-7pm.
This majestic complex overlooks the town. The façade is Classical and the interior was renovated in the 19th C. There is a pigeon-loft from which the château gets its name. It contains archaeological finds and a collection of paintings.

Musée de l'École des Mines

6, Avenue de Clavières,
☎ 04 66 78 51 69.
Open 15 June–15 Sept., daily except weekend, 2-6pm; out of season by appointment.
Admission charge.
It will take you an hour to see the 700 or so samples of rocks and minerals from all over the world out of the 5,000 stored here. Don't miss the Australian opal and a smoky

❀ LA MINE TÉMOIN

Chemin de la Cité-Rochebelle,
☎ **04 66 30 45 15.**
Open June–Aug., 9.30am-5.30pm; Sept.–May,
9am-12.30pm and 2-5.30pm.
Admission charge.
This is a retrospective of mining from the time of
Emile Zola to today. You wear a miner's helmet and
carry a lamp, wandering through 2,170 ft (650 m)
of tunnels. Pit-props, coal-cutting, removing it and
examples of coal faces will give you an idea of the
back-breaking work of mining a generation ago.

quartz from the Aveyron.
There are displays to explain
rock formations.

Wild mushrooms

Maison Lagarde,
1091, Avenue des
Maladreries,
☎ **04 66 86 11 41.**
Open Mon.–Fri., 9am-
noon and 2-5.30pm.
The oldest wild mushroom
cannery in France has been
operating since 1893. Ceps,
morels and other woodland
fungi are preserved for the
delight of connoisseurs. You
can also buy jams made from
figs, watermelons and peaches.

Saint-Ambroix

❀ Préhistorama

Musée des Origines et
de l'Évolution de
l'Homme, on the D 904
between Alès and Saint-
Ambroix
☎ **04 66 85 86 96.**
Open 1 Apr.–1 Sept.,
10am-7pm; March–Oct.,
2-5pm; closed Dec.
and Jan.
Admission charge.
A Scandinavian, Erik
Granqvist, has produced his
own version of the world of
our ancestors some 2 million
years ago. People and mam-

moths are all life-size and
there are scenes from everyday life. A combination of the
unusual, the humorous and
the scientific.

Parc Ornithologique des Îles, Saint-Julien-de-Cassagnas

☎ **04 66 25 66 13.**
Open daily, 9am-6pm or
7pm depending on the
season.
Admission charge.
Thousands of birds from the
tiny wren to the huge ostrich
live in this shady 6-acre (2.5-
ha) park. They were collected
by a former nurseryman.
You won't be able to see them
all on the same day, however.
You can picnic here and there
is also a snack-bar.

Spotcheck

E3

Gard

Things to do

La Mine Témoin (Mining
Museum)
Préhistorama
Wild mushroom cannery
Barjac antiques market

Within easy reach

Uzès, 33 km SE, p. 272.

Tourist office

Alès: ☎ 04 66 52 32 15

Château de Portes
☎ 04 66 34 35 90.
Open 1 Jul.–30 Sept,
Tues.–Sun., 9am-1pm
and 3-7pm; out of
season, same opening
hours. Sat. Sun.
Admission charge.
For centuries, this handsome
monument has guarded the
road between le Puy-en-Velay
and Saint-Gilles. It consists
of two very different parts:
one is medieval, the other
Renaissance, which gives it its
original silhouette. There is a
lovely view of the Lozère from
the terrace.

Grotte de la Cocalière
☎ 04 66 24 01 57.
Open 1 Apr.–1 Nov.,
10am-6pm.
Admission charge.

This cave contains rare **disc
stalagmites**, as well as **crystal-
clear pools** and a **prehistoric
gallery** which is well present-
ed. A bicycle race is held here
every year. You return to the
entrance on a little train along
a route lined with prehistoric
and geological remains.

*Around Mont
Bouquet*

Guidon du Bouquet
This peak is
reached via the
D 6, and at an
altitude of
2,100 ft (629 m)
it is the summit of
a chalk ridge. On
one side there is the
garrigue (scrubland)
and on the other
escarpments and
sheer cliffs below the
summit. At the very
top there is

a chapel and a 19th-C. statue
of the Admirable Mother.
The **view** extends over the
plain of Alès, the Cévennes,
the *garrigues* and, in the
distance, the Rhône valley,
Mont Ventoux and the Alps.

Château de Rousson
6¼ miles (10 km) from
Alès by the D 904,
☎ 04 66 85 60 31.
Open daily Easter–All
Saints' Day, 10am-7pm.
This massive 17th-C. building
has an impressive sculpted
and reinforced door. There
are lovely old tiles, period
furniture and

a superb cabinet from Uzès. The kitchen, with its huge fireplace and mantelpiece and bread oven, is well worth seeing. There is also an old pirate's chest. From the

terrace there is a lovely view over the Aigoual and Mont Ventoux.

Méjannes-le-Clap
Holiday and leisure complex

There are campgrounds, hotels, sports facilities, and signposted hiking trails for young and old, as well as the gorges of the Cèze with their beaches and naturist camps.

All these will particularly delight those holidaymakers who have opted for the *garrigue* rather than the seaside.

Especially for sports enthusiasts

If you can't decide, even for a single day, between hiking, mountain-biking, rock-climbing, potholing, canyoning, canoeing or kayaking,

Virgin of the Chapel of Guidon du Bouquet

contact Sud Loisirs, ☎ 04 66 24 40 94 or ☎ 04 66 24 10 70. Accompanied by experts, you can explore the Pont d'Arc or canoe in the white waters of the gorges de la Cèze or the Ardèche.

Anduze

Anduze rises like an amphitheatre on the banks of the Gardon, squashed between two cliffs. It is at the junction between the plain of Languedoc and the mountains of the Cévennes. It has narrow lanes with elegant covered entrances, numerous fountains, parks and potteries. Due to the quality of the local red clay, the town has made a name for itself as the creator of a particular kind of vase (see p. 58).

Tour de l'Horloge

The clock tower was built in 1320, and has the same architecture as the ramparts of Aigues-Mortes. When the rest of the ramparts were destroyed in 1629 the tower was spared. Nearby there is a Bicentennial Fountain erected in 1989 by an Anduzian.

Parc des Cordeliers

Avenue Rollin.
This park, which once belonged to a convent, has a superb avenue of bamboo cedar and magnolia. From the terrace, you can look out over the valley and see right to the Château de Tornac. A statue of a 12th-C. female

troubadour, Clara d'Anduze, erected in 1895, is a reminder of the cultural importance of the town.

Musée de la Musique

Route d'Alès,
☎ 04 66 61 86 60.
Open Jul.–Aug., daily, 10am-1pm and 3-7pm; June, Sept. and school holidays, Sun. and public holidays, 2-6pm. Guided tour every hour. *Admission charge.*
There are 1,000 instruments from all over the world, dating from the 16th C. to today and they can each be heard individually. There are also concerts, workshops and training courses.

The fountains

Many fountains decorate the town. The most extraordinary, **The Pagoda,**

The Pagoda Fountain

(1648), owes its glazed tiles and Oriental style to a local boy who went to the Orient in search of silkworm eggs.

Anduze pottery

Les Enfants de Boisset, Route de Saint-Jean-du-Gard,
☎ 04 66 61 80 86.
Daily visits to the workshops, 9am-noon and 2-7pm.
This family, which has been working with clay since 1610, supplies garden vases to stately homes. They all obey the same rules of shape and colour. There are nine sizes of vases, the largest of which measures 3.3 ft (1 m) by 31$^1/_2$ in (80 cm) and weighs 17 stone (110 kg)! The colours are

THE ANDUZE BAMBOO GROVE

**Prafrance, Générargues,
☎ 04 66 61 70 47.**
Open 1 March–31 Dec.
from 9.30am-7pm; closed
on Mon and Tues. in Nov.
and Dec.

**Bamboo was brought to
the Cévennes in the 19th
C. This bamboo grove,
created 150 years ago,
contains 150 species. The**
100-acre (40-ha) park is crossed by an avenue of
67 ft (20 m) high bamboos and giant sequoias
from California. Another avenue is lined with palm
trees and has a tulip tree from Virginia. There are
also magnolias, banana trees and ginkgo biloba.

Spotcheck
E3

Gard

Things to do

Musée de la Musique
The little steam train
Anduze pottery
Sauve and the Sea of Rocks

To do with children

Musée du Santon

Tourist Office

Anduze: ☎ 04 66 61 98 17

---

marbled, a mixture of honey
yellow, olive green and chestnut brown. Other craft potteries at Anduze include:
Poterie de la Madeleine
(☎ 04 66 61 63 44);
Le Chêne vert
(☎ 04 66 61 70 24);
La Draille
(☎ 04 66 61 83 59).

The little steam train

Open daily 15 June–end
of Aug.; 1 Apr.–15 June,
Tues.–Sun.
The little train runs from
Anduze to Saint-Jean-du-
Gard, covering 8 miles
(13 km) in 1¼ hours, including the cinder shower (the
carriages are open), with a
stop at the bamboo grove.

Around Anduze

From Anduze to Saint-Hippolyte-du-Fort

Some 37½ miles (60 km) of
road edged with *garrigues* end
in a bastion of Protestantism
and a silk-weaving centre
(p. 52). The Écomusée (open
Jul. and Aug. daily, 10am-
6.30pm, other opening hours
the rest of the year,
☎ 04 66 77 66 47) retraces
the history of these techniques (silkworm farming,
spinning, milling, weaving).
The Association pour le
Développement de la
Sériculture (☎ 04 66 77 66 47)
will tell you all about the **Silk
Road** (p. 53).

Sauve and the Sea of Rocks

A two-hour signposted route
will take you from this picturesque **medieval village** to
a landscape consisting of
hundreds of rocks which have
been eroded into many
strange shapes. After passing
the Château de Roquevaire,
you reach the Sea of Rocks, a
wonderful – or frightening –
sight.

Musée du Santon

**Place du Tilleul,
Générargues,
☎ 04 66 61 66 74.**
Open daily July.–Aug.,
10am-noon and 2-7pm.
Thanks to these little figures,
the life and occupations of
Cévennes and Provence are
represented here through 200
figurines, with the help of *son
et lumière*. There is a large
Christmas crib from
November to March.

Le Vigan
and the gorges of the Dourbie

Although you are at the foot of the Aigoual, you can't see it. This is still the Cévennes, although this sub-prefecture of the Gard is still redolent of the south. Spring water runs in many of the town's fountains and is even piped to the inhabitants. Schappe – thread woven from silk remnants – is no longer produced here, but has been replaced by socks and tights. Le Vigan has plenty of charm!

The town

Le Vigan is only 25 miles (40 km) from Mont Aigoual, along a **scenic route** which inspired the writer André Chamson. A guided tour of the village is organised by appointment (☎ 04 67 81 01 72); in 2½ hours you can visit the Musée Cévenol and the Parc des Châtaigniers, and discover its urban and industrial heritage.

Musée Cévenol

1, Rue des Calquières, ☎ 04 67 81 06 86. Open Apr.–end of Oct., daily except Tues., 10am-noon and 2-6pm;

Nov.–March, Wed. 10am-noon and 2-6pm. *Admission charge.* Three storeys are devoted to the **Arts and Traditions of the Cévennes and the Pays Viganais**, a land of sweet chestnuts and silk; a craft room shows glass-making and basket-weaving. In another room, there is a clog-maker and cooper.

Parc des Châtaigniers

This was a fairground in the Middle Ages. Unfortunately, many of the trees have been destroyed by disease but a few are 250 years old. There are also acacias, service-trees, red oak, sycamores, limes and Douglas fir.

From russets to socks

The golden russet is the queen of apples in Vigan. Buy the apples on Tuesday, Thursday and Saturday mornings. If your legs are cold, you can always buy stockings, knee-highs, socks or tights at

Bresson-Rande, 5, Quai du Pont (open 9.30am-noon and

1.30-6.30pm except Sun. and Mon., ☎ 04 67 81 66 66), or at the factory shop of the Weil brand in the Quartier Saint-Euzéby (open Tues., Thurs., Fri. 10am-noon, 2-6.30pm, Wed. and Sat. 10am-6pm).

Coluche in a sculpture

Strange but true, there is a statue of the French comedian Coluche in a garden behind the Caisse d'Épargne (savings bank, formerly the Hôtel de Ginestous). Christian Zénéré sculpted it and offered it to the Provençal village in which Coluche died.

They did not want it so the mayor of Le Vigan brought it here.

Around Le Vigan

Valley of the Arre

Leave Le Vigan by the D 999 towards Saint-Affrique.
On one side the valley runs along beside the escarpments of the arid Causse de Blandas, and on the other side it faces the wooded Lingas mountain. The road is lined with 18th- and 19th-C. silk mills. The village of Arre has always specialised in textile dyeing and the making of silk stockings. There is a lovely view at Esparon, a village on a rocky outcrop.

Gorges of the Dourbie

Leave from Le Vigan towards the Aigoual on the D 48.
After the Col du Minier (if the weather is good you can see as far as the Mediterranean) and before the Espérou, continue along the D 151 which winds like a corniche around the wild gorges in which many sweet chestnuts grow. The Dourbie, which flows between the Causse Noir and Le Larzac, is a stream abundant with fresh trout.

DONKEY RIDE

Mas Equestre, Les Magettes,
☎ 04 67 82 02 31.
Admission charge.
For a lovely family outing, come to the farm with your children (aged between 4 and 10 years old). You have the set menu and after coffee, you go for a walk in the *causse* (limestone plateau), while your child rides on a donkey's back. A delicious snack awaits you on your return. If you like, you can also travel through the plateau on horseback.

The old bridge of Le Vigan

Parc National des Cévennes

The Cévennes National Park was created to protect the landscape, wildlife and architectural heritage of this part of France. Take part in moving the flocks to their summer pasture, marvel at a martagon lily or carnivorous plants, cross fields of menhirs and the *dolines des Causses* (oases of fertility); there are so many ways of learning about the Cévennes. On the back of a donkey, on a mountain-bike, on foot or on horseback, the visitor can take in the varied landscapes, set with little hamlets, *gîtes* or traditional inns in which to stay.

Le Pont-de-Montvert

Ste-Énimie

Florac

Génolhac

Le Pompidou

Mt Aigoual

Meyrueis

L'Espérou

St-Jean-du-Gard

Why a national park?

In the early 20th C., local society in the Cévennes was on the verge of collapse. Two wars, sweet chestnut disease and the decline of the silk trade caused four-fifths of the population of the upper Cévennes to leave and look for work elsewhere. In this empty space, a few people became aware of the need to preserve both the natural and human heritage, which was in the process of disappearing forever. In 1956, the General Council of Lozère began campaigning for the creation of a national park in the region. The park was officially created in 1970.

An inhabited park

The park is a semi-mountainous region in the heart of the Cévennes crescent. Covering 226,000 acres (91,500 ha) it is the largest of the seven national parks in France. It is also the only national park that is inhabited (600 people) and is one of **UNESCO's World Biosphere Reserves**. The *raison d'être* of the park is not only to preserve nature but also to maintain a

landscape which has been strongly affected by human intervention for centuries. From the snow-capped peaks of the Monts Lozère and Aigoual to the low valleys sculpted in shale, via the limestone *causse* (plateau) of Méjean, the **flora and fauna** of the area are **unique.**

Rambles

The park authorities publish wonderful guides to help you understand what you are seeing as you walk. There are 16 educational paths which are

CELEBRATIONS

On the Sunday after the Feast of the Assumption (15 August), there is a big fair in the region. It starts with a market in the morning and continues all day with demonstrations of peasant skills (wood and stone carving) and workshops for young and old. You can learn to dance the *bourrée*, for instance. Every year, the park also organises a **Nature Festival** which includes guided walks, slide shows and lectures, workshops, fairs and peasant markets.

like Robert Louis Stevenson (p. 124), apply to Gentiane: (Christian Brochier, Castagnols-Vialas, 48220 Le Pont-de-Montvert, ☎ 04 66 41 04 16). Finally, as regards accommodation, we suggest you rent a **gîte rural**, like the one at Merlet (2,000 F a week for 2 to 4 people), or a 16th-C. hamlet, restored by Catherine et Philippe (Le Merlet, 48220 Pont-de-Montvert, ☎ 04 66 45 82 92). You will get helpful advice and delicious food.

Discovering a chestnut grove

The sweet chestnut has fed humans and animals for centuries and during the Middle Ages it was a typical feature of the landscape of the Cévennes. The entire tree is useful. The fruit,

easy to walk and even accessible by car (car park at the start of the route); **signposted paths** are also described in three booklets (Mont Lozère and Bougès, Causses-Cévennes, Aigoual-Lingas) which are circular tours of less than one day (the booklets cost 25 F in the park information centres at Florac, ☎ 04 66 49 53 01). You can go **pony-trekking**, for one or more days. Information at the École d'Équitation Pirouette (Le Pont-du-Tarn, Florac, ☎ 04 66 45 29 85. Open the whole year round). Some rambles are designed specially for children. If you want to cover the region on a donkey

Spotcheck
D2-E2-D3-E3

Gard et Lozère

Things to do

The Nature Festival
Hiking, mountain-biking, rambling
Visit a chestnut grove

Things to do with children

Pony-trekking

Within easy reach

Mont Lozère, p. 296, Causses lozériens, p. 298, Gorges du Tarn, p. 300.

Tourist office

Florac: ☎ 04 66 49 53 01

the leaves which were used as animal litter and fertiliser, and its hard wood which used in buildings (rafters, flooring, stairs and furniture). Hives could be dug into its trunk, baskets made from its split wood, not forgetting barrels and vine-stakes. To see a chestnut grove, take the **Sentier de la Roquette** which belongs to the Ecomusée de la Cévenne. Information from the National Park of the Cévennes, ☎ 04 66 49 53 01.

The Cévennes corniche

Florac

Le Mazel

St -Laurent-de-Trèves

N.D. de Valfrancesque

Barre-des-Cévennes

St-Étienne-Vallée-Française

Pont-Ravagers

Le Pompidou

Grotte de Trabuc

St-André-de-Valborgne

Col de l'Exil

Col-de-St-Pierre

St-Jean-du-Gard

T he corniche road, 33 miles (53 km) long, which runs between Florac and Saint-Jean-du-Gard between two peaks, is very picturesque. It was built in the 18th C. to enable Louis XIV's army to march deep into the Cévennes to fight the Protestants. The best time for a walk is late afternoon when the light is very beautiful. Then move on to the outskirts of Saint-Jean-du-Gard.

Écomusées des Cévennes
Information:
☎ **04 66 49 53 01.**
The Cévennes National Park has set up **three ecological museums**, the Mont Lozère Museum, the Cévennes Museum and the Museum of the Causse and the Gorges.

These museums preserve the heritage and collective memory of links forged between a land, a society and a culture. They offer itineraries for trips such as the Romanesque church circuit.

Le Can de l'Hospitalet and Le Col des Faïsses
Can means 'a high, flat area' which is characterised by underground rivers and pot-holes. The *can* here is crossed by a *draille* (road for taking the sheep up to pasture) of Margeride. The road is lined by tall standing stones, the *mont-joies*, which were once used to guide ancient travellers during snow or fog. You can enjoy a delicious, hearty lunch at the Ferme de l'Hospitalet.

A lone mont-joie *on the Can de l'Hospitalet*

THE TERRACES OF THE CÉVENNES

These are part of the Cévennes landscape and are called *bancels* or *faïsses*. They are narrow strips of land (some are only two steps wide) shored up with little walls and are the only cultivated areas, some of them laboriously dug out of the mountainside. They need constant maintenance to prevent the rain carrying away the soil. They are used mainly for growing vines, olive trees, mulberry trees and sweet chestnuts, but also grain and sweet onions.

Col de l'Exil and the Col de Saint-Pierre

The Col de l'Exil takes its name from the banished Protestants who took their last look at the Cévennes here. There is a lovely view of the Aigoual. At the Signal Saint-Pierre, orientation tables indicate the names of places in the landscape.

Vallée Borgne

To the south, at the foot of the Cévennes corniche, the Borgne valley forms a sort of cul-de-sac. The very beautiful road takes you through traditional hamlets, ruined châteaux and little Huguenot cemeteries.

Notre-Dame-de-Valfrancesque

Vallée-Française

This is the Cévennes of Robert Louis Stevenson's travels (see p. 124), an enclave in the midst of the preserved mountains. Places to see include **Notre-Dame-de-Valfrancesque**, an 11th-C. masterpiece of Romanesque Cévennes architecture, built in honour of Roland, Charlemagne's nephew, who vanquished the Saracens here. At **Pont-Ravagers**, an old forge contains a little local museum, Le Mazel, a 17th-C. château and the 11th-C. Tour du Canourgue. Visit the **Calberte Château**,

(see p. 124)

Spotcheck
D3-E3

Gard et Lozère

Things to do

Ecomusées des Cévennes (Ecological Museums)
Atlantide Parc
The Cévennes on horseback
Vallée Borgne

Within easy reach

*Mont Lozère, p. 296,
Causses lozériens, p. 298,
Gorges du Tarn, p. 300.*

Tourist Office

Florac: ☎ 04 66 49 53 01

(☎ 04 66 45 90 30) restored by Daniel Darnas, a carver and goldsmith, whose jewellery and sculptures are displayed in the castle keep.

Florac

Château de Florac

☎ 04 66 49 53 01.
Open daily Jul.–
Aug., 9am-7pm, or
Mon.–Fri. 9-11.45am
and 2-5.45pm;
weekends until 11 Nov.
and from May.

This large 17th-C. château, flanked by round towers, is the headquarters of the Parc National des Cévennes (numerous brochures available). From here you can wander through the old town.

L'Atelier du Sucre et de la Châtaigne

64 Avenue Jean Monestier,
04 66 45 28 41.
Open daily
9am-
12.30pm
and 3-
7.15pm.
Experience all the flavours and fragrances of the Cévennes. This shop sells foods based on chestnut flour: biscuits, spice bread with chestnut honey (21 F), *tuiles* with chestnuts (14 F for a 3 oz/80 g bag).

Saint-Laurent-de-Trèves

Prehistoric footprints

When the dinosaurs lived 200 million years ago, there was a lagoon here which was inhabited by grallators, bipeds about 13 ft (4 m) high. An **audiovisual show** in the old church retraces their life (open daily 3 Jul.–3 Sept., 10am-7pm, 10 May–2 Jul. and 4 Sept.–22 Oct., daily except Tues. 10am-noon and 2-6pm). Their traces are visible on the little plateau which dominates the village. There is a **lovely view** over the Causse Méjean and Monts Aigoual and Lozère.

Barre-des-Cévennes

The Church of Notre-Dame-de-l'Assomption

This long village lies 2 miles (3 km) off the corniche road. Its main street can hardly have

changed since the 16th C. with houses taller than they are wide and little terraced gardens. The church was built in the 12th C., but rebuilt in the Renaissance and again in the 19th C. It is worth a visit.

THE CÉVENNES ON HORSEBACK

Les Falguières,
☎ 04 66 85 18 15.
Open all year round.
Booking only.

By far the most pleasant way to discover the valley of the Gardon is on horseback. A two-hour ride will enable you to discover the site of la Borie. Circuits of 16 or 25 miles (25 or 40 km) are organised; you will then get a taste of life in the wild mountains of the Cévennes, crossed by numerous little streams and inhabited by a wide variety of wildlife. Children aged from three to six can also go on pony rides and stay at Les Falguières.

Saint-Jean-du-Gard

Taking your time

This little capital of the land of the *camisards* (Protestants) (p. 78), with its southern feel, is a former silk-weaving centre (p. 52). Take the time to walk down the **Grand-Rue** edged with houses with lovely entrances, including the Hôtel du Chevalier d'Algues which now contains the Tourist Office. The former spinning mill, called the Maison-Rouge, is richly decorated and is now a regional furniture factory. In summer there is a big market in the town on Tuesday mornings.

Musée des Vallées Cévenoles

95, Grand-Rue,
☎ 04 66 85 10 48.
Open daily except Sun. morning and Mon., 10.30am-12.30pm and 2-7pm. *Admission charge.* Life in the villages and the countryside is wonderfully reconstructed in this former 17th-C. inn. Tools, photos and documents as well as chestnut and silkworm cultivation are given due prominence.

✤ Atlantide Parc

Avenue de la Résistance,
☎ 04 66 85 32 32.
Open daily 9.30am-8pm. *Admission charge.* Imagine about 60 tanks in a reconstruction of the Palace of the Pharaoh Amenhotep III. Do not approach the electric eel too closely; it discharges a current of up to 1,000 volts. Fish swim among the mangrove roots.

Statue of Rameses II 17 ft (5 m) high and made of stucco, plaster and resin at the Atlantide Parc

Festival International de la Randonnée et de l'Aventure

Information,
☎ 04 66 85 17 94.
In memory of Robert Louis Stevenson, who crossed the Cévennes with his donkey Modestine, every year since 1990, a festival reserved for **non-motorised sports** is held on All Saints' Day (30 October) and Ascension Day (40 days after Easter). There are rambles, pony-treks and mountain-bike rides.

Mialet

The Musée du Désert

Mas Soubeyran (7 miles (11 km) S of Saint-Jean-du-Gard),
☎ 04 66 85 02 72.
Open 1 March–30 Nov., 9.30am-noon and 2.30-6pm, Jul.–Aug., 9am-6pm. *Admission charge.* This museum in a typical Cévennes hamlet with narrow paved streets, housed in the birthplace of the head of the *camisard* rebels, Pierre Laporte, alias Roland, celebrates the memory of the Huguenots. There is a remarkable collection of 16th-to 18th-C. bibles.

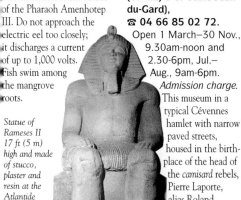

La Grotte de Trabuc

☎ 04 66 85 03 28.
Open 1 March–30 June and 1 Sept.–30 Nov., 9.30am-noon and 2-6pm; Jul.–Aug., 9.30am-6.30pm. *Admission charge.* There is a guided tour of this amazing cave 1,333 yards (1,200 m) long, which lasts approximately an hour. The black aragonite, emerald green Midnight Lake, Devil's Bridge, waterfalls – and a unique formation of 100,000 'soldiers', strange little stalagmites grouped on either side of the 'Great Wall of China'.

Cendras

Écomusée de la Vallée du Galeizon

Place Roger-Assenas,
☎ 04 66 30 21 83
(Ask for M. Anton).
Open all year round; daily during school holidays, except Sun., Mon. and Wed.; in summer, daily, 9am-noon and 2-6pm.
The Association Culturelle du Galeizon gives guided tours of this carefully protected valley of 19,800 acres (8,000 ha) whose population is only 2,500 inhabitants. The various types of landscape are described, as are the flora and fauna of a region that has been inhabited since early prehistory. The river is one of the purest in France and inhabited by beavers and otters. You can also help with farming activities.

Mont Aigoual

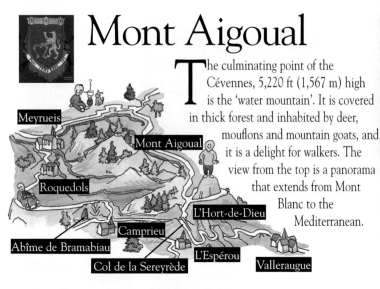

The culminating point of the Cévennes, 5,220 ft (1,567 m) high is the 'water mountain'. It is covered in thick forest and inhabited by deer, mouflons and mountain goats, and it is a delight for walkers. The view from the top is a panorama that extends from Mont Blanc to the Mediterranean.

Meyrueis

Mont Aigoual

Roquedols

L'Hort-de-Dieu

Camprieu

Abîme de Bramabiau

L'Espérou

Col de la Sereyrède

Valleraugue

The botanists path

One mile (1.5 km) before reaching the top of Mont Aigoual, there is a ½ mile (1 km) signposted path. This makes it possible to explore the three sides of the mountain by walking through mountain pastures above the Hort-de-Dieu arboretum and before moving to the east slope. The cold, windy north face is covered in beech and fir trees while the south face is planted with pines and spruce.

L'Espérou

Return to the Col de Sereyrède past the Hérault waterfall before you get to this village surrounded by forests and mountain pastures. A festival is held every year on the route to these pastures, when shepherds take their flock to spend the summer in the valley of the Dourbie. In winter, skiers meet at Prat-Peyrot.

Col de la Sereyrède

The peak is 4,330 ft (1,300 m) high at the line where the waters divide. In June, thousands of head of

sheep take this route from the *garrigues* to the pastures of the Aubrac or the Margeride (today these hardy beasts are sometimes taken there by truck!). There is a fine view over the Hérault valley. **Park Information centre** at the Maison Forestière.

Roquedols

Forest trees

1¼ miles (2 km) from Meyrueis. The castle is now the National Park Information Centre,

☎ 04 66 45 62 81.
Open Jul.–Aug.,
9.30am-12.30pm and
3-6.30pm, except Sun.
and Mon. morning.
This path teaches you about the forest (about a 30 minute walk) and introduces you to the pectin fir, Austrian oak, sycamore and sequoia.

Local products

**Les fermes des Jontanels,
from Meyrueis, take the D 996 in the direction of Florac, then the D 19 on the right.**
This hamlet was revived by cheese-makers from Lilles in the 1970s. It is also the home of Josiane Estève, who breeds angora rabbits.
(☎ 04 66 45 65 72). You can visit her farm and buy pullovers,

Château de Roquedols

berets and scarves, and you can taste her jams. The hamlet also produces cheese and charcuterie. You can watch cheese being made (daily around 11am) and goats being milked (from 5pm; ☎ 04 66 45 63 71).

Meyrueis
'In the midst of streams'

This little town is within the Aigoual, the Causse Noir and the Causse Méjean, at an altitude of 2,350 ft (706 m). It has some lovely houses including the 16th-C. Viguier house, the Belon house and the clock tower (home of the Tourist Office). If you take the D 986, it will take you 20 miles (32 km) all the way to the top (it takes about three hours).

Campieu
Abîme de Bramabiau

☎ 04 67 82 60 78.
Open 1 Apr.–11 Nov. daily, 9am-6pm or 7pm. *Admission charge.*

A stream called the Bonheur, rises in the mountain and disappears underground in a 4-mile (6.5-km) labyrinth. It then emerges loudly (apparently 'like a bull roaring') through a 267-ft (80-m) channel. You can climb up several hundred yards of its course in 1½ hours.

Vallerangue
Strenuous walks

The winding D 986, offers **exceptional views**. The steep slopes have been terraced on which the sweet onion or *raïolette*, is cultivated.

A path 'of 4,000 steps' takes you to the top in five hours of strenuous walks (a gradient of more than 3,333 ft/1,000 m).

Spotcheck
D3

Gard et Lozère

Things to do

The botanists' path
Down Mont Aigoual on a mountain bike
Visit a weather station
Sample and buy local produce

Within easy reach

*Mont Lozère, p. 296,
Causses lozériens, p. 298,
Gorges du Tarn, p. 300.*

Tourist Office

Roquedols:
☎ 04 66 45 62 81

DOWN MONT AIGOUAL ON A MOUNTAIN BIKE

Fremyc, Place Sully,
☎ 04 66 45 61 04.
Open Jun.–Sept., 8am-8pm.

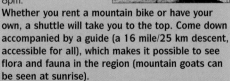

Whether you rent a mountain bike or have your own, a shuttle will take you to the top. Come down accompanied by a guide (a 16 mile/25 km descent, accessible for all), which makes it possible to see flora and fauna in the region (mountain goats can be seen at sunrise).

Weather station

☎ 04 67 82 60 01.
Open daily 1 June–30 Sept., 10am-7pm.
Free admission.

By visiting this weather station which is still operating, you will understand clouds, storms and masses of hot air and can admire equipment, old and new. Amateur meteorologists can buy thermometers, rain-gauges and other vital instruments for the study of the weather.

Mont Lozère

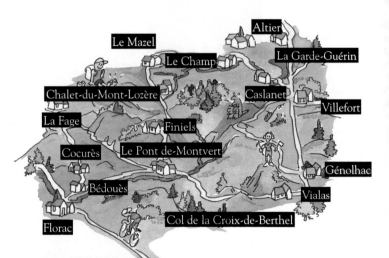

Le Mazel
Altier
Le Champ
La Garde-Guérin
Chalet-du-Mont-Lozère
Caslanet
Villefort
La Fage
Finiels
Cocurès
Le Pont de-Montvert
Génolhac
Bédouès
Vialas
Florac
Col de la Croix-de-Berthel

This bare mountain, between the highlands of the Massif Central, the valley of the Tarn, the waters of the Cèze and of the Lot, is a majestic granite bastion. A multitude of streams rise here. In June, the slopes are covered in beech and pines and bright with golden broom. The drosera, a carnivorous plant with bright red hairs, grows in the short grass. A 110-mile (176-km) tour should preferably take two days, the roads being narrow and winding.

La Cham des Bondons

This limestone plateau dominates the countryside north of Florac. Black marl is protected by a cap of limestone and dolomites. According to popular tradition, this is mud from the dirty clogs of Gargantua when he leapt from a neighbouring *causse* and shook them out on the foothills of Mont Lozère. More than a hundred granite menhirs are spread over the landscape. There is a path to take you to the most beautiful of them.

Between Bédouès and the Pont-de-Montvert

Leave Florac to take the D 998 which climbs the valley of the Tarn through fields and orchards. The old village of Bédouès is dominated

by the Church of Notre-Dame, a collegiate church founded in the 14th C., destroyed, and rebuilt in the 19th C., with a rather incongruous belltower. After Cocurès, the road climbs the valley, which narrows. The Tarn runs beside

Mont Lozère

the beech, oak, spruce and fir of the forest of Bougè, whose wildlife includes wild boar, mountain goats and grouse.

Écomusée du Mont Lozère

Le Pont-de-Montvert, ☎ 04 66 45 80 73. Open daily 15 Apr.–30 Sept. and All Saints' Day holidays, 10.30am-12.30pm and 2.30-6.30pm.

The **Maison du Mont Lozère** must be visited if you want to learn about the Lozère. As regards its traditions and inhabitants, the **Ferme de Troubat**, with its barns, cowshed and mill is ideal. From the Camargues farmhouse, a **path** takes you through pastures, moors and grassland of which the estate consists. There is lots of information about hikes, rambles, excursions, rivers and so on.

From Finiels to Altier

Passing through the little ski resort of Chalet-du-Mont-Lozère you will see the standing stones, along an old path, which once served as landmarks to travellers in the snow. At Mazel, old silver-bearing lead mines are reminders of how important mining once was in this region. Just before Altier, the Château du Champ provides a romantic little backdrop to the landscape.

Lac de Villefort

A dam 640 ft (192 m) long and more than 233 ft (70 m) high has created a run-off of about 1.23 million ft³ (35 million m³). **Bathing** and **windsurfing** are allowed on the lake. Visit the **Château de Castanet** (open daily May–Oct., 10.30am-12.30pm and 3-6pm; Apr.–May and Oct., Sat.–Sun., ☎ 04 66 46 81 11). Fortunately it has been saved from the floodwaters of the dam. Visit its well-furnished Renaissance rooms.

La Garde-Guérin

All that remains of the 10th-C. citadel which was besieged, razed and dismantled, is a tower 90 ft (27 m) high. Enter the church (12th–17th C.) to admire its hammer-beam roof and sculpted capitals. Walk through the cobbled streets and admire the lovely façades of the houses.

Génolhac, Vialas and the Col de la Croix-de-Berthel

Génolhac is a village with old granite houses (15th–17th C.) which was once home to the chief *camisard* Jouany. The Belvédère des Bouzèdes near the village has a wonderful **view** over the

Cévennes. Vialas is dominated by the crest of Rocher de Trenze, which is dotted with granite boles. The 3,627-ft (1,088-m) peak is on the route taken by sheep from the *garrigues* to the mountain pastures.

Spotcheck

D2

Lozère

Things to do

Écomusée du Mont Lozère
Lac de Villefort

Within easy reach

Cévennes National Park ,
p. 288,
Corniche des Cévennes,
p. 290,
Mont Aigoual, p. 294.

Tourist Office

Le Pont-de-Monvert:
☎ 04 66 45 81 94

SHANK'S PONY

The way to discover this region of moors, woods and remote villages is on foot. Visit the farms built of dry-stone. Take GR 68, if you have a week (69 miles/110 km). Otherwise, walk the 10 miles (16 km) of the GR 43 (5- to 6-hour walk) which separates Florac from La Fage, one of the loveliest villages in the region with its unique belltower.

The Causses Lozériens

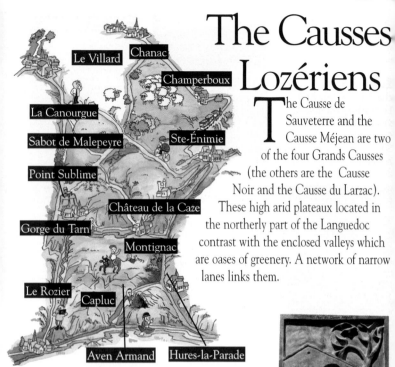

The Causse de Sauveterre and the Causse Méjean are two of the four Grands Causses (the others are the Causse Noir and the Causse du Larzac). These high arid plateaux located in the northerly part of the Languedoc contrast with the enclosed valleys which are oases of greenery. A network of narrow lanes links them.

Causse de Sauveterre

This is the least arid of the Grands Causses but each plot of arable land is carefully cultivated. The Canourgue was prosperous thanks to its abundant water. A few miles away on the D 46, see the Sabot de Malepeyre, a 100-ft (30-m) rock eroded by water.

La Canourgue

Furniture

RN 9, La Mothe,
☎ 04 66 32 81 51.
Open daily except Sun. and Mon. morning, 8.30am–noon and 2–7pm.

This was once a village of spinners, weavers, tanners and leather-dressers. Now you can visit the furniture workshop belonging to Charles Malet. These craftsmen have handed down from father to son the skill of making the Lozerian box or *cantou*, in walnut, cherrywood or oak.

Le Villard-Chanac

Le Domaine des Champs

☎ 04 66 48 25 00.
Open daily Jul.–Aug., 11am–7pm.
Admission charge.

Medieval life has been re-created in the Causse de Sauveterre, in a group of 14th-C. buildings. There are weaving and illumination workshops, a forge and a tavern, and two delightful medieval gardens.

Champerboux

The little train

☎ 04 66 48 50 73.
Open daily Jul.–Aug.
Admission charge.

Take a trip through the Causse above the medieval town of Sainte-Énimie, where prehistoric sites have been

PRZEWALSKI'S HORSE

Association Takh, Le Villaret,
☎ 04 66 45 64 43.
Przewalski's horse is the last truly wild horse in the world and it has never been domesticated. The breed is almost extinct and only 1,300 animals now survive in zoos. The Takh Association (*takh* in Mongolian means 'wild horse') transplanted 12 of these animals to 1,235 acres (500 ha) of the Causse Méjean. They acclimatised well, and are reproducing and living in natural herds. When ready, it is hoped that their descendants will be re-introduced into their country of origin,

discovered, including the Dolmen de Peyrelevade. Visit the mouflon park and stop to eat and buy local foods at the Ferme de Boisset.

The Corniches of the Causse Méjean

The Causse Méjean is separated from Sauveterre by the Canyon du Tarn. It is the

highest *causse* with the harshest climate (Siberian-style winters and torrid summers), hence its low population density. On the other hand, there are plenty of ewes (approxi-

mately 19,000). Starting from Rozier there is a **spectacular hiking trail** which can be covered in about 7 hours. Don't forget your water-bottle and lunch!

La ferme équestre de la Périgouse

At 1¼ miles (2 km) S from Champerboux,
☎ 04 66 48 53 71;
fax 04 66 48 54 67.
Open all year round.
This very pleasant farm in the Causses is situated in a hamlet whose stone roof tiles are now being restored. It offers pony-treks and rambles lasting several days. They are accompanied by guides and cover the Causse de Sauveterre, which is covered with wild iris in the spring, but is more arid in summer, though always full of grandeur. You can also stay overnight in the rooms that are let on this farm.

Hures-la-Parade
Hyelzas, an old-fashioned farm
☎ 04 66 45 65 25.
Open Easter–15 Oct., 9am-noon and 2-7pm (Jul.–Aug., 9am-7pm).
This is a traditional house and a restored farmhouse with furniture and agricultural machinery to match. In the nearby Fédou dairy, taste

Hyelzas farm

Things to do
Ride in a little train
Hyelzas farm
Le Domaine des Champes
Hiking on the Causse Méjean

Within easy reach
*Cévennes National Park, p. 288,
Corniche des Cévennes, p. 290,
Mont Aigoual, p. 294.*

Tourist office
Sainte-Énimie:
☎ 04 66 48 53 44

the charcuterie, sheep's milk and goat's milk cheese and desserts. You can also buy local products.

Aven Armand
☎ 04 66 45 61 31.
Open daily 9am-noon, 1.30-5.30pm or 7pm depending on the season.
Admission charge.
Descend 250 ft (75 m) by funicular to reach a chamber which resembles the central nave of the Cathedral of Notre-Dame-de-Paris: 150 ft (45 m) high, 370 ft (110 m) long, 170 ft (50 m) wide. The 'virgin forest' is the highlight: 400 stalagmites growing tall and narrow in various shapes like piles of plates, pine-cones or palm-tree trunks.

The Tarn and Jonte gorges

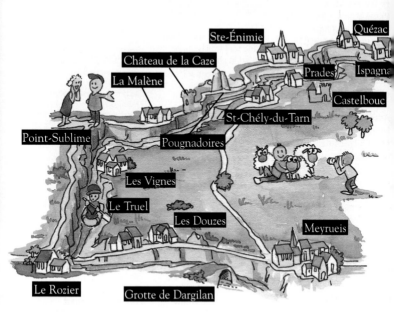

Quézac

Ste-Énimie

Château de la Caze

La Malène

Prades

Ispagna

Castelbouc

St-Chély-du-Tarn

Point-Sublime

Pougnadoires

Les Vignes

Le Truel

Les Douzes

Meyrueis

Le Rozier

Grotte de Dargilan

The gorges of the Tarn constitute an unbridgeable gap between Sauveterre and the Causse Méjean. The river runs deep down in a green valley, surmounted by reddish-orange cliff walls. You can follow its course by car or on foot, along a cliffside path. You can also take a boat down the river, a day trip that starts at Ispagnac. It can be extended in the neighbouring gorges of the Jonte, which are just as lovely.

Ispagnac
The entrance to the gorges

The gorges begin at the exit from the village which is in the 'Garden of the Lozère' which was famous for its fruits and vegetables. The **Romanesque church** with its octogonal cupola is one of the loveliest in Gévaudan. The Château of Châteauneuf-Randon houses an **Ursuline Convent**.

Quézac
Water town

Quézac stands on the opposite bank of the Tarn, reached by a Gothic bridge. The town is

The Church of Ispagnac

famous for its carbonated mineral water (p. 28) and a collegiate church, founded by Pope Urban V, which contains a statue of the Black

Virgin. There is a pilgrimage to the statue in September. Some of the houses in the town have attractive doors.

Window in Ispagnac church

FROM LA MALÈNE
BY BARGE

☎ 04 66 48 51 10.
Open Apr.–Oct.
The price includes return trip by taxi.
A 5-mile (8-km) barge trip along the Tarn between La Malène and the Cirque des Baumes takes about one hour. You go through the narrowest part of the gorges, the straits, where the cliffs are 1,670 ft (500 m) high. You can admire the plants and animals and the strange rock formation called 'Woman with a Parasol' due to its shape.

Charbonnières
Belvedere

This lookout post is at Castelbouc, one of the most famous of the gorges. The ruins of the feudal château dominate the village. A *son et lumière* show recalls the legend of the lord of Castelbouc.

He was the only man on the estate when the rest had gone to the Crusades and he assiduously pursued the women. He died of his excesses and as his soul left his body a large goat (*bouc*) was seen running around the manor house. Since then, there are strange bleating noises at night followed by murmurings.

Sainte-Énimie
Medieval village

Énimie, sister of good King Dagobert, was cured of leprosy

Spotcheck
D2–D3

Lozère

Things to do

Rambling through the gorges of the Jonte
The Tarn by barge

Within easy reach

The Cévennes National Park, p. 288,
Cévennes Corniche, p. 290,
Mont Aigoual, p. 294.

Tourist office

Sainte-Énimie:
☎ 04 66 48 53 44

by the water of the Burle spring, so she founded a **monastery** in the deepest of the gorges. All that is left is the refectory, a large building with a vaulted ceiling. The medieval village is paved with pebbles from the Tarn, occupies one of the narrowest passages of the gorge and has been classified as one of the **most beautiful villages in France**. From Sainte-Éminie, you can sail down the gorges of the Tarn for a whole day to La Malène, watching herons and beavers on the banks (information at the Tourist Office, ☎ 04 66 48 53 44.

✿ Utopix

☎ 04 66 48 59 07.
Open daily
Admission charge.
Jo Pillet, a slightly crazy builder, has spent about 35,000 hours building this strange village of igloos made of *lauzes* (local stone). He holds **sculpture and painting exhibitions** and organises games for children.

The village of Castelbouc beside the Tarn

Saint-Chély-du-Tarn
Between the cliffs

This superb site, ringed by high cliffs, contains a tiny village which seems to be stuck in a time warp. Access is via a bridge built in 1901 beside the church with its **Gothic portal**. Two streams cascade into the Tarn, the largest of which crosses the village. **Pougnadoires**, a nearby village lies in a *cirque*, a natural bowl, the houses being attached to its sides.

Château de la Caze

This late 15th-C. manor house stands in 320 acres (130 ha) of grounds and is now a luxury hotel, but is not open to the general public.

The Chambre des Nymphesis is a bedroom with a 17th-C. painted ceiling representing eight lovely girls from la Caze who were condemned by Heaven for their flirtatiousness to spend their nights wandering through the vale 'of eternal desire'.

La Malène
Beside the ravine

This picturesque village teeters at the edge of the sheer drop and seems to be crushed by the extraordinary striped rust-coloured wall. The paths trodden by sheep going up to the mountain pastures are now regularly used by tourists to get to the **canoes** in which they can paddle down the Tarn or to hike and ramble along the rocky ledges beside its pretty banks.

THE VULTURES OF THE JONTE

Vultures disappeared from the area in the 1940s, having been hunted to extinction because they ate poison meant for foxes or simply because there was no carrion for them to eat. They have been re-introduced, and the fawn vulture and monk vulture, both endangered species, now fly overhead. The landscape is perfect for their nesting sites, and they glide on the thermal winds. Look up from time to time and you may see one. At Les Terrasses (Le Truel) a Vulture House is dedicated to them.

Ruined bridge at Rozier

The Cave of Dargilan

From Meyrueis, 4 miles (7 km) along the D 39, then the D 139, ☎ 04 66 45 60 20. Open Apr.–Nov. 9am–noon and 1.30-6pm; in winter, daily during the school holidays visit at 3pm except 25 Dec. and 1st Jan. *Admission charge.* This two-storey cave was discovered in 1888 by Édouard-Alfred Martel. It includes formations called the Boulder Room, the Belfry, the Mosque, the Pink Room and the Corridor of the great petrified waterfall, 333 ft (100 m) long. A tunnel shortens the way back.

The Cirque des Baumes and the Point-Sublime

This natural semi-circle 3 miles (5 km) long is covered in rocks, cliffs, needles and trees. The valley widens out at the village of Les Vignes. Take the winding D 995 which leads to the Causse de Sauveterre. The Point-Sublime is a sheer rock, at the edge of the Cirque des Baumes. The view into the depths of the gorges is extraordinary.

Grandiose site
Le Rozier

Between Les Vignes and this village, the gorges run like an almost straight corridor. The landscape consists of **cirques, rocks and ruined hermitages.** At Le Rozier, the gorges of the Tarn end and those of the Jonte begin. Follow them for 12½ miles (20 km) to Meyrueis, along the corniche road above the waters.

The gorges of the Jonte

From Le Rozier, the road climbs up to the Les Terrasses lookout. From the car park (with facilities, admission charge) you have a wonderful view over the rocks, the green banks of the river and into the depths of the clear waters. You pass the picturesque village of Truel and reach the hamlet of Les Douzes.

Les Douzes

The Jonte, which disappeared into the limestone rock, now resurfaces as the Fontaine des Douze (meaning 'twelve mouths'). The Saint-Gervais rock, topped with a Romanesque chapel like a huge ruined tower, dominates the hamlet below.

Marvejols and the Aubrac

Marvejols, in the Colagne valley, has been an important industrial and commercial centre since the 12th C., dealing in wool and locally made cloth. In the 19th C., spinning, weaving and dyeing mills opened here.

But, in the 1960s, the last of these mills closed down. A sheep market is held here on the first and third Monday of the month, and the 'Marvejols en Scène' in July combines drama, dance and music.

Fortified gates

The gates stand as memorials to the eventful past of this city, which was destroyed by Admiral de Joyeuse in 1586 because it was a Protestant stronghold. They overlook three entrances to the old city. The **Porte du Soubeyran**, **Porte du Théron and Porte de Chanelles** are defended by two large circular towers linked by battlements and topped with machicolations and a stone-tiled roof. Inscriptions praise Henri IV, who restored 'Marvejols la brûlée' from the ashes.

Notre-Dame-de-la-Carce

The present church was built on the site of the former and dates from the 17th C. It has retained the venerated statue of the Happy Virgin Mary of Marvejols. The church is flanked by a massive bell-tower and has a handsome colonnaded entrance. Inside, there is a **Way of the Cross** painted by Louis Rigal, born in Marvejols, who won the Rome Prize in 1919.

From Henri IV to Jacques Secrétin

Look out for statues and busts of local celebrities during your walk around the town. In the Place du Soubeyran, Emmanuel Auricoste, a local sculptor, produced a statue of the saviour of the town; there is a bust of Savorgnan de Brazza, a famous explorer who married a local girl at the entrance to the public park. As for the table tennis champion, a square has been dedicated to him with a Boulevard de Chambrun in which there is an open-air ping-pong table to be used by anyone.

Around Marvejols

Lac du Moulinet

12¹⁄₂ miles (20 km) from Marvejols. Amid forests and meadows, the children can

Spotcheck
C1-C2-D2

Lozère

Things to do

The wolves of Gévaudan

Within easy reach

*Cévennes National Park,
p. 288.*

Tourist office

Marvejols:
☎ 04 66 32 02 14

float down the Aquagliss flume. As long as you bring your own equipment, you can fish, windsurfing or go canoeing or kayaking. A good opportunity for a swim. Information at the Tourist Office of Marvejols.

Chirac

Le Pompidou, Chirac – the region is full of villages with the names of French presidents! Chirac, at the foot of the Truc de la Fare, a large grassy, rocky hill, is worth visiting for its two **churches**, one containing Roman remains, the other a local history museum.

The Monastier

1¼ miles (2 km) S of Chirac.

The village developed around its Benedictine monastery,

Romanesque capital in the Church of Monastier

whose church was dedicated in 1095. The church gives the impression of harmony in

THE WOLVES OF GÉVAUDAN

**Sainte-Lucie, 5¼ miles (9 km) N of Marvejols,
☎ 04 66 32 09 22.**
Open daily 10am-4.30pm or 6pm, closed in Jan.
Admission charge.
A hundred or so wolves have been re-introduced here from Canada, Siberia, Mongolia and Poland, and they roam in semi-freedom thanks to the creator of this animal park, Gérard Ménatory. Even if you do not get to see them in the wild, they can be watched on video-cameras all over the park. The shop sells all types of gifts, books, photographs and objects with wolves on them.

dissymmetry. It is now square due to various renovations. Look for capitals depicting cupid harvesters and a bearded devil with donkey's ears.

L'Aubrac

The Monts d'Aubrac cover the area between the valleys of the Truyère and the Lot. Above 2,830 ft (850 m), they are a huge pasture, 'sanctuary of the pastoral life' as George Sands described them. This is

one of the least populated regions of France with only 14 inhabitants per square kilometre, against an average of 96. Nasbinals (pretty 11–12th-C. Romanesque Auvergnat church), Fournels and Saint-Germain-du-Teil (village of lime trees) are its three cantons. In *burons*, low stone structures, were dairies in which cows' milk was made into a raw curd cheese that was pressed into rounds.

Margeride
and the Gévaudan

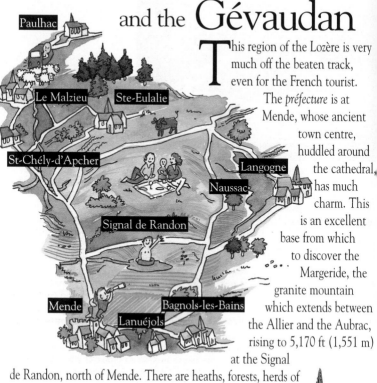

This region of the Lozère is very much off the beaten track, even for the French tourist. The *préfecture* is at Mende, whose ancient town centre, huddled around the cathedral, has much charm. This is an excellent base from which to discover the Margeride, the granite mountain which extends between the Allier and the Aubrac, rising to 5,170 ft (1,551 m) at the Signal de Randon, north of Mende. There are heaths, forests, herds of sheep and cattle, hamlets and small towns, fairs and markets.

Mende

The Cathedral of Notre-Dame-et-Saint-Privat

The cathedral was built in the 14th C. by Pope Urban V and restored in the early 17th C. Its imposing mass dominates the town. Inside, there are

The Cathedral of Notre-Dame-et-Saint-Privat

JAMS AND PRESERVES FROM MAISON GRIBET

1, Avenue Conturie,
☎ **04 66 69 06 84.**
Open daily in season, 9am-7pm.
You have to come to Lozère to see where these wonderful jams are made. Maison Gribet has supplied them to Fauchon, the luxury grocer in Paris, for 25 years. Fauchon's customers love the wild strawberry jams and preserves made from wild fruits and flowers, especially dandelions and wild pansies.

Spotcheck
D1-D2

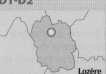

Lozère

Things to do

Fishing at Langlade mill
Health trips
Bison Nature Reserve
Water-sports and mountain-biking

Within easy reach

Cévennes National Park, p. 288.

Tourist office

Mende: ☎ 04 66 65 60 00

lovely carved wooden choir-stalls and eight **Aubusson tapestries** (1708) of scenes from the life of the Virgin. The cathedral once had the largest bell in the whole of Christendom, the Non-Pareille, which weighed 20 tonnes. All that remains is the clapper (by the porch).

Le Pont Notre-Dame

This very narrow bridge was built in the 12th C. and was called the Pont Peyrenc ('of stone') at first. It has three wide arches, which enabled it to withstand the flooding of the river Lot. There is a **good view** of the town from here.

Maison Paul-Majorel

2, Rue de l'Abbaye,
☎ **04 66 65 00 47.**

Open Tues.–Sat., 2.30-7pm. Closed 15–30 June and 10–30 Sept.
This prize-winning bakery, famous throughout Lozère, has a speciality for which the recipe has been transmitted from father to son for three generations. It is the **croquant**, a crunchy biscuit

made with almonds and hazelnuts. You can taste it in the tea-room and buy some to take home (23 F for a 9 oz/ 250 g bag).

Tour des Pénitents

The former Tour d'Auriac is the last vestige of the town's ramparts. In the 17th C., it was made into a belltower, and topped with a little belfry with two arches.

Le Falisson

☎ **04 66 47 08 31.**
Open daily by appointment. *Free admission.*
Fabrice Gautier will tell you all (or almost all) there is to know about converting clay into artefacts. But his expertise with the dampers, the

trap-doors in the chimney, are what gives his pots their flame colour.

Lozère shopping

Coopérative des Artisans et Paysans de Lozère,
4, Rue de l'Ange,
☎ **04 66 65 01 57.**
Open daily except Sun., 9am-noon and 2-7pm.
Boutique des Artisans Créateurs,
3, Rue Notre-Dame,
☎ **04 66 49 00 42.**
Open daily except Sun., 9.30am-12.30pm and 2.30-7pm.

Both these shops sell large wooden furniture, chairs with rush seats or winter items, as well as honey, jam, terrines, mushrooms or folkweaves, jewellery and wooden toys. Plenty of lovely souvenirs to take home.

Fishing at Langlade mill

Commune de Brenoux,
☎ **04 66 48 02 75.**
Open daily, in summer 9am-8pm, in winter 9am-noon and 2-6pm.
You can fish in the stream that feeds the fish-farm, in which rainbow trout, salmon-trout and Arctic charr swim in large numbers. The Arctic charr lives in the waters of Fontmaure spring. Fish as much as you intend to eat because you have to pay for what you catch. You can buy

smoked or fresh trout, fish portions and various canned products from the mill.

Mont Mimat and the Saint-Privat Hermitage

½ mile (1 km) SW of Mende.
On foot, sign-posted path, or by car.
The hermitage dominates the town from its position on the hillside. It has a lovely view over the valley of the Lot. Crude steps lead up to the two superimposed caves in which Privat was martyred by the Alamans in the 3rd C. (He is buried in the crypt of the cathedral). Mont Mimat is 3,560 ft (1,067 m) high and from the top there is a great view of the city.

Lanuéjols

Bassulus and Balbinus

6 miles (9 km) via the D 25 and the D 41.
The village has a 12th C. **Romanesque church** but is best-known for its **Roman mausoleum** (below the main road), an architectural masterpiece. Over the 12-ft (3.70-m) long stone lintel of the gate, a Latin inscription explains that Lucius Julius Bassianus and Pomponia Regola erected this tomb in memory of their two sons, Bassulus and Balbinus, who died of the same wasting disease.

Bagnols-les-Bains

The Valley of the Villaret

Allenc,
☎ **04 66 47 63 76.**
Open daily from Easter–15 Sept., 10am-7pm; 16 Sept.–All Saint's Day, Sat.–Sun. 10am-7pm.
Admission charge, except for children

❀ SAINTE-EULALIE-EN-MARGERIDE BISON NATURE RESERVE
☎ **04 66 31 40 40.**
Open daily, in summer 10am-7pm; in winter 10am-noon, 2-5pm.
Admission charge.
European bisons were recently re-introduced here and live semi-wild in 445 acres (180 ha) of unspoiled landscape. Go and see what the largest European mammal looks like. The bison, which disappeared in Europe 1,500 years ago, is a rare survivor from pre-historic times. You can watch the animals from observation posts. If you are on foot, you can explore the area in the same way that pre-historic people did (from 1 May to 31 August) or you can ride in a carriage or sledge depending on the season (reservations required).

under 40 in (1 m) tall.
This park is ideal for a family outing. The circular route around it is 1¼ miles (2 km) long. It is a lovely adventure playground in the wild, with trails and walks, suspension and rope bridges. There are exhibitions, a snack-bar and a shop midway along the route.

Health trips

Les Chemins Francis,
☎ **04 66 47 60 04,**
fax: 04 66 47 62 73.
In summer and winter, Les Chemins Francis organise **health cures with hikes** to get you back into shape. The mornings are reserved for **spa treatments** (p. 101). In the afternoon, accompanied hikes take you into the Cévennes National Park, Mont Lozère, to learn about the local flora, old villages and the shepherds and their flocks. In July and August, six nights with full board start at 2,540 F.

Langogne
The Church of Saint-Gervais-et-Saint-Protais

This is one of the most remarkable churches in the area, despite its rather austere façade. It is built in Burgundian Romanesque style but rebuilt extensively between the 15th and 17th C. **Sculpted capitals**

decorate the pillars in the nave, with angels and demons fighting over the lost souls or evoking the vices. When you leave, go to the market in the **Halles** which were built in 1765 (14 sturdy granite columns support a stone-tiled roof). They were used for housing cattle and for the corn exchange. There are lots of nice walks or mountain-bike trails in the area (information at the Tourist Office,
☎ 04 66 69 01 38).

Filature des Calquières

23, Rue de Calquières,
☎ **04 66 69 25 56.**

Admission charge.
The four stories of this 19th-C. factory-museum contain carding, spinning and twisting machines for making yarn, all run by a huge paddle-wheel. The woollen yarn produced was and is still used for home knitting. There are temporary exhibitions, a weaving workshop and a shop.

The Beast of Gévaudan

In 1764 and for three years thereafter, in the region of Langogne, Malzieu, d'Aumont, about 100 people, mainly women and children, were the victims of an extraordinary beast. There were wolves in the region, but could it have been God punishing human beings for their sins? Huge searches were conducted but in vain. It was not until 1767 that Jean Chastel killed this terrible beast near Saugues. People are still asking themselves today what on earth it might have been.

Naussac
Water-sports centre

☎ **04 66 69 21 28.**
Open 15 Apr.–15 Oct.
The reservoir of Naussacis is an ideal place for all sorts of **water-sports.** The centre teaches yachting, offers wind-surfing board and dinghy rental and organises canyoning and rafting trips. For the less daring there is a swimming pool and flume. There is also mountain-biking, rock-climbing and tennis.

This guide was written by BETTY DER ANDRÉASSIAN, MARIE-ANGE JOULIA-DEMORY and ALINE SIBONY-ISMAIL, with additional help from JACKIE BALDWIN, MARIE BARBELET, DENIS HILL, EVE LAMASSÉ, FRÉDÉRIC OLIVIER, FRANÇOISE PICON and ISABELLE ROMAIN.

Illustrations: FRANÇOIS LACHÉZE

Illustrated maps: STÉPHANIE HUMBERT-BASSET

Cartography: © IDÉ-INFOGRAPHIE (THOMAS GROLLIER)

Translation and adaptation: CHANTERELLE TRANSLATIONS, LONDON (JOSEPHINE BACON)

Additional design and editorial assistance: BOOK CREATION SERVICES, CHRISTINE BELL

Project manager: LIZ COGHILL

We have done our best to ensure the accuracy of the information contained in this guide. However, addresses, telephone numbers, opening times etc. inevitably do change from time to time, so if you find a discrepancy please do let us know. You can contact us at: hachetteuk@orionbooks.co.uk or write to us at Hachette UK, address below.

Hachette UK guides provide independent advice. The authors and compilers do not accept any remuneration for the inclusion of any addresses in these guides.

Please note that we cannot accept any responsibility for any loss, injury or inconvenience sustained by anyone as a result of any information or advice contained in this guide.

First published in the United Kingdom in 2000 by Hachette UK

© English translation and adaptation, Hachette UK 2000

© Hachette Livre (Hachette Tourisme) 1999

Distributed in the United States of America by Sterling Publishing Co., Inc. 387 Park Avenue South, New York, NY 10016-8810

A CIP catalogue for this book is available from the British Library

ISBN 1 84202 008 0

Hachette UK, Cassell & Co., The Orion Publishing Group, Wellington House, 125 Strand, London WC2R 0BB

Printed in Spain by Graficas Estella

Voucher section

Wherever you see this symbol ❀ in the guide, you will find a voucher in this section which will entitle you to a discount or special offer. If you find a voucher here you want to use, the corresponding page number in the guide is there for your reference.

On presentation of this Vacances guide

Le Domaine Sarda Malet

(vineyard)

p.137

A free bottle of 'la gamme Rivesaltes'
Offer exclusive to customers placing an order at the Domaine de Sarda Malet

Offre une bouteille de la gamme Rivesaltes
Offre réservée aux personnes passant une commande au Domaine de Sarda Malet

Le Domaine Sarda Malet
Mas Saint-Michel, Chemin Sainte-Barbe
66000 PERPIGNAN
☎ 04 68 56 72 38

On presentation of this Vacances guide

Le Musée de Tautavel Centre Européen de Préhistoire

(Prehistoric Museum)

p.138

Tickets for only 30F for adults and 10F for children aged 7–14

Propose l'entrée à 30 F pour les adultes et à 10 F pour les enfants de 7 à 14 ans

Musée de Tautavel
16, route de Vingrau
66720 TAUTAVEL
☎ 04 68 29 07 76

On presentation of this Vacances guide

L'Aquarium

(aquarium)

p.141

Buy two entry tickets, get one free

Offre une entrée gratuite
pour deux entrées achetées

Aquarium
Boulevard de la jetée
66140 CANET-EN-ROUSSILLON
☎ 04 68 80 49 64

On presentation of this Vacances guide

Le Musée du Jouet

(Toy Museum)

p.141

Buy two entry tickets, get one free

Offre une entrée gratuite
pour deux entrées achetées

Musée du Jouet
Place de la Méditerranée
66140 CANET-EN-ROUSSILLON
☎ 04 68 73 20 29

On presentation of this Vacances guide

Le Delta Club Aude et PO

(aeronautic club)

p.153

A free turn on a flight simulator

Offre une séance de simulateur de vol Delta

Delta Club Aude et PO
64, rue de la République
66400 CERET
☎ 04 68 87 25 54

On presentation of this Vacances guide

La Cavale

(B&B/hotel in Mantet)

p.157 and p.161

10% discount on all overnight stays in their short-stay gites or B&Bs

Offer valid for stays of 3 nights or more

Offre 10% de réduction sur les nuitées en gîte d'étape ou chambre d'hôtes

Offre valable pour les séjours à partir de 3 nuits

La Cavale
66360 MANTET
☎ 04 68 05 57 59

On presentation of this Vacances guide

Gruissan Windsurf

(windsurfing)

p.187

10% discount

Offer limited to the following activities: windsurfing, funboarding, catamaran and 'optimist'

Offre 10% de réduction

Offre limitée aux activités de planche à voile, funboard, catamaran et optimist

Gruissan Windsurf
Boulevard du Pech Maynaud B.P. 49
11430 GRUISSAN
☎ 04 68 49 88 31

On presentation of this Vacances guide

L'Aquarium du Cap-d'Agde

(aquarium)

p.214

One free child entry ticket (0–18 years)

Offre une entrée gratuite pour un enfant (0-18 ans)

Aquarium du Cap d'Agde
11, rue des Deux-Frères
34300 LE CAP-D'AGDE
☎ 04 67 26 14 21

Agropolis Musuem

(Agricultural Museum)

p.228

Buy one entry ticket, get one free

Offre une entrée gratuite pour une entrée achetée

Agropolis Museum
951, avenue Agropolis
34394 MONTPELLIER Cedex 5
☎ 04 67 04 75 04

La Cave de Rabelais

(wine cellar)

p.235

5% discount on all purchases

Offre 5% de réduction
sur vos achats

Cave de Rabelais
B.P. 514
34114 MIREVAL Cedex
☎ 04 67 78 15 79

On presentation of this Vacances guide

Le Château de Flaugergues

(Flaugergues castle)

p.237

Group rates for individual entry tickets

Propose l'entrée au tarif de groupe

Château de Flaugergues
1744, avenue Albert Einstein
34000 MONTPELLIER
☎ 04 67 65 51 72

On presentation of this Vacances guide

La Source Perrier

(Perrier spring)

p.258

Buy one entry ticket, get one free

Offre une entrée gratuite
pour une entrée achetée

Source Perrier
Les Bouillens
30310 VERGÈZE
☎ 04 66 87 61 01

On presentation of this Vacances guide

Les Domaines de Listel

(vineyard)

p.265

A free bottle of their own label

Offrent une bouteille de leur production

Domaines de Listel
Domaine de Jarras
30220 AIGUES-MORTES
☎ 04 66 51 17 00

On presentation of this Vacances guide

La Bouscarasse

(aquatic park)

p.275

10% discount on entry tickets

Offre 10% de réduction
sur le prix d'entrée

La Bouscarasse
KM 8, Route d'Alès
30700 UZES
☎ 04 66 22 50 25

On presentation of this Vacances guide

La Mine Témoin d'Alès

(mine)

p.281

A free drink or a selection of 4 postcards

Offre une boisson
ou un lot de 4 cartes postales

Mine Témoin d'Alès
Chemin de la Cité Sainte-Marie
B.P. 49
30101 ALÈS Cedex
☎ 04 66 78 49 10

On presentation of this Vacances guide

Le Préhistorama

(Prehistoric Museum)

p.281

Group rates for individual entry tickets

Propose l'entrée au tarif de groupe

Préhistorama
La Croix de Fauvie
30340 ROUSSON
☎ 04 66 85 86 96

On presentation of this Vacances guide

L'Atlantide Parc Aquarium Tropical Géant

(tropical aquarium and park)

p.293

Adult entry for only 38F

Propose l'entrée adulte à 38 F

Atlantide Parc Aquarium Tropical Géant
Avenue de la Résistance
30270 ST-JEAN-DU-GARD
☎ 04 66 85 32 32

On presentation of this Vacances guide

Utopix

(sculpture village)

p.301

15% discount

Offre 15% de réduction

Utopix
La Sirvente
48210 SAINTE-ÉNIMIE
☎ 04 66 48 59 07

La Réserve de Bisons

(bison reserve)

p.308

Reduced price entry tickets

Propose l'entrée au tarif réduit

La réserve de Bisons
Village
48120 SAINTE-EULALIE-EN-MARGERIDE
☎ 04 66 31 40 40

*All these promotional offers are exclusive
to our readers, and are valid until 31st March 2002*

*Ces offres promotionnelles sont reservées à nos
lecteurs, et sont valables jusqu'au 31 mars 2002*

NOTES

NOTES